HYBRIDITY
ON THE GROUND
IN PEACEBUILDING
AND DEVELOPMENT

CRITICAL CONVERSATIONS

HYBRIDITY
ON THE GROUND
IN PEACEBUILDING
AND DEVELOPMENT

CRITICAL CONVERSATIONS

EDITED BY JOANNE WALLIS, LIA KENT,
MIRANDA FORSYTH, SINCLAIR DINNEN
AND SRINJOY BOSE

Australian
National
University

PRESS

PACIFIC AFFAIRS SERIES

ANU PRESS

Published by ANU Press
The Australian National University
Acton ACT 2601, Australia
Email: anupress@anu.edu.au
This title is also available online at press.anu.edu.au

A catalogue record for this
book is available from the
National Library of Australia

ISBN(s): 9781760461836 (print)
9781760461843 (eBook)

Cover design and layout by ANU Press

Contents

Section One — Theorising Hybridity

Section Two — Hybridity and Peacebuilding

Foreword

A group of scholars based at several Australian universities have long been influential in the development of our understanding of hybrid political order. The term was first used in relation to peacebuilding (to the best of my knowledge) by Kevin Clements, Volker Boege, Anne Brown, Wendy Foley and Anna Nolan in a now seminal paper published in 2007 called 'State Building Reconsidered: The Role of Hybridity in the Formation of Political Order' in *Political Science*. A bolt out of the prescriptive liberal blue, it turned this field of debate on its head.

Discussions of agency, particularly local agency, of the possibility of new political forms—of resistance, but also of the risks of neocolonial forms of administration—suddenly swung into our view. They formed part of a broader and emerging intersection between liberal, Marxist and postcolonial thought, and the use of this concept has proliferated enormously ever since. It is now the mainstay of policy thinking in conflict-affected societies around the world, as well as the target of much academic debate. Hybridity is nothing if not highly complex and controversial, but it has attracted the interest of many academic and policy quarters because of its intuitive and easily observable empirical dimensions: relationality in a rapidly globalising and fluid world. It also points to power inequalities and injustices, to the painful yet plausible potential of rubbing along together after conflict, as well as to the prescriptive over-reach of liberal interventionism on the post–Cold War world. Somewhere between the liberal peace, its interventionary nature and individualist/constructivist rationalities and the older concepts associated with anti-colonialism and non-alignment, a real sense of the current reality of peace and order in the periphery began to emerge, with both unnoticed positives as well as obvious dangers.

Thus, it is very apt that this important discussion is carried forward in this volume, including by some of the concept's original scholars. What has become clear over the time that this concept has come into use is that it can be used in negative ways (to indicate or even camouflage neo-trusteeship or counter-insurgency) and in positive ways, where it takes an important place in the production of new political orders, in which rights are expanded and peace is more sustainable. In my own work I have used the notion of post-liberalism to point to this potential as a way of escaping problems in particular relating to the limits of liberalism in Eurocentric form.

At a workshop in Canberra in December 2015 (where I was present) held to discuss the draft chapters for this volume, it became clear how widely entangled the dynamics of hybridity are, across so many issues from rights, identity, indigeneity, materiality, local governance, justice, reconciliation, sustainability, the nature of the state and international system, globalisation and the commons, to name but a few. It begins to bring a far more complex view of peace and order, one that accentuates the open and hidden violence of more parsimonious approaches. Indeed, as an epistemological framework, with methodological–ethical sets of tools, it offers a completely new ontology of relationality across at least four dimensions as opposed to the black-and-white world of rational self-interest. Due to the work of the scholars included in this study, it is gradually becoming clear that another world is not just 'possible' but is already in existence and that concepts and thinking about peace and peacebuilding need to respond. This volume continues this important research agenda.

Oliver P. Richmond

Preface

The further we advance into the twenty-first century, the broader spreads the realisation that we are moving deeper into a 'post-Western' world. Ideas and institutions developed in Europe and North America, which came to dominate global orders and expectations, are becoming less and less authoritative as new, non-Western centres of power rise and as precolonial ideas and institutions reassert themselves. The big question, of course, is what a post-Western world will look like. For those of us sceptical of a future shaped by a 'clash of civilisations', our contemporary world provides abundant evidence of the interplay and mutual influence of different cultural approaches to order—or as the scholars writing in this book call it, 'hybridity'.

This collection of essays represents the product of a sustained intellectual conversation that took place over the course of a seminar series and a workshop held at The Australian National University during 2015. Like many fruitful academic collaborations, this one had its gestation in informal conversations and deliberations among a group of scholars based at the time in the ANU Coral Bell School of Asia Pacific Affairs. This group applied for, and was awarded, a small grant to organise the Bell School's inaugural Horizons Seminar Series in 2015. The Horizons Series aims to nurture interdisciplinary conversations and research collaborations among scholars working on diverse aspects of social and political change in the Asia–Pacific region. 'Hybridity: History, Power and Scale' was the theme chosen for the inaugural seminar series.

The seminar series brought together scholars from a range of disciplinary backgrounds whose work engaged in some way or another with the concept of hybridity. Areas of research represented included peacebuilding, state formation, legal pluralism, transitional justice, security governance and development. The series culminated in an international workshop in December 2015 that engaged critically with core themes that had emerged during the course of the seminar series. As well as those who had presented seminars, the organisers invited a number of additional speakers and participants, including Oliver Richmond, one of the foremost authorities on hybridity in the critical peacebuilding field, and Hilary Charlesworth, a leading scholar in the fields of international law, human rights and gender. Other participants included Anne Brown and Volker Boege, who, along with other colleagues at the University of Queensland, had developed the concept of 'hybrid political orders'; Helene Maria Kyed, who has utilised the concept of hybridity in the context of policing and legal pluralism; Shahar Hameiri, who has undertaken extensive critical analysis of contemporary statebuilding practice; Peter Albrecht, who has examined the nature of hybrid authority at the level of local governance; Matthew Allen and Sinclair Dinnen, who have deployed the concept of scalar politics as an analytical alternative to hybridity in exploring ongoing processes of state formation; and Damian Grenfell, who has examined the relevance of the concept of hybridity in the context of gender-based violence.

The essays in this volume have thus emerged from an intensive process of presentation, discussion, critique and reformulation. Most, though not all, argue that the concept of hybridity has heuristic value for thinking about the uncertain 'post-Western' world we are entering. While they pose more questions than they answer, together they point the way to rich and ongoing conversations across disciplinary and geographic boundaries and to exciting future collaborations.

Michael Wesley
Dean
College of Asia & the Pacific
The Australian National University

Introduction

Lia Kent, Srinjoy Bose, Joanne Wallis,
Sinclair Dinnen and Miranda Forsyth

Hybridity as a conceptual tool has long been discussed in a range of disciplines including the biological sciences, social sciences and even literature and literary criticism. In its literal sense, and as used in biology, the term 'hybrid' refers to the product of a process of mixing or combining two or more distinct elements. The concept originated in the biological and zoological sciences, where it was appropriated into the highly controversial pseudoscientific theories of race that informed debates about European imperialism in the nineteenth century. In the social sciences, hybridity later became prominent in discussions of identity,[1] culture,[2] economic and power relations, and political systems,[3] and has been characterised as the outcome of encounters between hegemonic practices and attempts to decolonise peoples, territories and knowledge. In the field of postcolonial studies, for example, hybridity was first articulated to help understand complex processes of sociopolitical interaction and relationships[4] between colonial powers and colonised subjects. Critical of the coloniser's or intervener's aims to reform the 'Other' (that is, attempts to mould the colonised in the image of the coloniser or intervener), Bhabha stressed themes such as resistance to domination and the agential power of the colonised or subaltern subjects.[5] Similarly, Kapoor argued that hybridity recognises the strategies of those who resist overt and subtle forms of

---

1   Barry, *Beginning Theory*; Young, *Colonial Desire*.
2   Ashcroft et al., *The Empire Writes Back*; Ashcroft et al., *Post-colonial Studies*; Bhabha, 'Signs Taken for Wonders'; Bhabha, *The Location of Culture*; Spivak, 'Can the Subaltern Speak?'.
3   Boege et al., *On Hybrid Political Orders and Emerging States*.
4   Bhabha, 'Signs Taken for Wonders'.
5   Ibid.; Bhabha, *The Location of Culture*.

colonisation.[6] This framework was subsequently developed and applied to international relations and development literatures, specifically studies in conflict resolution, intervention and peacebuilding.[7]

In conflict resolution, hybridity implies a combination of elements from different—seemingly incompatible and inharmonious—world views. A hybrid order comprises a mixed structure of informal and formal institutions of power. Hybridity is 'a state of affairs in which liberal and illiberal norms, institutions, and actors coexist'.[8] Viewed in this way, the 'state' is only one institutional actor and source of power among others within a 'hybrid political order', and 'state order' is only one of a number of competing orders claiming to provide security, frameworks for conflict regulation and other forms of welfare provision.[9] Today, as Millar has noted, conflict resolution (and the associated concepts of peacebuilding, development, transnational justice and so on) lies at the heart of most debates on intervention, with many scholars problematising the roles of external interveners and local agential power.[10] More specifically, the term hybridity has been used in critiques of the spate of 'liberal' peace interventions that occurred during the second half of the 1990s and the first decade of the new millennium. Focusing on the externally driven, state-centric, technical and formulaic orientation of these interventions and their neglect of local contexts, some recent critiques have adopted the notion of 'hybrid peace' to denote the interactive and contested quality of the processes involved in such encounters.[11] This usage seeks to capture the 'intertwined relationship between the global and the local, the formal and the informal and the liberal and the illiberal'[12] that characterises the actual practice of contemporary peacebuilding, as opposed to the assumptions of its underpinning (liberal peace) theory. It is argued that the outcome of these interactions—the 'hybrid peace'—is both a more accurate depiction of the complex realities on the ground, and more legitimate than the

---

6   Kapoor, 'Acting in a Tight Spot', 568.
7   See Mac Ginty, *International Peacebuilding and Local Resistance*; Mac Ginty, 'Hybrid Peace: How Does Hybrid Peace Come About?'; Richmond, 'De-romanticising the Local, De-mystifying the International'.
8   Belloni, 'Hybrid Peace Governance', 22.
9   Boege et al., *On Hybrid Political Orders and Emerging States*; Clements et al., 'State Building Reconsidered'; Donais, *Peacebuilding and Local Ownership*; Richmond, *A Post-liberal Peace*.
10   Millar, 'Disaggregating Hybridity'.
11   Mac Ginty, 'Gilding the Lily?'; Mac Ginty, 'Hybrid Peace: The Interaction between Top-Down and Bottom-Up Peace'.
12   Björkdahl and Höglund, 'Precarious Peacebuilding', 293.

liberal peace because it taps into local agency and knowledge, thereby broadening the peace constituency and more effectively capturing the dynamic and interactive processes involved.[13]

The term hybridity has also gained significance in policy discourse and practice set against the backdrop of growing international interventionism in recent decades.[14] A notable example is the *World Development Report 2011: Conflict, Security, and Development*, in which the World Bank acknowledged that in those parts of the global South in which state institutions are weak and much of the population lives according to local sociopolitical beliefs and practices, it might be necessary for international actors to move away from unilinear processes of institutional transfer from the global North and instead adopt flexible 'best fit' approaches that draw upon 'combinations of state, private sector, faith based, traditional, and community structures for service delivery'.[15] These developments suggest there has been a shift away from seeing local sociopolitical practices and institutions primarily as hurdles or spoilers to achieving a universal model of liberal democracy, towards a greater recognition of their potential strengths in advancing larger goals of peacebuilding and development.

The growing prominence of the hybridity concept in the conflict resolution and peacebuilding literatures, and in policy discourse and practice, helps to explain the current emphasis on interactions between the 'international' and the 'local'. The hybrid approach was introduced to unsettle the statist,[16] Eurocentric and linear logic of liberal peacebuilding, and locates peace both in the agency of the local, and in the hybrid formations of liberal and non-liberal institutions and values resulting from such encounters.[17] Hybridity denotes 'how local actors attempt

---

13 Ibid.
14 Chesterman, 'Ownership in Theory and Practice'; Paris, *At War's End*.
15 World Bank, *World Development Report 2011*, 106.
16 According to Nadarajah and Rampton, the hybrid approach characterises international peacebuilding as coercive, top-down, technocratic and blind to the conditions of the local environment. Thus, liberal peacebuilding is held to favour the interests of statists (those who favour the interests of local elites and international interveners) rather than the majority who suffer the weight of both conflict and peace engagements. The latter are systematically alienated from statebuilding and peacebuilding processes. This renders the liberal peace illegitimate and drives various resistances that make impossible its advance and sustainability. Nadarajah and Rampton, 'The Limits of Hybridity', 54.
17 Ibid., 49–50.

to respond to, resist and ultimately reshape peace initiatives through interactions with international actors and institutions'.[18] Nadarajah and Rampton argue that hybridity allows the 'liberal peace' to be:

> transcended and its narrow ethnocentric boundaries, technocratic tendencies and fixation with state and institution-building overcome to produce a more empathetic, responsive, culturally sensitive and ultimately radical peace encompassing the local, indigenous and quotidian experience, especially that of the subaltern categories, within conflict-affected spaces and societies.[19]

As noted above, hybrid processes arise from resistance to hegemony. The resistance may manifest itself in outright violence, active reform of introduced practices, co-optation and so on. Some within the policy and academic communities have tended to perceive obstacles to peace as lying primarily in deficiencies in local and state institutions in contemporary contexts of interventions.[20] But does this view not smack of older and discredited colonial epistemologies? Richmond reminds us that grassroots-level actors often have a more nuanced understanding of the limitations and potential of both their own frameworks and those promulgated by international authorities.[21] He argues that blaming local actors for their own ills and conditionality is common among interveners, and that this imbues these interventions with a neocolonial character.[22] Others, drawing on Spivak's work,[23] have argued that the colonised/intervened are active agents in creating, maintaining and modifying the colonial and postcolonial sociopolitical orders. They argue that local actors can be equipped to play an active role in statebuilding and peacebuilding processes and discourse. Quoting Duffield[24] and Richmond,[25] Wallis remarks that 'critiques converge on the emerging consensus that statebuilders should seek to engage in "unscripted conversations"[26] with ordinary people, about the design of their state'.[27] Writing in a postcolonial studies tradition, Bhabha is somewhat more critical, arguing that material power

---

18   Richmond and Mitchell, 'Introduction—Towards a Post-liberal Peace', 8.
19   Nadarajah and Rampton, 'The Limits of Hybridity', 53.
20   See, for example, Paris, 'Saving Liberal Peacebuilding'.
21   Richmond, 'The Dilemmas of a Hybrid Peace'.
22   Ibid., 51.
23   See Spivak, 'Can the Subaltern Speak?'.
24   Duffield, *Development, Security and Unending War*.
25   Richmond, 'Becoming Liberal, Unbecoming Liberalism'; Richmond, 'A Post-liberal Peace: Eirenism and the Everyday'.
26   Duffield, *Development, Security and Unending War*, 234.
27   Wallis, 'A Liberal–Local Hybrid Peace Project in Action?', 736.

imbalances between the (typically Western) hegemon and (typically non-Western) subaltern ensures that the latter are structurally incapable of modifying existing power dynamics and relations.[28]

Alongside the growing prominence of hybridity as a concept is an emerging critique of hybridity.[29] One aspect of the latter is its focus on the paradoxical ways in which the concept of hybridity can often serve to reinscribe the problematic binaries it seeks to overcome. Discussions of hybridity have often focused on the relationship between the 'international' and 'local', characterising their interactions in dichotomous terms: 'liberal' versus 'illiberal', 'modern' versus 'traditional', 'Western' versus 'non-Western', 'state' versus 'non-state', 'coercion' versus 'resistance', 'insurgent' versus 'government', and 'peace' versus 'conflict'. Such binaries are unhelpful[30]— they homogenise categories, oversimplify complex contexts and milieus,[31] and essentialise local (and international) groupings.[32] By contrast, several scholars have highlighted the *multiplicity of outcomes* that can occur when two entities meet and interact. This critique also points to the extent to which, given the historical influences of colonialism and globalisation, both 'international' and 'local' actors and institutions are themselves the products of earlier processes of hybridisation. Pitting the international against the local therefore distorts the multifarious and continuous processes of interaction that characterise all human and societal exchange. Pieterse, cognisant of the role of globalisation, comments that hybridity indicates profound changes brought about by mobility, migration and multiculturalism.[33] In other words, hybridity reminds us that categories are the site of contestation and negotiation, yet also stresses the fluidity within and between categories. Anthropologists have long argued that local practices are never static; they are constantly evolving,[34] particularly when encountering the forces of intervention and globalisation. Petersen argues that it is the shift away from these binaries and absolutes that appears as the primary appeal of hybridity.[35] While nuanced analyses seek to do

---

28   Bhabha, *The Location of Culture*, 330.
29   Chandler, 'Peacebuilding and the Politics of Non-linearity'; Millar, 'Disaggregating Hybridity'; Newman, 'A Human Security Peace-building Agenda'; Peterson, 'A Conceptual Unpacking of Hybridity'.
30   de Guevara, 'Introduction: The Limits of Statebuilding'; Peterson, 'A Conceptual Unpacking of Hybridity'; Heathershaw, 'Conclusions: Neither Built Nor Formed'.
31   Moreiras, 'Hybridity and Double Consciousness'; Millar, 'Disaggregating Hybridity'.
32   Peterson, '"Rule of Law" Initiatives'; Peterson, 'A Conceptual Unpacking of Hybridity'.
33   Pieterse, 'Hybridity, So What?', 221.
34   Brown, 'Security, Development and the Nation-building Agenda', 155.
35   Peterson, 'A Conceptual Unpacking of Hybridity', 12.

justice to these complexities, contemporary usage of the term 'hybridity'—accentuated by the limitations of our available vocabulary—often serves inadvertently to reinscribe binaries even as it seeks to unpack them.

A second criticism relates to the frameworks used to discuss hybridity. Millar suggests that the literature on hybridity can be characterised as either 'prescriptive' or 'descriptive'.[36] Descriptive accounts explain what hybridity is (and isn't) and how it comes about. This usage of hybridity offers a mechanism for viewing the outcomes of interchange between external actors and complex local contexts, as well as for understanding the critical role of local agency in mediating external interventions. Prescriptive accounts, on the other hand, examine how hybridity can be purposefully *designed* into statebuilding, peacebuilding and governance projects.[37] Many have warned that prescriptive accounts give licence to external intervention, including ambitious and intrusive projects of social engineering.[38] More importantly, perhaps, critical scholars have expressed doubt as to whether hybridity can be harnessed to implement stated objectives and goals; some go so far as to suggest interveners should not even attempt to harness hybridity.[39] Millar is also critical of prescriptive approaches, arguing that 'prescriptive hybridity assumes that administering hybrid institutions will foster predictable peace-promoting experiences'.[40] Others stress the importance of prescriptive hybridity, arguing, for example, that customary norms, values and institutions need to be incorporated into new structures designed to promote peace, stability and development if the goals of creating capable, effective and legitimate states are to be realised.[41] They argue that while it is a necessary starting point, a merely descriptive use of hybridity—describing how things are—fails to address more fundamental questions about the power imbalances and inequality underlying particular hybrid configurations and how these might be overcome.[42] Politically, a hybrid approach considers hybridity as a space where local and international practices are continuously negotiated in interactions of differential power; hence, when merely observing the pluralistic outcomes of these interactions, the underlying differentials in power that animate these outcomes are often glossed over.

---

36 Millar, 'Disaggregating Hybridity', 501.
37 Ibid.; Peterson, 'A Conceptual Unpacking of Hybridity'.
38 Mac Ginty and Richmond, 'The Fallacy of Constructing Hybrid Political Orders'.
39 Visoka, 'Three Levels of Hybridisation Practices'; see also Hameiri and Jones, this volume.
40 Millar, 'Disaggregating Hybridity', 502.
41 Clements et al., 'State Building Reconsidered', 48.
42 Pieterse, *Ethnicities and Global Multiculture*.

What these critiques highlight is that the use of hybridity in both descriptive and prescriptive accounts can serve to mask underlying injustices and power differentials between international and local actors, as well as within each of these spheres. A purely institutionalist approach that privileges the processes and outcomes of institutional interaction can thus render them devoid of their inherently political character. For example, a pure focus on the hybrid features of a hybrid court can detract attention from the constrained political circumstances in which these courts are established or from questions about whose interests these models serve in practice. There are also concerns that attempts to instrumentalise 'hybrid governance' can be appropriated as part of broader neoliberal agendas and used to hollow out already 'weak' states by outsourcing the provision of public goods to international actors, private providers or, indeed, to poor communities themselves.[43] Likewise, there are well-founded concerns about 'romanticising the local' and downplaying significant power differentials at the local level based on gender, age, ethnic or other significant divisions. All of this suggests that if the hybridity concept is used without sufficient attention to the power dynamics and conflictual elements in the specific context in question, it can ultimately serve to reproduce existing patterns of hierarchy, domination and prevailing relations of power.

History, power and scale

Against the background of the growing prominence of the hybridity concept and the emerging critiques, it seemed to us as a group of scholars engaged in these issues that questions of history, power and scale had not been adequately examined. The seminar series, which along with the workshop provided an important part of the genesis of this edited collection, set out to probe these questions in greater detail. For example, we asked presenters to consider whether hybridity describes a relatively new undertaking, or whether it merely crystallises processes of interaction and syncretism that have deep historical roots. We similarly challenged them to reflect on whether focusing on hybridity as a potential 'solution' to enduring problems of conflict and instability obscures important questions of power and agency that are inherent in contested sites of institutional transformation, thereby risking potentially unintended and

---

43   Meagher, 'The Strength of Weak States?'.

undesirable outcomes. Finally, we asked presenters to analyse the role of scale in relation to hybridity, including whether and how interactions play out differently at local, national, regional and international levels.

Participants at the workshop were asked to reflect on the extent to which their work resonates with one or more of six central themes that had emerged during the seminar series. The first of these was 'plurality'. Many speakers at the seminar series noted the need to broaden the conventional state-centric focus of disciplines such as political science, international relations, development studies and law in order to recognise a more comprehensive spectrum of state and non-state actors, institutions and practices. We asked speakers to consider whether this plurality poses difficulties in terms of disentangling different scales of intervention spanning 'local', 'national' and 'transnational' levels. How might analyses of hybridity work to decentre the conventional focus on the state? How might they adequately recognise the complex of linkages, relationships, frictions and shifting scales between international and local institutions, actors and discourses in particular contexts? Might these relationships and frictions also contain emancipatory or generative potential?

The second key theme that emerged during the seminar series was that of 'history'. The role of history, including colonialism, was identified repeatedly as playing a fundamental role in the determination of present-day relationships between institutions in postcolonial societies and, indeed, in many cases, their very existence. Much analysis of hybridity in disciplines outside history, however, tends to be 'history blind'. Policy discourse, in particular, is often narrowly focused on current circumstances and priorities with scant attention to historical precedent. The problematic historical uses of hybridity in the discipline of anthropology and its unhelpful connotations of essentialism was also raised. Might a more historically grounded approach problematise and enrich the concept of hybridity?

The third key theme was 'power'. The prevalence, but also the potential invisibility, of power dynamics within and between a wide range of groups emerged as a key theme in the seminar series. Some speakers noted that the concept of hybridity can mask underlying injustices and power differentials between international and local actors, as well as within each of these spheres. In this regard, there was an echoing of the concerns raised in the emergent critique of hybridity including a tendency to romanticise the 'local' and neglect local power differences. Other speakers noted that international and national actors and institutions disproportionately shape the terms of hybrid arrangements because of structural imbalances in the distribution of power and control of resources. Might it be possible for analyses of hybridity to pay more attention to conflictual elements and power dynamics? While other orders exist, should the particular power and resources of the state be analysed differently?

The fourth theme was that of 'scale', drawing, in particular, on the insights of human geographers, and was one that resonated with many speakers from different disciplines. Consistent with the 'local turn' in peacebuilding scholarship, much of the hybridity literature has an explicit orientation towards the most local level in contexts of intervention. Given continuing assumptions about the centrality of the nation-state as the normal way of organising social and political life, this growing sensibility to the significance of subnational scales provides a welcome corrective. We nevertheless need to avoid being constrained by artificial categorisations of space and scale that obscure the realities of the flow of ideas, people, resources and politics across all such categories including 'the local'. While assumptions about the centrality of states remain deeply entrenched in disciplines like international relations, political science, law and development studies, the lived realities of contemporary globalisation are much less static and spatially fragmented owing to the dynamic flows across what many continue to view as bounded spaces. Analysing these fluid and multilayered complexities requires a new spatial imaginary freed from such artificial boundaries.

The fifth theme was that of 'reinscribing binaries'. Another point raised during the seminar series was the fact that the hybridity concept often reinscribes problematic binaries even as it seeks to unpack them (for instance between the global/local). Given the historical influences of colonialism, globalisation and intervention, it is often argued that actors and institutions are continuously negotiating and renegotiating a range of locally derived and non-localised norms and in this sense are already 'hybrid'. Does this suggest the need for a different term? Do terms such as pluralism, syncretism, the third space, intersections or friction offer more theoretically adequate alternatives to the hybridity concept?

The sixth and final theme was 'conceptual tools'. During the seminar series, many speakers identified that ambiguities exist in relation to the ways in which the hybridity concept is 'operationalised' through policies in areas including rule of law and statebuilding and peacebuilding. In some ways, the most superficial of these insights has been exploited by those driving reforms as a way of co-opting more resources and undermining potential opposition. However, the more profound insights about the need to engage more equitably with systems, institutions and individuals operating on the basis of fundamentally different principles, values and world views has been overlooked. We asked speakers to consider what conceptual tools might enable the translation of the hybridity concept into more meaningful and equitable policy development.

The chapters

Reflecting themes raised in the chapters, we have divided this book into four sections. The first, 'Theorising Hybridity', contains six chapters which interrogate the conceptual foundations of hybridity. Anne Brown's chapter sets the theoretical scene for the book, as she traces the 'family trees' of the concept of hybridity, ranging from biology to postcolonial studies. While Brown notes that neither the concept nor phenomenon of hybridity is new, she describes how it emerged in the context of specific debates about statebuilding and peacebuilding to bring fresh attention to the 'dense layering of interactions, relations and institutions that make up political community and constitute the basis of state formation'. She analyses how hybridity has been used in three primary ways in the statebuilding and peacebuilding literature: descriptively, aspirationally and instrumentally. Brown concludes by proposing more dialogical ways of seeking to understand peacebuilding that are grounded in 'processes and habits of open-ended exchange'.

Paul Jackson and Peter Albrecht's chapter interrogates the concept of hybridity by focusing on the 'power of local actors to resist the imposition of liberal statebuilding processes'. They are particularly interested in including 'the political' into analyses of hybridity, in order to recognise how hybridity during statebuilding and peacebuilding can be 'moderated by the political power of local elites'. They are also concerned that much of the hybridity literature 'reifies and idealises "the local"', thereby overlooking the power structures and political processes of inclusion and exclusion that they involve.

Charles Hunt's chapter analyses the concept of hybridity from the perspective of a relational approach that recognises the multilayered nature of sociopolitical orders in conflict-affected societies. Using a case study of Liberia, Hunt illustrates the complexity of these societies and the importance of analysing the relationships between different providers of order, security and justice. He concludes by arguing for a relational approach to hybridity based on a 'performative-based, liminal and integrative understanding of hybrid sociopolitical order'.

Miranda Forsyth's chapter considers whether the concept of hybridity should be used normatively as well as descriptively. She proposes that hybridity should be developed to 'answer questions about how legal/ regulatory systems *ought to be*, as well as describing how they currently work'. Forsyth then makes proposals concerning how this might occur, identifying three starting points: 'focus on the values and objectives at stake, concentrate on the processes of change, and analyse the relationships between and within different legal orders'. She concludes that developing the concept along normative lines can 'facilitate change agents in helping to steer hybrid legal orders in positive and emancipatory directions'.

Joanne Wallis's chapter traces how a sense of humility within Western governments and international institutions regarding liberal peacebuilding has facilitated the emergence of the concept of hybridity in statebuilding and peacebuilding in order to achieve 'good enough' outcomes. She considers how hybridity has operated during peacebuilding in Timor-Leste and identifies a number of challenges it has faced. She concludes by arguing there is evidence that many Timorese desire a role for modern liberal state institutions 'as a response to the inequality, exclusions and injustices that can occur under local practices and institutions', and consequently that while the concept of hybridity should not be abandoned, building liberal state institutions may retain a place in contemporary peacebuilding.

Shahar Hameiri and Lee Jones's chapter takes a more radical stance, arguing that the concept of hybridity is 'unfit for purpose and must be entirely jettisoned' in the study of statebuilding and peacebuilding. They argue that the hybridity literature has been 'unable to escape binaries based on dichotomised categories of the illiberal-local and liberal-international', which they conclude 'distorts empirical analysis'. Instead, they propose an alternative framework based on a Gramscian understanding of the state and other governance institutions as 'condensations of social power relations'. They argue that this approach helps to recognise the 'politics of scale' of 'hierarchised social, political and economic territorial spaces', including how power and resources are distributed among different scales during statebuilding and peacebuilding interventions.

Section two of the book consists of five chapters that engage with the concept of hybridity in the postconflict settings of Bougainville, Solomon Islands, Timor-Leste and Mozambique respectively, with reference to broader processes of peacebuilding and statebuilding in these different contexts. Drawing on extensive fieldwork in Bougainville, Volker Boege's chapter proposes a relational understanding of hybridisation in peacebuilding as a fluid and dynamic process of interaction between 'local' and 'international' actors. His chapter documents the extent to which Bougainvillean agency was able to mediate and shape the implementation and outcomes of the international peacebuilding agenda. This includes the ways in which 'local' agency was able to appropriate the resources of the latter according to Bougainvillean's priorities, logic and understanding of the islands' unique political economy. Boege also reflects on the impacts of these interactions on the international actors and how these contributed to the 'turn to the local' in regional peacebuilding practice and the emergence of a more reflective discourse around 'relational sensibility'.

Sinclair Dinnen and Matthew Allen use a case study of rural Solomon Islands to reflect critically on the value of 'hybridity' as a concept for understanding and engaging with the complex and ongoing processes of state formation—as distinct from statebuilding—underway in this island nation. While seeing value in engaging with 'local' forms of authority and regulation in localities where state presence is weak, Dinnen and Allen share many of the concerns raised by critics of 'the local turn' in peacebuilding and development. They also point out that attempts to instrumentalise hybridity are by no means confined to international and national-level actors but are also apparent in the strategies of local-level actors. Their chapter emphasises the multiple scales at which processes of hybridisation take place, with an explicit critique of the privileging of 'the local' scale in much of the hybridity literature. The authors also question assumptions that local-level actors naturally prefer local forms of authority and organisation over state and transnational forms. On the contrary, they argue that many rural Solomon Islanders are demanding greater engagement with Weberian-like institutions that are perceived—rightly or wrongly—as being more emancipated from what are viewed as the corrosive and corrupting influence of local social and power relations.

Drawing on her research into transitional justice in Timor-Leste, Lia Kent's starting point is the need to pay more attention to the ways in which individuals and communities deal with the legacies of the violent past outside formal institutional contexts and dispute resolution forums. She argues that these subtler actions and practices are critical to ongoing processes of reconstructing social life in postconflict Timor-Leste and are better understood as part of a process of 'everyday' reconciliation where those with limited power 'make do' with resources, tactics and possibilities. In doing so, she seeks to widen the scope of what has hitherto been encompassed in analyses of hybrid transitional justice by proposing a richer conception that goes beyond a focus on institutions, structures and conflict resolution 'events' and pays more attention to the ongoing process of rebuilding everyday life and renegotiating relationships following conflict. Central to Kent's conception of hybrid transitional justice is a relational understanding of individuals as 'socially constituted' and 'attached to others'. As she argues, this more dynamic understanding is particularly relevant in kinship-based societies such as Timor-Leste, where maintaining good relations is not only important to an individual's social standing, but is absolutely critical to sustaining viable social life, security and economic survival.

Victor Igreja's chapter examines what he terms 'post-hybridity bargaining' and 'embodied accountability' in postwar Mozambique, where he has undertaken periodic fieldwork over the past two decades. Following the country's protracted and bloody civil war (1976–1992), state authorities took no steps to hold the perpetrators of serious acts of violence accountable for their actions. Igreja's focus on 'post-hybridity bargaining' examines the participation of war survivors, community leaders and spiritual agents in struggles for accountability and justice in particular rural localities. Sometimes this involves negotiations with individual representatives of state authority, such as police officers. At other times, this kind of bargaining entails ignoring or manipulating state agents and each other in order to pursue personal and more culturally meaningful forms of accountability and justice. State authorities similarly shift between taking diverse community actors seriously to ignoring and manipulating them, and, on occasion, violently abusing them. For Igreja, the continuously shifting and unpredictable quality of 'post-hybridity bargaining' serves to unsettle notions of hybridity that assume a relatively stable state of co-existence and overlap between different political orders. Any attempt to formalise or render more predictable the outcomes of such fluid and malleable processes of negotiation is fraught with risk, not least given that these very qualities are key sources of social innovation and change. In his view, policy engagements in this area must themselves be experimental in order to have any chance of success.

The last chapter in this section, by James Scambary and Todd Wassel, returns the reader to Timor-Leste and the challenges of national and international peacebuilding efforts, particularly following serious disturbances in Dili in 2006, in such a dynamic social landscape. It draws on the practical fieldwork experiences of both authors in Timor-Leste over the past ten years. Echoing key strands in the emergent critique of hybrid peacebuilding, Scambary and Wassel highlight the limited understanding of Timor-Leste's complex, nonlinear and rapidly changing social systems, as well as the highly localised scale and endemic nature of conflict in this country. Using a case study approach to trace the evolution of peacebuilding efforts since 2006, the authors strike an optimistic note in illustrating how recent initiatives have been based on nuanced analyses of local forms of authority and organisation and, indeed, different forms of hybridity. These efforts have met with some success in reinvigorating community networks going beyond preconceived ideas about 'traditional leadership' and are open to engaging with a variety of other actors including clandestine associations, youth groups and church organisations.

The third section consists of two chapters that examine hybridity in relation to broader issues of security and politics. Drawing on the canons of (Western) war studies, as well as contemporary strategic and security studies, Gavin Mount's chapter adopts a 'hybrid sensibility' to explore the blurred boundaries between war and peace. His survey of the canonical texts shows how a reflexive analysis of dominant binary categories of 'war' and 'peace' can be used to elucidate the hybrid dynamics of power, legitimacy and identity in conflict-affected societies. A focus on the interstitial period between states of war and relative peace demonstrates that these conditions exist on a continuum and that both categories are firmly anchored in shared notions of the 'political'. For Mount, the conceptual or heuristic value of hybridity in thinking about war and peace relates to how it allows analysts to reinscribe rigid boundaries while simultaneously revealing significant nuances and overlapping understandings.

Imelda Deinla's chapter draws on research undertaken by herself and colleagues in the Autonomous Region of Muslim Mindanao, an area of the southern Philippines that is well known for its ethnic and religious divisions and longstanding pattern of conflict. Hybrid justice mechanisms have developed in this region as ways of coping with insecurity arising from actual and perceived injustices. These mechanisms are drawn from a plurality of customary, Islamic and state justice practices and work through informal networks. They appear to do so in a relatively coordinated way and serve to prevent conflict escalation while providing a level of justice and security provision to local populations. As well as being locally initiated, innovations are now also evident in respect of some national initiatives responding to local demands for more timely, flexible and adequate dispute resolution. These forms of hybrid justice emanating from national or state-level sources offer insights into how professional and culturally attuned justice provision can provide a better alternative to locally initiated mechanisms that remain susceptible to capture by local elites and discriminatory practices against vulnerable groups such as women.

The chapters in the fourth and final section examine hybridity in relation to gender. In different ways, each chapter draws attention to how hybridised environments can offer both opportunities and constraints to women, and highlights the need for analyses of hybridity to pay more attention to gendered power relations. The first chapter, by Damian Grenfell, draws on long-term fieldwork to examine the thorny issue of violence against women in Timor-Leste. Taking as his starting point the idea that 'customary' and 'modern' forms of spatiality co-exist in Timor-Leste, Grenfell suggests that while modern space tends to be treated as 'secular, empty, commodifiable, transferrable', customary space is understood very differently, and is characterised by genealogical and kinship connections between living people and, in turn, their relationship with the ancestors. Critical of the ways in which international development agencies 'render' Timor-Leste as patriarchal—a move that labels the population negatively and deems it in need of 'modernising'— Grenfell argues that modern forms of spatiality may be just as gendered as customary forms of spatiality. To illustrate his argument, Grenfell shows that in Timor-Leste's capital, Dili, modern modes of production work to 'contain' women to the private sphere in ways that often exacerbate their dependence on intimate partners. He concludes by arguing that the interaction and overlap between customary and modern spatialities may at times compound women's experiences of violence rather than enabling pathways away from it.

The next chapter by Nicole George is a study of Fiji, specifically of the gendered consequences of the hybridised security environment. George focuses on the ways in which the operations of 'state security agencies in Fiji are shaped by, and intertwined with, powerful institutions of customary and religious authority'. While at first glance the fusing of state and indigenous authority structures might suggest that state policing is more locally resonant, George argues that the interplay between 'bottom-up' and 'top-down' sites of authority generates its own gendered exclusions and restrictions. George deploys Nils Bubant's concept of 'vernacular security' to explore how threats to security are framed and legitimised. Specifically, she shows how the Methodist faith and custom both 'sustain a sense of distinctive Fijian unity and identity' and simultaneously give rise to 'fears about Fijians' ultimate survival and need for vigorous state protection of indigenous custom and the centrality of their church'. In this context, women's identity and behaviour are rigorously policed to ensure that gendered norms, which are viewed as foundational to the achievement and maintenance of social order, predominate. George concludes with a call for more nuanced thinking about the 'vernacularised ontologies of uncertainty and insecurity that are generated in hybridised environments' which, in the Fijian context at least, have resulted in forms of policing that are deeply gendered.

The final chapter, by Ceridwen Spark, on Papua New Guinea, offers a more optimistic perspective on the potential of hybrid spaces to open up possibilities for women. Spark explores the French-owned Duffy cafe in Port Moresby, which is frequented by expatriates and well-to-do Papuan New Guineans, as a site of hybridity. Spark argues that it would be erroneous to see the cafe merely as the embodiment of wealth, privilege and consumerism, suggesting that to some extent it has also become a site where 'new sociospatial practices and identities' are produced that challenge the dominant constructions of class and gender in Port Moresby. Spark illustrates these dynamics by drawing on photos and commentary shared by a Papuan New Guinean woman, 'Karuka', who now lives in Melbourne, Australia. Through the eyes of Karuka and other women interviewed by Spark, we are able to see that Duffy enables some 'women to construct themselves as friends and customers—rather than daughters, wives or sisters—and in doing so provides momentary liberation from the ordinary constraints of life in Port Moresby'.

Conclusion

As the hybridity concept becomes ever more popular among academics and policymakers working in the interrelated fields of development, security studies and peacebuilding, nuanced reflections on its utility are increasingly necessary. A notable strength of the contributions to this edited collection is that they are grounded in in-depth knowledge of specific local contexts. This enriches the analyses, and allows the messy, awkward and dynamic realities of hybridity—the power dynamic, and diverse actors, ideas, practices and sites that shape it—to be brought into full view. This, in turn, provides rich insights into the possibilities and limitations of hybridity as a conceptual tool.

Section One — Theorising Hybridity

1

The 'Hybrid Turn': Approaches and Potentials

M. Anne Brown

Introduction

Hybridity, the hybrid turn and hybrid political orders have become increasingly common as terms in debates around peacebuilding, state formation, governance and, to some extent, counter-insurgency and security in postcolonial states. While circulating in scholarly debate, where they are best exemplified in the work of Oliver Richmond,[1] Volker Boege, Roger Mac Ginty and others, these terms, or approaches associated with them, now also appear regularly in policy and practice arenas,[2] where they have emerged as part of a response to what is seen as the relative failure of many international postwar reconstruction, statebuilding and security interventions to establish stable, relatively peaceful and well-governed states in many postcolonial regions.[3] As the word implies, hybridity in the first instance is concerned with interaction and change across significant difference—in the context of these debates, the difference in question relates to the making and experience of political community, in the fullest

---

1   There is an extensive opus of work by Oliver Richmond, including, for example, 'Resistance and the Post-liberal Peace' and *A Post-liberal Peace*.
2   OECD-DAC, *OECD DAC Handbook on Security System Reform*, 17; World Bank, *World Development Report 2011*.
3   Ramsbotham et al., *Contemporary Conflict Resolution*.

sense of that term, across time and always engaging questions of power. Hybridity offers a way of bringing focus to the struggles, entanglements, patterns of occlusion and exclusion, processes of reworking, and ways of doing things engendered by the interaction of sometimes profoundly different logics of social and political order, sources of legitimacy and patterns of collective meaning.

How sociopolitical orders approach significant difference is a longstanding and ongoing challenge which has been understood and managed very differently across changing historical and sociocultural contexts. This discussion of hybridity is part of these wideranging and fundamental debates about how we collectively live, and more specifically about the desired nature of the state, and it carries implications for these debates. Nevertheless, as the later discussion of the emergence of the current exchange regarding hybridity indicates, the use of hybridity here has a more particular focus and purpose. Here hybridity is a response to the standardising drive dominating statebuilding and associated governance agendas in international development and peacebuilding contexts.

Varied family trees can be traced for hybridity, from biology to postcolonial studies.[4] At the same time, 'hybridity' is an everyday word with all the mutability that common usage brings; in scholarly and policy contexts there can be sharply different uses and meanings at work.[5] This chapter is not endeavouring to patrol the boundaries of a word at play in such a range of contexts. Nevertheless, the expression has become significant in a spectrum of interrelated debates and practices because references to hybridity enable certain kinds of discursive work to occur; they make possible certain conceptual insights, linkages and moves; and they open the way for particular practices. In the context of international peacebuilding, statebuilding and development, there is arguably a desperate need to recognise the reality of profound difference both between the sociopolitical models predominantly carried by such international endeavours and the lived reality of the recipient populations but also within the recipient states, to understand and give weight to that difference in new ways, and to craft ways of working creatively with and across it. Hybridity could thus open the potential for new ways of thinking about relations within states, but also across political communities within and among states.

---

4   See, for example, Bhabha, 'Signs Taken for Wonders'.
5   See, for example, Mac Ginty and Richmond, 'The Fallacy of Constructing Hybrid Political Orders', for a discussion of different approaches.

The contexts in which references to hybridity and the hybrid turn have again gained prominence (touched on later) cast light on some of these moves and practices. It is also important to reflect critically on the significantly different ways that hybridity can be used, and therefore the different kinds of work that the term can be undertaking and the different trajectories that work is embedded within. A reference to hybridity does not automatically bear the same potential or significance from one use to another. This is not only a matter of conceptual clarity, but also of following the threads of practical, political and ethical potential and effect.

As a phenomenon, hybridity is not new. There is nothing novel in complex, dynamic enmeshments across difference, including friction and transformation across struggles for power. Negotiating profound difference seems likely to be a fundamental and potentially creative part of collective human experience and activity, across millennia of migrations, trade, wars, occupations and marriages; it is also often deeply challenging, frequently unchosen and repeatedly violent. All sociopolitical formations could be understood as 'hybrid' in this very general use of the term. As a broadly theoretical term, postcolonial studies then bring to this generic insight a more particular focus on the long history and deeply formative ongoing experience and legacy of colonialism, for all parties.[6] Many studies explore the long, complex and often self-contradictory collective and individual relations, identities and psyches shaped by centuries of colonial interaction. Even while recognising the deformations produced by deep structural violence, these accounts, often of resistances and radical reappropriations, offer critically important alternatives to analyses that produce simply oppressors and victims.[7]

Contexts of emergence

The uses of hybridity discussed in this chapter emerged more specifically in the context of debates around statebuilding, state-strengthening, governance and peacebuilding efforts undertaken by international and external state agencies. In such debates, the state is not surprisingly taken to be the fundamental vehicle for political life, and so for stability, governance and prosperity.[8] A distinguishing factor in this current usage

---

6   Appiah, *In My Father's House*; Braithwaite, *The Development of Creole Society in Jamaica*.
7   Nandy, *The Intimate Enemy*.
8   Paris and Sisk, *The Dilemmas of Statebuilding*.

of the term, then, is a focus on how the state and political community take shape, change and consolidate (or not),[9] whether or not 'the state' features prominently in any particular analysis. The hybrid turn, however, arguably marks a shift towards more complex, but perhaps also more grounded, notions of what in fact constitutes a working state, in contrast to the more technocratic models favoured by statebuilding interventions. Hybridity as an analytical approach brings a focus on the state not solely from the more common perspective of state institutions, but rather in terms of the dense layering of interactions, relations and institutions that make up political community and constitute the basis of state formation, in which state institutions play key roles.[10]

Indeed, the hybrid turn more often engages with community, customary or more generally societal efforts regarding security, justice, peace, welfare, conflict resolution or governance—dynamics that are rarely centre stage in international statebuilding agendas. Nor is 'the state' assumed to exist according to the narrative of the secular, legal-institutional architecture forged for it in statebuilding exercises. The world of the unseen—of the dead, the sacred, of spirits, ghosts and the powers of nature—can be and often is a fundamental part of political community, including of its play of power.[11] Whether 'the state' is understood as the institutional and legal framework for regulation, however, or whether it is understood more broadly as potentially encompassing the political communities across an entire population (living and perhaps also the dead), this complex, multivalenced world of sociopolitical life is what the state is part of and what it must work with, across and for. For many people in postcolonial states, who are both inevitably building on but also struggling with the colonial legacy, the encounter with the state is the ongoing effort to craft their own working political order, perhaps simply to continue cultivating their own place, but in effect to contribute to shaping their own state in the context of a dynamic, dangerous and interconnected world. This effort involves not only matters of self-rule, security and wellbeing but also identity and meaning, and it is always fought out across and as part of the power dynamics in play.

---

9   That is, the hybrid turn focuses on broader processes of 'state formation' rather than the narrower, more technical focus of 'statebuilding' which relies on the essentially technical processes of institutional transfer and 'capacity building' over short time frames.

10   Grenfell et al., *Understanding Community*; Wiuff Moe, 'Hybrid and "Everyday" Political Ordering'.

11   Ellis and ter Haar, *Worlds of Power*; Grenfell, 'Remembering the Dead'.

Hybridity in this context then refers to the complex co-existence, exchange and entanglement between often incommensurate logics of social, political and sacred order in the ongoing process of state formation and shaping political community: between, on one hand, the various prevailing values and practices of particular peoples and, on the other hand, the various norms and practices embedded in the dominant legal-institutional models of state operation, neoliberal modes of economic rationality and what could loosely be called 'modern' social formations and constructions of the person. Notions of hybridity thus begin as a pointer to, and a lens on, the need to take profound difference as fundamental in the dynamic of political order and as embedded in the very structure and working life of most postcolonial states (and perhaps increasingly, in all states). In this case, difference is not simply a matter of competing interests or antagonistic ethnic or religious identities, but refers to what are often profoundly different ways of knowing and being in the world. As well as some anthropologists and ethnographers, theorists of radical indigeneity point to this depth of difference well.[12] Nevertheless, this is a difference of logics or of ways of knowing—actual empirical institutions, groups and even individuals can be deeply shaped by both: hence hybridity. A working chief in Ghana might have a masters degree from a British or United States university; the head of a government department in Vanuatu can be deeply embedded in very traditionally operating kinship networks from a remote island; a community and customary leader from Bougainville might be trying to forge viable responses to contemporary political dilemmas, drawing on customary and parliamentary political dynamics, and so forth. While some groups live overwhelmingly in one 'world' or another, and many activities circulate within one set of meanings, many interweave different domains on a daily basis. Identity is never uniform or homogenous, and is perhaps always marked by difference with itself.[13] Despite this interweaving, however, negotiating profound difference in the context of forging political community or state formation throws down fundamental political, practical and ethical dilemmas. It intensifies the questions of how we live together across difference, questions that are arguably one of the drivers of the enterprise of the modern state, but takes them into another register altogether.[14] These questions are also relevant to a wide range of national contexts.

---

12 See, for example, Alfred, 'What Is Radical Imagination?'; Smith, *Decolonizing Methodologies*.
13 Derrida, *Writing and Difference*.
14 Tully, *Strange Multiplicity*.

One strong initial motivation for talking about hybridity and hybrid political orders was the effort to move away from a preoccupation with state failure as the framework for analysis of political instability and violence in postcolonial states.[15] Some of the relatively early uses of the term, for example, emerged through research and practice engagements in Bougainville, Solomon Islands, Vanuatu and Timor-Leste, where a focus on state failure or incapacity, while certainly yielding insights, failed to capture both the complexity, dynamism, broader resilience and capacity of political community and social order, but also significant underlying sources of disorder.[16] Stepping aside from frameworks of state failure is not a rejection of the idea that the architecture of state governance can fail (presuming it has ever actually operated) as such, but marks an effort to investigate more comprehensively the actual forms of authority, legitimacy, order and disorder in play. This involves a more complex and open-ended imagination of the state, and opens new perspectives on its 'failure'. At a simple but fundamental level, the reference to hybridity is a refusal to judge whole regions primarily in relation to their conformity or otherwise to an idealised version of the rational-legal state—to models of what those in the Organisation for Economic Co-operation and Development (OECD) states might like to portray themselves officially as being. Such narrow grounds of assessment cannot be expected to yield a strong understanding of what is at stake in the region concerned, and only in very particular circumstances could be the basis for good policy.[17]

An emphasis on hybridity then entails taking seriously deeply held collective values, forms of knowledge and ways of life, in their dynamism, struggles and continuities, as part of a living political context. This enables sources of order that would in official terms be seen to lie outside state institutions to become more clearly visible and open to exploration—not predominantly as an anthropological engagement, but as a current political exchange. Such exploration does not imply endorsing or condemning those forms of order but, rather, requires paying full attention to them. In the countries or regions mentioned, everyday security, food security, social welfare, conflict management and justice provision are substantially underpinned by customary and community forms of order, which may

---

15   See, for example, Wainwright, *Our Failing Neighbour*.
16   Boege, 'Bougainville and the Discovery of Slowness'; Boege et al., 'State Building Reconsidered'; Boege et al., 'States Emerging from Hybrid Political Orders'; Dinnen, 'The Solomon Islands Intervention'.
17   Brown, 'Security and Development'; Dinnen and Peake, 'More than Just Policing'.

themselves be understood as part of a larger cosmic order.[18] In many respects, the working sociopolitical order of 'the state' exists by virtue of villages and customary or kin patterns. Villages, and the political fabric which enables them to work, need, then, to come more fully into view, not as a signifier of what is parochial or of the past, but as a functioning way of contemporary life. Considering hybridity also, however, brings more clearly into focus the profound forms of disorder, alienation, manipulation and sociopolitical dysfunction that can be generated in the context of disjunction and deep ambiguity between prevailing social values and official state institutional systems and norms.[19]

A focus on state failure, by contrast, approaches questions of order and disorder through the lens not of the state as political community, but of a narrow conception of the state modelled around (in effect) the ideal forms of state institutions. This identification of the state with government and juridical institutions—an identification that to a significant extent conceptually underpins institutional transfer processes[20]—posits both a categorical distinction between state and society, and a fundamental uniformity between the values, life-worlds and political vocabulary of state and society, and across society. The idea of the state carried by much statebuilding embeds an assumption that the narrow, idealised forms of state institutions and of the notional public sphere of the liberal state are sufficiently grounded on universal reason to be beyond 'culture' and difference.[21] For this fundamental form of intervention and the powerful idea of the state that is associated with it, the ideal form of sociopolitical life has already been determined and simply awaits implementation. While such assumptions may work well enough where the structure and processes of state institutions substantially share underlying cultural understandings with a broadly homogenous population, they are considerably less effective for (the increasing number of) states where that is not the case.[22] Beyond programs of education and training, predominant statebuilding and peacebuilding narratives offer few tools for working with the relationship between government or international institutions and societal networks, or for exploring the complex interplay between prevailing cultural norms of obligation, accountability and appropriate behaviour with liberal

---

18 Grenfell et al., *Understanding Community*; Hicks, *Tetum Ghosts and Kin*.
19 Ellis and ter Haar, *Worlds of Power*.
20 Lamour, *Foreign Flowers*.
21 Eriksen, 'State Effects'; Tully, *Strange Multiplicity*.
22 Dodson, 'The Human Rights Situation of Indigenous Peoples'.

rights norms and legal-institutional models of behaviour, or for even understanding why such work might be important.[23] It is common for forms of sociopolitical order that are neither government nor civil society (often, although not solely, customary forms) to be seen as in competition with, undermining or corrupting state institutions, inherently exploitative or violent or simply as too fragmentary to act as viable sources of order. Often they are implicitly cast as the 'dark shadow' of the past from which modern life has progressed and against which it marks its progress. This is to rule them out from serious engagement from the start. It can be these institutions and networks, however, that actually enable key forms of sociopolitical life and in effect underpin the state.[24]

Notions of hybridity thus support a move away from taking the legal-institutional, broadly Weberian models of the state as the definitive standard of political community, and as the sole source or form of political goods such as accountability, participation, legitimacy, justice and ethics. They call for more complex understandings of what might constitute political order and political community and for processes for defining and achieving collective goods and shared understanding across profound difference.[25]

Terminologies and scales

The difference of sociopolitical logics to which hybridity refers is sometimes characterised as one between 'state' and 'society' and sometimes as the interaction of 'international' and 'local' (whether because exchanges between international agencies and local people in the context of international peacebuilding or statebuilding are the focus of analysis, or because the state itself is seen as an internationalising force). Or the difference might be understood as one between customary, modern or other possible social formations.[26] The first two of these characterisations, however, have a shorthand quality, and all are more relevant to certain situations than others. Categories of society, state, local, national, international are fundamental to how contemporary politics is thought; they situate each other in a network of constitutive references, arranged

---

23   Hohe, 'The Clash of Paradigms'.
24   Grenfell et al., *Understanding Community*; McWilliam, 'Customary Governance in Timor-Leste'.
25   Mac Ginty and Richmond, 'The Fallacy of Constructing Hybrid Political Orders'.
26   For example, see Grenfell, this volume.

in vertical hierarchies.[27] Perhaps in part because of their fundamental nature, such categories are not so stable when pushed empirically or theoretically. A state is not simply a 'domestic' entity experienced (and to varying extents constructed) by those living within a defined territory and in principle subject to its laws, institutions and requirements—although it is certainly that. As a political and legal form the state is a globalised phenomenon and effectively enforced as such—for peoples wishing to exercise a particular level of self-rule and sovereignty, or even simply security from invasion or domination by violent others, there is as yet no alternative to being a state. Even when borders are in effect notional, the state is by definition the hinge point of articulation between domestic and international, 'inside' and 'outside', by virtue of which these spaces are constituted.[28] The encounter with the state, and the architecture of political, social and economic modes of practice it references, is (albeit to varying degrees) an encounter with a globalising drive as much as with a 'domestic' or national one. The 'local' is meanwhile saturated by, and interwoven with, international and global influences and forces.

A spectrum of approaches

This chapter distinguishes among three different ways of using notions of hybridity as a theoretical tool. A key distinction turns on the question of instrumentalisation and therefore on the nature of relationships between what could be called the subjects and the objects of the approach enabled by notions of hybridity.[29] As will become clearer, this focus on instrumentalisation and relationship has important epistemological, practical, political and ethical dimensions.

The first use of hybridity is as an analytical or descriptive category, broadly in line with the orientations set out above. That is, it is not in the first instance normative, does not point to something to be aimed for, and does not denote a good or a bad state of play in itself. In this usage, hybridity simply marks a recognition of the co-existence of diverse sources of order (and disorder) within the make-up of political community, without judging such co-existence to be inherently negative, and so opens a space to investigate the prevailing ecology of relationships.

---

27 Escobar, *Territories of Difference*; Ferguson and Gupta, 'Spatializing States'.
28 Walker, *Inside/Outside*.
29 See also Mac Ginty and Richmond, 'The Fallacy of Constructing Hybrid Political Orders'.

Research informed by this approach—into questions of everyday security, for example—might explore with people in communities, towns and across an array of relevant institutions and community positions common sources of insecurity, who or what is seen to provide security or to counter insecurity and how they go about it, avenues for accountability, patterns of exclusion and inclusion, patterns of vulnerability, how providers of security might link outwards geographically or institutionally, and so on. The answers to such questions often concern social order generated by complex networks of groups; they often include customary networks as fundamental lines of connection and modes of practice, but can also include elements of state institutions and regional governments; they might include church or religious groups, but also community-based organisations and neighbourhood associations. Such work often focuses more on the everyday production of life and less on elites, whether these are elites claiming state platforms, or their rivals (e.g. warlords), although such figures are certainly key actors and might feature in the chain of connections. While the perspectives opened by hybridity as an approach can provide sharp insight into dysfunction and violence, one consequence of this line of enquiry is that it is possible to discover that rather more is working than often appears to be the case.[30]

This approach is somewhat different from an emphasis on political economy. While both might seek to drill deep into the nature of interactions among a wide range of players, an emphasis on hybridity might look not only at the complex dynamics of power, but also at profoundly different understandings of what constitutes power, of what its sources might be, and what might operate as checks upon it. Hybridity or the hybrid turn involves a much greater recognition of what is sweepingly and reductively called 'culture' in the generation and circulation of power. As it is understood here, the hybrid turn also carries quite particular implications for and orientations to practice, even if that is simply the comportment of self-reflective research.

While an emphasis on hybridity is not, in this first and fundamental approach, normative, it can have significant normative implications, as implied earlier. Moreover, these dimensions can be pushed far. The key element here is the importance of paying attention, of taking people's own values, beliefs, emotions, practices and self-understanding

---

30   See, for example, Boege, 'Bougainville and the Discovery of Slowness'; Dinnen and Peake, 'More than Just Policing'.

seriously. After the manner of Simone Weil, attention may be what we fundamentally have to offer each other.[31] This does not mean accepting or endorsing those values, or preclude critiquing them, if that seems relevant, but it does require serious engagement. While this certainly has significance in a research context, it becomes even more pressing in a practice engagement. The critical question becomes one of mutuality and dialogic exchange with the normative point including the question of how might 'we', as researchers, practitioners or 'intervenors', engage? This shifts focus from being only on 'others' elsewhere to the nature of the exchange and perhaps the history of the exchange; it thus includes ourselves, as reflective researchers and practitioners.[32]

This shift thus involves self-reflection regarding the nature and impact of our individual but also collective agency and actions, including the history of actions that we, perhaps unwittingly, represent to those we are interacting with; it involves a move away from the 'delivery' mode that dominates development, and from imagining that 'our' work is technical and neutral, to an emphasis on participation and the quality of relationship. It involves recognising others as interlocutors, as co-creators of knowledge and action and demands a capacity to enter into difficult conversations and exchange. Perhaps most challenging, it involves stepping back from a demand to control. If we are seeking some form of change in others, not only do we need to understand (as well as we can) people's sources and forms of practice, we might also need to be open to change ourselves—even if that change is primarily in the ability to enter into more mutual forms of engagement.[33] In this, such modes of engagement echo the loosening of those discourses of the state, centralised to the sovereign point at which control ultimately resides and from which it radiates. The normativity of the hybrid turn in this iteration does not, therefore, concern how to achieve hybridity, but how to support the more familiar goals of wellbeing, reasonable safety, food security, reduction of violence, greater justice and so forth, but doing so in ways that place priority on paying attention to the people involved, their own goals, what is valued, by whom, the range of views on how it might be achieved, and the nature and quality of the exchange.

---

31 Weil, *The First and Last Notebooks.*
32 Lederach, *The Moral Imagination*; Schon, *The Reflective Practitioner.*
33 Brown, *Human Rights and the Borders of Suffering.*

A second use of hybridity, which is more prominent in the peacebuilding literature, casts it as something to be aimed at. In practical terms this approach emerges from the very reasonable effort to encourage international agencies or national elites to give greater recognition or weight to widely prevalent forms of sociopolitical order. A subtle shift takes place, however, from working with communities' own approaches to (for example) achieve less violent everyday security provision to seeking to achieve 'hybridity'. This approach appears to be the result of setting up the argument as a chequerboard of moves in a narrative of development, shaped by the logic of the positive dialectic, from which synthesis ideally emerges. The emphasis shifts from the process of mutuality to an imagined outcome—a newly constructed hybridity. 'Hybridity' then becomes a conceptual space, and a prefigured, notional or narrative solution to a profound, ongoing set of concrete issues about how we live together. This is the design of hybrid institutions to which Gearoid Millar refers.[34] It appeals to the desire (or the bureaucratic need) for a 'form of words' or a repeatable 'place holder' able to stand in for concrete responses to particular conundrums. Instead of being an orientation and openness to complexity, it stands as a solution. Such a solution may be premature and reified, however, and so obscure more than it reveals. In practical terms it may endanger the challenge and potential of an emphasis on hybridity, as the need to recognise and (where relevant) work with the grain of complex, dynamic situations.

What I identify as the third approach is the effort to devise hybrid solutions, far from the mutuality of exchange, in the distant capitals of international agency such as New York or Geneva or even Kabul, in order to provide what is hoped will be predictability and uniformity. The focus here shifts to questions of control from abstract capitals and to finding more effective forms by which places and peoples can be managed so that they do not pose problems for those capitals. Hybrid sources of order and authority are recognised, but in terms of whether and how they might be manipulated. This approach represents a highly instrumentalised form of relationship, reminiscent of colonial mechanisms of 'indirect rule' whereby colonial administrations used local customary systems as a low-cost means 'to maintain order … enforce production of cash crops and collect taxes'.[35] As Richmond and Mac Ginty note, this approach is in line

---

34 Millar, 'Disaggregating Hybridity'.
35 Aning and Aubyn, 'Challenging Conventional Understandings'; Dunn, *Timor: A People Betrayed*, 54.

'with a post-Iraq and Afghanistan curtailed liberal interventionism, and is also in keeping with neoliberal mores of shifting responsibility and lowering intervention costs'.[36] Counter-insurgency also provides a developed arena of policy and practice that exemplifies this third approach to 'hybridity'. United States counter-insurgency efforts in Somalia, for example, have operated under a 'dual track' policy of engaging with a wide range of 'non-state actors' opposed to Al Shabaab.[37] Similar policies have been adopted in Afghanistan in the struggle against the Taliban, and elsewhere. This kind of approach to 'hybridity' has a very long history.

Instrumental approaches and logics are not in themselves a problem; there is no criticism intended here of the effort to achieve outcomes and the need for management of people and things in order to do so. Nor is any criticism intended of the effort to understand the power dynamics of others. The issues at stake in discussions of hybridity, however, entail working across, and in a context of, significant difference, often severe fragmentation, perhaps violence and highly unequal, coercive power dynamics. This establishes a very different context from one of managing others where a substantial political or social vocabulary and mechanisms of redress are already shared; the presence or otherwise of such contexts of exchange makes a significant difference to the nature of the instrumentalisation. The researcher or practitioner could ask how those involved at different points in the process are engaged—what is the scope for exchange, participation, accountability or even safety? How deeply are people objectified, or treated as interlocutors, and is this to engage only with the powerful, or with the spectrum of those involved in the issue at hand?

Whether or not there are reasons to argue for this instrumentalisation and objectification of people under conditions of violent insurgency, such an approach constitutes a radically different approach to hybridity. A highly instrumentalised use of hybridity may have tactical benefits, but is unlikely to be productive in situations where the international intervenors are trying to build or achieve something sustainable, such as forms of legitimacy that are not essentially coercive. Peacebuilding or statebuilding endeavours are often trying to do just this, however. A highly instrumentalised approach is unlikely to be able to build broadly based trust, or long-term relations which generate some levels of mutual respect,

36   Mac Ginty and Richmond, 'The Fallacy of Constructing Hybrid Political Orders', 220.
37   US Department of State, 2010, in Wiuff Moe, 'The "Turn to the Local"', 132.

yet it may be in the context of such relations that change regarding violent social practices (such as female genital mutilation, for example) are most likely to become possible.[38]

Moreover, it seems likely to be this instrumental third approach to hybridity that is most vulnerable to becoming seriously compromised through 'going along' with deeply violent assertions of power that can pass themselves off as an expression of 'culture' or 'tradition'. A contemporary example might be the practice of 'boy play', where powerful men use young boys as sexual slaves in Afghanistan.[39] This practice has come to international media attention over the past few years, perhaps because it has occurred among Afghan military personnel on United States (US) bases in Afghanistan. The US military hierarchy, apparently seeking not to disrupt relations with its allies, has at best 'looked the other way' and at worst offered partial protection by sidelining or dismissing those US servicemen who have objected.[40] 'Boy play' emerged from, and has been shaped by, prevailing social relations in Afghanistan, as in different ways violent paedophilia is present, and frequently 'overlooked', in countries across Europe, the Anglosphere and elsewhere. It was and is also seen across Afghanistan as abhorrent; 'overlooking' it does not build good relations nor earn respect. The hybrid turn is not a rationale for collaboration with deeply violent practices. At its best, it might rather be an opportunity to collaboratively reflect on and work with the various forms of violence that mark all our cultures.

Dialogue and its implications

As Foucault has pointed out, the ways we understand and experience the knowing subject and the processes of knowing, and the ways we understand the state, are deeply enmeshed.[41] Both are shaped around the figure of the sovereign self, the central knower, who sees and shapes the world around him. The argument that is at least implicit in notions of hybridity is that we need increasingly to explore different practices of statehood

---

38   On the basis of field research by the author in 2015, the work of the Carter Center on female genital mutilation in Liberia, for example, offers an instance of a long-term, respectful engagement that is seeking to shift this entrenched practice, with what appears some success. The Carter Center has already contributed to changes in the practice of trial by ordeal in Liberia.

39   Sahak, 'Afghanistan's Enslaved Children'.

40   Ibid.

41   Foucault, *The Archaeology of Knowledge*.

and open up richer ways of being a state—ways that cannot be generated by or assimilated into prevailing modes and practices of imagining and reproducing statehood.[42] This is not a matter of abandoning goals and principles of participation, accountability, justice, fairness, inclusion, safety, respect and so forth, but about acknowledging and working with the multiple ways that we are people in the world. Richer ways of talking and doing political community may come less from the texts of theorists, and more from experimentation and exchanges already taking place on the ground, as they are in regions around the world, where towns, villages and districts are often struggling to deal with the complex problems confronting them. Such exchanges, however, need to be taken seriously by national governments, international bodies and scholarship, and to be considered and weighed for what they might make possible or illuminate. Richer ways of understanding the state as political community (and the person as citizen) come also from supporting processes and habits of open-ended exchange that can emerge as people and institutions seek to deal with the challenges of co-existence across very different practices of political community. Such processes can emerge in the face of pressing problems communities or regions are facing. While crafting practical responses to problems can be extremely valuable, an equally valuable outcome of such processes can be the gradual creation of habits and networks of exchange and listening, the experience of being taken seriously, and the flexibility involved in sitting with profoundly different logics, cosmologies and ways of engaging in dialogue. For those representing state institutions or central elites, it requires letting go of the imperial habits of thought and practice[43] in which we have been trained, letting go of needing to know the outcome beforehand, and being prepared not always to try to control outcomes.

This need not constitute a revolution in institutional frameworks (although it might), as much as in processes and methods of engagement. Nevertheless, it would represent a major change in the ways we understand and enact the state, from a centralised 'empire of uniformity'[44] to perhaps a network of relations among and across overlapping institutions and communities, in which government has important and particular roles. This is far from a call for a 'good enough' state.[45] Rather, it represents the

---

42 Tully, *Strange Multiplicity*, 43.
43 Tully, *Strange Multiplicity*. The literal quote is 'imperious habits of thought and behaviour', 19.
44 Ibid., 58.
45 World Bank, *World Development Report 2011*.

effort to gradually craft differently calibrated, more relational and mutual ways of knowing the person and political community.[46] The challenges of crafting linkages and constructive adaption across difference, adaption that enables exploring and giving substance to key political goods such as justice, accountability, participation and mutual respect, rest not only with the usual recipients of international statebuilding efforts, but with all of us.

---

46   See Hunt, this volume, for further discussion of relational approaches.

2

Power, Politics and Hybridity

Paul Jackson and Peter Albrecht

Introduction

Hybridity and hybrid political orders form part of a body of literature that critiques the fragile-state discourse through which the modern state is contrasted with traditional or non-state modes of ordering in the global South.[1] The notion of hybridity proposes an alternative lens that aims to move beyond normative notions of fragility and failure and beyond dichotomous thinking that articulates states and non-states as discrete and independent actors and institutions. Instead, the concepts of hybridity and hybrid political orders offer starting points for comprehending the processes at work between diverse and competing structures of authority, sets of rules, logics of order and claims to power that co-exist, overlap, interact and intertwine. The blending of these spheres is the explicit focus of the hybridity lens.

Despite its burgeoning popularity, hybridity itself is undertheorised and is applied by different scholars to mean a number of things. For instance, it has been used as a means of viewing interaction between the international and the local,[2] to analyse the space of intervention;[3] it has been used descriptively by some scholars and prescriptively by

---

1   Wiuff Moe and Albrecht, 'Hybridity and Simultaneity in the Global South'.
2   Mac Ginty, *International Peacebuilding and Local Resistance*.
3   Charbonneau and Sears, 'Fighting for Liberal Peace in Mali?'.

others. This chapter regards the development of prescriptive hybridity as lacking conceptual clarity and developing approaches that assume the international community can construct hybridity through external, international program planning.

The emergence of hybridity is really a response to the failure of intervention in postconflict environments where complex social, political, economic and cultural conditions co-exist with an international approach dominated by liberal, Western thinking. Furthermore, the experiences also show there are both considerable local variations in the outcomes of such interventions, but also difference in degrees of local ownership and involvement. Hybridity contains promise within this framework by providing a critique of the binaries involved in such interventions, notably between international/modern and local/traditional. As such, it is commonly presented as a means of merging these two worlds into a mutually created political, social, economic and cultural world where the international and the local co-exist and co-produce hybrid political orders.

In addition, these hybrid orders are both locally and internationally owned, opening up the possibility of continuing external and international intervention and a new prescription for international agencies seeking to program and manage. Programming in this area typically assumes that hybridity can be planned within projects, to produce 'hybrid programming' and to make programming better through increasing legitimacy and trust. The argument follows that hybridity within political systems can improve both of these by using local networks and providers with the aim of increasing cooperation and increasing legitimacy, a role that is, in fact, very similar to colonial indirect rule.[4] Alongside this is a desire to equip local actors so they can play a more constructive role in statebuilding more broadly through incorporation (absorption?) of traditional norms and institutions into the constructing of conventional liberal states.[5] Hybridity, therefore, attempts to show that violence and the alternative governance systems that arise from it are part of an authentic and legitimate process of state formation that enjoys greater popular legitimacy than the (attempted) international imposition of Weberian state systems.[6]

---

4   Johnson and Hutchison, 'Hybridity, Political Order and Legitimacy'.
5   Clements et al., 'State Building Reconsidered'.
6   Boege et al., *On Hybrid Political Orders*.

Before continuing, we need to provide a short caveat on the international/ local dichotomy. We recognise that in many ways this is problematic, not least because national elites and national concerns do play a role within both international and local spheres of (political) activity. However, this chapter focuses on the interaction between the international and the local, recognising that any idea of the 'national' aggregates several different experiences. At the same time, the term 'local' encompasses communal and individual experiences of security and justice that we are interested in, whereas the overwhelming involvement in the design, application and evaluation of development programming is by an 'international community' of wealthy states and multilateral institutions.

Recognition of 'the local' as important in what has been termed 'the local turn in peacebuilding',[7] especially political science, is to be welcomed. It is also important to keep in mind that in itself this is not new, and Menkhaus, among others, has drawn attention to 'the obvious but often overlooked observation that local communities are not passive in the face of state failure and insecurity, but instead adapt in a variety of ways to minimize risk and increase predictability in their dangerous environments'.[8] The local turn has shifted the literature towards a far more positive view of these societal adaptations and their legitimacy as sources of power, even a somewhat romantic notion of local non-state orders as inherently positive models of governance. This has in some cases led to reification of the local as a defence against the ostensibly hegemonic order of the liberal state.[9] The work of Richmond,[10] for example, moves beyond seeing the liberal state itself as being hybrid and towards hybridity as a form of resistance and survival to externally imposed ideas. At the same time, he uses the concept of everyday peace as a means to move beyond hybridity as just a description of two things combined and towards an approach that sees hybridity as a set of 'practices'. As Millar points out, however, this does not provide a way out of the core issue of how to establish peace without external intervention and international management and control of hybridity.[11]

---

7   Mac Ginty and Richmond, 'The Local Turn in Peace Building'.
8   Menkhaus, 'Governance without Government in Somalia', 75.
9   See, for example, Richmond, *A Post-liberal Peace*.
10   Ibid.
11   Millar, *An Ethnographic Approach to Peacebuilding*.

This chapter interrogates the concept of hybridity by exploring security and justice systems across a number of African contexts and how they are conditioned by power and politics. As such, the chapter has an explicit focus on the power of local actors to resist the imposition of liberal statebuilding processes. It shows that some hybrid structures do provide a means to subvert externally imposed statebuilding but, importantly, access to these approaches is controlled and moderated by the political power of local elites. In addition, prescriptive hybridity makes assumptions about the nature of local institutions that are not grounded in the reality of those institutions themselves. The implication is that much current thinking on hybridity reifies and idealises 'the local'. It assumes representation, legitimacy and equilibrium, and underrepresents power struggles and political processes of inclusion and exclusion from decision-making and resource allocation.[12]

In the following, we make a case for explicitly including the political into the notion of hybrid orders. This is because most prescriptive forms of hybridity assume that the local can be managed and manipulated without acknowledging the political agency of local institutions.

Origins: Hybridity and peacebuilding

Hybridity as a way of conceptualising resistance to liberal statebuilding has been an emerging theme within both development and peacebuilding literatures. On one hand, hybrid approaches derive from a well-established recognition among development scholars and practitioners that conventional Weberian state models do not reflect realities on the ground and are incompatible with local structures of power.[13] On the other hand, within the peacebuilding literature it has been recognised that state-centric approaches to postconflict reconstruction commonly are exclusionary and often do not develop into stable and peaceful situations.[14] An additional literature on the effects of security and justice reform efforts challenges the state-centric approaches of many international agencies, reflected mainly within evaluations and case studies.[15] They do not necessarily use the

---

12   Albrecht and Kyed, *Policing and the Politics of Order-Making*.
13   See, for example, Hagmann and Péclard, 'Negotiating Statehood'; Meagher, 'The Strength of Weak States'; and Menkhaus, 'Governance without Government in Somalia'.
14   Boege et al., *On Hybrid Political Orders*; Mac Ginty, 'Hybrid Peace'; Richmond, *A Post-liberal Peace*.
15   Albrecht et al., *Perspectives on Involving Non-state and Customary Actors*.

hybridity label, but convey a similar message of how state institutions and other actors interact with traditional leaders and non-state groups more generally, suggesting there are some complex empirical challenges to ideas of 'state-centric' approaches and simple state/non-state dichotomies.[16]

Many scholars go beyond this, making the assumption that a combination of individuals and processes from both the local and the international will improve the prospects for peace, moving beyond the institutional gap between existing experiences of internationally led statebuilding and local realities. However, there is an underlying assumption that there is a direct causal relationship between programming and results on the ground that can be planned and predicted. In addition, there are a set of assumptions about the nature of the local that are rooted in the political agendas of peacebuilding and the representation of the local that goes beyond local people's experience of those institutions.[17] Finally, there is a tendency to assume a 'static' quality to many 'traditional' authorities and local political structures, without recognising that all of these institutions and structures are political and evolve as a consequence of internal dynamics, but equally through interaction with the outside world, including the international system.

Hybridity as a concept contributes to the articulation of the fluidity and networked quality of social systems and orders. Mac Ginty provides the most institutionally structured analysis of hybridity and, as he points out, it is useful for moving analytically beyond romanticised and purist notions of 'pristine systems', recognising that all social orders by definition are 'tainted with the "original sin" of hybridity'.[18] This shifts the focus away from dichotomous approaches with clear divides between state/non-state and international/local to an explicit focus on the political-cum-power dynamics and interactions between international and local systems that are always already hybrid and represent 'grey areas' of interaction. For instance, Richards points out that the inclusion of traditional authorities in the central government of Somaliland merges external demands and internal necessities, but itself produces complex sets of interaction between actors that are more unpredictable than formal, bureaucratic state institutions.[19]

---

16 Albrecht and Buur, 'An Uneasy Marriage'; Baker, 'Beyond the Tarmac Road'.
17 Hirblinger and Simons, 'The Good, the Bad, and the Powerful'.
18 Mac Ginty, 'Hybrid Peace', 398.
19 Richards, 'Bringing the Outside In'.

Current approaches to policy and, indeed, much scholarly work, take a simple starting point as the relationship between state and non-state actors. This is hardly surprising given the peacebuilding roots of hybridity as it has evolved over the past 10 years in peace and conflict studies,[20] which is at least partly guided by the imperative to recreate or reconstruct a functioning state in the face of armed challenges to its sovereignty. Part of the issue with this conceptualisation is the lack of clarity about what is actually non-state, whether there is a simple dividing line or whether non-state actors can be more legitimate than state ones in particular circumstances. The example of South Sudan is interesting, in that a non-state challenge of the Sudanese state in the form of the Sudan People's Liberation Army[21] eventually became the government of South Sudan that gained independence in 2011, and now faces challenges to its own authority. What this shows is that the categories of state and non-state are fundamentally fluid.

Looking more closely, it can also be observed that some actors, networks and institutions are more fixed than others, and some actors, for example, can be both state and non-state at the same time. A paramount chief in Sierra Leone, for instance, is a traditional authority, but is also defined within the constitution and has a formal role. This type of fluidity has led scholars like Albrecht, in the case of chiefs in Sierra Leone,[22] as well as Visoka in the case of Kosovo, to concentrate on processes of hybridity rather than hybrid actors. They do this to move away from a notion of hybridity that involves taking two separate entities and combining them to make a new (hybrid) order.[23]

Local elites and the politics of resistance

The notion of hybridity as process has led Mac Ginty and others to argue that hybridity is largely produced through interactions between the local and the international and is a result of active resistance by local people.[24]

---

20 Boege et al., *On Hybrid Political Orders*; Mac Ginty, 'Hybrid Peace'; Richmond, *A Post-liberal Peace*.

21 The Sudan People's Liberation Army was renamed South Sudan Defence Forces in May 2017.

22 Albrecht, 'Hybridisation in a Case of Diamond Theft in Rural Sierra Leone'.

23 Visoka, 'Three Levels of Hybridisation Practices in Post-conflict Kosovo'.

24 Mac Ginty, *International Peacebuilding and Local Resistance*.

This implies that any analysis must understand the explicit balance between alternative sources of legitimacy and authority. Who, for example, has the power to resist and in what way? Is all resistance positive and for whom?

The answers to these questions are all political in the sense that all hybridity is partly a political choice and partly the result of institutional pressures that arise from institutional constraints. A realistic analysis of hybridity must, therefore, involve analysis of the empirical dimension of domestic politics, or the 'politics of the everyday'.[25] Recent literature has begun to examine the nature of these local political interactions and their role in shaping, resisting and constraining international projects. Pouligny[26] and Autesserre,[27] for instance, focus on peacekeeping from below, while there is a growing literature on the role of domestic elites in taking opportunities to benefit from international intervention, but also in developing international approaches to democratic transition.[28] This leaves a number of unresolved issues concerning legitimacy and political power at the local level. Part of any analysis of a hybrid system therefore has to include a focus on where power lies within such systems, who exercises power and how, a dynamic that is not well captured by the analytically homogenising effects of prescriptive hybridity approaches.

Accepting Mac Ginty's premise that hybridity is variable according to context, and also the overarching premise that local actors are capable of resistance to international intervention, makes the concept of hybridity difficult to categorise with one simple theory. Millar also adds another important element beyond agency: 'some areas of social life in any context … are inherently resistant to purposeful planning—the ritual and the conceptual—but … do not demand wilful action on the part of local actors to serve as points of resistance'.[29] In other words, there are always local political and social structures rooted in belief systems that are going to be difficult to manipulate or manage in the context of Western liberal intervention. This would include the admission of magical or secret society beliefs in court, aspects of cultural practice or even the use of specific rituals. Millar identifies four types of hybridity—institutional, practical,

---

25   Roberts, 'Everyday Legitimacy and Postconflict States'; Schroeder and Chappuis, 'New Perspectives on Security Sector Reform'.
26   Pouligny, *Peace Operations Seen from Below*.
27   Autesserre, *The Trouble with the Congo*.
28   Hensell and Gerdes, 'Elites and International Actors in Post-war Societies'; Sending, 'The Effects of Peacebuilding'; Tansey, *Regime-Building*.
29   Millar, *An Ethnographic Approach to Peacebuilding*, 4.

ritual and conceptual—that are progressively difficult to manipulate. This conceptual typology is useful to illustrate a spectrum of hybridity from institutional/legal elements that can be changed through to belief systems that are resistant.[30]

Of course, these elements themselves do not sit independently of power structures at the local level. Belief systems may constrain certain actions of chiefs at the local level, for example, but this does not stop chiefs from seeking to manipulate them or interpret them in ways that maintain local power structures and hierarchies. Indeed, some actors may even gain from political disorder or resistance as a source of political power, as well as being in a constant state of flux and renegotiation of position.[31] In some places those in charge of delivering justice may be those most responsible for insecurity in the first place,[32] or alleged agents of insecurity may be providing a particular form of security.[33] This means that the concept of hybridity may be more useful as a tool to critique liberal approaches to peacebuilding than to offer a credible alternative strategy or practical approach.[34]

It could be questioned whether the term hybridity represents a useful alternative analytical framework, or whether it is simply a way of describing empirical complexity and as such appears to have little practical utility to practitioners of statebuilding. Goodfellow and Lindemann[35] point out in the case of Uganda that the mere co-existence of different institutional forms does not by definition mean that a hybrid system emerges. Indeed, for them it is the distinction between the Buganda Kingdom and the bureaucratic state of Uganda that is partly a source of power for those who operate within Buganda.

This does not mean that Buganda and Uganda operate at arms-length from each other, but the relationship is not a simple one. Goodfellow and Lindemann[36] therefore have a point when they suggest substituting 'hybrid' for 'complex' and using hybridity to describe institutional multiplicity.[37] These considerations further negate the concept of hybridity as giving

---

30   Millar, 'Disaggregating Hybridity'.
31   Chabal and Daloz, *Africa Works: Disorder as Political Instrument*.
32   Baker, 'Beyond the Tarmac Road'.
33   Goodhand and Mansfield, 'Drugs and (Dis)Order'.
34   Luckham and Kirk, 'Security in Hybrid Political Contexts'.
35   Goodfellow and Lindemann, 'The Clash of Institutions'.
36   Ibid.
37   Hesselbein et al., 'Economic and Political Foundations of State Making in Africa'.

rise to a single integrated system but also add the idea that an end user of security or justice, for example, is faced with a series of competing institutions, each linked and each exhibiting different forms of hybridity. The end user may therefore be faced with a series of institutional choices each leading to different consequences and with different sources of legitimacy, power and agency. In the topography of such an institutional landscape, there are choices between different linked, but also potentially competing, providers. For example, in Sierra Leone someone seeking compensation in a court may look to a chiefdom court first, but then use local paralegals to access a district court. This could then lead to formal legal proceedings, or alternatively to an improved offer from the chiefdom court. This form of 'justice shopping' may be empowering to some end users.

This is an important conceptual clarification of an institutional landscape that has been continually shaped, partly by local actors and customs, and partly by external influences, including resources of the international community.[38] At the same time, reification of the local through use of the label 'hybridity' in fact underestimates the flexibility, pragmatism and fluidity of many local systems, at least partly by seeing 'the local' as one thing rather than several different sets of processes. Using hybridity as an analytical tool does not allow a distinction to be made between what Meagher refers to as 'constructive' and 'corrosive' elements of hybridity.[39] Indeed, hybridity has been associated with state making and state breaking,[40] conflict increase[41] and conflict decrease.[42] This evidently weakens the analytical vigour of hybridity, since an inability to predict or differentiate between effects when hybridity is present suggests that hybridity itself might not lead to one specific outcome, but may act as a mediating factor in underlying state formation that is not predetermined but contextual.[43]

The value of hybridity, then, lies in moving away from binary conceptualisations of the world and towards recognition of all governance systems as the product of numerous sources of authority that are drawn

---

38   Albrecht and Wiuff Moe, 'The Simultaneity of Authority'.
39   Meagher, 'The Strength of Weak States'.
40   Renders and Terlinden, 'Negotiating Statehood in a Hybrid Political Order'.
41   Ganson and Wennmann, 'Operationalising Conflict Prevention as Strong, Resilient Systems'.
42   Williams, *Chieftaincy, the State, and Democracy*.
43   Balthasar, 'From Hybridity to Standardization'.

upon simultaneously.[44] External influences on those processes, such as those involved in justice reform, will change their dynamics and not simply replace them. The exercise of power in this case then becomes the process of negotiating the relative influences of intervention and resistance and it places much power in the hands of those who control processes at the local level, including chiefs, local headmen, religious leaders and the leaders of other local institutions such as secret societies.[45] One of the most common institutions exercising power at the local level in Africa is the chief. The role and scope of chiefs varies considerably across the continent, although most commonly chiefs act as regulators of traditional social controls, frequently over access to land or other aspects of social life such as marriage.

Drawing on our own fieldwork in Sierra Leone, it is clear that chiefs play an important role in everyday politics.[46] Chiefs in Sierra Leone frequently play the role of 'opinion formers' within communities and have considerable powers, yet most of these power relationships are not established in writing. The role of the chief is thus flexible and not always clearly specified, even if there are strong local traditions within which chiefs operate. Despite their central role, chiefs remain empirically underrepresented in much of the literature on statebuilding, while this very literature recognises that capable democratic states must be based on shared social values and that this might be achieved by incorporating indigenous institutions and norms, while adapting those systems to international expectations.[47] The nature of the local political system means that incorporation, or even harmonisation, into a formal state institutional system as espoused by statebuilding, remains extremely difficult, even if it is actually desirable at all.[48] Chiefs themselves equate their control of local justice mechanisms to a source of power rather than a means of dispensing justice.[49] It is the nature of this approach that is particularly interesting, since it is essentially a conservative way of maintaining social cohesion. Justice is primarily about the maintenance of social control rather than conceptualised as an abstract aspiration or value.

---

44 Wiuff Moe and Albrecht, 'Hybridity and Simultaneity in the Global South'.
45 Albrecht, 'Secrets, Strangers and Order-Making in Rural Sierra Leone'.
46 Albrecht, 'The Chiefs of Community Policing'; Albrecht, 'The Hybrid Authority of Sierra Leone's Chiefs'; Jackson, 'Chiefs, Money and Politicians'; Jackson, 'Reshuffling an Old Deck of Cards?'.
47 Crook et al., 'Popular Concepts of Justice and Fairness in Ghana'; Jackson, 'Chiefs, Money and Politicians'.
48 Baker, 'Beyond the Tarmac Road'; Piot, *Remotely Global*.
49 Jackson, 'Reshuffling an Old Deck of Cards?'.

Importantly, the local regulations within which the chief operates comprise a system designed to maintain social cohesion and so the exercise of traditional law is about maintaining social control. This has a number of effects, including the maintenance of social structures in which an elite has a vested interest and where dissent among groups that do not benefit from such social conformity (youth, women and other excluded groups) takes the form of silence where conformity is taken as consent or absence of power conflict. In other words, local justice systems reinforce the social systems they are derived from, including providing a mechanism for a local elite to reinforce and maintain their own power.

The inclusion of such power at a local level begs questions about the predictability of hybrid approaches to intervention, as well as the nature of everyday approaches to local structures of peacebuilding and justice. Even the concept of justice may be resistant to Western ideas of just outcomes, reflecting more the maintenance of particular forms of social hierarchy in which some experiences of the everyday are less benign than others. Unfortunately the literature to date gives comparatively little attention to the politics at play within these relations at the level of everyday practice. Indeed, making order is more often than not done with efforts to concentrate power and consolidate particular power positions.[50]

Conclusion

Citizens across Africa seeking justice face a multilayered and fluid set of choices. However, those choices are limited by local power structures and relations, and specifically self-perpetuating elites. Such elites manage what local justice and order mean as an integral part of maintaining and reproducing their own power/dominance, with justice having the aim of conserving social control and conformity. As such, local justice systems become a method of maintaining security for the state, but at the price of potentially alienating specific groups or ensuring their continued subordination. International reform efforts across Africa have overlooked the inherent political dimensions of justice provision, which are deeply embedded in informal social structures, including kinship relations and secret societies, but which have also been influenced by more recent local

---

50   Albrecht and Kyed, *Policing and the Politics of Order-Making*, 5.

government reforms and the continuing influence of chiefs. This raises questions of whether a hybrid system is emerging or whether there is a multiplicity of institutions that co-exist and compete.

Most people need to navigate a complex network of institutions operating between a formal state system and resilient local systems at the local level, which may or may not be codified or even visible to external observers. These institutions constantly change and are subject to a variety of controlling bodies that regulate the meaning and enforcement of common law. Indeed, even the formal institutions of local and magistrate's courts draw on customary law rather than formal law in many of their cases, and this is open to interpretation and influence according to changing local customs and agency. Different social structures exercise influence over justice processes and outcomes. Local power is at least partly exercised through the appointment to courts and through the role of elders within villages. This leads to institutional bias within the customary system, particularly against women and youth.

This political process at the local level is about preserving power and conserving institutions and hierarchies rather than social transformation, even if political processes inevitably have a transformative effect. This can have significant benefits in environments where social cohesion has been destroyed, and in activities that require some form of social development following trauma, such as peacebuilding. However, there is an issue here of how to treat those who do not conform. In practice these are people who are effectively alienated from the benefits of those communities and are isolated from political participation and justice. It is these norms that may clash with international ideas of human rights, partly because international law tends to try individuals for crimes that are perceived to hold some degree of individual responsibility, whereas most local systems are really about social conformity.

This leads to a dilemma for international support in the justice sector. Some argue that international support should place less emphasis on formal, Western justice and support the local systems.[51] However, there are considerable issues with this style of justice. Indeed, abuses of this system may have significantly contributed to war in the first place, as was

---

51   Baker, 'Beyond the Tarmac Road'.

the case in Sierra Leone.[52] For the powerless, this means they have no effective access to justice, while justice is accessible for those from the indigene kinship group or for those who can afford suitable recompense.

The analysis of power at the local level raises questions about who actually exercises ownership, since the implication of hybridity is that some local owners can be incorporated into broader reform processes, but these will tend to be elites who are able to control local power systems rather than those who are excluded from those systems. In the short term, this may be acceptable—indeed it may be the only choice—but the question for international donors must be how far they are willing to provide support for those who navigate these systems locally. This is especially the case with respect to those who are excluded, as opposed to elite agents who may be able to exist in and use the formal system on one level and also control a traditional system on another. The question of who resists and why is thus partly answered by looking at local elites who are in a position to resist in the first place. In turn, the question for donor agencies is whether the maintenance of local elites was what they had in mind by introducing and operationalising the notion of hybrid orders.

---

52   Jay and Koroma, *From 'Crying' and Clientelism to Rights and Responsibilities.*

3

Hybridity Revisited: Relational Approaches to Peacebuilding in Complex Sociopolitical Orders

Charles T. Hunt[1]

Introduction

In recent years, hybridity has received a great deal of attention in the peacebuilding and development literature. This 'rediscovery' of a concept with strong roots in critical and postcolonial theory[2] has emerged in critical peace studies as a compelling lens with which scholars can better understand the empirics of sociopolitical order and the forms of peace produced through international interventions in conflict-affected states. To a growing extent, these formulations are beginning to find their way into the documents, frameworks and even practices of the organisations who design and implement policy in these areas.[3] Notwithstanding its appeal and traction, hybridity has come in for a range of critiques regarding its content as well as its use in both scholarship and praxis. Some have cautioned about the risk of instrumentalisation in practice while others have identified potential ethical and political implications associated with

1   The work for this chapter was supported by a grant under the Australian Development Research Awards Scheme (DFAT agreement 66442).
2   Bhabha, *The Location of Culture*.
3   See, for example, World Bank, *World Development Report 2011*.

its (mis)use. Of particular interest here, hybridity has also been subject to criticism for its perceived ontological and epistemological biases manifest in the persistence of reductive analytical binaries and a preoccupation with entities over and above the relationships between them.

This chapter picks up on these critiques, and argues for an augmented concept of hybridity that embraces a relational approach to the theory and practice of peacebuilding and development. I argue that such an approach to understanding and working with conflict-affected societies provides a means to overcome the biases that hybrid approaches can produce. The chapter begins by articulating the nature of hybrid sociopolitical order in many conflict-affected societies and outlines the salient criticisms directed at the hybridity concept. It then proposes a relational account of multilayered sociopolitical order. Drawing on examples from fieldwork and research in Liberia, I identify the value that a relational approach could bring to the concept of hybridity in understanding and working in complex adaptive systems. The final section reflects on how an analytical framework informed by these conceptual moves can handle perceived deficiencies in hybridity relating to treatment of power relations, dynamics, and notions of space and territoriality in conflict-affected societies.

Hybrid sociopolitical orders, binaries and blind spots

In keeping with a number of other chapters in this volume,[4] I argue that empirical pluralism characterises the provision of governance, security and justice in the majority of the world's conflict zones. In postcolonial states of sub-Saharan Africa in particular, social order is the product of the work of myriad actors who provide critical services and ultimately contribute to the formation of political community and social peace. When it comes to everyday public safety, dispute resolution and community harmony, the institutions of government such as the national police, courts and corrections facilities play an important role in this regard. However, they are at most only part of the plural security and justice landscape.

---

4   Such as Boege, Brown, etc.

What Ostrom calls 'polycentric governance' connotes an order (or more accurately a system of overlapping/intersecting orders) where these government institutions are often complemented by a range of societal bodies that are deeply involved in providing for the everyday needs of the majority of people.[5] This cast of players does not fit neatly into any single umbrella category such as Western notions of civil society.[6] For instance, while this often includes traditional authorities and autochthonous agencies such as chieftaincies and councils of elders, it also stretches to incorporate providers such as citizen militia groups and private security forces as well as less obviously coercive elements such as trade unions, private-sector entities and more community-based—occasionally 'secret'—societies.[7]

Local populations often favour this collection of actors providing conflict management and social services beyond the strict purview of central government. This can be for a combination of reasons related to access, cost, timeliness and cultural sensitivity. Ultimately, these preferences translate into high(er) levels of public familiarity and trust.[8] Recent studies reinforce the empirical reality that in conflict-affected states security and justice needs are addressed through these means for the majority of people most of the time.[9] While this is often generalised to be a rural or 'hinterland' phenomenon, similar patterns pertain in urban spaces where, despite displacement and heterogeneity, authority and legitimacy remain multifaceted.

The result is fundamentally different systems of social and political ordering. This sits in stark contrast to a Weberian ideal type where 'the state'—narrowly defined—possesses a rational bureaucracy and holds (or at least claims) a monopoly on the legitimate recourse to violent means to retain order. These multilayered systems operate according to different logics of governance whereby legitimacy is derived from a range of sites and the construction of authority is a dynamic process.[10] This plethora of providers inhabits what is, in effect, a hybrid sociopolitical order that emerges from the intricate interactions across this assortment of actors.[11]

---

5   Ostrom, 'Polycentricity (Parts 1&2)'.
6   Richmond and Mitchell, 'Introduction—Towards a Post-liberal Peace', 13.
7   Raeymaekers et al., 'State and Non-state Regulation in African Protracted Crises', 8.
8   Baker and Scheye, 'Multi-layered Justice and Security Delivery', 512.
9   OECD-DAC, 'Improving Security and Justice Programming', 22, fn15. See also Albrecht and Kyed, 'Introduction: Non-state and Customary Actors'.
10   Boege, 'Legitimacy in Hybrid Political Orders', 10–12; Boege et al., *Addressing Legitimacy Issues in Fragile Postconflict Situations*.
11   Boege et al., *On Hybrid Political Orders and Emerging States*.

In recent years, a growing number of critical peace and security scholars have embraced 'hybridity', championing its conceptual and explanatory potential for informing analysis of conflict-affected societies.[12] More recently, the language and ideas around hybridity have begun to appear in policy documents and programs aimed at building peace and supporting development in so-called fragile states.[13] However, despite its growing popularity, efforts to apply concepts of hybridity to the analysis of these settings have met with a number of critiques.[14] Among other things, the normative intent of hybridity or scholars who promote it has been challenged.[15] This in turn has precipitated debates in the literature over inconsistent and divergent applications and the relative opportunities and challenges associated with descriptive, prescriptive and instrumental applications of hybridity.[16] Notwithstanding the central ethical, political and practical dilemmas these debates throw up, a range of criticisms has also emerged that relate to the ontological and epistemological orientations of hybridity.

First, some scholars have argued that hybridity models perpetuate the reification of arbitrary categories. Efforts to understand the plural nature of security and justice provision in conflict-affected societies tend to categorise providers as 'one' or 'other' in a coterie of analytical binaries. It is common for particular agents to be described as state or non-state, formal or informal, traditional or modern, or local or international. Furthermore, it is often implicit that these dichotomies map to ideas of actors operating in spaces or ways deemed to be licit versus illicit or liberal as opposed to illiberal. This is more than a semantic issue as the use of these labels can generate significant ethical, political and practical challenges.

---

12   See, for example, Boege et al., 'Building Peace and Political Community'; Mac Ginty, *International Peacebuilding and Local Resistance*; Richmond and Mitchell, *Hybrid Forms of Peace*.
13   For example, DFID, *Policy Approach to Rule of Law*; World Bank, *World Development Report 2011*.
14   For extended discussion of critiques, see Kent et al., 'Introduction', this volume.
15   See, for example, Cassani, 'Hybrid What? Partial Consensus and Persistent Divergences'; Chandler, 'Peacebuilding and the Politics of Non-linearity'; Heathershaw, 'Towards Better Theories of Peacebuilding'; Meagher, 'The Strength of Weak States?'; Nadarajah and Rampton, 'The Limits of Hybridity'.
16   See, for example, Brown, this volume; Forsyth, this volume; Mac Ginty and Richmond, 'The Fallacy of Constructing Hybrid Political Orders', 224–228; Millar, 'Disaggregating Hybridity'; Wallis et al., 'Political Reconciliation in Timor Leste', 162.

Proponents argue that hybridity can provide the conceptual framework necessary to transcend and do away with analytical binaries.[17] For instance, Mac Ginty and Richmond argue 'the concept of hybridity, if used as a post-colonial, post-territorial and post-biological construct, liberates us from the dominant policy script of goodies and baddies, states and non-states and West and non-West'.[18] However, others argue that efforts to develop the utility of hybridity in understanding fragile/conflict-affected societies—particularly where it has appeared in peacebuilding and development policies and praxis—have actually served to 're-inscribe' these binaries.[19] For example, Moreiras argues that despite good intentions hybridity literature has a tendency to fall back on problematic binaries to describe and understand the roles and influence of the different providers involved in the production of order.[20] The malignance of this dichotomous version of reality can have a number of negative consequences.[21]

It is true that binary categories are difficult to avoid when analysing different types of actors. Indeed, these categorisations can perform some useful function when conducting analyses. For example, drawing boundaries around different nodes of providers of social order can help in the process of identifying relationships between them.[22] However, it has been argued that one of the downsides of continued use of such analytics is uncritically essentialising and/or romanticising actors deemed to be autochthonous or local, underplaying the ethical and accountability issues associated with their function.[23] This approach invariably focuses on what qualities and characteristics distinguish providers from each other and risks exaggerating the veracity of the dichotomies.[24]

---

17   Boege, this volume; Peterson, 'A Conceptual Unpacking of Hybridity', 12. See originally Mac Ginty, 'Hybrid Peace: The Interaction between Top-Down and Bottom-Up Peace'; Mac Ginty, 'Hybrid Peace: How Does Hybrid Peace Come About?'.
18   Mac Ginty and Richmond, 'The Fallacy of Constructing Hybrid Political Orders', 220.
19   Hameiri and Jones, this volume. See also Heathershaw, 'Towards Better Theories of Peacebuilding', 277; Laffey and Nadarajah, 'The Hybridity of Liberal Peace', 417; Sabaratnam, 'Avatars of Eurocentrism', 261–263.
20   Moreiras, 'Hybridity and Double Consciousness'.
21   Bliesemann de Guevara, 'Introduction: The Limits of Statebuilding'; Heathershaw, 'Towards Better Theories of Peacebuilding; Millar, 'Disaggregating Hybridity'; Peterson, 'A Conceptual Unpacking of Hybridity'.
22   The author is grateful to the editors for this point.
23   Bliesemann de Guevara, 'Introduction: The Limits of Statebuilding'; Meagher, 'The Strength of Weak States?'; Peterson, '"Rule of Law" Initiatives'.
24   See also Ojendal et al., 'The "Local Turn" in Peacebuilding'; Randazzo, 'The Paradoxes of the "Everyday"'.

Second, and related to this endurance of analytical binaries, hybridity has met with criticism for being problematically reductive in the way it accounts for the construction of authority and the production of order. For instance, Dirlik states 'hybridity reduces all complexity to a "statement of mixture"' and goes on to problematise the fact that this leaves out some of the specifics of *what* is being mixed.[25] Moreover, by depicting complex social order as a 'mixture' of agency, a hybridity lens can oversimplify or obscure how this 'mixing' occurs and exactly how (and what sort of) sociopolitical order emerges. As a result, hybridity has faced criticism for being undertheorised,[26] failing to reveal power dynamics,[27] underplaying the perpetuity of change, and being inadequate for handling different territorialities/levels of analysis.[28] By extension, this critique contends that such an approach can also mask the potential for malevolent emergence and hybrid outcomes.[29] Consequently, it is argued that imprecision may limit the utility of hybridity for explaining how (dis)order emerges and evolves over time.

These criticisms point to a problematic focus on actors and their features at the expense of seeking out how myriad providers are linked, the ways in which they relate, and how they are at times intrinsically dependent on each other to achieve their objectives. The allegation is therefore that hybridity's analytical imprecision renders the empirical relationships between these actors underexamined and often misunderstood.[30] Where hybridity literature does elevate the relationships between key actors, it tends to focus primarily on the interface between the 'international' and the 'local' or Western and non-Western actors.[31] The preoccupation in the hybridity literature with this particular encounter inhibits a more nuanced rendering of the relationships between all providers at multiple levels across the system, particularly those between inhabitants in the local sphere.[32]

---

25 Dirlik, 'Bringing History Back In', 106.
26 Millar, 'Disaggregating Hybridity', 501.
27 Meagher, 'The Strength of Weak States?', 1078; Peterson, 'A Conceptual Unpacking of Hybridity', 14; see also Pieterse, 'Hybridity, So What?'; Tanikella, 'The Politics of Hybridity'.
28 See, for example, critiques of Mac Ginty's 2011 hybridisation model by, inter alia, Millar.
29 Meagher, 'The Strength of Weak States?', 1073.
30 Frödin, 'Dissecting the State', 271.
31 Sabaratnam, 'Avatars of Eurocentrism', 269.
32 Paffenholz, 'Unpacking the Local Turn in Peacebuilding'.

In order to accurately reflect complex forms of social (dis)order in conflict-affected societies our conceptual and analytical tools need to be as agile and dynamic as the systems we seek to track and understand. However, as a result of the aforementioned shortcomings, current uses of the concept of hybridity struggle to apprehend the nuanced, mutable and context-specific relationships between a diverse array of providers of governance, security and justice. The following section turns to insights from complexity theory in order to develop a more relational focus in the application of hybridity.

Complex social order and a primacy of relationships

The hybrid sociopolitical orders described above display the characteristics of a complex social system. According to complexity theory, a social system (society) is 'complex' if it displays the following features and properties. Interacting parts of the system produce *intricate interdependence* between constituent elements. This dictates that the actions of one part of the system can impede another or indeed the whole system. The interactions are changing and it is the degree of 'connectivity' (i.e. interdependence) that controls how change occurs through the system. This contingency produces *feedback processes* that can drive or inhibit system change. It is through this feedback that properties and behaviours at the system level are relayed to their original source and other elements of the system. This in turn causes often unpredictable outcomes known as the *emergent properties*—that is, the behavioural patterns of the system as a whole. Emergence is therefore contingent on and produced by the myriad of possible interrelationships between elements within the system. This *emergence* is difficult to predict based on the characteristics of constituent parts and the archetypal feature of a complex system.[33]

These particular characteristics dictate that change in system-level outcomes occurs in three key ways. First, change occurs in a *nonlinear* fashion where outcomes are not directly proportionate to variations in the inputs and resources available.[34] A multiplicity of influencing factors means that causal relationships are difficult to identify and cannot be

---

33   Mitchell, *Complexity: A Guided Tour*.
34   Stacey, *Complexity and Creativity in Organizations*, 23–28, 65.

assumed. Second, adaptive agents comprise the complex social system and as conscious agents have the ability to 'know' and adjust their behaviour according to information gleaned and lessons learned. This means that, as a result of human agency, complex social systems have an intrinsic capacity to *self-organise*.[35] Consequently, and third, they are in a continuous process of *coevolution* in relation to each other as well as to the broader systemic environment, reproducing along trajectories that are influenced but never fully determined by any one of a large number of factors.[36] In this reading of the context, it is the relationships between providers of security and justice that are constitutive of emergent order. Therefore, to understand how hybrid (dis)order emerges requires a more nuanced understanding of the type of relationships between providers more than a deep grasp of the features of the providers in a complex social system.

In hybrid orders, the whole gamut of providers are interacting and evolving in relation to each other. As Albrecht and Kyed have argued, 'there may be full recognition and close collaboration, limited partnership, unofficial acceptance, competition and even open hostility'.[37] It is these relationships that generate the entanglements symptomatic of hybridity and generative of emergent sociopolitical order. The next section uses examples from the case of Liberia in West Africa to elaborate on the range of relationships at play.

Complexity in practice: The case of Liberia

The relationships between the institutions of central government and a range of other providers of security and justice in a hybrid order are often explained in terms of competition.[38] For instance, Charles Taylor's armed insurrection through the 1990s is perhaps more clearly understood as a predatory zero-sum battle with the sovereign government it sought to overthrow. However, both were fundamental to providing basic public goods and social order (such as it was) in the territories they controlled. In this case, a warlord controlling strategic locations and trade routes was viewed as a threat by a central state bunkered and restricted to an isolated urban capital in Monrovia. The central government's efforts to extend

---

35 Heylighen, *The Science of Self-organization and Adaptivity*, 4–5.
36 Garnsey and McGlade, *Complexity and Co-evolution*.
37 Albrecht and Kyed, 'Justice and Security', 2.
38 Bayart et al., *The Criminalization of the State in Africa*.

its authority over the national sovereign territory also clearly constituted a threat to Taylor's authority. Actors whose authority is contingent on different sources and logics can at times directly contest each other for political capital and resources.

However, there is invariably a good deal more interdependence and cooperation between government and a range of other actors. Accommodation here can be both formal and more informal but the nature and content of these relationships are vital in the co-production of order.[39] For example, in rural Liberia, where government institutions do not reach or would not be well tolerated, societal bodies such as councils of elders or secret societies often provide essential services.[40] Chiefs, for instance, are commonly seen as a significant authority in the community, drawing on customary sources of legitimacy. However, through state-sponsored customary law they also play a role in the formal dual legal system and consequently lend significant support to central government in the production of order.[41] Furthermore, delineations of statutory and customary law or rules are not strictly adhered to in practice. Customary courts are constitutionally empowered to handle civil but not criminal cases; however, this division of labour is not always adhered to. In effect the central government is dependent on community-based actors for maintaining everyday social order.

Similarly, vigilantes, citizen militia or 'community watch groups' are ubiquitous across Liberia.[42] While such entities are often understood as challenging the state's monopoly on legitimate violence, they have also proven to be a vital source of providing protection and defence of towns and communities.[43] Moreover, the relationship between the Liberian National Police and these groups has ranged from tacit acquiescence to formal approval, partnership and even the provision of training and material support.

---

39   Baker, *Security in Post-conflict Africa*, 32–35.
40   Reports from focus groups and key participant interviews conducted as part of fieldwork for author research project 'Understanding and Working with Local Sources of Peace, Security and Justice in West Africa' (Australian Government Department of Foreign Affairs and Trade). See also Jaye, *Understanding and Explaining Hybridity*.
41   Lubkemann et al., 'Justice in a Vacuum'.
42   Kantor and Persson, *Understanding Vigilantism*.
43   Isser et al., *Looking for Justice*.

In these cases, entities conventionally thought of as non-state or informal can behave in very 'state-like' ways. The central government not only tolerates their conduct but by outsourcing service provision to them affords a certain degree of legitimacy to these actors. In these cases, the relationships between state institutions and societal bodies can be mutually beneficial. Accurate recognition of this variation in relationships across state and non-state providers is critical to analysts and peacebuilders for a number of reasons. First, this elaborates the degree of hybridisation that has already occurred and led to current conditions. Second, a more accurate grasp of cooperation as well as competition between these stakeholders feeds understanding of the nature of emergent everyday peace and security.

Those providers who do not derive authority directly from the writ of the state will also have a diverse range of relationships among them. These, too, matter fundamentally to the everyday experiences of (dis)order. For instance, in Liberia, the relationships between town, quarter, clan and village chiefs can often be discerned through known hierarchies and territoriality. However, the way that these same chiefs relate to other elders in their community, secret societies such as the Poro, and those who are deemed to have access to the ancestral realm (e.g. *juju* men) is less visible but no less important to the way in which order is sustained.[44] Similarly, in the settlement of disputes at the local level, resolution may depend on a network of actors. For instance, a town chief may not be able to pass judgement on a dispute unless the witch doctor is able to remove a curse from one of the disputants.[45] The satisfactory settlement is contingent on a range of functional relationships among a number of societal actors.[46] It is the unique way in which theses interactions occur that produces an outcome and contributes to emergent order.

During Liberia's civil war there was a struggle for authority between some of the elders and those participating more actively in the fighting. In particular, youth who became empowered through membership of militia challenged the traditional gerontocratic structures of society.[47] This obviously had a significant impact on people's everyday security during

---

44 Focus group report from fieldwork in Liberia, Australian Development Research Awards.
45 Herman and Martin-Ortega, 'Narrowing Gaps in Justice', 146; Lubkemann et al., 'Neither State nor Custom'. See also Ellis, *The Mask of Anarchy*, 225.
46 Flomoku and Reeves, 'Formal and Informal Justice in Liberia'.
47 Sawyer, 'Social Capital, Survival Strategies, and Their Potential for Post-conflict Governance in Liberia'.

the years of conflict. However, to this day, the relations between chiefs, elders and ex-combatants—demobilised and reintegrated into society to varying degrees—continues to shape the contours of everyday order.[48]

While Liberia is only a single case and the above discussion is far from exhaustive, it bears a strong resemblance to other conflict-affected societies in West Africa—neighbouring Sierra Leone and Côte d'Ivoire.[49] Furthermore, these relational dynamics can be seen as emblematic of a wider set of postcolonial states emerging from violent conflict where peacebuilding efforts have been attempted and met with mixed results. Emphasising the importance of relationships between providers may seem common sense. However, such recognition eludes extant mainstream thinking and praxis around peacebuilding—focused, as it overwhelmingly is, on ontological questions of what entities exist and their characteristics rather than how all pertinent entities interrelate and co-produce order. This risks overlooking the forms of peace that emerge as the result of feedback between intertwined providers. Moving beyond a taxonomy of providers, it is the nature of the linkages between myriad providers— irrespective whence they derive their legitimacy or authority—that is central to emergent (dis)order. Therefore, in keeping with some recent developments in the peacebuilding literature,[50] I argue that what is needed is a relational approach when articulating hybrid forms of peace and order.

Operationalising a relational approach

Translating and working in line with a relational approach requires new and tailored conceptual tools. These can take the form of theoretical but also analytical frameworks. One such analytical framework based on these ideas has been developed elsewhere by this author.[51] The framework elaborates on a set of 'symbiotic relations' between myriad providers of social order. Borrowed from biology, *symbiosis* refers to the state of entities 'living together'. The framework explains three categories. The first, *predatory-amenalism*, incorporates confrontational relationships between providers. The second, *commensalism/parasitism*, includes relationships

---

48 Focus group report from fieldwork in Liberia, Australian Development Research Awards.
49 Fawole and Ukeje, *The Crisis of the State and Regionalism in West Africa*.
50 See, for example, Brigg, 'Relational Peacebuilding'. See also Gadinger et al., *Relational Sensibility and the 'Turn to the Local'*.
51 Symbiosis framework developed in Hunt, 'Beyond the binaries'.

between providers characterised by sustainable asymmetry. The third, *mutualism*, refers to those relationships that are characterised by mutual benefit and 'complementarity'. These categories capture the ways in which relations embody a continuous process of contestation, accommodation or outright cooperation in the construction of authority and distribution of resources.

The framework categories allow the multiverse of connectivities and subtleties of interaction to be more accurately depicted. In doing so, this approach offers a corrective to three substantive criticisms of extant models of hybridity and hybridisation.[52] First, these bonds are not fixed nor meant to imply rigidity. On the contrary, the systems of sociality at play are dynamical where elements are adapting and evolving in relation to each other as a result of ongoing feedback processes. Alliances are ephemeral and changeable; history and context matter hugely, such that the relationship that applies to particular providers will have multiple potential equilibria and the type of relationship is therefore mutable. The dynamical nature of the system means that relations are shifting and continuously renegotiated—characterised by ongoing processes of exchange between and across different elements of the system. The feedback intrinsic to these relations renders all actors in coevolutionary processes, altered as a result of the interactions and influence on each other such that they cannot be static or unchanging. This leads to a conception of hybrid order that is emergent, self-organised and a dynamic coevolutionary sociopolitical system.

Second, the relations articulated through the framework are imbued with power. That is, the bonds between providers reflect the political economy of power in conflict-affected societies. It is these relationships that therefore shape, empower and at times constrain the extent to which social systems are resilient. The construction of authority is embedded in the relationality revealed through the framework. Any changes to who is providing security and justice services will in turn entrench or redistribute power in significant ways. Far from ignoring or trying to obfuscate questions of power, this framework tackles the aforementioned criticism of hybridity by revealing and integrating rather than concealing and obscuring power dynamics. It supports a more nuanced rendering of power but moreover creates the space for a potentially profoundly different conceptualisation

---

52   See, for example, the critique of Mac Ginty, *International Peacebuilding and Local Resistance*, in Millar, 'Disaggregating Hybridity'.

of power. This promises to better reflect how it is mediated, contested and ultimately shared in the symbiosis at play. Gaining clarity on the circulation of power within the local sphere is a precondition for understanding who has the capacity and resources to interact with international actors in order to be heard and make claims—potentially shaping outcomes through blocking, contaminating or enabling different formations of peace.[53] It is, nevertheless, important to note that those who are not possessed of visibility and voice are not necessarily without agency or influence. On the contrary, with nonlinear change the norm in complex systems, more detailed articulations of power can also inform more convincing explanations for unpredictable outcomes and modalities better prepared to expect the surprising. This can in turn form a backdrop for subsequent analyses of the hybrid forms of peace that emerge as a result of strategies and tactics of acceptance, hybridisation, co-optation and resistance by locals in the face of international interventions.[54]

Third, and following from above, the framework enables an approach that is not simply about understanding and working with the often-obscured actors inhabiting the 'local' arena. By opening up questions of relationality, this approach offers a way of understanding the system holistically. This is consonant with the spatial turn in state theory/political geography, bringing in the different levels at which politics takes place and requiring a certain incorporation of the 'politics of scale'. The framework not only allows for assessments of networked relationality across different providers within particular strata but also across providers at different levels. This means that the significance of agency in the local arena can be understood in the context of provincial and national settings. As with the discussion relating to power, this also opens up possibilities for more finely grained analysis incorporating stakeholders at the international and transnational levels. This multilevel and multidimensional approach allows for assessments that ask which, if any, levels and interfaces are most significant in the emergence of (dis)order.[55]

This is all to argue that the plurality of providers of social order and the realms they inhabit do not simply co-exist alongside each other or only interact through unavoidable overlap. On the contrary, they have

---

53   Richmond, 'The Paradox of Peace and Power'. See also Peterson, 'A Conceptual Unpacking of Hybridity', 17.
54   Richmond and Mitchell, 'Introduction—Towards a Post-liberal Peace', 8–10.
55   For discussion of the relative weight of different interfaces see Debiel and Rinck, 'Rethinking the Local in Peacebuilding'.

genuinely symbiotic relationships that are constitutive of emergent and hybrid order. The everyday exchanges that occur between providers of services, and between them and 'end users', are actually generative of the agency at play and therefore critical to the imaginary of what constitutes political community for conflict-affected populations as well as its substance and dynamics.

While it is not entirely new to acknowledge the networked nature of providers,[56] the symbiosis framework discussed here constitutes an example of how a relational approach could be realised in tangible ways that can further inform theorising and praxis relating to hybridity. Such an approach and others like it—grounded in relational understandings of the societies on the receiving end of international intervention—offer the possibility of redressing the lack of empiricism that besets current international efforts to reform and rebuild security and justice sectors in developing and conflict-affected contexts. What is critical is that these tools and analytical frameworks are promulgated in ways that are accessible to researchers and practitioners.

Conclusion

Overall, the analysis described here contributes to the argument for a relational approach—for a performative-based, liminal and integrative understanding of hybrid sociopolitical order and how this can inform peacebuilding theory and practice. While such a shift presents many opportunities, it also presents ethical, political and practical challenges for research and policy.[57] It is therefore important to acknowledge that greater understanding of the emergence of everyday order in conflict-affected states can be instrumentalised or co-opted by international peacebuilders, just as those on the receiving end of their interventions can also divert and manipulate the material support brought from the outside. A relational approach could also create rationales to support malevolent emergence that inadvertently empowers entities and practices that propagate rather than transform violent and discriminatory practices.

---

56   See, for example, Forsyth, 'Spinning a Conflict Management Web in Vanuatu'.
57   See, for example, Chandler, 'Peacebuilding and the Politics of Non-linearity'.

Notwithstanding the challenges, a relational approach promises to enhance our understanding of the way in which (dis)order emerges in complex social systems affected by conflict. It also provides a way of revealing and conceptualising the agency of people affected by conflict and elaborating on how their everyday experiences are shaped.[58] It furnishes us with a way of taking seriously the strengths and weaknesses of those processes in the pursuit of peacebuilding objectives. Such an approach requires innovative conceptual tools, such as the symbiosis analytical framework discussed herein, to realise its potential. Rather than attempting to displace hybridity, the relational approach proposed here is intended to extend and augment it. The symbiosis framework and other conceptual tools like it have the potential to bring additional analytical leverage and shed further light on the empirical realities that the hybridity lens already brings to our attention. A framework for analysis based on these insights can help reveal the nature of the multiplicity of relationships among the range of providers of security and justice. It can also point to the significance of these relations in the construction of authority and the production of emergent (dis)order. This may have the potential to enhance the utility of hybridity as a conceptual and analytical tool for both scholars and practitioners of peacebuilding. Doing so should help us move beyond the deployment of limited and limiting binaries that do not stand up to scrutiny, underplay the nuance and variation of the relations between providers, and fundamentally miss how (dis)order emerges in the complex social systems pertaining in conflict-affected societies. As well as better tools, such a relational approach demands more humble, realistic and pragmatic expectations from the advocates and agents of peacebuilding about what can be achieved and in what time frame. This is in keeping with calls for 'slower and more open processes' that are 'dialogical and organic' while 'patient and sensitive to different temporal sensibilities'.[59] Moves in that direction may also contribute to opening up discourse and our imaginaries of political community that can in turn offer ways of escaping the teleological visions for the 'state' that dominate current orthodoxy in peacebuilding.

---

58   Bleiker, 'Conclusion—Everyday Struggles for a Hybrid Peace', 300–303.
59   Comments made, respectively, by Damian Grenfell, Anne Brown and Volker Boege (all contributors to this volume) during the workshop that led to this book.

4

Should the Concept of Hybridity Be Used Normatively as well as Descriptively?

Miranda Forsyth

Introduction

This chapter explores the question of whether it is possible and useful to develop the concept of hybridity to answer questions about how legal/regulatory systems *ought to be*, as well as describing how they currently work. This was a question that arose many times during the seminar series and workshop that this collection is based upon. It also reflects a tension that is often present in interdisciplinary contexts, particularly where anthropologists and lawyers are involved as their basic orientation (descriptive versus normative) is often so different. This chapter uses examples from Melanesia, primarily Papua New Guinea and Vanuatu, where I have conducted research in the area of law and development since 2002.

Approaches to law through a hybrid orientation

There are a number of ways of theorising about law that are shared by many who adopt a hybrid approach to law. For the purposes of this chapter, it is helpful to sketch these out initially to clarify what is encompassed by such an approach, as many different concepts of hybridity exist in the literature.[1] First, the concept of hybridity in the legal context involves a recognition that even in Western countries, and certainly and most obviously in indigenous communities and postcolonial national states, law also exists outside statutes and case law.[2] Second, law is seen to be constructed by a wide range of institutions, and it is increasingly recognised that even individual legal subjects are 'law inventing' as well as 'law abiding'.[3] Third, there is acknowledgment that multiple legal orders co-exist in different overlapping spatial dimensions and typically shape one another through ongoing interaction. The relationship between legal orders—which are often neither entirely internally coherent nor externally differentiable—is dynamic, mutually constitutive and mutually dependent. This process has been characterised by a variety of different terms—interlegality,[4] interactional law,[5] transnational legal orders,[6] critical legal pluralism[7] and hybridisation.[8] The differences that exist between these different approaches is beyond the scope of this chapter. I will refer to a hybrid approach which should be taken to encompass the abovementioned insights, with the additional benefit of centring focus on the dynamic and porous nature of the relationship between legal orders.

These approaches to law unsettle the commonly held view of law as being created exclusively by legislatures and courts. However, departing from that well-trodden foundation raises a number of difficult questions: *What is law? (And when does a social norm become law?) Who are the agents of law? (And whose voices and needs are privileged and whose are overlooked?)*

---

1 Many people use the term 'hybrid' in a narrow legal sense to refer to hybrid institutions, such as village courts in Papua New Guinea. See, for example, Evans et al., 'The Hybrid Courts of Melanesia'. This is not the sense the term is used in this chapter. For more description see Brown, this volume.
2 Merry, 'Legal Pluralism'; Moore, 'Law and Social Change'.
3 Kleinhans and MacDonald, 'What Is Critical Legal Pluralism?'
4 Santos, 'Law: A Map of Misreading'; Santos, *Towards a New Legal Common Sense*.
5 van der Burg, *The Dynamics of Law and Morality*.
6 Halliday and Shaffer, *Transnational Legal Orders*.
7 Kleinhans and MacDonald, 'What Is Critical Legal Pluralism?'
8 Snyder, 'Colonialism and Legal Form'.

What time periods are involved in bringing about legal change? What requirements for legitimacy exist in different legal systems? Where is law constructed? The concept of hybridity thus leads us onto uncertain ground, with more and more gaps and questions opening up the further one travels. Recognising that there are multiple different change agents, all operating in a semi-autonomous way, makes any deliberate program of positive social change through regulation highly challenging. This is the reason for seeking to develop analytical and conceptual methods to assist in both explaining the development of hybrid legal orders, and also in answering questions about if and how such developments can be steered in an emancipatory direction.

Should hybridity be developed to answer the 'ought' as well as the 'is' questions?

This brings us to the important issue of 'is' versus 'ought' or 'fact' versus 'norm' or, as many in the hybridity literature express it, questions of 'descriptive hybridity' versus 'instrumental hybridity'.[9] The concept of hybridity has been widely accepted as being useful for answering the 'is' question; that is, how *is* law or regulation done in practice? It encourages legal reformers to move away from a positivistic and state-centric approach to law as being solely limited to legislation or case law, or, for that matter, customary law being conceived of as a coherent system of rules.[10] For example, applying such a perspective to the issue of the regulation of intangible cultural heritage in Vanuatu, I have identified that rights are claimed and disputes are managed as a result of a variety of regulatory forces, including the need to maintain relationships, fear of the supernatural, avoidance of shaming and customary sanctions.[11] A hybrid analytical framework provides a far wider view of regulatory forces than a myopic focus on written or unwritten norms, and assists in understanding the empirical reality of the various forces at play in the relevant social field.

---

9   Mac Ginty and Richmond, 'The Fallacy of Constructing Hybrid Political Orders'.
10   I term this customary positivism.
11   Forsyth and Farran, *Weaving Intellectual Property Policy in Small Island Developing States*.

Much more contested is whether the concept of hybridity is also relevant for answering the 'ought' question; that is, how *ought* hybrid legal frameworks operate? This is often referred to as instrumental hybridity; I prefer the more value neutral term of normative hybridity. It should be noted in passing that in legal jurisprudence there is a history of debates over the relationship between empirical facts and normative questions of law (for example, the famous debate between Ehrlich and Kelsen),[12] and so this tension has a long tradition.

A strong critique of instrumental hybridity has emerged quite recently in both the law and development and peacebuilding literature.[13] This critique is in response to the embrace of hybrid approaches by international agencies and donors in the past decade, especially in the context of rule of law and statebuilding programs in conflict-affected and so-called fragile countries where the reach of the state is often limited and lacking in legitimacy. Moving away from a narrow state-centric framework has been seized upon as offering creative ways to overcome limitations of capacity on the part of state actors and to provide existing mechanisms that can be used to do the work that state agencies are not able to do.[14] In some respects, this pragmatic use of hybridity resonates uncomfortably with colonial techniques of indirect rule, which involved mechanisms such as native courts, district assessors and the enrolling of local chiefs into the state justice system.[15]

Such instrumental approaches to hybridity have been criticised as involving 'jurisprudential technology', a 'set of templates and models through which the non-state legal orders are regulated and authorized'[16] or 'hybrid programming' in the peacebuilding and development fields.[17] These critiques point to the extent to which such approaches 'give license to intervention—giving credence to prescriptive approaches and legitimizing top-down technocratic solutions'.[18] They are seen to facilitate the implementation of Western models in a local disguise, by creating institutions that are given a cloak of legitimacy as they purportedly comprise elements of both systems. There is also the concern that the

---

12   van Klink, 'Facts and Norms'.
13   See Hameiri and Jones, this volume.
14   Tamanaha et al., *Legal Pluralism and Development*.
15   Rodman, 'Men of Influence, Men of Rank'.
16   Porter, 'Some Implications on the Application of Legal Pluralism to Development Practice', 168.
17   Millar, 'Disaggregating Hybridity', 503.
18   Ibid., 511.

'turn to the local' in international engagements—whether peacebuilding, statebuilding or development more broadly—facilitates or is in sympathy with external neoliberal agendas aimed at subcontracting state functions to non-state actors, thereby further hollowing out already weak states.[19] A further difficulty identified by critics is that in the construction of institutional hybrids 'there is a reduction of complex social processes to simple rules or norms that mimic formal law'.[20] Reflections of this sort have led critical peacebuilding scholars such as Mac Ginty and Richmond to announce they are 'sceptical of the possibility of instrumentalizing hybridity' and that attempts to instrumentalise hybridity 'evades ethical questions relating to social and distributive justice'.[21] Boege has similarly declared that 'hybrid political orders, hybrid security governance and hybrid peace cannot be instrumentally designed, crafted or constructed'.[22]

There is not the space here to discuss the substantive validity or otherwise of these critiques of previous uses of hybridity.[23] The point I wish to make is that the way in which the concept *has* been used as an instrument of legal reform should not be a reflection on whether it *should* or *could* be used to answer normative questions about social justice (the 'ought' question). In other words, previous (for argument's sake, misguided) instances of using the concept in a normative way should not preclude future attempts to develop the conceptual insights of hybridity to better answer 'ought' questions concerning social justice.

There are a number of reasons to support this argument. The first is that those arguing against instrumentalised hybridity appear to base their argument on the grounds that those 'doing' hybridity are always outsiders or international actors, characterised as 'elites intent on modernization and marketization'[24] and who get 'local actors to work in the service of strategic and liberal internationalist goals'.[25] This characterisation ignores the broader view of agency that is one of the advances of hybridity; namely that regulatory change involves the conscious and unconscious interweaving of different aspects of different legal systems at many

---

19   Meagher, 'The Strength of Weak States?'.
20   Jayasuriya, 'Institutional Hybrids and the Rule of Law as a Regulatory Project', 152–153.
21   Mac Ginty and Richmond, 'The Fallacy of Constructing Hybrid Political Orders', 220.
22   Boege, this volume.
23   It is relevant in assessing such critiques that 'prescriptive hybridity' has been anchored in a larger critique of 'the liberal peace' that has characterised international peacebuilding over the past two decades.
24   Mac Ginty and Richmond, 'The Fallacy of Constructing Hybrid Political Orders', 230.
25   Ibid., 225.

different levels and is driven by many different actors. As such, it involves both internal and external change agents, and often shifting coalitions of both, a point demonstrated by other chapters in this collection (for example, Dinnen and Allen). This is also something that has been thoroughly explored and documented by historical anthropology.[26] One has only to look in Melanesia at the various initiatives at a customary level—such as the adoption of constitutions and by-laws by chiefly councils, the appointment of minute takers and even the creation of uniforms and letterhead for non-state justice processes—to see that hybridity is in no way limited to outside agents of change.[27] It is also incorrect to characterise external agents as uniformly driven by neoliberalising motivations and internal agents as not; it is abundantly clear that forces for and forces against capitalism and neoliberal development models exist along every part of the local to global continuum.

Second, in arguing against normative hybridity there is a failure to perceive a role for regulation, in the sense of 'the intentional activity of attempting to control, order or influence the behaviour of others'[28] or for governance, meaning 'steering the flow of events within a social system'.[29] Richmond distinguishes between a negative hybrid peace, which 'may represent the outsourcing of power and norms from the international to the state or society', and a positive hybrid peace that 'implies that significant legitimacy and agency emerge from the local scale'.[30] However, they imply that it will largely be a matter of happenstance, context and power dynamics that will lead to either one or the other. In other words, there is no room for conscious and informed regulatory design in steering or influencing movement towards particular hybrid formations (and any move in that direction is doomed to failure). I am puzzled by this; hybrid arrangements occur at least in part due to various degrees of conscience or deliberate reform by a range of actors. It may be that the intentions and actions of such change agents are thwarted at times by geopolitical or local power dynamics, but this should not rule out the possibility of directed positive change all together. It seems a worthwhile endeavour to enquire into, and theorise about, what sorts of processes of change and regulatory tools bring about what types of hybrid arrangements in which contexts.

26   Akin, *Colonialism, Maasina Rule, and the Origins of Malaitan Kastom*.
27   Forsyth, *A Bird That Flies with Two Wings*.
28   Black, 'Critical Reflections on Regulation', 25.
29   Gunningham, 'Confronting the Challenge of Energy Governance', 120.
30   Richmond, 'The Dilemmas of a Hybrid Peace', 51.

Generating such insights will surely be of relevance for all those engaged in reform projects involving hybrid legal orders, and can help to avoid the shallow engagement with the concept that has been so problematic. In answer to the concerns of Mac Ginty and Richmond, I argue that it is precisely *through* such theorising that ethical questions relating to social and distributive justice associated with hybrid legal orders can be asked and debated.

A third argument is that the relationship between 'is' and 'ought' is itself highly interwoven, making separating the two problematic.[31] This is supported by Braithwaite and Pettit who argue that we need to work harder to make our normative and explanatory theories work better together. They contend:

> Any normative theory that works with a category that lacks explanatory resonance is likely to be utopian and it will serve our policymaking badly. Any explanatory theory that fails to connect with a normative concern is likely to be unguided and it will be incapable of serving policymaking at all.[32]

Developing normative hybridity further will therefore also enhance the value of hybridity as an explanatory concept.

How could hybridity be developed to answer the 'ought' question?

Having set out why it is worthwhile to consider how hybridity can be theorised on a normative level, I turn now to the question of how to do so. Once we start to think through the many questions involved it is not long before we run smack bang into issues of power and privilege. A useful theory of hybridity must therefore focus on these at its heart. Other and related issues are: *Who decides which norms to pursue? Who has the authority and the power to bring about change in any legal system? If there are multiple legal systems, how can they all be taken into account if each system has only a partial perspective and conflicting objectives?*

---

31   For instance, merely describing the existence of other normative systems—even to the extent of calling them 'law'—often creates a layer of additional legitimacy.
32   Braithwaite and Pettit, *Not Just Deserts*, 161.

These are all large questions and the aim of this chapter is just to identify a few leads in beginning to develop a richer conceptual framework. I identify three starting points: focus on the values and objectives at stake, concentrate on the processes of change, and analyse the relationships between and within different legal orders.

Focus on the values and objectives at stake

Previous attempts to bring about social change using concepts that underpin hybridity have heavily focused on questions of structure, institutions and instruments (for example, written laws, police officers and customary compensation payments). This focus on institutional form[33] and other more easily identifiable aspects of the regulatory system often leads to the overlooking of values or principles that underlie different regulatory systems and reform agents. These values are often hidden through what Gramsci termed cultural hegemony[34] and others assumptive normality, the process by which certain values come to be seen as 'natural' and hence taken for granted. This process has been identified by postcolonial scholars in relation to concepts such as human rights, the rule of law and development.[35]

Using hybridity to answer 'ought' questions requires explicit identification of the values, principles and objectives of any reform project and space created for debate over them. It thus brings to the forefront issues that often remain hidden in reform projects through generalised references to 'rule of law', 'capacity building' and 'peace'. What is required is a conscious reflexivity about the use of such terms, even those that are apparently widely accepted, such as 'justice'. Such a term can involve connotations associated with Western 'justice' systems, such as the importance of individual rights, consistency in judgements, a fair and open trial, impartial judges and the right to present a defence. However, in countries where I work, such as Vanuatu, these may not be the priorities of conflict management; rather, concepts such as the re-establishment of peace and harmony in the community and the restoration of relationships are often prioritised. The use of the term 'justice' may mask these fundamental

---

33 See Andrews, *The Limits of Institutional Reform in Development*.
34 Lears, 'The Concept of Cultural Hegemony'.
35 Escobar, *Encountering Development*; Pahuka, *Decolonising International Law*; Rajagopal, *International Law from Below*.

differences in agenda, creating the assumption that all systems are reading from the same page when in reality there might be considerable divergence of opinion in what priorities should be pursued.

It is also important to highlight the tendency to underestimate the difficulty that everyone (aid and development practitioners, villagers, government officials) has in truly understanding new value systems or ontological realities (and in identifying them beneath the institutional form). This is often because values and principles are not explicitly articulated in many contexts—the focus is more on institutions and programs and processes (strengthening the justice system, for example). Many times concepts like 'justice' and 'rights' and 'victims' are understood very differently by different interest groups but this is often not perceived; a situation I and a colleague have elsewhere identified as being the 'false friends' problem.[36] This borrows a linguistics concept that describes a situation of striking resemblance between two words in two different languages, leading speakers of each language to assume, incorrectly, that they understand the word's meaning in the other language. Even more problematically, the misunderstanding is hidden by the assumption of understanding.

For instance, in my work on sorcery-related violence in Melanesia, I have observed there is fundamental disagreement between international and local actors about what 'problem' requires regulation, and who the 'victims' of sorcery and witchcraft are. These disagreements are often not even realised as those with differing ideologies 'talk past' each other. For those who do not believe in the existence of sorcery, the 'problem' is the violence related to sorcery or witchcraft accusations, and the victims are those accused of *being* witches or sorcerers. For those who do believe, although there is often concern about sorcery accusation–related violence, the 'problem' is also (and for some primarily) the harm that sorcerers and witches do to their communities, killing and harming innocent people. From this perspective, the victims are those people who have been killed or hurt through sorcery or witchcraft. This spiritual/rational ontological divide is also observed in Boege's chapter in this volume, where he notes that spiritual rehabilitation was critical to the Bougainvilleans but only dimly understood by the international peacekeepers.

---

36 Forsyth and Haggart, 'The False Friends Problem for Foreign Norm Transplantation in Developing Countries'.

In many ways, this is why issues such as sorcery, treatment of youth and gender-based violence are so important: they raise in stark relief these differences in value systems that otherwise remain covered over. So while such issues may seem to be particularly difficult for hybrid legal orders, they may in reality be the relatively low-hanging fruit—far more work needs to be done in *other* contexts in unearthing the different value systems because they are more deeply hidden.

It must be stressed that a focus on values and objectives should not imply that these are fixed, static or uncontested. The insights of hybridity apply equally here: values are in a constant process of adaptation/ mutual permeation and change and often involve power contestations. The suggestion here is simply to make these visible in order to facilitate more informed debate and include more voices, particularly those which are silenced by assumptions about the universality of values. A normative approach to hybridity must accept there will be disagreement about which norms to pursue and who gets to decide, but this will perhaps be easier to negotiate if there is generalised understanding about what is at stake.

Focus on the processes of change

Local-level hybrid arrangements are often seen as being more legitimate, authentic and positive than those 'designed' or constructed by the state or international actors. It is useful to unpack the reasons for this to understand if it is *just* because they are locally driven, or whether there are other explanatory processual factors behind this. Such factors may include the time span of the change (incremental or sudden), the underlying values in new regulatory arrangements, and whether existing power dynamics are reinforced and unchallenged. Understanding in detail which processes of change have which effects and *why* will give clearer insights into how better outcomes can be achieved through reform activities in hybrid legal contexts. It should also avoid lip service being paid to notions of 'consultation', 'local ownership' and 'bottom-up change'.

A much-needed dimension of research in this field is therefore the systematic identification of hybridising processes that enable positive/ liberal social change (acknowledging that what is 'positive' will always be relative and contingent). This will also involve identifying the agents of change, the values, implicit and explicit, being promoted and the extent to which all parties are in agreement over them, as well as how disagreements are managed. It is useful here to include processes that have led to successful hybridisation through conscious reform endeavours, and also hybridisations that have been less obviously directed. The question of who or what possesses intentionality and its role and limits in processes of change is highly relevant.[37] Change impacts upon and is directed by structural factors, cultural prejudice and political, economic and ideological hegemony, and the extent to which these interplay with subjective intention requires further investigation.

My own research suggests positive reform in hybrid legal contexts is facilitated by the creation of spaces or forums that allow for active and well-informed debates about the objectives of particular reform projects, and the values and principles that underlie the desire to change. This notion comes from a number of different directions, including both the advocates of interculturality within the decolonial movement and from Habermas's concept of communicative action.[38] Quijano argues that in order to clear the path for 'new intercultural communication' there must be 'epistemological decolonization'.[39] In other words, he suggests there can only be true communication between those from different cultures, and hence possessed of different ontologies or world views, if each party to the dialogue recognises the partiality of their perspective. Applying this notion to a legal context as an illustration, Tobin describes intercultural legal pluralism as 'a world of legal interfaces that cannot be imposed but must be negotiated, tested and modulated in response to the realities of differing worldviews, value systems and legal visions'.[40] Drawing these insights together means that such forums need to be places where difference is embraced; there is a willingness or incentive to learn; different value systems and ontological frameworks are explicitly articulated; each party to the dialogue recognises the partiality of their perspective; and there is an understanding that behind all regulatory systems are distinct logics, rationalities, customs and knowledge that must be taken into account. This is illustrated in some community development practices such as 'community conversations' around HIV in Melanesia.[41]

---

37   Latour's insights that it is not just people who have agency are highly relevant here. See Latour, *Reassembling the Social.*
38   Habermas, *Theory of Communicative Action.*
39   Quijano, 'Coloniality and Modernity/Rationality', 177.
40   Tobin, 'Bridging the Nagoya Compliance Gap', 161.
41   Reid, 'Re-thinking Human Rights and the HIV Epidemic'. See also Berman, 'Jurisgenerative Constitutionalism'.

Those making conscious reforms in hybrid spaces need to find ways to create such spaces. This is in fact a space that academics can help to create through the holding of conferences, particularly in the countries where the issues involved are occurring, and including both scholarly and non-scholarly participants. One example of this I have been involved in was the holding of a series of conferences on the issue of sorcery accusation–related violence in Papua New Guinea. These have led to the creation of a coalition of local and international change agents and the development and passage of a new national policy to address this violence.[42] The conferences also allowed for the working through of many of the difficult ontological issues associated with this area, such as how to address the violence while not denying people the right to their customary beliefs and practices.

The convening of conferences in a way that successfully creates such spaces is vastly more likely to be successful if international and local scholars, researchers and activists are able to plan, convene and publish together. It also requires proceedings of conferences to be made available and accessible (i.e. in plain English or where relevant translated) to those who will have practical need of them. This may involve creative approaches, such as publishing short summaries online, producing podcasts, holding information sessions or radio sessions, or other means. These are all real challenges for scholars in Western educational institutions where the political economy creates disincentives for these types of engagements, for example, pressures to publish single-authored papers in prestigious academic journals.

A concomitant part of the creation of such spaces is a recognition that no single approach works in every situation and there is intrinsic value in the mere fact that there are different ways of doing things. For example, a commitment to human rights principles may work wonderfully in relation to requiring everyone to be accorded a trial before conviction. However, it may end up being liberty depriving in dealing with gender-based violence in contexts where state agencies are themselves abusers of human rights. Other approaches may better ensure safety. There is also a need for recognition that notions such as human rights and rule of law are not a fixed-package option—people often do 'pick and mix' to use Helene Kyed's lovely term,[43] in ways that to an outsider may be

---

42   Forsyth and Haggart, 'The False Friends Problem'.
43   At the workshop.

unexpected, but seem to work in practice. For example, my research into dealing with sorcery-related violence in Melanesia indicates that one of the most effective ways for local leaders to deflect violence is to stress the absence of proof, a concept imported in this form from the state justice system.

Focus on relationships between and within different legal orders

Finally, there is a need to pay attention to the nature of linkages or relationships, formal and informal, between different legal systems or regulatory nodes within hybrid legal arrangements.[44] As Baker has observed, relational ties within a network are crucial to determining the 'strength, cohesion, collaborative intensity and sustainability'[45] of the network as a whole. Such a statement is equally applicable to hybrid legal contexts which can be seen as a variety of network.

Focusing on relationships can involve looking at them both within legal orders and between legal orders through a range of different sections (in the sense of slicing up a specimen to look at under a microscope). This can be looking at all legal orders involved in a particular problem (such as domestic violence or intellectual property regulation) or all the legal orders involved in a particular geographical location. It can also be sliced temporally, to look at a particular moment in time or to take a long historical perspective.

Further, rather than stopping at the analytical stage, I am interested in the potential that exists to consciously change the nature of these relationships. A number of different regulatory theories have been developed in a Western context that may have relevance to such a project. Regulatory theories are not prescriptive about regulatory design; rather, they articulate insights about general principles that can be used in certain contexts to create regulatory systems that are more legitimate and less dominated by those with power. Below, I set out two that have the potential to be developed further in this context.

---

44   This is a topic on which much legal pluralism literature exists. See, for example, the discussion in Berman, 'Jurisgenerative Constitutionalism', where he identifies dialectical legal interactions, margins of appreciation, subsidiary schemes, hybrid participation arrangements and jurisdictional redundancies.
45   Baker, 'Linking State and Non-state Security and Justice', 600.

The first is responsive regulation, which is based on the empirical insight that ensuring compliance with a particular regulatory objective can sometimes be achieved with persuasion and education, and sometimes requires heavier sanctions. It is based on the idea of a regulatory pyramid that gives the cheaper and more respectful options (education, mediation, community conversations) a chance to work first, while keeping the more costly punitive attempts at control in reserve for those cases where persuasion fails.[46] Responsive regulation was designed in developed economies, but has recently started to be expanded to the developing world. In such a context it can be usefully supplemented with a networked or nodal governance dimension.[47] This means that rather than dealing with a particular regulatory problem by itself, the state enrols a range of other actors (community organisations, civil society, church organisations, other states, United Nations organisations, academic institutions) in its efforts to ensure compliance. This is a potentially valuable approach in developing countries where the state does not have sufficient justice resources and there is a range of non-state actors offering assistance, especially in relation to issues such as gender-based violence. The challenge is for all the initiatives at work to be developed into an effective regulatory pyramid, so they meaningfully support each other. Responsive regulation coupled with network governance has clear relevance for situations of hybrid legal arrangements. It would need to be adapted further, however, to integrate the dynamic and coproducing nature of hybrid legal orders and also to deal more explicitly with questions of power, differences in ontology and the avoidance of domination.

The second regulatory theory of potential relevance is a conflict web concept I have developed[48] that draws on network theory,[49] nodal governance[50] and regulatory space metaphors.[51] The key features are as follows: first, it focuses on identifying, strengthening and, where necessary, building mutually supporting linkages between actors and institutions actively involved in conflict management (or indeed any other field). This avoids the adoption of a hierarchical, state-centralist approach to reform and frees up reform initiatives to consider how, for example, state

---

46   Braithwaite, 'Responsive Regulation and Developing Economies', 887.
47   Drahos, 'Intellectual Property and Pharmaceutical Markets'.
48   Forsyth, 'Spinning a Conflict Management Web in Vanuatu'.
49   Wellman, 'Network Analysis: Some Basic Principles'.
50   Shearing and Wood, 'Nodal Governance, Democracy, and the New "Denizens"'.
51   Scott, 'Analysing Regulatory Space'.

institutions can be positively influenced by and kept in check by non-state actors and institutions.[52] It also helps to ensure that agents of reform (be they state governments or international donors) are not duplicating the efforts (or worse, inadvertently undermining the efforts) of another reform project.

Second, this framework emphasises the sharing of information about what reform initiatives work and why between various state and non-state actors in the field and also donors, non-government organisations and academics. This will foster homegrown adaptation and innovation to replace the current tendency to look immediately outside for ideas and models. In turn, this is likely to increase the legitimacy of conflict-management institutions and actors, which has been identified as an important issue in statebuilding and reducing conflict and violence.[53] Action learning and reflection are thus central to the framework, meaning that those involved in reform should regularly assess the benefits of their projects to inform themselves, and others in the web, about how to better implement reforms.[54]

Conclusion

This chapter has argued that the concept of hybridity can and should be developed to answer questions of how hybrid legal orders *ought* to be, a dimension to the concept termed here normative hybridity. It suggests three initial ways forward in developing these elements of the concept; namely a focus on the values at stake, a focus on the processes of change, and a focus on the relationships between and within different legal orders. It also suggests two regulatory theories that may prove useful for further developing this concept, noting that these ideas are as yet undeveloped and there is a need for further empirical testing and development. Developing the concept of hybridity in this way can facilitate change agents in helping to steer hybrid legal orders in positive and emancipatory directions.

---

52 Ibid., 337.
53 World Bank, *World Development Report 2011*, 84.
54 A collaboration-strengthening pyramid such as suggested by Braithwaite may also assist in this evaluation and strengthening process. See Braithwaite, *Restorative Justice and Responsive Regulation*, 115–127.

5

Is There Still a Place for Liberal Peacebuilding?

Joanne Wallis[1]

For the past 20 years the concept of liberal peacebuilding has ostensibly guided the efforts of Western governments, the United Nations and other international institutions to stabilise and rebuild conflict-affect states.[2] Liberal peacebuilding sought to build state institutions that adhere to the key tenets of the 'liberal peace': democracy, the rule of law and human rights, and which provide the conditions for capitalist market economies to flourish. The concept was based on the assumption that liberalism was inherently attractive and offered the most likely path to peace and prosperity. Its authority was buttressed by the claim that promoting liberal peace would also end conflict between states, based on the democratic peace thesis.[3]

While critics have argued that the wide variety of contemporary peacebuilding interventions have not been exercises of liberal peacebuilding,[4] and instead interveners have aimed for 'regulatory stability and regional and domestic security',[5] the 'rhetoric, if not the practice,

---

footnotes
1   The research leading to this chapter was generously funded by Australian Research Council Discovery grant DP160104692, 'Doing State-building Better? Practising Hybridity in Melanesia'.
2   United Nations, *An Agenda for Peace*.
3   Doyle, 'Three Pillars of the Liberal Peace'.
4   Hameiri, 'The Crisis of Liberal Peacebuilding'; Zaum, 'Beyond the "Liberal Peace"'.
5   Chandler, 'The Uncritical Critique of 'Liberal Peace', 148; Hameiri, 'The Crisis of Liberal Peacebuilding'.

is most firmly liberal and in the Wilsonian tradition'.[6] Data from Peace Accords Matrix also suggests that 'liberal ideals have been embedded in the vast majority of post-1989 peace accords'.[7] Yet, there is remarkably little consensus regarding what the liberalism that guides liberal peacebuilding actually is, with 'competing and often contradictory claims' made about its content.[8] This has meant that neoliberal peacebuilding has instead been implemented, guided by an emphasis on individual autonomy removed from basic principles of justice.

(Neo)liberal peacebuilding has not built sustainable peace in most places where it was attempted. There are also new ideological challenges to Western conceptions of the liberal peace. The first comes from China, which, despite resisting the temptation towards liberal political reforms, seems to demonstrate that authoritarian capitalism can deliver prosperity. The second comes from the new form of transnational political actor represented by Da'esh, which raises existential questions about liberal peacebuilding; despite the massive efforts to build stable liberal democracies in Iraq and Afghanistan, Iraq now hosts the Da'esh insurgency against the fundamental principles of liberalism and the concept of sovereign statehood. The third comes from disruptions to the West's pragmatic approaches to international order; after the Arab Spring, Western states realised they could no longer credibly support longstanding authoritarian allies in the face of popular demands for democracy, but as a consequence had to contemplate the possibility of hostile groups taking power. These challenges have underlined emerging questions about whether the liberal peace, or even liberalism as a political ideology, is inherently attractive in all contexts and offers the only path to prosperity, recognition of identity or stability.

Accordingly, there is a palpable sense of hubris within Western governments, the United Nations and other international institutions, which now pursue the more modest goal of 'good enough' outcomes that may involve 'combinations of state, private sector, faith-based, traditional, and community structures for service delivery'.[9] This move away from liberal peacebuilding might be interpreted as an instrumental lowering of the liberal peace standards sought during peacebuilding, such

---

6   Richmond and Mac Ginty, 'Where Now for the Critique of the Liberal Peace?', 174.
7   Ibid., 177–178; Peace Accords Matrix, Kroc Institute for International Peace Studies, peaceaccords.nd.edu/about.
8   Bell, 'What Is Liberalism?', 687.
9   World Bank, *World Development Report 2011*, 106.

as shifting from attempting to hold 'free and fair' elections to merely holding 'credible' ones, in order to reduce the burden on the international community of the expense and time required to institutionalise liberal democracy during interventions. Yet it also reflects the emergence of the concept of hybrid peacebuilding in the academic literature, which seeks to negotiate elements of the liberal peace in a local context by advocating 'an intersubjective mediation between local and international scales and norms, institutions, law, right, needs and interests, depending on both power and legitimacy'.[10] Ideally, this will generate a 'positive hybrid peace', 'rooted in accommodation, reconciliation, emancipation, autonomy, social justice and a sense of liberation'.[11]

But, how does the turn away from liberal to hybrid peacebuilding operate in practice? Is there still a place for liberal peacebuilding? I seek to answer these questions using a case study of Timor-Leste.[12]

Timor-Leste is a small state with a population of 1.17 million people. It was a Portuguese colony from the early eighteenth century to 1974, when the Portuguese withdrew and a group of Timorese leaders declared independence in November 1975. In December 1975, Indonesia invaded the territory and occupied it for 24 years. Various Timorese groups opposed the occupation and a long and bloody independence struggle followed. That struggle culminated in the Timorese people being given the opportunity to vote on their political future in a United Nations–run referendum in August 1999. An overwhelming majority (78.5 per cent) opted for independence, rather than autonomy within Indonesia (21.5 per cent). After the result of the vote was announced the Indonesian military and its supporting Timorese militia engaged in a scorched earth campaign in which thousands were killed and almost three quarters of buildings and infrastructure were destroyed.[13] An Australian-led intervention force stabilised the territory, and the United Nations Transitional Administration in East Timor engaged in what was described as a liberal peacebuilding operation to build the new state for its independence in May 2002. However, in response to challenges that emerged following independence, since 2004 the government has attempted to engage with local sociopolitical practices

10   Richmond, 'The Dilemmas of a Hybrid Peace', 51.
11   Ibid., 60.
12   Fieldwork was conducted in Timor-Leste in 2009, 2010 and 2013. As Timor-Leste is a conflict-affected state, all interviews are anonymous to protect the confidentiality of interviewees.
13   CAVR, *Chega!*

and institutions in certain areas. Although the government's attempts are neither systematic nor coherent, in Timor-Leste what can be described as an attempt at hybrid peacebuilding has emerged in relation to areas such as decentralisation and justice.[14]

I begin with a brief outline of hybrid peacebuilding and the questions it raises. The core of this chapter is a case study about how hybrid peacebuilding has operated in practice in Timor-Leste, with a focus on decentralisation and justice. I conclude by arguing there may still be a place for liberal peacebuilding in Timor-Leste.

Hybrid peacebuilding

As described in the Introduction, the hybrid peacebuilding literature starts from the observation that diverse sociopolitical practices and institutions can 'co-exist, overlap, interact, and intertwine' in conflict-affected societies.[15] Hybrid peacebuilding is taken to imply more than mere co-existence of these practices and institutions;[16] they must instead merge, integrate or syncretise into a 'fusion policy'.[17] While the literature has been criticised for oversimplification by drawing a neat distinction between the 'local' and 'liberal' or 'international',[18] it does not seek to create artificial binaries,[19] as 'hybrid forms are never simply a mix of two otherwise pure forms, but are perennially ongoing processes of amalgamation and dissolution'.[20]

In much of the literature the 'local' is taken to refer to 'customary law and indigenous knowledge, as well as traditional societal structures—extended families, clans, tribes, religious brotherhoods, village communities—and traditional authorities such as village elders, clan chiefs, healers, big men, and religious leaders' that determine 'the everyday social reality of large parts of the population … particularly in rural and remote peripheral areas'.[21] Although some analyses tend to attribute the local with 'spatial

---

14   Brown and Gusmao, 'Peacebuilding and Political Hybridity in East Timor'; Wallis, 'A Liberal–Local Hybrid Peace Project'.

15   Boege et al., 'Hybrid Political Orders, Not Fragile States', 17.

16   Goodfellow and Lindemann, 'The Clash of Institutions'.

17   Mac Ginty, 'Hybrid Peace: The Interaction between Top-Down and Bottom-Up Peace', 406.

18   Björkdahl and Höglund, 'Precarious Peacebuilding'.

19   Heathershaw, 'Towards Better Theories of Peacebuilding'.

20   Albrecht and Wiuff Moe, 'The Simultaneity of Authority', 5.

21   Boege et al., 'Hybrid Political Orders, Not Fragile States', 15.

characteristics',[22] local practices and institutions need not 'operate in a geographically and politically defined sub-national and sub-regional space',[23] but can also be 'de-territorialised, networked and constituted by people and activity rather than place'.[24] This is because the local 'may not be local at all, but transnational or global, based upon relationships of kinship, trade, occupation, religion or leisure, mediated by direct interaction between mobile bodies, or via various types of media'.[25]

Criticisms of hybrid peacebuilding

Yet, as the Introduction to this volume notes, the hybrid peacebuilding literature has attracted criticism. The aspect of the hybrid peacebuilding literature which has attracted the most criticism is its potential to be used prescriptively or instrumentally.[26] There are warnings that it may be used to 'give license to intervention' and to legitimise 'top-down technocratic solutions'.[27] Indeed, rather than responding to local demands, the shift to hybrid or good enough outcomes during peacebuilding is more and more driven by international interveners, multinational corporations and aid agencies.[28]

The literature is also concerned that hybrid peacebuilding may have perverse consequences, as by emphasising local agency it might only provide the 'illusion of local ownership'.[29] This may see the determinants of peacebuilding attributed to the local level and overlook broader structural challenges,[30] such as its often discriminatory and distorting political economy.[31] Indeed, hybrid peacebuilding may focus too heavily on ideational issues and institutions and overlook the influence of material factors of social welfare and human security.[32] There is also a risk that it can be used to legitimate actions by practitioners and

---

22   Hirblinger and Simons, 'The Good, the Bad, and the Powerful', 422.
23   Baker, 'Justice and Security Architecture in Africa', 29.
24   Mac Ginty, 'Where Is the Local?', 841.
25   Hughes et al., 'The Struggle versus the Song', 821.
26   Mac Ginty and Richmond, 'The Fallacy of Constructing Hybrid Political Orders', 220.
27   Millar, 'Disaggregating Hybridity', 511.
28   Meagher et al., *Unravelling Public Authority*.
29   Björkdahl and Höglund, 'Precarious Peacebuilding', 291.
30   Chandler, 'Peacebuilding and the Politics of Non-linearity'.
31   Hameiri, *Regulating Statehood*.
32   Nadarajah and Rampton, 'The Limits of Hybridity'; Newman, 'A Human Security Peace-building Agenda'.

policymakers focused on the 'resilience' of local communities as a 'cure-all status'.[33] In this regard, there is the suggestion that international actors may instrumentally embrace hybrid peacebuilding because it 'lessens the burden on the state and donors and lessens the burden on reform processes', which highlights concerns that hybrid peacebuilding aimed at 'good enough' outcomes may be used as a cloak for merely attempting to institutionalise the liberal peace with lower standards.[34] However, it must be acknowledged that local actors are sometimes able to either 'benefit from international intervention, or to resist intentional intervention, while enacting oppressions of their own'.[35]

The literature frequently cautions about the need to resist the temptation to romanticise the local practices and institutions engaged with during hybrid peacebuilding,[36] as they often include 'a range of non-traditional and often unsavoury actors, including warlords, militias, gang leaders, millenarian religious movements and organized crime'.[37] Local practices and institutions can also obscure issues of injustice and differential power relationships, based on factors such as gender and class.[38] This highlights the potential dark side of hybridity 'in which violent and oppressive social practices become embedded in officially recognised governance systems'.[39] Local practices and institutions should also not be essentialised; they are not immutable relics of the 'pre-contact' past, since the cultures in which they exist are constantly evolving living organisms.[40]

Hybrid peacebuilding in Timor-Leste

Although the United Nations claimed it was conducting liberal peacebuilding in Timor-Leste, in substance it engaged in neoliberal peacebuilding; that is, it focused on building highly centralised institutions, limiting public expenditure, creating financial liberalisation and reducing the role for the state.[41] Consequently, the 80 per cent of

33   Chandler, 'Resilience and the "Everyday"'; Mac Ginty, 'Everyday Peace', 559.
34   Richmond and Mitchell, 'Peacebuilding and Critical Forms of Agency', 334.
35   Hughes et al., 'The Struggle versus the Song', 820.
36   Richmond, 'The Romanticisation of the Local'.
37   Meagher, 'The Strength of Weak States?', 1080.
38   Peterson, 'A Conceptual Unpacking of Hybridity'.
39   Meagher et al., *Unravelling Public Authority*, 5.
40   Boege et al., 'Hybrid Political Orders, Not Fragile States', 15.
41   Wallis, 'A Liberal–Local Hybrid Peace Project'.

Timorese residing in rural areas and living subsistence lifestyles were left out of the peacebuilding process and continued to follow local sociopolitical practices and institutions centred on their village (*suku*) or hamlet (*aldeia*). Indeed, a 2002 Asia Foundation survey found that 61 per cent of respondents favoured their *suku* chief or traditional leader for resolving problems with their neighbours, and 65 per cent favoured their *suku* chief or traditional leader for mediating property disputes, while 54 per cent favoured their *suku* chief as the source of political information.[42] In recognition of these facts, with the encouragement and assistance of international interveners and donors, from 2004 the Timor-Leste Government began to engage with local practices and institutions in certain areas in a process that can be described as hybrid peacebuilding. I focus on decentralisation and justice, as these are two of the most notable areas in which this has occurred.

Decentralisation

In 2004 the Timor-Leste Government introduced limited administrative and political decentralisation. A wide range of political and administrative functions were decentralised to the *aldeia* and *suku* leaders and *suku* councils,[43] which are characterised as 'community leaders'. As a result of this characterisation, *aldeia* and *suku* leaders and *suku* councils are 'not included in the public administration'.[44] Therefore, they can access few resources, are given limited support and have little influence over higher levels of government.[45] This has restricted their capacity to exercise their mandate and generated a degree of frustration and 'confusion' concerning their status.[46]

There are questions about the performance of local leaders. Many *suku* leaders have 'good coordination with the community',[47] and 'are very active in meeting their responsibilities'.[48] However, their capacity to plan

---

42 Asia Foundation, *Timor Lorosa'e National Survey of Citizen Knowledge*.
43 *Decree Law on Community Authorities No. 5/2004*; *Law on Community Leaderships and Their Election No. 3/2009*.
44 *Law on Community Leaderships*, section 2(3).
45 Interview with a governance adviser, 18 July 2013; interview with a subdistrict administrator, 28 August 2013.
46 Interview with a member of civil society (b), 4 September 2013; interview with a governance adviser, 18 July 2013; interview with a public servant, 3 September 2013.
47 Interview with a governance adviser, 18 July 2013.
48 Interview with a member of civil society (c), 17 July 2013.

and implement projects has varied.[49] Some *suku* leaders 'don't do a good job and many communities complain',[50] others make decisions that favour their personal interests,[51] and some *suku* councils fail to meet regularly.[52] A World Bank report even claimed that some local leaders displayed 'authoritarian characteristics'.[53] These issues may be partly explained by the fact that many *sukus* are large both in terms of geographical size and population (the average size is 2,000 to 3,000 people), or are socially fractured, which means that it can be difficult and expensive to generate societal trust.[54] In addition, because local leaders are often selected based on traditional power structures and ritual authority, their levels of literacy and numeracy can be low, which means that some struggle to manage the technical requirements of administrative activities and decentralised development projects.[55]

There are concerns that local sociopolitical practices which influence *aldeias* and *sukus* can discriminate against women and young people, since it is generally elder males who have authority.[56] To combat this, the *suku* councils reserve seats for women and young people to ensure their participation. However, there are structural and material barriers to women taking leadership positions. The small incentive local leaders receive can be economically prohibitive for women, as they usually do not have an independent source of income and are required to complete significant domestic and agricultural work.[57] Even when women do take a leadership role, it is difficult for them to influence decision-making,[58] partly because local sociopolitical practices often perpetuate a patriarchal approach.[59]

---

49   Everett and Ragragio, *Decentralisation in Timor-Leste*; interview with a member of parliament, 30 September 2010; interview with a *suku* leader, 28 September 2010; interview with a governance adviser, 23 April 2010.
50   Interview with a member of civil society (c), 17 July 2013.
51   Cummins and Maia, *Community Experiences of Decentralised Development*; interview with a member of civil society (c), 17 July 2013; interview with a governance adviser, 18 July 2013.
52   Interview with a member of civil society (a), 4 September 2013; interview with a member of civil society (c), 17 July 2013.
53   Butterworth and Dale, *Local Governance and Community Development Initiatives*, 13.
54   Cummins and Maia, *Community Experiences of Decentralised Development*.
55   Ibid.
56   Hicks, '*Adat* and the Nation-State'; interview with a women's leader, 29 April 2010.
57   Cummins, 'The Problem of Gender Quotas'; interview with a women's leader, 18 July 2013.
58   Interview with a member of civil society (a), 4 September 2013; interview with a women's leader, 18 July 2013.
59   Cummins and Maia, *Community Experiences of Decentralised Development*; interview with a member of civil society (a), 17 July 2013; interview with a member of civil society (c), 17 July 2013.

In this regard, while introducing elections for local leaders appears to have extended democracy to the local level, elections might actually have reduced political participation,[60] as they occur only every four years and *suku* leaders and councils do not necessarily consult their communities in between.[61] Moreover, the first round of *suku* elections in 2005 and 2006 was highly politicised. The introduction of party politics at the local level contributed to friction, hampered the ability of many *suku* leaders and councils to operate, affected the perceived legitimacy of leaders and undermined local sociopolitical practices.[62] As a result, the 2009 local government law prevented political parties from running in the 2009 *suku* elections[63] and provided that *suku* councils would be elected as 'packages', rather than as individuals. Yet this change has had unintended consequences, as powerful local figures are now said to compile packages from their families, which can allow one family to dominate *suku* affairs, leading to the election of people who lack capacity or are inefficient.[64] It has also generated social jealousy and inequalities in the distribution of benefits and opportunities.[65]

The opportunities to use local government positions to dispense benefits has been enhanced by the developmental decentralisation introduced in 2009,[66] which has distributed significant resources, created jobs and provided communities with the opportunity to undertake local decision-making.[67] The quality of these projects has differed, primarily due to variable local capacity, poor planning and project choice, lack of opportunities for local feedback and at times limited opportunities for

---

60   Pereira and Koten, 'Dynamics of Democracy at the *Suku* Level'.

61   Interview with a member of civil society (a), 4 September 2013; interview with a member of civil society (c), 17 July 2013.

62   Interview with a governance adviser, 18 July 2013; interview with a member of civil society, 18 July 2013.

63   *Law on Community Leaderships*, section 21. Anecdotal evidence suggests that parties were still active.

64   Interview with an academic, 18 July 2013; Asia Foundation, *Reflections on Law No. 3/2009*.

65   Interview with a governance adviser, 18 July 2013.

66   *Pakote Referendum* (Referendum Package) in 2009; *Pakote Dezenvolvimentu Desentralizasaun* (Decentralised Development Package) and *Planu Dezenvolvimentu Suku* (Suku Development Plan) in 2010; *Programa Dezenvolvimentu Dezentralizadu* (Decentralised Development Programs) in 2011; *Planeamentu Dezenvolvimentu Integradu Distrital* (Integrated District Development Plan) (*Decree Law on Integrated District Development No. 4/2012*) and *Programa Nasional Dezenvolvimentu Suku* (National Program for Village Development) (*Government Resolution Approving the Establishment of a National Mechanism to Accelerate Community Development No. 1/2012*; *Ministerial Decree on Elaboration of District Investment Plan No. 9/2012*) in 2012.

67   Interview with a governance adviser, 18 July 2013; interview with an academic, 18 July 2013.

local input.[68] There are also claims that the central government overrides the development priorities identified by the *sukus*, which has led to frustration.[69] The relatively weak links between the local level and the central government also mean there is insufficient oversight of decentralised development projects, with claims of collusion and nepotism common.[70] This highlights the danger of hybrid peacebuilding being used as an excuse for lowering standards of governance. This has created a perception that the government has used developmental decentralisation as 'a strategy to execute the budget, so it can report that it executed well, even though there have been no outcomes'.[71]

Justice

The Timor-Leste Government has also taken steps to decentralise activities relating to justice, such as implementing community policing and working with local justice mechanisms.[72] Yet, there are claims that community policing remains 'a vague ambition rather than an immediate priority' as it is 'chronically under-resourced'.[73] There is also inadequate oversight of local justice mechanisms,[74] partly because there is no clear framework establishing the relationship between state institutions and local mechanisms.[75] The role of *suku* leaders when settling disputes is also unclear, as is how this role fits with that of state institutions.

In this regard, the recognition of local justice mechanisms has been criticised as sending 'mixed messages' that may undermine the rule of law.[76] Local mechanisms co-exist with state justice institutions and often enforce customary law rather than state law, which results in legal pluralism, whereby 'two or more legal systems co-exist in the same social

---

68 Interview with a member of civil society, 18 July 2013; interview with a *suku* leader, 3 September 2013; interview with an academic, 18 July 2013; interview with a governance adviser, 18 July 2013.
69 Interview with a subdistrict administrator, 28 August 2013; interview with a district administrator, 29 August 2013; interview with a district administrator, 31 August 2013; interview with a district administrator, 1 September 2013; interview with a *suku* leader, 3 September 2013.
70 Interview with a member of civil society (a), 17 July 2013; interview with a member of civil society (c), 17 July 2013.
71 Interview with a member of civil society (a), 17 July 2013.
72 *Organic Law of Timor-Leste's National Police (PNTL) No. 9/2009*; *Law on Community Leaderships*, section 11.
73 Belo and Koenig, *Institutionalizing Community Policing in Timor-Leste*, 1.
74 USAID, *Rule of Law in Timor-Leste*.
75 Asia Foundation, *Timor-Leste Law & Justice Survey 2013*.
76 Grenfell, 'Promoting the Rule of Law in Timor-Leste', 228.

field'.[77] As the system currently operates it 'does not serve the rule of law because it operates without any of the checks or balances' as there are 'no formal avenues of appeal and thus minimal accountability and transparency'.[78] This challenge is exemplified by the fact that people can receive customary sanctions under a *tara bandu*, 'an agreement among the community regulating aspects of behaviour and relationships among people, between people and natural resources, and economic life',[79] and then face punishment under the state system for the same crime.[80] There is also the risk that people may be sanctioned under *tara bandu* for behaviour that does not contravene state law. As a solution, efforts could be made to minimise the contradictions between *tara bandu* and state law, so that they can be seen as 'complementary'.[81] Moreover, a draft customary law provides for appeals from local mechanisms to state justice institutions, which gives people the opportunity to access state law if they are dissatisfied with the outcome of the local mechanism.[82] This draft law has been under development as a partnership between the United Nations Development Programme and Timor-Leste Government for several years, with little sign that it will be adopted.

The use of customary sanctions raises questions concerning the human rights implications of recognising local justice mechanisms. There are concerns over the neutrality of local justice decision-makers, the consistency of their decision-making and their treatment of women, particularly in cases of sexual assault and domestic violence.[83] For example, a 2008 Asia Foundation survey revealed that 58 per cent of respondents disapprove of women being able to speak for themselves in local justice mechanisms, although this number had shrunk to 39 per cent in 2013, reflecting changing community attitudes.[84]

This last point highlights the fact that local justice mechanisms should not be romanticised, nor should state justice institutions be 'automatically disregarded as imposed, harmful and culturally inappropriate'.[85] While local mechanisms can provide a 'check on the inability of state law to

---

77 Merry, 'Legal Pluralism', 870.
78 Grenfell, 'Legal Pluralism and the Rule of Law in Timor-Leste', 307.
79 Brown and Gusmao, 'Peacebuilding and Political Hybridity', 67.
80 Belun and The Asia Foundation, *Tara Bandu*.
81 Interview with an academic, 17 July 2013.
82 Interview with an international justice adviser, 14 May 2010.
83 Hohe and Nixon, *Reconciling Justice*; UNOHCHR and UNMIT, *Facing the Future*.
84 Everett, *Law and Justice in Timor-Leste*; Asia Foundation, *Timor-Leste Law & Justice Survey 2013*.
85 Mac Ginty, 'Indigenous Peace-Making Versus the Liberal Peace', 150.

grapple with contextual injustices in a local language in which citizens can understand the proceedings', state justice institutions can be 'a check on the failure of traditional justice to guarantee' liberal human rights.[86] There is potential for state justice institutions to supervise local mechanisms, such as through reviewing whether penalties are proportionate and comply with constitutional human rights protections. In this regard, there are proposals to empower the *provedor de dereitos humanos e justica* (human rights and justice ombudsman), who is mandated to investigate complaints against 'public bodies',[87] to monitor local mechanisms. In addition, education programs could assist communities adapt to the constitutional human rights protections.[88] Indeed, the consultation process on a draft customary law indicated that, once it was explained how local practices conflict with liberal human rights, communities were prepared to alter their local practices.[89]

There is also evidence that many Timorese want state justice institutions to play a more active role at the local level. In the 2008 Asia Foundation survey 85 per cent of respondents said that they wanted a court official to help settle disputes, which was echoed by 80 per cent of respondents when asked the same question in 2013.[90] Consequently, reflecting the government's turn to the local, pilot mobile courts that hold hearings at the local level now function in four districts, although the quality of justice they deliver has been questioned.[91] In a 2013 Asia Foundation survey, 96 per cent of respondents also recorded a high level of confidence in the effectiveness of the police force (Polícia Nacional Timor-Leste; PNTL).[92] Indeed, there is an increasing preference to the PNTL for violent crimes; in 2008, 91 per cent of respondents agreed that someone who kills another person should go to jail, while only 5 per cent favoured the traditional remedy of compensation.[93] Similarly, if threatened by a gang, 51 per cent would request assistance from the PNTL, 21 per cent from the *suku* leader and 13 per cent from the *suku* council or elder.[94]

---

86   Braithwaite et al., *Networked Governance of Freedom and Tyranny*, 218.
87   Constitution, section 27.
88   Grenfell, 'Legal Pluralism and the Rule of Law'.
89   Interview with an international justice adviser, 14 May 2010.
90   Everett, *Law and Justice in Timor-Leste*.
91   IPAC, *Justice at the Crossroads*.
92   Asia Foundation, *Timor-Leste Law & Justice Survey 2013*.
93   Wassel and Rajalingam, *A Survey of Community-Police Perceptions*; Everett, *Law and Justice in Timor-Leste*.
94   Wassel and Rajalingam, *A Survey of Community-Police Perceptions*.

The above discussion raises a number of questions about how hybrid peacebuilding has operated in Timor-Leste. The Timor-Leste Government appears to have instrumentally engaged in decentralisation to local institutions in order to lessen the burden of certain political, administrative, developmental and justice functions. Yet this transfer is not accompanied by sufficient linkages between the central government and local level, or the development of capacity and resources at the local level, in order for local leaders to perform their roles. Although the government has adopted policies which seek to engage with local practices and institutions, it also frequently acts as a spoiler to these hybrid frameworks, particularly by ignoring or undermining local decision-making in relation to decentralised development projects. This highlights the danger that governments or international peacebuilders use the language of hybrid peacebuilding either as a cloak for shifting the burden of state functions to the local level, or as an excuse for lowering the standards of governance. There are also concerns that local institutions can be discriminatory or undemocratic, which underscores the risk that an uncritical emphasis on local agency can obscure issues of injustice and differential power relationships, particularly the marginalisation of women. Problems with the implementation of developmental decentralisation also highlight the risk that emphasising local agency might see the determinants of the success of peacebuilding attributed to the local level, which may overlook broader structural problems.

Space for liberal peacebuilding in Timor-Leste?

Despite these challenges, hybrid peacebuilding in Timor-Leste has increased opportunities for political participation and the delivery of public goods at the local level. Therefore, the Timor-Leste case suggests that, by foregrounding the importance of local agency, hybrid peacebuilding offers an important correction to the top-down, technocratic approach that has characterised neoliberal peacebuilding.

However, there is emerging evidence that many Timorese desire a role for modern liberal state institutions as a response to the inequality, exclusions and injustices that can occur under local practices and institutions. While local sociopolitical practices and institutions remain influential in Timor-Leste, it may be that they were an attractive alternative to Timorese in the immediate aftermath of the 1999 referendum and in the first decade of independence, not because state institutions were inherently illegitimate, but because they were highly centralised, under-resourced and lacked capacity. The effectiveness and reach of state institutions is slowly improving, which has increased their legitimacy and attractiveness. However, calls by Timorese for state institutions to play an increased role in their lives should not necessarily be interpreted as implying that those institutions are unproblematic. Instead, they might indicate a desire for those institutions to work more effectively and to be more locally legitimate.

An advocate of hybrid peacebuilding might argue that Timor-Leste has only achieved a negative hybrid peace, which rests 'mainly on hybrid forms of politics which reify existing power structures and hierarchies' and leans 'too far towards the preferences of internationals, state elites or global capital'.[95] Indeed, it does appear that the government has instrumentally engaged with local practices and institutions in relation to decentralisation and justice, which has undermined the legitimacy and effectiveness of its attempt at hybrid peacebuilding.

However, for many Timorese at least some aspects of the liberal state seem genuinely attractive, which suggests that building state liberal institutions may retain a place in contemporary peacebuilding. Therefore, the assumption that populations prefer their local practices and institutions to those of a liberal state may not necessarily hold in the long term, nor may the assumption that populations favour the fusion of local and state practices and institutions envisaged by hybrid peacebuilding. Instead, much will depend on how the government engages with local practices and institutions. Alternatively, it may be that people are more concerned with having effective and legitimate institutions that will meet their needs, than about whether these institutions are local, liberal or hybrid.

Two challenges have contributed to liberal peacebuilding falling from favour. First, in much of the academic and policy literature liberalism has been 'used promiscuously to explain a broad range of often contradictory policy perspectives and practices across very differing circumstances and with very differing outcomes'.[96] Indeed, even in the political theory literature there is remarkably little consensus regarding what liberalism

---

95   Mac Ginty and Richmond, 'The Fallacy of Constructing Hybrid Political Orders', 230.
96   Chandler, 'The Uncritical Critique of "Liberal Peace"', 145.

actually is. This has created space for what has essentially been neoliberal peacebuilding, guided by an emphasis on individual autonomy removed from basic principles of justice, to be described as liberal peacebuilding. Neoliberal peacebuilding has strayed far from most understandings of liberalism, which recognise that individuals may have conflicting—as well as common—interests and therefore need to be offered the protection of basic principles of justice.[97]

Second, while the failures of neoliberal peacebuilding have led Western states and international institutions to conclude that people do not want liberalism, what it actually means is that people do not want the shallow, ineffective, distant and corrupt governments that neoliberal peacebuilding has built. Instead, the liberal needs to be restored to peacebuilding, with peacebuilding guided by the liberal principle of popular sovereignty, which implies that people should consent to the manner in which their political unit is governed, including deciding the extent to which it reflects liberal and local principles and incorporates state and local institutions, in the form of a 'social contract'.[98] Existing political and legal pluralism should neither be rejected as uncivilised nor accepted uncritically, but instead brought into critical dialogues in discussions of how society will be organised. Therefore, liberal norms can be 'renegotiated in context, producing hybridity'.[99] Elsewhere I have argued that a participatory constitution-making process can provide an opportunity for this negotiation to take place.[100] That is not the only forum in which this can occur, as there can be multiple opportunities for people to exercise their popular sovereignty during peacebuilding, such as during transitional justice processes and elections for their new institutions.

Critics may accuse me of advocating 'hybridity *for* liberal peace'[101] or say that I am trapped in a 'paradox of liberalism' that 'sees the liberal peace as oppressive but the only true source of emancipation'.[102] My response has two parts: first, I question what alternatives these critics propose in order to achieve truly emancipatory peace; to date no one has made a sustained attempt to make such a proposal in either theoretical or

---

97 Rawls, *A Theory of Justice*.
98 Rousseau, *The Social Contract and Other Later Political Writings*.
99 Richmond, 'The Dilemmas of a Hybrid Peace', 56.
100 Wallis, *Constitution Making During State Building*.
101 Nadarajah and Rampton, 'The Limits of Hybridity'.
102 Sabaratnam, 'Avatars of Eurocentrism'.

empirical terms.[103] Second, I question why critics assume that many conflict-affected populations will not see a place for—and indeed may even favour—liberal state institutions. Although liberalism has its roots in Europe, the idea that individuals have political autonomy and that government should be based on a population's consent in order to be legitimate is not necessarily attractive only to Europeans. It seems to me that much of the critical literature is not really critical of liberalism per se, but of how liberalism has purportedly been implemented by neoliberal peacebuilding interventions as occurred initially in Timor-Leste. By advocating for mediation between the local and liberal, hybrid peacebuilding provides ways to limit the neocolonial and negative power dynamics that commonly arise during neoliberal peacebuilding.

In conclusion, my case study of Timor-Leste reveals that many of the critiques of hybrid peacebuilding have merit. This does not mean that we should abandon hybrid peacebuilding, which offers an important correction to neoliberal peacebuilding by foregrounding the importance of local agency. However, the assumption that populations prefer their local practices and institutions to those of the state may not hold in the long term, nor may the assumption that populations favour the fusion of local and state practices and institutions. Instead, my research in Timor-Leste suggests that liberalism may retain a place in contemporary peacebuilding.

---

103 Paris, 'Saving Liberal Peacebuilding'.

6

Against Hybridity in the Study of Peacebuilding and Statebuilding

Shahar Hameiri and Lee Jones[1]

Introduction

In recent years, 'hybridity' has emerged as a fashionable concept, primarily used for describing the outcomes of the interaction between international interveners and target societies. Several related literatures have grown rapidly, focusing on hybrid peace, hybrid governance and hybrid political orders. Its popularisation is part of a wider 'local turn' in the study and practice of intervention, with attention shifting from the refinement or critique of interveners' ideas and modalities towards examining how recipients' ideas, culture, institutions and agency shape intervention outcomes.[2] This refocusing stemmed from the evident failure of most peacebuilding and statebuilding interventions to attain their desired political and governance ends, or even pacify target societies.

1   The research leading to this chapter was generously funded by an Australian Research Council Discovery Project, grant DP130102273, 'The Politics of Public Administration Reform: Capacity Development and Ideological Contestation in International State-building'. Shahar Hameiri would also like to thank the organisers of the 'Interrogating Hybridity' workshop, The Australian National University, 2–4 December 2015, for inviting him to attend, as well as the workshop's participants for their comments on an earlier draft. The authors would like to thank Ryan Smith for his assistance in copyediting the manuscript, as well as Anna Chapman and Melissa Johnston for their research assistance. The usual disclaimers apply.
2   Hughes et al., 'The Struggle versus the Song'; Mac Ginty and Richmond, 'The Local Turn in Peace Building'; World Bank, *World Development Report 2011*.

This research agenda is far superior to the earlier, narrow preoccupation with interveners' official agendas. Doubtless, we cannot understand or normatively evaluate the widely divergent outcomes of international interventions without considering how the interveners and intervened-upon interact. The concept of hybridity, however, is a highly problematic approach to this objective and, in our view, it should be replaced by better frameworks. Hybridity does not accurately describe the effects of international interventions on local politics, so it cannot explain their uneven outcomes or serve as a basis for normative evaluation. Despite incessant proclamations to the contrary by hybridity scholars, and several recent efforts to nuance the concept, hybridity intrinsically dichotomises and reifies 'local/traditional' and 'international/liberal' ideal-typical assemblages of institutions, actors and practices. Conflicts between these binary assemblages are seen to generate hybrid orders. This approach is descriptively inaccurate insofar as some 'locals' support some 'international' peacebuilding and statebuilding intervention agendas, while others resist. Nor do 'internationals' always promote 'liberal' agendas while 'locals' favour 'traditional' ones. Although recognised by some hybridity scholars, these complex realities are impossible to address coherently within an inherently dichotomising framework. Moreover, merely locating intervention outcomes on a 'local–international' spectrum, as the hybridity scholarship tends to do, does not explain why particular modes of governance emerge or whose specific interests they serve. Hence, hybridity's analytical purchase is very limited.

In this chapter, we first show how hybridity scholarship is unable to escape binaries based on dichotomised categories of the illiberal-local and liberal-international, despite considerable efforts to do so. We then demonstrate why the binary view produced through the concept of hybridity distorts empirical analysis. We conclude by outlining an alternative framework that overcomes hybridity's fatal flaws.

Hybridity: Trapped in binaries

In the peacebuilding literature, 'hybridity' denotes how:

> local actors attempt to respond to, resist and ultimately reshape peace initiatives through interactions with international actors and institutions … hybrid forms of peace arise when the strategies, institutions and norms

of international, largely liberal-democratic peacebuilding interventions collide with the everyday practices and agencies of local actors affected by conflict.[3]

Hybridity is thus 'a state of affairs in which liberal and illiberal norms, institutions, and actors coexist'.[4] It emerges because of a 'gap',[5] or 'agonism'[6] between the agendas of 'liberal' international interveners and those of 'non-liberal' target societies.

Hybridity is used both to describe intervention outcomes, and to prescribe the incorporation of local priorities into peacebuilding and statebuilding interventions to achieve success.[7] Scholars often suggest that 'hybrid' outcomes, being more locally legitimate, create greater stability.[8] For some, hybridity is even potentially 'emancipatory', though critical scholars increasingly doubt that interveners can simply harness local agency towards predictable or desirable ends, or should seek to do so.[9]

Before its adoption in peacebuilding, hybridity was already widely used in cultural and postcolonial studies, where extensive criticism created an 'anti-hybridity backlash'.[10] Peacebuilding scholars therefore attempted to avoid well-recognised pitfalls with the concept, particularly accusations that it depends upon, and thus reifies, prior, 'pure' social categories and identities. They thus strongly deny that hybridity essentialises or dichotomises the 'international'/'local' distinction, or romanticises 'local' institutions and norms. For example, Boege, Brown and Clements state:

> there are no clear-cut boundaries between the realm of the exogenous 'modern' and the endogenous 'customary'; instead processes of assimilation, articulation, transformation and/or adoption are at the interface of the global/exogenous and the local/indigenous.[11]

---

3   Richmond and Mitchell, 'Introduction—Towards a Post-liberal Peace', 8, 33.
4   Belloni, 'Hybrid Peace Governance', 22; Boege et al., 'Hybrid Political Orders, Not Fragile States'; Mac Ginty, *International Peacebuilding and Local Resistance*.
5   Belloni, 'Hybrid Peace Governance', 23.
6   Richmond and Mitchell, 'Introduction—Towards a Post-liberal Peace', 26.
7   Millar, 'Disaggregating Hybridity', 501.
8   Belloni, 'Hybrid Peace Governance', 35; Boege et al., 'Hybrid Political Orders, Not Fragile States'; Chopra and Hohe, 'Participatory Intervention'; Kumar and De la Haye, 'Hybrid Peacemaking'.
9   Mac Ginty and Richmond, 'The Fallacy of Constructing Hybrid Political Orders'; Millar, 'Disaggregating Hybridity'; Visoka, 'Three Levels of Hybridisation Practices'.
10   Pieterse, 'Hybridity, So What?'.
11   Boege et al., 'Hybrid Political Orders, Not Fragile States', 15.

Hybridity scholars repeatedly disavow binaries like 'local/international', 'Western/non-Western' or 'modern/customary', emphasising their interaction instead.[12] Similarly, they claim that the 'local' is 'neither monolithic nor necessarily incompatible with liberal norms'.[13]

However, as Heathershaw rightly notes, despite being 'caveated to the point of defensiveness', in practice, hybridity accounts *still* rely 'on the bifurcation between ideal-types of local-indigenous and international-liberal'.[14] To demonstrate this we focus closely on the work of Roger Mac Ginty,[15] who has gone furthest of all hybridity scholars in denying that hybridity reifies binary categories. He argues:

> Hybridity is taken as the composite forms of social thinking and practice that emerge as the result of the interaction of different groups, practices, and worldviews. It is not the grafting together of two separate entities to create a third entity. Instead, it is assumed that norms and practices are the result of prior hybridisation. This helps move us away from notions of discrete categories that are somehow pristine and insulated from social negotiation and interaction over the millennia.[16]

For Mac Ginty, every actor—whether local actor or international statebuilder—is always 'already hybridised'; '[f]urther hybridisation [then] ensues as (the already hybrid) local and international interact, conflict and cooperate'.[17] This conceptualisation supposedly 'frees [analysts] from the static thinking of binaries'.[18]

In practice, however, as Heathershaw highlights, Mac Ginty actually reinstates other dichotomous (binary) categories when establishing his analytical framework.[19] In the statement just quoted, outcomes result from how the 'local and international' interface—a binary. Likewise, in the framework that guides his case studies, Mac Ginty states that hybridised peacebuilding outcomes reflect tensions between two sets of forces: (1) the 'compliance' and 'incentivising powers' of 'liberal peace agents' and

---

12   Peterson, 'A Conceptual Unpacking of Hybridity', 12; see also Mac Ginty, 'Hybrid Peace', 397.
13   Belloni, 'Hybrid Peace Governance', 23; Mac Ginty and Richmond, 'The Local Turn in Peace Building'; Richmond and Mitchell, 'Introduction—Towards a Post-liberal Peace', 11.
14   Heathershaw, 'Towards Better Theories of Peacebuilding', 277; see also Hirblinger and Simons, 'The Good, the Bad, and the Powerful', 424.
15   Mac Ginty, *International Peacebuilding and Local Resistance*.
16   Ibid., Introduction.
17   Ibid.
18   Mac Ginty and Richmond, 'The Fallacy of Constructing Hybrid Political Orders', 223.
19   Heathershaw, 'Towards Better Theories of Peacebuilding'.

(2) the ability of 'local actors, networks and structures' to 'resist, ignore, or adapt liberal peace interventions' and 'present and maintain alternative forms of peacebuilding'.[20] Thus, the outcome is a struggle between the 'liberal' interveners and the 'locals'—another dichotomy. Likewise in his theorisation of hybridity, Mac Ginty states: 'hybrid spaces and forms develop as external and internal agents, ideas, and processes interact, and new meanings are attached to existing entities'—another dichotomy, this time between 'external' and 'internal'.[21] Mac Ginty immediately insists (again) on 'prior hybridisation', such that 'internationally sponsored and resourced peace interventions' cannot simply be labelled '"external", "exogenous", "international", or "western"'; and yet he has clearly just used one of these labels himself.[22] Even in his most recent work with Oliver Richmond, binaries abound: 'liberal peacemaking' versus 'stubborn locals', 'the modern and traditional', 'the formal and informal', 'the "local" and the "social"' versus 'top-down forms of power (the state or the international)', 'subaltern subjects' versus 'external actors' and so on.[23] Thus, while Mac Ginty tries to evade the criticism that his concepts are dichotomised by invoking 'prior hybridity', this merely provides the cover to continue using those exact same dichotomous categories. He apparently recognises the contradiction between insisting on prior hybridisation yet continuing to use these dichotomous categories, but simply declines to resolve it:

> If … everything and everyone is a hybrid, then concepts such as endogenous and exogenous, indigenous and international risk losing their currency. The stance adopted in this book is to recognise the shortcomings of concepts and language but to move on.[24]

Mac Ginty further states that, notwithstanding his apparent rejection of dichotomies and insistence on 'prior hybridisation', we can still recognise that 'some actors, societies, and processes are more hybridised than others … it is possible to identify degrees of hybridisation'.[25] It is this emphasis on 'degrees' or 'levels' that apparently avoids dichotomous thinking. Yet, if we accept Mac Ginty's caveat that everything is already hybridised, and there are no pure categories, how can anything ever be identified as 'more' hybridised than something else? In reality, assessing

---

20   Mac Ginty, *International Peacebuilding and Local Resistance,* Chapter 3.
21   Ibid.
22   Ibid.
23   Mac Ginty and Richmond, 'The Fallacy of Constructing Hybrid Political Orders', 222, 223, 230.
24   Mac Ginty, *International Peacebuilding and Local Resistance*, Chapter 3.
25   Ibid.

the 'degree of hybridisation' always involves identifying some point on a spectrum between two binaries. Thus, Mac Ginty suggests, some 'local' actors, like national governments, might become 'more' hybridised than others, as their actions come to 'reflect the mores of the external peace champions'.[26] How do we know they are 'more hybridised' than other 'local' actors? We observe how far they *move away from one pole* (the 'local') *towards the other pole* (the 'external'). Similarly, 'it is possible to think of some actors and norms as being more locally constituted than others (a "local local" as opposed to an "international local" that is patterned by global forces)'.[27] How do we know whether a 'local' actor/norm is 'more local'? Because they are closer to the 'local' end of the spectrum than the 'international/global' end.

Mac Ginty's problem here is intrinsic to the concept of hybridity itself. *By definition*, hybridisation is the mixing of two (or possibly more) distinct entities in order to produce something new. Even if those entities are themselves also the product of prior hybridisation, there is simply nothing capable of being 'hybridised' unless at least two *distinct* things previously exist. Notwithstanding protestations to the contrary, then, hybridity as a concept is *inherently* 'based on the existence of two oppositional and apparently dialectically related forces'.[28] As Visoka writes (citing Canclini, whose definition is frequently used by hybridity scholars):

> hybridisation should be seen as a process whereby 'discrete structures or practices, *previously existing in separate form*, are combined to generate new structures, objects and practices' [emphasis added].[29]

Accordingly, assessing the *degree* of hybridity, as Mac Ginty proposes, *must always* rest upon the degree to which entity x has moved away from its original form by adopting some aspects of entity y. Consider Mac Ginty's statement:

> hybridisation helps visualise the dynamics in societies undergoing liberal interventionism as a series of balances (for example, a balance between mainly internal and mainly external thinking on how to organise the economy). Such a visualisation discourages thinking about absolutist categories.[30]

---

26   Ibid.
27   Ibid.
28   Heathershaw, 'Towards Better Theories of Peacebuilding', 277.
29   Visoka, 'Three Levels of Hybridisation Practices', 25.
30   Mac Ginty, *International Peacebuilding and Local Resistance,* Chapter 3.

In fact this visualisation clearly relies entirely on dichotomous categories (here, 'internal' and 'external') that a society is supposedly 'balancing' between. Despite Mac Ginty's endless caveats and contortions, it is clearly impossible to escape the need for 'absolutist' and 'binary' categories while using the concept of hybridity: it is hardwired into the concept's DNA.

Why it matters: The distortion of empirical analysis

The inability of even hybridity's most sophisticated theorists to evade its intrinsically dichotomising approach has seriously negative consequences for how peacebuilding and statebuilding interventions are described and their outcomes explained or evaluated. Hybridity encourages analysts to draw binary, dichotomising contrasts between 'local' and 'international' actors and to explain outcomes as stemming from conflict and cooperation between these two forces. This considerably distorts empirical reality, which simply does not fit into such binary frameworks. What we instead observe is different forces, located across multiple territorial scales, promoting, contesting or rejecting different governance interventions depending on their interests and agendas.

The easiest way to apprehend the problems of hybridity for empirical analysis is to consider the problem scholars have specifying 'the local' half of their equation. Sometimes, 'local' means everything not-international, with scholars lumping entire target societies together, as in formulations focusing on the '"contact zone" … between local and external'[31] or 'the melding of the "international" with the "local"'.[32] Elsewhere, however, 'local' seems to denote something more subnational, as in dichotomous presentations of 'non-state indigenous societal structures and [externally] introduced state structures'.[33] Here, 'local' means 'traditional, indigenous and customary',[34] denoting social relations 'at an individual or communal level rather than at the national level'.[35]

---

31 Peterson, 'A Conceptual Unpacking of Hybridity', 11.
32 Millar, 'Disaggregating Hybridity', 502.
33 Boege et al., 'Hybrid Political Orders, Not Fragile States', 17.
34 Mac Ginty, 'Hybrid Peace', 391.
35 Millar, 'Disaggregating Hybridity', 502.

Neither definition is satisfactory. The first approach clearly cannot account for the presence, in every target state, of some groups that collaborate with international actors and support their projects. This is what leads to such awkward and unhelpful formulations as 'local local' and 'international local' that seek to recognise the existence of 'local' collaboration with intervention, yet remain straitjacketed by dichotomising categories. However, the second approach is no better, because it arbitrarily locates resistance at a subnational level, where 'tradition' and 'custom' supposedly hold sway, while assuming that the 'national' level is amenable to intervention. Whatever definition is adopted, then, hybridity compels the analyst to homogenise whichever group is defined as 'local' ('traditional', 'customary', etc.) and set it in opposition to that which is 'international' ('modern', 'liberal', 'Western', etc.) as an explanation for why a particular intervention encountered difficulties. This produces crude generalisations about how 'local' actors think and behave that seriously distort reality.[36]

Consider Millar's treatment of Sierra Leone. Millar defines hybridity as 'the melding of the "international" with the "local"'.[37] He recognises, though, that national elites play a role in interventions, and prefers the term 'local' to 'national' as it allegedly permits the disaggregation of 'local' actors. Millar is also sensitive to Mac Ginty's 'prior hybridisation', describing how many revered, supposedly traditional practices in Sierra Leone were previously externally introduced. Nonetheless, Millar explains difficulties encountered by Western-led efforts to demobilise child soldiers by invoking 'the concept of "childhood" in Sierra Leone', stating that 'local concepts' are 'defined quite differently from [those in] the West'.[38] In practice, then, Millar does not really disaggregate 'the local', but makes sweeping claims about how all Sierra Leoneans (and indeed all Westerners) view childhood. Millar admits that some militias may have used these notions strategically to recruit children, but does not explore this. Armed groups simply thrived because they met the locally defined 'needs of … young people and provided them … with something they deeply wanted'.[39] This absurd claim fails to explain why thousands of children had to be abducted, drugged or brutalised into joining militias. In reality, it was the *erosion* of 'traditional' kinship structures (and associated family control over youths), induced by economic and political crises,

---

36   Hirblinger and Simons, 'The Good, the Bad, and the Powerful'.
37   Millar, 'Disaggregating Hybridity', 502.
38   Ibid., 507–508.
39   Ibid., 508–509.

that paved the way for child soldiering.[40] Most importantly, Millar fails to investigate or even identify *any* Sierra Leonean resistance to these notions about childhood, or their use by militias. As Shepley shows, while militias certainly exploited cultural norms to recruit children, most Sierra Leoneans were 'dismayed' by child soldiering, and many children were press-ganged only when their resisting parents were threatened, tortured or killed.[41] However, in Millar's account, the need—imposed by hybridity as an organising concept—to explain outcomes with reference to a local/international dichotomy leads Sierra Leoneans to be falsely homogenised.

The reality that, in every target society, some actors will support some aspects of intervention while others resist is never adequately captured by a *spatial* definition of 'the local', whether this encompasses the entire society or just those residing (presumably) in rural areas. Henrizi critiques the first approach through a case study of Iraq.[42] Contrary to hybridity approaches that restrict 'local' agency to resistance of 'the international', Henrizi shows how Iraqi women's non-government organisations selectively embraced international peacebuilders' gender programs after 2003 to resist the restoration of highly patriarchal social relations sought by many Iraqi men—who have, contrariwise, resisted this intervention.[43] Similar complexity exceeds the dichotomising grasp of the hybridity framework in Visoka's essay on Kosovo.[44] Typically, Visoka defines hybridisation as interaction 'between local and international agents', reflecting the 'disconnect between the Western liberal agenda and local indigenous practices, needs and interests'.[45] As usual, dichotomies abound: local/international, Western-liberal/local-indigenous. Ironically, however, Kosovo's reality simply does not fit into these binary categories. Visoka discovers 'local' people resisting *both* 'local *and* international governance' [emphasis added].[46] A Kosovar social movement, Lëvizja Vetëvendosje (which opposed compromise with the Serbian minority), and Kosovo Liberation Army (KLA) veterans demanding legal immunity and welfare payments, challenged *both* the United Nations Mission in Kosovo *and* the KLA regime. Similarly, 'local' people are observed engaging in tax dodging and informal economic activity, defying other 'locals' trying

---

40 Zack-Williams, 'Child Soldiers in the Civil War in Sierra Leone'.

41 Shepley, 'The Social and Cultural Context of Child Soldiering in Sierra Leone'.

42 Henrizi, 'Building Peace in Hybrid Spaces'.

43 Ibid.

44 Visoka, 'Three Levels of Hybridisation Practices'.

45 Ibid., 24.

46 Ibid., 29.

to make the formal economy function. Clearly, the conflicts shaping intervention outcomes are too complex to be reduced to the dichotomies imposed by hybridity. As Visoka belatedly admits, outcomes are instead 'shaped by multiple actors interacting at different societal levels'.[47]

An even clearer indication of this comes from Hirblinger and Simons' study of peacebuilding in Burundi and South Sudan.[48] These authors rightly attack the simplistic depiction of 'the local' in hybridity studies, showing that 'the local' cannot be objectively identified. Rather, what counts as 'the local'—what actors, practices, institutions and so on are considered 'legitimate'—is a discursive construct that is contested by different actors.[49] In Burundi, for example, Hirblinger and Simons show how some international statebuilders promoted the decentralisation of conflict resolution to 'traditional', 'local' institutions called 'Bashingantahe', but this was resisted by the national government, which instead promoted 'modern', local 'hill councils', recruiting a rival set of local collaborators.[50] This was because the Bashingantahe were seen as instruments and bulwarks of the previous regime, whereas the new government wished to cultivate its own local power bases. This example shows there is no clear or necessary divide between the local/traditional/customary and the international/modern/liberal, however one defines them. Certain international actors allied with certain 'local', apparently 'traditional', actors (the Bashingantahe, which had previously been co-opted into a modern system of rule), while elites at a national scale allied with rival 'local' forces, promoting an apparently more 'modern' and 'liberal' mode of governance. The real cleavage here was not 'local' versus 'international' but rather involved two coalitions of actors, comprising groups located at multiple territorial scales, struggling over which mode and scale of governance should prevail, and whose interests would be privileged thereby.

East Timor presents yet more evidence of these complex, inter-scalar alliances and dynamics. This again defies the territory's dichotomised depiction by hybridity scholars, who widely attribute the failures of the United Nations Transitional Authority in East Timor (UNTAET) to a 'clash of paradigms' between liberal-international statebuilders and the

---

47 Ibid., 33.
48 Hirblinger and Simons, 'The Good, the Bad, and the Powerful'.
49 See also Randazzo, 'The Paradoxes of the "Everyday"'.
50 Hirblinger and Simons, 'The Good, the Bad, and the Powerful', 430–434.

'tribal-traditional' Timorese, producing an 'empty shell' state.[51] Since, supposedly, most villagers' 'only experience [is] of customary governance', they rejected the nation-state imposed by internationals, producing a 'major "gap" between government decision-makers and … people in the villages'.[52] For example, the World Bank's Community Empowerment Project (CEP), implemented during UNTAET's rule, sought to establish local elected councils empowered to disburse small development budgets. These excluded traditional village elders but guaranteed women and youth representation. Hybridity scholars claim CEP failed miserably because, being based on international-liberal principles, it 'lack[ed] … local legitimacy' and 'could not compete with the authority exercised by [customary] leaders'.[53] In reality, far from being uniformly rejected by tradition-bound 'locals', CEP was enthusiastically embraced by many women and youths as a way of wresting power and control from male elders.[54] It was also supported by Conselho Nacional da Resistencia Timorense leaders, who were keen to sideline local chiefs. Yet, it was opposed by UNTAET and, unsurprisingly, by village elders.[55] Thus, we see two multi-scalar alliances contesting postconflict governance in East Timor: one comprising some internationals, some national actors and some village-level actors; and another comprising some internationals and some village-level actors.

The reasons behind these configurations are relatively simple but are obscured by dichotomisation imposed by hybridity analysis. Contrary to claims that 'local' Timorese uniformly respected traditional elders and customary law, Cummins notes that Timorese village life had been radically transformed by colonialism and capitalism, such that several key groups—notably women, youths and national political leaders—reject traditional attitudes.[56] However, because Cummins is hidebound by the hybridity framework, she is nonetheless compelled to homogenise the Timorese in explaining outcomes, as the above citations of her work show. Thus, she insists that *lisan* is 'central to people's lives', 'every' Timorese

---

51 Grenfell, 'Governance, Violence and Crises in Timor-Leste'; Hohe, 'The Clash of Paradigms'; Lemay-Hébert, 'The "Empty-Shell" Approach'.
52 Cummins, *Local Governance in Timor-Leste*, 34, 38.
53 Ibid., 35–36. See also Ospina and Hohe, 'Traditional Power Structures and the Community Empowerment Project and Local Governance Project'.
54 Ospina and Hohe, 'Traditional Power Structures', 16, 93, 109, 115, 117–120, 138–142, 153.
55 Totilo, 'Development in the Shadows', 76–83.
56 Cummins, *Local Governance in Timor-Leste*, 48, 57, 85–91, 110–111.

favours its retention and 'in general, customary authorities are well-respected and their roles are actively relied upon', even though her own findings undermine such claims.[57]

Such self-contradictions are not generated by misunderstanding or inadequate research; they are imposed by the hybridity framework, which drives analysts to group actors, institutions and values into two homogenised, opposing camps with crude, inaccurate, spatial labels. This framework clearly struggles to accurately describe the forces contesting statebuilding and peacebuilding projects so it cannot hope to adequately explain their outcomes, let alone guide normative evaluation of international interventions.

Conclusion: What is the alternative?

This chapter has shown that hybridity, despite repeated caveating and refinement, remains intrinsically bound by binaries, mainly between the illiberal-local and liberal-international, which fatally compromises its utility in describing and explaining the outcomes of intervention—its purported objective. The concept, therefore, is unfit for purpose and must be entirely jettisoned by scholars of peacebuilding and statebuilding. Fortunately, a good alternative is available. Given space constraints, we cannot fully develop it here, but only present its broad outlines.[58]

A first step is to jettison 'hybridity' in favour of a Gramscian understanding of the state and other governance institutions as condensations of social power relations.[59] Institutions distribute power, resources and political opportunities. Consequently, they are endlessly contested by sociopolitical forces—classes and class fragments; state-based groupings; distributional coalitions; ethnic, religious and regional groups; forces based in international agencies and overseas; and so on. These groups struggle over power, resources and ideational goals, seeking to mould institutions to favour themselves and their allies. What emerges in practice is a contingent outcome of this struggle. Typically, leading groups must make material and ideological concessions to subordinate groups to stabilise their hegemony or domination. Accordingly, institutions reflect an uneven compromise

---

57   Ibid., 44, 47, 104.
58   The approach is elaborated in Hameiri and Jones, 'Beyond Hybridity to the Politics of Scale'.
59   Jessop, *State Power*; Poulantzas, *State, Power, Socialism*.

between different forces. Thus, even when international statebuilders are materially preponderant, what emerges is still a result of struggle, accommodation and compromise.[60] This is arguably what 'hybridity' has unsuccessfully sought to capture. A Gramscian approach is superior since it has no need to reify binary categories or insist on analysing outcomes as an accommodation between two poles. It admits as many different parties to a conflict as there exist. It does not inaccurately lump together actors into 'local' or 'international' or any other reductive category but insists on studying the real sociopolitical coalitions that coalesce around particular governance projects.

This approach deals with the particular, spatialised nature of struggles around peacebuilding and statebuilding by incorporating a 'politics of scale' approach, as urged by Hirblinger and Simons.[61] This provides a far more sophisticated way of grasping what is at stake in struggles invoking 'the local'. In political geography, 'scale' denotes hierarchised social, political and economic territorial spaces, each denoting 'the arena and moment, both discursively and materially, where sociospatial power relations are contested and compromises are negotiated and regulated'.[62] Scale matters in peacebuilding and statebuilding interventions because interveners inevitably seek to reallocate power and resources among different scales, for example, embedding international disciplines into a centralised national state,[63] or decentralising power to subnational, state-based or 'traditional' agencies.[64] A 'politics of scale', then, refers to struggles to define the power exercised and resources controlled at different territorial tiers and by associated governance institutions. In analysing this contestation, crucially, political geographers do not reify or dichotomise scales and associated sets of actors, unlike hybridity scholars. For example, 'locals' do not automatically prefer 'local' modes of governance, and indeed what counts as 'local' is always open to contestation. Scales are not fixed or pre-given but are rather 'the product of economic, political and social activities and relationships; as such, they are as changeable as these relationships themselves'.[65] Thus, we avoid dichotomies like 'local' and 'international' altogether, foregrounding instead specific

---

60   Hameiri, *Regulating Statehood*; Jones, 'State Theory and Statebuilding'.
61   Hirblinger and Simons, 'The Good, the Bad, and the Powerful'.
62   Swyngedouw, 'Neither Global nor Local', 140.
63   Hameiri, *Regulating Statehood*.
64   Hirblinger and Simons, 'The Good, the Bad, and the Powerful'.
65   Smith, 'Remaking Scale', 228.

sociopolitical groups whose orientation to specific intervention projects varies according to their particular interests, agendas and strategies. Where a given scaled mode of governance is potentially favourable to a particular group, the intervention will likely be supported or adapted; where an intervention is deleterious, it will likely be resisted. Accordingly, different 'locals', even those co-located in a given spatial setting—in the same village, for example—will potentially have very different attitudes to specific intervention projects, generating complex, multi-scalar alliances and contestation. These produce variegated outcomes for international intervention, depending on the particular project examined and the relative strength of the coalitions assembling in each case.

Our preferred framework may not be adopted by everyone. Yet all scholars of international intervention should certainly cease refining frameworks stemming from the flawed concept of hybridity, and instead shift their attention to other, more fruitful, avenues.

Section Two — Hybridity and Peacebuilding

7

Hybridisation of Peacebuilding at the Local–International Interface: The Bougainville Case

Volker Boege

Introduction

This chapter builds its argument on a relational understanding of hybridity, focusing on hybridisation—of peace, governance, security, sociopolitical order—as an ongoing process of *becoming* through mixing, reconverting, leaching and blending. The concept of hybridisation tries to capture the fluid, dynamic, emergent and relational quality of the reality it is meant to grasp.[1] Talking about the *process* of hybridisation allows us to shift attention from fixed entities to relations.[2] Let us be reminded that protagonists of the hybridity approach initially introduced the term into the scholarly debate about peacebuilding not least with the aim of overcoming reductive dichotomies, to open space for reflection about enmeshment, permeation, interpenetration, liminality, entanglement, fluidity, slippage, ambiguity, in-betweenness, dynamics and relations, with the shift away from binaries as 'the primary appeal of hybridity and hybridisation'.[3]

---

1   See Hunt, this volume.
2   This in turn allows us to respond to the critique that the hybridity approach merely perpetuates thinking in dichotomies and distinct entities. For the latest iteration of this critique see Hameiri and Jones, this volume.
3   Peterson, 'A Conceptual Unpacking of Hybridity', 12.

So, although this chapter's title can be read as again reifying entities—'the local/s' and 'the international/s'—the terms 'hybridisation' and 'interface', which also figure in the title, signal a relational understanding of the issues at stake.[4] I shall nevertheless start by indeed talking about 'locals' and 'internationals': in the Bougainville peace process there are actors who present themselves as, and are perceived as, 'locals' and 'internationals'. These two 'camps' are highly diverse in themselves, of course, with all kinds of internal differences and frictions. But for purposes of tracing processes of peace formation it is worthwhile paying special attention to the local–international interface. It is of particular significance, shaping the actual processes and their outcomes substantially, because the actors involved in peace formation position themselves as 'local' or 'international', and from this position define 'the other' and engage with this other when trying to 'build peace'.[5] Peacebuilding therefore is itself imbued with behaviour, actions, norms, interests that stem from this positioning. There are of course other differentiations that matter for peace formation: between male and female, rural and urban, young and old and between classes and language or other social and political groups. It is no doubt important to take these and their specific interests and agendas into account in comprehensive analyses of peace formation. Nevertheless, I think a case can be made for a particular focus on the local–international interface as I'm trying to demonstrate with this short piece on Bougainville. I will show how in Bougainville local actors affect the implementation of the internationals' predetermined peacebuilding agenda through various forms of agency, and how they appropriate international agendas and resources for their own purposes, according to their own functional logic and political economy.[6]

4   For different types of relational approaches in (the study of) peacebuilding see Brigg, 'Relational Peacebuilding'. Brigg opts for a 'thick relationality' approach which 'reverses the prevailing priority of entity over relation in mainstream social science to focus attention on how entities continually arise or emerge through relations and processes' (61). In this chapter, I follow the more modest path of 'thin relationality', which 'draws attention to underappreciated relations among entities' and 'reaffirms the centrality of relationships of all types to peacebuilding' (66). Hunt, this volume, also builds a case for an ontology of relationships.
5   Of course, actors present themselves and are seen also along other delineating categories, for example, as 'woman' or 'Australian' or 'NGO' or 'UN'. But the identification as 'local' or 'international' is always present and effectual: a local woman, an international from Australia (or from the UN), a local (or an international) NGO.
6   Mac Ginty and Richmond, 'The Local Turn in Peace Building'; Richmond, A Post-liberal Peace; Richmond and Mitchell, Hybrid Forms of Peace.

Local–international relations and interactions hybridise processes of peace formation. This plays out in the locale, taking the form of ongoing processes of interchange, entanglement, permeation, reassemblage and reconfiguration, which involve a host of local and international actors and institutions.[7] In this understanding, the local 'becomes a verb as well as a noun or a simple descriptor of place. It is interpreted in its own right, and not as a mere adjunct to the somehow more important levels of analysis such as the state, the region or the metropolis'.[8] In other words, the locale (in this case Bougainville) is conceptualised not just as another 'level' or a 'place', but a site of societal contestation—including contestation about what is and who is 'local'.

In the following, I'll present some aspects of how this plays out in the Bougainville case.

Internationals and locals in Bougainville

Peace formation on Bougainville is in its 17th year, with a critical new phase ahead, namely preparations for and conduct of a referendum on independence, most probably in 2019. In general, Bougainville is seen as a peacebuilding success story (so far), both by external observers and stakeholders directly involved in the peace process. And it is generally acknowledged that international intervention—which compared to other endeavours was a 'light intervention'—played a modest, but indispensable role.[9]

New Zealand supported the commencement of the peace process by offering facilitation services, providing logistical assistance, hosting the initial rounds of peace talks and negotiations, and creating a warm atmosphere for negotiators.[10] With the consent of the conflict parties, neighbouring

---

7   Albrecht and Wiuff Moe, 'The Simultaneity of Authority'; Mac Ginty and Richmond, 'The Local Turn in Peace Building'.
8   Mac Ginty, 'Where Is the Local?', 848. In this understanding, the local is not separate from the international, and vice versa. International actors thread themselves into the local fabric, they operate from their own local positions, and their actions have to be channelled through a couple of interlinked localities; local actors and activities make their presence felt and have an impact in the international realm. The locality includes local–international relations; it is not static and territorially bound, but a dynamic and de-territorialised network. On the spatial dimension of these processes of interchange see Hameiri and Jones as well as Dinnen and Allen, this volume.
9   Regan, *Light Intervention*.
10   Braithwaite et al., *Reconciliation and Architectures of Commitment*, 46–49.

states and the United Nations (UN) conducted a peacebuilding mission on Bougainville. The UN sent a small contingent, first known as the UN Political Office in Bougainville (UNPOB, August 1998 to 2004) and then as the UN Observer Mission in Bougainville (UNOMB, 2004 to June 2005). Its symbolic value, demonstrating the international community's commitment, its contribution to the weapons disposal process and its role as mediator in negotiations between conflict parties, were significant. Not least, the UN provided the external interveners with international legitimacy.[11] A regional Truce Monitoring Group (TMG), which later became the Peace Monitoring Group (PMG), arrived on the island in late 1997 and stayed until June 2003. It was followed by a small, entirely civilian Bougainville Transitional Team until December 2003.

The TMG/PMG was an unarmed force of both military and civilian personnel comprising men and women from Australia, New Zealand, Fiji and Vanuatu. New Zealand led the TMG and Australia led the PMG, with Australia providing the bulk of personnel and resources.[12] The TMG/PMG's mandate was to support the peace process 'through logistics, monitoring, verification, mediation and confidence building'.[13]

Later, after the stabilisation of the security situation on the ground, a considerable number of foreign development agencies, international non-government organisations (INGOs) and UN programs and institutions became active on Bougainville in support of reconstruction, rehabilitation and peacebuilding. Australia's development agency was and is the biggest of these external players. Others involved are the aid agencies of Japan, New Zealand and the United States, the European Union, the World Bank and the Asian Development Bank, as well as several UN agencies: UNDP, UNHCR, UN Women and UNICEF. Save the Children, World Vision and Oxfam are among the INGOs present. Currently it looks as if this international engagement will increase even further in the near future, with the impending referendum on independence.

---

11   Regan, 'The Bougainville Intervention', 202.
12   For a comprehensive account of the TMG and PMG see Adams, *Peace on Bougainville*; Braithwaite et al., *Reconciliation and Architectures of Commitment*; Breen, *The Good Neighbour*; Regan, *Light Intervention*; Wehner and Denoon, *Without a Gun*.
13   Australian Civil-Military Centre, *Partnering for Peace*, 20.

So here you have the camp of the 'internationals'. It is self-evidently highly diverse.[14] The Bougainvilleans, the 'locals', however, see these institutions and actors as outsiders, foreigners, strangers, internationals, expats—and these actors themselves know that they are seen that way, and they define themselves as such. They came in from the outside (or some of them actually operate from the outside) and they will leave and go 'home' (wherever that may be) sooner or later—or they have gone already (the PMG, the UNOMB); and others may come in, for example, for preparation and conduct of the independence referendum.

On the other hand, the internationals are not just 'outsiders', as they get more or less enmeshed in local networks. It is obvious that internationals on peacebuilding support missions can operate only by entering the locality; and by being present in the locale they become part of its social fabric. While most of the internationals stay for relatively short periods of time (months), some (a few) are around for longer (years), and this affects their status as 'internationals' or 'outsiders'. They become 'localised' to a degree, entangled in local configurations and with local actors. This affects their way of being and operating not only in the local context, but also in the context of the external entity that they come from and are part of, be it an international organisation, a sending state or an INGO.

Let's turn to the locals. Like the internationals, the locals are far from being homogenous, neatly delineated or static: among the locals are differences of power, age, gender, political affiliation, social status and so on. Some are 'local' in a pan-Bougainville context (for example, as members of the Autonomous Bougainville Government), some are 'local' in a spatially rather narrowly circumscribed context, for example, as inhabitants of a village in the mountains of central Bougainville. Connections that link the local(s) with the world beyond the locale are plenty; quite a number of locals frequently move across borders, regions and roles. Nevertheless, a significant marker of being 'local' in the Bougainville context is the

---

14 Disentangling 'the internationals' not only means differentiating between different types of international actors and their different approaches to, and roles in, peacebuilding (for example, the UN and its various arms and agencies, regional organisations, international financial institutions, INGOs). Nor does it only mean differentiating between intervening countries (Australia – New Zealand), or between military and civilian personnel, but also between the different layers of international institutions, from the metropolitan 'headquarters' through the 'base camp' in the country where the intervention takes place to the 'bush offices' in the field (Schlichte and Veit, 'Coupled Arenas'). Actors at these different levels engage differently with the local(s), and this impacts on, and is processed within, the international institutions with regard to understanding, conceptualising and implementing their peacebuilding mission. Available space constrains further discussion of this topic here.

sense of belonging—to a specific place and a group of people bound by kinship ties, shared customs and culture, with a deep connection to 'land' (with 'land' being not just a material/physical reality, but imbued with cultural, spiritual and metaphysical qualities) who think of themselves as locals and are perceived as such by outsiders. 'Outsiders' can mean 'internationals' (from overseas), or people from other parts of Papua New Guinea, or people from the other side of the mountain range, depending on context.

Nonetheless, the locals cannot be conceptualised as merely local apart from the international. In Bougainville these days you can find locals who have worked for an INGO or for a UN agency for longer periods of time; they remain locals, embedded in, and loyal to, their kinship networks, while at the same time taking on the rationale and agenda of 'their' INGO or UN agency, becoming 'internationalised' and 'liberalised' to a certain extent. This affects their way of being and operating not only in their professional 'international' environment, but also in the context of the locale they come from.

But then you also have the 'local locals' as Oliver Richmond has called them,[15] among them most notably customary leaders of communities and social groups, such as chiefs, elders, prophets, healers. In the dominant liberal peace discourse, these actors are either not seen at all because they do not fit into the Western liberal format of 'state', 'civil society' or 'business/economy', or they are labelled as 'traditional', implying they are 'anachronistic', 'illiberal', 'undemocratic' or 'just cultural', that is, unfit or irrelevant for peacebuilding. In fact, they play important roles in processes of peace formation and formation of political community. This is particularly so in Bougainville where 'kastom' is still strong and 'traditional' leaders—chiefs, elders—are very much in charge of dispute resolution and governance in the context of rural communities.

The local/international interface

In contrast to many other peacebuilding interventions around the globe, the extent and content of the activities of the internationals who came in to support peacebuilding could be largely controlled by the leadership of the Bougainville conflict parties. They were successful in their insistence

---

15 Richmond, 'A Pedagogy of Peacebuilding', 116.

on having an unarmed intervention, despite initial concerns of the interveners, who felt uneasy about going into a volatile postconflict situation unarmed. This arrangement meant that the interveners were dependent on the locals for their security and protection. The locals developed strong feelings of responsibility for the safety of their international 'guests' (and, in fact, TMG/PMG personnel were hardly ever threatened and never attacked).[16] This arrangement provided a rather robust security guarantee for the internationals. On the other hand, it affected the power relations between the internationals and the locals in the latter's favour.[17]

The presence of the internationals opened a secure space for former enemies to come together. The internationals played an important role in initiating conversations between the conflict parties and keeping conversations going, even in critical stages of the peace process.[18] Hence it was not only the internationals' mandate in a narrow sense—to 'monitor' (TMG/PMG), to 'observe' (UNOMB)—that made their contribution to peacebuilding so valuable, but the reassurances for the locals that came with the internationals' presence, based on a plethora of activities and collateral goods that reached well beyond the formal mandate.

Actually, the 'way the intervention developed was not so much a matter of careful planning, but rather a product of complex interactions of numerous often distinct interests among both international and local actors'.[19] In the following I'll try to give a glimpse of these 'complex interactions' (which were not confined to the realm of just 'interests').

The intervention set out with the conventional liberal peacebuilding agenda, but it turned out that this did not align neatly with local understandings and practices. This holds true not least regarding the conceptualisation of peace itself. One peace monitor says:

---

16 Regan, *Light Intervention*, 69. In hindsight, the Australian side concedes that 'the arrangements under which local parties would provide security to unarmed monitors worked well. An unanticipated benefit was that it also encouraged the members of the Truce and Peace Monitoring Groups to place greater importance on building good relationships with local leaders and communities so as to prevent misunderstandings that might result in threats of violence against the operation' (Australian Civil-Military Centre, *Partnering for Peace*, 34).

17 Regan, *Light Intervention*, 156.

18 Braithwaite, 'Partial Truth and Reconciliation in the *Longue Durée*'.

19 Regan, *Light Intervention*, 162–163.

I began to realize that my understanding of 'peace' was too narrow to encompass its much more complex meaning for many Bougainvilleans. We peace monitors tended to define peace in terms of the formal truce and cease-fire agreements … We went to villages with copies of the Burnham, Lincoln and Arawa agreements … We poorly grasped that peace meant dealing with … less tangible elements … On a more complex level, which I only glimpsed, Bougainvilleans seemed committed to 'spiritual rehabilitation'. Calls for 'spiritual rehabilitation' were linked to attempts to articulate the kind of society that they wanted to build.[20]

The last sentence indicates how misleading liberal peacebuilding notions of 'local culture' as apolitical are, and it hints at the fundamental political significance of culture, emotion and spirituality.

The difference in understanding 'peace' played out in various dimensions of the local–international exchange, particularly in areas that are easily discredited as 'soft' and 'non-essential' by internationals. To mention just three:

First, the spiritual aspect. Another peace monitor reported: 'I experienced one healing ceremony, two crusades and a number of discussions with women who had just talked with Jesus'.[21] For internationals coming from a Western secular, presumably enlightened and rational, background, it is difficult to earnestly engage with the spiritual, to actually become open to emotional and spiritual sensation and intuition and appreciate the role of myth and ritual for peacebuilding—not to speak of magic, sorcery and witchcraft. On Bougainville, however, God, the spirits of the ancestors and the unborn, the holy bushes and trees and the totem animals of the clans, who are embedded in networks that transcend the culture–nature divide and the human–non-human divide, are 'actors' in their own right, with the capacity to make a difference in the visible world (which for Western internationals by and large is the only 'real' world, while for locals it is intrinsically connected to the invisible world). Accordingly, peace cannot be conceptualised without taking this non-human, invisible dimension of the world into account. The Ni-Vanuatu, the Fiji i-Taukei and the Maori in the New Zealand contingent had far fewer problems engaging with the spiritual dimensions than did the white Australians and New Zealanders.

---

20 Ruiz-Avila, 'Peace Monitoring in Wakunai', 98–99.
21 Parry, 'Peace Monitoring in Wakunai', 106.

Second, 'gender issues'. A female monitor explains that the mission 'risked missing the boat with a key peace process resource—the women. We had applied our European attitudes to Bougainville and had not realized the role that women had customarily played'.[22] This observation refers to the fact that most Bougainville communities are matrilineal, which translates into a rather powerful social status for women, and that women played crucial roles in the transition from war to peace in the local contexts. Engaging with the women led to significant recalibration of exchanges between interveners and locals. Given that male and female spheres are to a large extent separate in Bougainville society, male peace monitors were not capable of building the relationships that their female colleagues were able to forge.

Third, different conceptualisations of time. On Bougainville, as in other international peacebuilding interventions, the external actors tried to impose their own (tight) time frames. But at the end of the day they had to adjust to 'Melanesian time'. The Australian military commander of the PMG, for example, makes the point that 'Canberra' (that is, the Australian Government) presented the PMG with over-ambitious timetables. He says: 'But I learned that Melanesian clocks differ from other timepieces … I quickly adapted to the Melanesian approach … [and] although there was significant early pressure from Canberra to speed up the process, I learned that it had to progress at the pace' of the locals.[23] Nevertheless, 'many in the Australian system did not really understand why the peace process moved at what, to them, seemed a frustratingly slow pace'.[24] On the ground, the locals disapproved with the rushed approach initially taken by PMG patrols. As a result, 'over time patrols spent longer in villages … Patrols took the time to listen to stories, appreciating the world of villagers and creating empathy and trust'.[25]

The focus on process and long time frames also shaped the 'high-level' political peacebuilding process, the negotiations conducted in its course and the process of disarmament and demobilisation. This is very much in line with local customary principles and methods of peacebuilding. At the same time it poses a major challenge for the international actors, whose mindset is determined by the notion of achieving 'outcomes' and getting

---

22 Castell, 'Opening Doors', 121.
23 Osborn, 'Role of the Military Commander', 52–53.
24 Regan, *Light Intervention*, 79.
25 Breen, 'Coordinating Monitoring and Defence Support', 47.

things done as quickly as possible. Overall, the locals largely succeeded in maintaining their pace of doing things and adjusting the international's planned timetables to local needs and customs.

These examples demonstrate that everyday processes of local–international exchange resulted in the recalibrations of relationships and involved the active renegotiation of the content and strategies of the peace intervention. In this way, the intervention was hybridised due to the agency of the locals who transformed the liberal peace agenda according to their norms, interests and ways of doing.[26] It can be argued that this was an outcome of the internationals' relative weakness, and at the same time a strategy of the internationals to regain and reconfigure control and power in the international–local relationship. For example, making adjustments regarding 'gender sensitivity' can be seen as appreciation of formerly marginalised voices and as an expression of a more participatory and inclusive approach. But it also can be seen as a means to fill a gap in the intervention so as to reconfigure and expand the interveners' control and power. When presenting the success of the PMG to the outside world, the male political and military leadership of the intervention managed to bolster its image by stressing the female component, but this was originally not in the plan. In fact, it was initially met with widespread ignorance and even some resistance in the context of the military as a dominantly masculine hierarchical organisation. Only in the everyday exchange with the locals did the gender dimension emerge as a factor of major political significance.

In a similar vein, the participation of personnel from Fiji and Vanuatu (and a strong Maori component in the New Zealand contingent) can be seen as an expression of the acknowledgement of the significance of cultural context and of cultural sensitivity, but it also can be seen as a clever tactical move to increase the acceptability of the TMG/PMG to the locals.[27] In an official assessment of peacebuilding interventions from 2012, an Australian Government document reads: 'Australia recognizes that its personnel rarely match the cultural skills, understanding of context and appropriateness of approach of our Pacific Island partners in regional settings'.[28]

---

26   The other side of this hybridisation is of course the transformation of local norms and ways of doing in the course of engaging with the protagonists of the liberal peace agenda. Space does not allow elaboration of this point.

27   Regan, 'The Bougainville Intervention', 193.

28   Australian Civil-Military Centre, *Partnering for Peace*, 43.

Or take the aspect of religion/spirituality. Engaging with this dimension was not planned for either. However, sitting through five-hour-long church services, for example, or bringing in more padres (the so-called 'God squad'),[29] changed the character of the international–local interaction. The internationals realised how useful this was for building relationships with the devout locals. It was not necessarily an indication that locals and internationals actually had a common understanding of the significance of religion and spirituality.

Or, again, the time factor. The PMG commander in the quote above speaks about the difference between 'Melanesian clocks' and 'other timepieces'. This way of talking implies a shared universal concept of time as linear and measurable. A different cultural understanding of time, however, can have profound impacts on peacebuilding, for example, if past events of linear clock time (the time of the internationals) are still 'present'. In Bougainville the spirits of the dead fighters of the war are still fighting today, because their bodies were not laid to rest according to the appropriate customary burial and reconciliation ceremonies. For many Bougainvilleans this is a major obstacle to achieving peace. There can only be peace once the bodies have been retrieved and buried according to custom. Time is not a universal given—it is something different for peacekeepers, villagers in the mountains of Bougainville, politicians in Canberra or at UN headquarters in New York. Being forced not to rush things and allow for more time to get things done is valuable in itself but might not dig deep enough.

So, even though in the course of everyday interaction with the locals the internationals' peacebuilding agenda changed, one cannot escape the impression that the internationals' engagement with local understandings of peace(building) remained within their own cultural and epistemological comfort zone, with 'the other', the local ways of being, doing and knowing (conflict, peace, culture etc.) merely seen to challenge and/or enrich liberal ways. The power of the internationals to set the paradigm within which peace is to be understood and seen as meaningful and legitimate remained unabated. On the other hand, it also has to be acknowledged that the local–international exchanges instigated self-reflection processes in the internationals' camp and led to a renegotiation of the liberal peacebuilding agenda, resulting in outcomes more conducive to the

---

29   Mortlock, 'A Good Thing to Do', 78.

locals' interests, needs, norms and understanding of peace. The seemingly all-powerful liberal peace approach was re-articulated by its 'recipients' on the ground, who turned out to be not simply grateful and abiding subjects of external agendas and strategies, but powerful actors in their own right, maintaining autonomy and agency, neither merely adopting the liberal peace agenda nor resisting it totally. The result is hybrid peace formation.

The too-often misused phrase 'local ownership' has substance in the Bougainville case, with local ownership *taken* by the locals rather than 'granted' and 'nurtured' by the internationals.[30] One aspect of the locals' agency that rarely attracts attention is that they were very smart in utilising the capacities provided by the internationals for purposes that at first sight were diverting resources from the 'real' peacebuilding tasks. For instance, transport by PMG helicopter was extensively used by chiefs and others to get them to and from meetings; villagers made comprehensive use of the PMG medical facilities or used the paper of the leaflets, flyers and newsletters distributed by the PMG for rolling their bush tobacco. So it was not only the 'core business' prescribed by the liberal peacebuilding agenda (supervise the ceasefire, assist in weapons disposal, etc.) which made the intervention useful for the locals, but also the 'collateral goods' that its presence provided—surely a distinct form of 'under the radar' local ownership.[31]

Of course, there were also changes on the side of the locals. Local understandings of peace, governance and legitimacy change due to the interaction with others/outsiders who have different understandings. Locals not only exploit the presence of the internationals, opportunistically adjusting to the peacebuilding and good governance talk in an instrumental manner so as to gain access to resources, but they (some, not all) genuinely change behaviours, practices and values; locals partially and selectively accepted, adopted and adapted to liberal attitudes and norms—they were more or less 'liberalised'. These processes also are expressions of the hybridisation of peace formation.

---

30   Krogstad, 'Local Ownership as Dependence Management'.
31   Ibid.

Conclusion

The Bougainville case demonstrates how in the everyday local–international exchange peace formation emerges as hybridised, with outcomes that are neither liberal nor illiberal/indigenous, but hybrid (that is, preserving elements of both the liberal and the local and at the same time transforming it into another quality). The realm of such hybrid peace formation is the locale/the locality, which is co-created and shared by a variety of interacting local and international actors and institutions, hybrid and emergent in itself. And in the context of the locale, the boundaries of 'the international' and 'the local' become porous and blurred or, as Laura McLeod puts it, 'the categorization of "local" and "international" is one with inherent slippage, and hybridity is a concept capturing this very slippage while still allowing an exploration of the interactions between local and international actors'.[32]

A final word on the practical political implications of all this: the encounters in Bougainville have contributed to a debate among internationals at home (in this case, in Australia and New Zealand) about the need to rethink and recalibrate one's own understandings of the international–local interface in peacebuilding.[33] This has, for example, triggered reassessments of the relationship between customary and statutory law, restorative and punitive justice, or state and non-state providers of security. Hence it can be posited that the Bougainville experience in the long run contributed to the 'turn to the local' and to the emergence of a discourse on 'relational sensibility' among international peacebuilders. This more recent interest in the local, hybridity and relationality in policy circles is evidence that there is merit in studying and talking about international–local relations in processes of peace formation also for practical political purposes. If one has the ambition to use one's research to change politics for the better, in other words, if one wants to do policy-relevant research, one has to engage with the sphere of international organisations, governments, INGOs and other political forces which are—as 'internationals'—pursuing what they call 'postconflict peacebuilding'. There can be no doubt that the findings of

---

32   McLeod, 'A Feminist Approach to Hybridity', 51.
33   See, for example, Australian Civil-Military Centre, *Partnering for Peace*, as an official document that is touched by the spirit of relational sensibility, cultural sensitivity and acknowledgement of local cultural context. For a scholarly discussion of this emerging trend see Hughes et al., *Forging New Conventional Wisdom Beyond International Policing*.

such research can be used—misused, as the researcher would say—for purposes that, and by actors whom, the researcher does not agree with; this also has happened to the hybridity approach, now that it has crossed into the policy world as Oliver Richmond and Roger Mac Ginty put it in their latest piece on this topic.[34] The 'hybrid turn' in the world of actual politics is open in both directions: it can potentially lead to more emancipatory peacebuilding practices beyond the liberal peace approach (as the best case), or to a refinement of counterinsurgency strategies (as the worst case) as Afghanistan, for example, shows.[35]

Although the latter trend gives reason for serious concern, the good news is that hybrid political orders, hybrid security governance and hybrid peace cannot be instrumentally designed, crafted or constructed. Any endeavours of internationals will always be nothing but (more or less benign or malign) elements in a complex and fluid web of relationships and interactions in a much broader mix of processes of peace formation and the emergence of political community.

---

34   Mac Ginty and Richmond, 'The Fallacy of Constructing Hybrid Political Orders'. We have to keep in mind, though, there is still a huge gap between the scholarly debate and political practice. Criticism of the 'local', 'hybrid' and 'relational' turns in peacebuilding as pursued mainly for instrumental or rhetorical reasons remains valid (Mac Ginty and Richmond, 'The Local Turn in Peace Building', 771). On the 'significantly different ways that hybridity can be used' see Brown, this volume.
35   Albrecht and Moe, 'The Simultaneity of Authority'; Mac Ginty and Richmond, 'The Fallacy of Constructing Hybrid Political Orders'.

8

Reflections on Hybridity as an Analytical Lens on State Formation: The Case of Solomon Islands

Sinclair Dinnen and Matthew Allen

Introduction

In this chapter we draw on a case study of rural Solomon Islands to reflect critically on the value of the concept of 'hybridity' in understanding processes of social, economic and political change underway in this small but socially complex archipelagic Pacific island nation. In foregrounding these processes of change, we draw attention in particular to the inherent tension between contemporary understandings of statebuilding, on one hand, and state formation, on the other.[1] The former, which tend to dominate policy discussions and some areas of academic debate, are often framed in terms of linear, technical and largely ahistorical projects, with a significant focus on the role of international actors. The latter has its antecedents in historical studies of the emergence of the post-Westphalian state and generally views state formation as a predominantly organic, contingent and highly contested process. Our analysis of change

---

1   Allen and Dinnen, 'Solomon Islands in Transition?', 393–394.

in Solomon Islands adopts a state formation lens and in this chapter we specifically ask what the concept of hybridity might contribute to our understanding of this process.

Hybridity has been used recently in Solomon Islands with reference to the pluralistic social and regulatory environment that prevails at 'local'[2] levels in rural areas, where 'traditional'[3] and state forms of authority overlap and intersect. As an idea, hybridity serves to highlight the myriad interactions between different institutional forms and value systems that cumulatively shape the character of everyday regulation and ordering at these local levels, particularly in terms of dispute resolution and community governance.[4]

While this usage seeks to describe how social regulation actually works for predominantly rural populations living in areas of limited statehood, the concept of hybridity has also attracted growing attention among policy and development actors in recent years with a more instrumental interest in improving service delivery to dispersed populations in parts of the global South, particularly in respect of justice and security provision.[5] In this regard, the main focus has been on how to improve the linkages and alignment between 'local' community-based mechanisms and the encompassing administrative and regulatory systems of the modern state. This interest has arisen most prominently in relation to international engagements with so-called fragile and conflict-affected states. The latter, which would include Solomon Islands, are characterised by the weakness of their formal institutions, constrained fiscal circumstances and, often, the social complexity and conspicuous level of normative pluralism found in many postcolonial settings. In such cases, external interveners are urged to extend their engagement beyond state actors to include, for example, 'traditional' and religious leaders, as integral to the larger statebuilding project.[6]

---

2   We use inverted commas here to signal the problematic treatment of this term/category—and the concept of scale more broadly—in much of the hybridity literature, a critique that we develop in a later section of the chapter.

3   We also use inverted commas here to acknowledge the problematic usage of the notion 'traditional' in much of the literature, often misleadingly implying a category that is bounded, static and oppositional to 'modern'.

4   See, for example, Allen et al., *Justice Delivered Locally*; Dinnen and Haley, *Evaluation of the Community Officer Project in Solomon Islands*; Evans et al., 'The Hybrid Courts of Melanesia'.

5   See Luckham and Kirk, 'Security in Hybrid Political Contexts'; World Bank, *World Development Report 2011*.

6   Smits and Wright, *Engagement with Non-state Actors in Fragile States*.

We certainly see merit in attempts to address particular problems—such as high rates of family and sexual violence or chronic levels of substance abuse—through engagement with these 'local' systems of authority and regulation in places like Solomon Islands and have made recommendations to this effect in our research on justice delivery in that country's rural provinces.[7] At the same time, we also share many of the concerns raised by critics of 'the local turn' in peacebuilding and development,[8] including in respect of the uncritical embrace of more instrumentalised forms of hybridity—what we have dubbed 'designer hybridity'—as a novel and innovative approach by external interveners to institutional reform. In the grounded case study that follows we elaborate on some of these concerns and, in doing so, make a number of points that connect with the broader themes—history, power and scale—of the workshop which provided the genesis for this edited collection.[9]

In the first place, we note that attempts to create linkages between different social orders and institutional forms have a long history in Solomon Islands, including through the experience of the indirect administration introduced initially by British colonial authorities, and that this longer history has had a significant influence on contemporary efforts to promote hybridity. Second, we note that such attempts have by no means been confined to international or national-level actors seeking to instrumentalise top-down processes of domination or reform but are also apparent in the actions of local actors seeking to connect and negotiate with the latter. These local agendas for hybridity have also been profoundly shaped by longer histories of interaction with external actors and processes, as have the local social orders that are driving them.

Third, and as pointed out by many others,[10] these interactions are invariably infused and mediated through existing power relations and contests, serving particular interests and neglecting or militating against others. Related to this, our fourth point draws attention to the scalar dimensions of these processes of hybridisation and the need to move beyond the crude scalar binaries (such as 'local–supranational' or 'local–liberal') that have characterised much of the hybridity literature in order to adequately engage with the hierarchies of power that animate them.

---

7   See, for example, Allen et al., *Justice Delivered Locally*.
8   Björkdahl and Höglund, 'Precarious Peacebuilding'; Meagher, 'The Strength of Weak States?'; Peterson, 'A Conceptual Unpacking Of Hybridity'.
9   See the Introduction to this volume for more information.
10   For example, Nadarajah and Rampton, 'The Limits of Hybridity'.

We acknowledge that some of our own work has been guilty on this count, although we have previously flagged scale as a problematic concept in the hybridity literature.[11] What we are seeking to do here through emphasising the importance of scalar analysis is to draw attention not only to the subnational scales of social and political organisation that are frequently overlooked in the hybridity discourse, such as the scale of the island province in the case of Solomon Islands and other archipelagic territories, but also to the various ways in which power has been rescaled, and new scales produced, in the context of successive phases of political economic struggle.

The final point from our research in Solomon Islands, and one that we have made previously,[12] questions the assumption in much of the existing literature that local-level actors have a natural preference for local forms of authority, organisation and regulation over those of state and transnational forms. Instead, we have found a strong desire among many of our Solomon Islander interlocutors for greater engagement with Weberian-like institutions that are perceived—whether rightly or wrongly—as being more emancipated from corrosive and corrupting dimensions of contemporary social and power relations. While neotraditional institutions such as those associated with chiefly authority continue to enjoy widespread legitimacy, the apparent demand for Weberian institutions, especially police and courts, is, in large part, based on a growing recognition among Solomon Islanders of the increasing frailty and politicisation of these 'local' institutions in the face of contemporary change.[13]

These five points can be distilled down to what we see as three critical limitations to the analytical value of hybridity as a lens with which to view the process of state formation; limitations, we suggest, that have resonance well beyond Solomon Islands. First, hybridity's crude approach to scale is blind to the vertical power dynamics that are becoming increasingly animated by globalised processes of political and economic change. Second, it is not only national and supranational actors that may attempt to instrumentalise hybridity; a raft of subnational actors may also engage with such agendas both discursively and materially. Third, it is wrong to assume that the 'local' is always synonymous with the 'non-state' or the 'traditional'. In elucidating these limitations with reference to our case study from Solomon Islands, we also demonstrate the indispensability

---

11   Dinnen and Allen, 'State Absence and State Formation in Solomon Islands'.
12   Ibid.
13   See Wallis, this volume.

of attention to history and power relations to any robust analysis of state formation. In this sense, history and power relations provide crosscutting, or encompassing, themes for our reflection upon the limits of hybridity as an analytical lens on state formation.

The first section of our chapter introduces the Solomon Islands case study, paying particular attention to the historical and geographical complexities of state formation in this archipelagic and socially diverse postcolonial and postconflict nation-state. We also define what we mean by the politics of scale and map out the (hierarchically ordered) scales of political and social organisation that we suggest are essential to any adequate and historically grounded analysis of state formation in the Solomons context. We then turn to the three main arguments we introduced above, providing brief sections on hybridity and the politics of scale, 'local' agendas for instrumentalist hybridity, and agency and the growing 'local' demand for emancipated institutions. In our concluding section we suggest that the three limitations to hybridity that we elucidate are by no means terminal. On the contrary, we see much that is analytically useful in the concept of hybridity for understanding processes of state formation. Indeed, the data we draw upon in this brief reflection demonstrates the value of descriptive hybridity as a methodological tool in the tradition of grounded ethnographic research. By drawing attention to the three limitations expounded here it is our intention that future hybridity research and practice might explicitly engage with them, thereby enriching and advancing the hybridity project and its—albeit qualified—utility as an analytical lens on state formation.

Understanding the complexities of state formation in Solomon Islands

These islands, lying 1,800 kilometres off Australia's north-east coast, possess the extraordinary ethnolinguistic diversity that is characteristic of Melanesia, with 80 languages spoken by a population of around 600,000 people. Rates of urbanisation are low, with most people living in rural hamlets and villages where contemporary forms of 'community' are based on complex interplays of kinship and exchange relations, 'traditional' and neo-'traditional' governance structures, friendships, membership of Christian churches and myriad claims to customary land of which genealogical descent is only one. Intense social diversity, geographical fragmentation and a widely dispersed population have long problematised the extension of centralised authority.

Commencing with colonisation by Great Britain, successive forces both external and internal have shaped the nature of the state and its interactions with society. These have included projects of pacification, missionisation, labour commodification, direct and indirect rule, institutional modernisation, globalised natural resource capitalism, patronage, structural adjustment and, most recently, a major liberal peacebuilding intervention in the form of the Australian-led Regional Assistance Mission to Solomon Islands (RAMSI). First deployed in 2003 and finally withdrawn in mid-2017, RAMSI came about largely in response to a period of violent internal conflict known locally as the 'ethnic tension'. The tension involved a complex interaction of historical factors, motivations and actors at different geographical scales and was, in fact, like many other recent conflicts, the manifestation of multiple local conflicts that mutated and escalated over time.[14] However, for concerned Australian policymakers in the early 2000s, it was viewed primarily through the global lens of 'state failure' and the threat this ostensibly posed to Australian and regional security.[15]

While central government could be said to have effectively collapsed during the tension period, changing relations between the political centre and rural periphery since independence meant that the state was already widely perceived as absent from rural areas before the outbreak of the tension in 1998.[16] However, while this narrative of state withdrawal is embraced by many rural Solomon Islanders it remains a contested one. Even if the state is interpreted primarily in terms of service delivery and development,[17] the depiction of its uniform and linear retreat from rural regions demands qualification because there has, in fact, been an expansion of some government services, notably health and education, in the postcolonial period. Fourteen years of substantial investment by RAMSI has also seen improvements in this regard. Significantly, there are also compelling political economy grounds for contesting the state-withdrawal narrative. These relate to the exponential expansion of

14   Kalyvas, 'The Ontology of "Political Violence"'.
15   Fry and Kabutaulaka, 'Political Legitimacy and State-building Intervention in the Pacific'.
16   Herlihy, 'Always We Are Last'; McDougall, 'Sub-national Governance in Post-RAMSI Solomon Islands'.
17   Bierschenck and de Sardan, 'Studying the Dynamics of African Bureaucracies'.

discretionary constituency development funds (known as CDFs) at the disposal of individual national members of parliament such that these now dwarf national grants to provincial governments.

For some observers, the latter development is indicative of a fundamental reordering of power that has taken place in Solomon Islands over the past few decades.[18] However, this reordering could also be seen as a form of rescaling: the consolidation of power in the hands of national-level political elites. This has involved the progressive evisceration of the middle (provincial) and local levels of government. In the case of the former, the division of responsibilities between provincial and national tiers has always been unclear, while provincial administrations have been subjected to perennial underfunding from the political centre.[19] The system of local-level government was effectively dismantled when the former area councils were officially suspended in 1998 as a consequence of both domestically and internationally driven structural adjustment programs against the larger backdrop of the Asian financial crisis.

Building upon and, in many ways, exacerbating historical patterns of uneven development introduced initially under colonialism, globalised extractive resource capitalism, in the form of the logging industry and a more recent intensification in mining activity, has also been a powerful animator of rescaling and reordering. The nexus between the notoriously corrupt logging sector and the larger pattern of political patronage that has shaped political development in the post-independence period has been well documented.[20] As has been the case in neighbouring Papua New Guinea, including in its Autonomous Region of Bougainville, the encounter with extractive resource capitalism has produced 'customary landownership' as a new and potent scale in both horizontal and vertical power struggles, especially over economic benefits, at the same time that it has animated the island province as scale for collective political action in benefit-sharing struggles.[21]

We suggest that despite its significant engagement over 14 years, RAMSI left many of these political economy dynamics alone and, in doing so, may have inadvertently served to reinforce and accentuate them by reifying

---

18   Craig and Porter, 'Political Settlement in Solomon Islands'.
19   Cox and Morrison, 'Solomon Islands Provincial Governance Information Paper'.
20   Bennett, *Pacific Forest*; Dauvergne, 'Corporate Power in the Forests of Solomon Islands'; Kabutaulaka, 'Rumble in the Jungle'.
21   Allen, 'Melanesia's Violent Environments'; Filer, 'Compensation, Rent and Power in Papua New Guinea'.

and reinforcing the national scale as the key locus of political power. In this sense RAMSI was, in effect, if not necessarily by design, aligned with a rescaling of power under CDFs that was already taking place before the intervention, a point that has been made by Hameiri.[22] While it would be unfair to hold the regional mission responsible—its objectives were altogether more modest—the fact remains that this substantial liberal intervention did little to shift the existing political economy of natural resource extraction. It also left unchallenged the exclusionary and dysfunctional political settlement that provides the setting for continuing grievances, including many that contributed to the original conflict. In this respect, Craig and Porter have demonstrated how the clientelism that continues to characterise relations between Solomon Islands' political and economic elites has had a profoundly corrosive impact on policy processes and contributes to enduring instability.[23]

At this juncture it is necessary to define what we mean by 'the politics of scale'. Briefly, drawing upon work in political and economic geography, we see scale as socially produced and constantly reconfigured through sociopolitical struggle.[24] Relationality and hierarchy are key defining characteristics of scale, though, importantly, these hierarchies can be reconfigured and scale, in this sense, is not fixed. Lastly, scalar politics are deployed regularly in political power struggles, both as 'tactics' by less powerful social groups and as 'strategies' by elites, to draw on Michel de Certeau's distinction.[25] In the case of Solomon Islands, we see the following scales as pertinent to an analysis of the politics of scale:

- *Very local.* The village level and, even below that, the kinship group, clan or tribe.

- *Regional/sub-island.* For example, geographically circumscribed social movements such as the Christian Fellow Church in parts of Western Province.[26] This scale might be conterminous with language boundaries and/or national constituencies.

---

22   Hameiri, 'Public Administration Reform and the Politics of Scale'.
23   Craig and Porter, 'Political Settlement in Solomon Islands'.
24   Brenner, 'The Limits to Scale?'; Smith, *Uneven Development*, 160–178; Swyngedouw, 'Neither Global nor Local'.
25   See Kent, this volume. For de Certeau, 'strategies'—typically employed by elites—usually involve official plans and defined frameworks for achieving desired goals, while 'tactics' are the more flexible approaches tailored to immediate contexts likely to be used by less powerful groups. De Certeau, *The Practice of Everyday Life*.
26   Hviding, 'Re-placing the State in the Western Solomon Islands'.

- *Provincial/island.* Most provinces (subnational jurisdictions) in Solomon Islands are geographically conterminous with a large island and the island province, due to its unique territorial qualities, is an especially potent, though problematic, scale for collective political action through the mobilisation of island-wide identities.

- *National.* The scale at which political power is being increasingly concentrated through the growth of CDFs and various forms of rent seeking.

- *Supranational.* This scale is critically important in the case of Solomon Islands because of the recent RAMSI intervention, the economic dominance of globalised extractive resource capitalism, and the legacies of earlier (colonial period) forms of intervention and statebuilding.

Hybridity and the politics of scale

Building upon an earlier article,[27] we contrast our analysis of state formation against existing scholarship on Solomon Islands that has tended to privilege the ascription of agency at one particular scale: either the very local or sub-island (taking the form of detailed ethnographic analyses of particular communities or social movements);[28] the national (such as the political settlement interpretations with a focus on national elites);[29] or the supranational (in the form of analysis that sees supranational actors as the primary driver of change in Solomon Islands).[30] Without detracting from the insights provided by these studies, our objective here is to bring an explicitly multi-scalar sensibility to bear on both processes of state formation and the analytical utility of hybridity for understanding them. This requires the facility to navigate between scales.

As mentioned in the introduction, much of the hybrid peace literature operates within a crude spatial ontology in which the 'local' appears as an extremely fuzzy and imprecise category that is primarily constructed in opposition to the supranational and/or the liberal. This clumsy scalar binary leads to much definitional slippage: in some instances the 'local' appears to refer to what we have identified above as the very local scale; in others it seems to refer to the national scale; and in yet others, it is taken

---

27   Dinnen and Allen, 'State Absence and State Formation in Solomon Islands'.
28   For example, Timmer, '*Kastom* and Theocracy'.
29   For example, Craig and Porter, 'Political Settlement in Solomon Islands'.
30   For example, Hameiri, 'State Building or Crisis Management?'.

to mean everything that is not supranational and/or liberal. Moreover, hybridity's scalar binary is also blind to the inherent dynamism of the politics of scale: it is unable to account for the reconfiguration of existing scales, and the production of new ones, that has occurred during different historical phases of political and economic struggle. Another aspect of the politics of this construction is how 'the local' is often represented in a manner that renders it as remote, marginal or 'marked by absence'.[31] This construction can, in turn, have consequences in terms of the ways in which policymakers approach particular locations.

We have already noted that CDFs can be usefully interpreted as a rescaling of power and that the advent of extractive resource industries has produced customary landownership as a new scale of political economic contestation at the same time that it has animated benefit-sharing tensions between the national and provincial scales. We are reminded that Solomon Islands has a long history of these sorts of scalar dynamics. The introduction of capitalist social relations under colonialism, especially in the form of international and domestic plantation labour trades, and subsequent patterns of uneven capitalist penetration (in conjunction with colonial cartographies that territorialised large islands into subnational jurisdictions for the administrative convenience of colonial authorities) has produced and reproduced the island province as a potent scale in political economic power struggles.

These politics of scale have found expression in longstanding tensions and debates about political devolution and decentralisation, and were an important factor in the origins of the 'ethnic tension'.[32] Set against the long haul of state formation, the tensions between national and subnational scales remain an important area of continuity as witnessed by an enduring agenda for constitutional change and the proposed adoption of a federal system of government that would see not only devolution of functions and powers subnationally, but also the formalisation of the many and varied subnational projects of instrumentalist hybridity that will be discussed below. The draft constitution contains significant scope for local accommodation, inflection and agency—provinces and 'community governments' will have considerable scope to do their own

---

31   See, for example, Gupta and Ferguson, *Culture, Power, Place*. We are grateful to a reviewer of our draft chapter for pointing this out and introducing us to the relevant literature.

32   The issue of centre–periphery relations (that is, between Honiara and the rest of the country) has been a critical fault line in Solomon Islands politics since decolonisation. See, for example, Larmour and Qalo, *Decentralisation in the South Pacific*.

thing.[33] Hybridity, in this sense, remains a useful lens for looking at these national/subnational tensions but only after its unsophisticated and defective approach to critical spatial/scalar dimensions has been remedied. Put bluntly, hybridity's crude scalar binary runs the risk of glossing over, or simply failing to see, critically important political contestation and dynamism between the national and multiple subnational scales that we have identified. Nor is hybridity alert to the production of new, previously unimaginable, scales of political economic struggle.

'Local' agendas for instrumentalist hybridity

This brings us to our second critique of the hybridity literature as it has been applied to the theory and practice of peace building and statebuilding. That is, the assumption that instrumentalist agendas for hybridity are the exclusive domain of actors at the supranational or national scales. The growing critique of instrumentalised or 'designer' hybridity in the critical peacebuilding literature is largely directed at the international actors involved in these interventions and questions the practicality, efficacy and ethics of such endeavours, including the high risks of unintended consequences.[34] While the recent RAMSI mission was almost exclusively focused on building/rebuilding the central agencies of state (and rightly criticised for this narrow focus), our work in rural Solomon Islands indicates there are extensive efforts being directed towards forms of instrumentalised hybridity at the very local, sub-island and provincial scales—particularly in areas of dispute resolution, policing and governance. What this research clearly demonstrates is that it is not only supranational actors that have been actively pursuing instrumentalist hybridity agendas.

A number of points have emerged in our analysis of these subnationally driven agendas for hybrid institutions. The first is the sheer range of subnational actors who are engaged in instrumentalised hybridity and the diverse forms that these innovative activities assume.[35] They include extensive experimentation in informal governance arrangements at the very local level including a proliferation of village 'committees',

---

33 'Constitution of the Federated Democratic Republic of Solomon Islands', 2nd draft, 6 May 2014.
34 See, for example, Meagher, 'The Strength of Weak States?'; Peterson, 'A Conceptual Unpacking of Hybridity'.
35 Allen et al., *Justice Delivered Locally*, 69–78.

'councils' and 'associations'. 'Traditional', predominantly male, leaders or 'chiefs' continue to have a prominent role in these local structures, but there is also evidence of participation by representatives of other groups, including women, youth and churches. Another manifestation lies in the proclamation of elaborate, often written, community 'rules', 'laws', 'by-laws', 'ordinances' and, in some cases, constitutions. Some of this activity may involve mimicry of state forms aimed at enhancing the visibility and legibility of local structures to actors at other scales such as governments and donors,[36] with the hope of initiating productive relations with them. There is also a strong element of self-help and local problem solving that is largely substitutive in the absence of tangible and effective linkages to more encompassing administrative and service delivery systems.

Experimentation is also evident at the provincial scale, with a number of provinces actively exploring ways of improving downward linkages with structures at the most local levels. These have been influenced by the wider and longstanding debates about constitutional reform and federalism, as well as by pressure from rural communities for improved service delivery and local development opportunities. The hybrid character of these provincial initiatives is evident in deliberate attempts to integrate state, church and 'traditional' forms of authority into provincial or island-wide governance models, as with Isabel's well-known 'tripod' system.[37] These locally and provincially driven efforts to reconfigure what are already hybridised governance arrangements also serve to blur the distinction between 'descriptive' and 'instrumentalised' hybridity that recurs in the broader literature.[38]

Following on from above is our observation that these contemporary examples of experimentation with hybrid governance at local and provincial levels have themselves been profoundly shaped by a much longer colonial and postcolonial history of hybridisation across different institutional forms, value systems and types of social ordering.[39] The clearest historical example of instrumentalised hybridity was the introduction of 'indirect rule' by the British colonial authorities, working through 'chiefs', 'headmen' and various local intermediaries, as well as

---

36   McDougall, 'Customary Authority and State Withdrawal in Solomon Islands'.
37   Baines, 'Beneath the State'.
38   Millar, 'Disaggregating Hybridity'.
39   McDougall, 'Customary Authority and State Withdrawal in Solomon Islands'.

through the establishment of 'native courts' to administer 'customary law'. Syncretism between 'introduced' Christianity and local normative systems is evident in the long history of missionisation. Christianity, *kastom* and state forms have also been interwoven in the social movements that have appeared throughout Solomon Islands modern history, often as explicit alternatives to the social and political ordering of the colonial and postcolonial state. These movements, including Maasina Rule in Malaita,[40] the Moro Movement in Guadalcanal[41] and, more recently, the Christian Fellowship in parts of Western Province,[42] represented an early form of re-territorialisation and deployed *kastom* as an ideology of resistance. The Western 'breakaway' movement during decolonisation and, as noted in our rural research, the current phenomena of 'colonial nostalgia' and 'state withdrawal' similarly serve to highlight the historical and hybrid aspects of political contestation within and between different scalar levels.[43]

The critical question, as we see it, is not so much about the instrumentalisation of hybridity per se, as it is about the actors and interests promoting these agendas and, specifically, who stands to benefit—and who stands to lose—from their advocacy and realisation. In short, analytical focus should be upon the power relations that animate the pursuit and shape the outcomes of these instrumentalised approaches to hybridity and the manner in which they play out at different scales. In the case of Solomon Islands, this remains an important priority for continuing and future research.

Agency and the growing 'local' demand for emancipated institutions

In our earlier article[44] we were critical of some aspects of the 'local turn' literature, notably for the assumption that the local level would automatically privilege 'local' over 'national' or 'supranational' forms (an assumption that has, in turn, generated a critique of 'the

40   Akin, *Colonialism, Maasina Rule, and the Origins of Malaitan Kastom*.
41   Davenport and Çoker, 'The Moro Movement of Guadalcanal'.
42   Hviding, 'Re-placing the State in the Western Solomon Islands'.
43   Allen et al., *Justice Delivered Locally*.
44   Dinnen and Allen, 'State Absence and State Formation in Solomon Islands'.

romanticisation of the local').[45] The more complex picture that emerged from the research we reported in that paper was the desire at all subnational scales for statebuilding with a strong local inflection and degree of local autonomy, on one hand, and a strong desire for aspects of Weberian or liberal statehood, particularly in relation to the management of newer forms of conflict stresses, on the other. Rather than being mutually exclusive, these simultaneous demands for local autonomy and an explicit acknowledgement of a particular role for certain institutions of liberal statehood indicated a strong desire for more effective articulation between local and state regulatory systems that would enhance the effectiveness of both, as well as the alignment between them.

The views expressed by rural villagers recognised the increasing frailties of local institutions and structures in the face of contemporary globalisation and, in particular, the socially disintegrative and frequently violent effects of resource extraction. The attraction of certain aspects of Weberian or liberal statehood at local levels was expressed in the preference for RAMSI (that is, international) police over the Royal Solomon Islands Police Force, in the desire for local non-state actors to be backed by the 'shadow of the law', as well as in the mimicry of state forms intended to attract external recognition and engagement, and in the widespread nostalgia for an older system of indirect rule that was believed to have effectively connected the legitimacy of local leaders with the functional authority of the state. As in other cases of 'colonial nostalgia', the underlying sentiment rests more on discontent with the ethnographic present than with any real desire to return to the colonial past.[46] While the historical veracity on which this nostalgia is based is certainly open to question, it reflects a contemporary situation where local elites or 'chiefs', as well as many police units operating in rural areas, are all too often deeply compromised in the current political economy through their entanglements with logging and other commercial extractive operations. This situation again highlights the significance of the underlying power relations informing the configuration and outcomes of hybrid forms of regulation in practice.

Another dimension of the frequently encountered nostalgia for the colonial system of indirect rule is the perception that colonial institutions, such as that of the district officer, were impartial and effectively impervious to potentially corrupting social relations, especially those that drove,

---

45   Richmond, 'De-romanticising the Local, De-mystifying the International'.
46   Bissell, 'Engaging Colonial Nostalgia'.

and continue to drive, loyalty to one's own kinship or language group (commonly expressed in contemporary parlance as *wantokism*). Our research demonstrates that RAMSI police are seen in a similar light: they are perceived as being immune from the social and political economic relations that can imperil the partiality of local police.[47] In this manner, we once again see the importance of history in informing and framing contemporary discourses around regulation and institutional development more broadly. Moreover, despite the growing recognition among rural Solomon Islanders of the frailties of their local institutions, such as those associated with 'chiefs', these institutions continue to enjoy a significant degree of legitimacy as reflected in widespread calls to empower 'chiefs' and link them into formal governance and law and order structures.

Conclusion

This brief reflection on the analytical utility of the concept of hybridity as a lens on state formation has drawn upon a case study of Solomon Islands to highlight three deficiencies with the concept: its clumsy and problematic treatment of scale, its tendency to see projects of instrumental hybridity as the exclusive purview of national and supranational actors, and its assumption that 'local' actors will automatically privilege the 'traditional' over the 'liberal'. In concluding, we suggest that if these deficiencies are explicitly recognised and addressed, hybridity remains a useful lens, among others, to bring to bear upon processes of state formation. This point is perhaps best illustrated with reference to the politics of scale. Other contributors to this volume have suggested that hybridity be dispensed with entirely in favour of a scalar understanding of institutional change in the context of political and economic contestation.[48] However, our view is that this would simply substitute one form of methodological and theoretical, and perhaps ontological, privileging with another.

We are very sympathetic to the proposition that new scales are produced, and existing scales reconfigured, in the course of political economic struggle. Indeed we have argued that the politics of scale is a salient lacuna in the literature on hybridity and statebuilding and peacebuilding. However, we have also demonstrated in the case of Solomon Islands that these

---

47   Dinnen and Allen, 'Paradoxes of Postcolonial Police-Building'.
48   See Hameiri and Jones, this volume.

scalar dynamics have critical social and cultural inflections. This applies, for example, to the emergence of customary landownership as a scale in the contentious politics of extractive resource industries, to the types of institutions that have emerged at the scale of the island province, and even to the rescaling of power that has occurred with the advent and rapid growth of CDFs. In this sense neither scale nor hybridity are, on their own, sufficient to achieve interpretive and analytical rigour. In concert, however, these lenses may start to provide a more robust perspective on state formation, even more so when the other limitations to hybridity that we have highlighted—especially its problematic treatment of agency—are explicitly addressed. And, of course, with agency comes questions of structure, contingency, history and power relations. In the final analysis, then, all of these things matter if we are to develop solid understandings of processes of state formation in highly complex postcolonial and postconflict settings. Hybridity, in this sense, is not a panacea.

9

Engaging with 'The Everyday': Towards a More Dynamic Conception of Hybrid Transitional Justice

Lia Kent

Introduction

Just as critical peacebuilding scholars are increasingly engaging with the concept of hybridity, so too are scholars working in the closely related field of transitional justice,[1] which is concerned with the mechanisms and practices used by states, communities and individuals to address the legacies of violent conflict. A clear manifestation of this is the growing number of studies that consider the potential of local or customary dispute resolution practices to help deliver justice to victims and promote reconciliation. In Timor-Leste, for instance, the local dispute resolution practice known as *nahe biti* (literally, 'stretching the mat') has received a great deal of scholarly attention, particularly since aspects of this practice were incorporated into the nationwide community reconciliation process that was implemented by the Commission for Reception, Truth and

---

1   Transitional justice is a rapidly expanding field of scholarship and practice. It is concerned with a broad range of measures such as criminal trials, truth commissions, reparations policies, institutional reform, lustration (the vetting of public officials), memorialisation and reforms to police, prisons and the judiciary.

Reconciliation.[2] There has been similar interest in the Sierra Leone Truth Commission, which was authorised to involve traditional and religious leaders in its hearings, and Rwanda's *gacaca* courts, which saw the transformation of local dispute resolution practices into a nationwide system for resolving cases of serious crimes.[3]

While I recognise the value of these analyses, the starting point of this chapter is that more attention is needed to the ways in which individuals and communities deal with the legacies of conflict *outside* formal institutional contexts and dispute resolution forums. I draw here on my observations of Timor-Leste, where the legacies of the 24-year Indonesian occupation continue to reverberate and where people often appear to be negotiating them through subtle actions, practices and tactics that do not involve direct forms of confrontation between perpetrators and victims.[4] In this chapter, I aim to draw out some of these practices and tactics that, I suggest, are critical to the ongoing process of reconstructing social life in the wake of the occupation, and which might be understood as part of a process of ongoing, 'everyday' reconciliation. I use the term 'everyday reconciliation' to describe the ways in which individuals, families and communities are seeking to resume patterns of communication, exchange and sociality, resist threats to their existence and wellbeing, and exert a degree of control over their lives. Building on my observations of the Timor-Leste context, I explore the potential of the concept of the everyday—and everyday reconciliation—to widen the scope of what tends to be encompassed in analyses of hybrid transitional justice.

In essence, what I am proposing here is the need for a richer, more dynamic, conception of hybrid transitional justice that goes beyond a focus on institutions, structures and dispute resolution 'events' and pays more attention to the ongoing process of rebuilding everyday life, and renegotiating relationships, in the wake of conflict. Central to this

---

2   For example, see Braithwaite et al., 'Transitional Justice and Reconciliation'; Kent, 'Community Views of Justice and Reconciliation in Timor-Leste'; Larke, '"… And the Truth Shall Set You Free"'; Zifcak, 'Restorative Justice in Timor-Leste'.

3   Waldorf, 'Mass Justice for Mass Atrocity', 3–4. This interest dovetails with developments in the policy sphere. For example, two key United Nations reports acknowledged the significance of indigenous and informal traditions for administering justice. These were the 2004 report of then UN Secretary General Kofi Annan, titled *The Rule of Law and Transitional Justice in Conflict and Post-conflict Societies*, and the 2011 report of the same name by UN Secretary General Ban Ki Moon.

4   This process included a truth commission—the Commission for Reception, Truth and Reconciliation—and a 'hybrid' or internationalised tribunal known as the Special Panels for Serious Crimes that prosecuted cases of 'serious crimes'.

conception is the recognition (that has long been a feature of feminist thinking and the work of anthropologists) that individuals are not isolated, independent, entities but are 'socially constituted bodies, attached to others'.[5] The dynamic conception of hybrid transitional justice that I propose is informed, then, by a relational understanding of selves as integrally connected to others. This understanding is particularly salient in the context of kinship-based societies, where maintaining good relations with one's kin is not only important to one's social standing, but is also essential to viable social life, security and economic survival.

This chapter proceeds in three parts. Part one provides a brief discussion of the concept of the everyday as it is being used within the peacebuilding literature before considering why, despite some take-up, it remains relatively neglected within the transitional justice scholarship. Part two draws out several practices and tactics of everyday reconciliation in Timor-Leste and explores their significance with reference to Audra Mitchell's concepts of 'worldbuilding' and 'threatworks'.[6] The third part offers some thoughts on how greater attention to the everyday could enrich scholarship on hybrid transitional justice. What I aim to emphasise here is not that the current interest in local dispute resolution practices should be abandoned, but that, by situating these practices in the realm of the everyday, it is possible to imagine transitional justice as a far richer—more dynamic, ongoing and relational—process. What should also become clear is that, while my understandings of the everyday are informed by the insights of critical peacebuilding scholars, many of whom highlight the everyday as a site of resistance, I argue that more attention is needed to the everyday as a site where those with limited power 'make do' with the resources, tactics and possibilities at hand.

Peacebuilding, transitional justice and the everyday

The term 'everyday' evokes the quotidian, the routine, the familiar, a sense of ordinariness, repetition and stability.[7] Yet, for conflict-affected societies, these aspects of everyday life cannot necessarily be taken for granted.

---

5   Butler, *Precarious Life*, 20. See also Robbins, 'Recognition, Reciprocity, and Justice'.
6   Mitchell, 'Quality/Control', 1623.
7   Alcala and Baines 'Editorial Note', 387.

Rather than being a space of security and comfort, the everyday might appear as 'bristling with dangers'.[8] These realities call for an understanding of the everyday as dynamic rather than stable, as a 'lively space in which emotions, interactions, tensions, power struggles, tactics of domination and resistance and small and big ceremonial routine events occur'.[9] They also suggest the need for a recognition of the significant effort or *labour* that is required by those living in conflict-affected societies to achieve some measure of stability and routine in everyday life.[10]

In recent years, critical peacebuilding scholars have begun to engage with the everyday in this dynamic sense of the word, as part of a broader critique of, and response to, the limitations of liberal peacebuilding.[11] Particularly illuminating are the insights of Audra Mitchell, who describes the everyday as the 'set of experiences, practices and interpretations through which people engage with the daily challenges of occupying, preserving, altering and sustaining the plural worlds that they occupy'.[12] Such practices, which Mitchell describes as 'worldbuilding',[13] tend to be oriented towards the meeting of daily challenges, such as interacting with or caring for family members, friends and community, working, and exchanging goods.[14] They may include the celebration of traditional holidays or the resumption of patterns of communication and exchange.[15] They also comprise 'threatworks', a set of 'practices, institutions and customs' that are used by a range of different actors to 'exchange, acknowledge, evade, manoeuvre, contest and otherwise resist' perceived threats to their existence.[16] Examples of threatworks include the erection of barriers or walls or the ostracism or segregation of particular members of the community.[17] As Mitchell notes, threatworks are perceived by the actors involved as integral to maintaining their quality of life and some

---

8   Das, 'What Does Ordinary Ethics Look Like?'.
9   Alcala and Baines, 'Editorial Note', 387.
10   See Ross, *Raw Life, New Hope*, 70. See also Das, *Life and Words*.
11   See, for example, Mac Ginty 'Everyday Peace: Bottom-Up and Local Agency in Conflict-Affected Societies'; Mitchell, 'Quality/Control', 1623; Richmond, 'A Post-liberal Peace', 557; Richmond and Mitchell, 'Introduction—Towards a Post-liberal Peace', 1.
12   Mitchell, 'Quality/Control', 1624.
13   Mitchell uses the term 'world' not to refer to the 'terrestrial earth but rather to refer to the unique spaces in which human groups create and sustain their collective lives, interacting with their material environment'. Ibid, 1624.
14   Mitchell 'Quality/Control', 1625.
15   Ibid.
16   Ibid., 1641.
17   Ibid.

form of control over it.[18] Threatworks also have an important relationship to violence, in many cases playing a role in preventing and controlling cycles of violence.[19]

The work of Michel de Certeau exerts a prominent influence in this scholarship, in particular, his 1984 book, *The Practice of Everyday Life*.[20] Here, de Certeau highlights the ways in which seemingly ordinary practices such as walking and dwelling can be central to the ways that individuals navigate societal control of their actions. De Certeau describes these practices as 'tactics' through which individuals attempt to carve out spaces for themselves while taking into account the institutions of power.[21] This term is an attempt to capture the way in which, despite official plans, goals and visions, individuals can create alternative visions, contest these plans or negotiate around them, by using the subtle, flexible and resourceful tactics at their disposal.[22] Central to de Certeau's work is the distinction between 'tactics' and 'strategies'. While strategies imply 'concerted action, enabled by rules, order and control over production, towards desired goals', tactics 'have a quality of flexibility to the immediate contexts'.[23] Tactics tend to be subtle and small, and are often shifting and transient as they must 'seize on the wing the possibilities that offer themselves at any given moment'.[24] What this distinction makes clear, then, is that strategies are the domain of the powerful, while tactics are the art of the less powerful.[25]

Building on de Certeau's insights, much of the scholarship on everyday peace is interested in the everyday as a site of resistance to liberal interventions and/or as an alternative site of knowledge for peacebuilding.[26] Understood in this way, the everyday, like the closely related concept of hybridity, provides an important corrective to the 'technocratic turn' that characterises the study and practice of peacebuilding, by bringing to the fore the role of local knowledge and agency in grounding the legitimacy of

---

18   Ibid.
19   Ibid., 1642.
20   de Certeau, *The Practice of Everyday Life*.
21   Ibid, xi.
22   Richmond and Mitchell, 'Introduction—Towards a Post-liberal Peace', 16.
23   Ross, *Raw Life, New Hope*, 124.
24   de Certeau, *The Practice of Everyday Life*, 37. See also Vinthagen and Johansson, '"Everyday Resistance"', 17.
25   de Certeau, *The Practice of Everyday Life*, 37.
26   See Richmond, 'A Post-liberal Peace', 571.

the peace.[27] This scholarship is also increasingly attuned to what Mitchell refers to as 'deep ambiguity of everyday life'.[28] What she means by this is that there is a growing recognition that the everyday is not only a 'space of resistance, agency, transcendence and the enhancement of life' but is also vulnerable to control, domination and manipulation by powerful external actors, both domestic and international.[29]

Another increasingly recognised set of ambiguities relates to the acknowledgement of the everyday both as a source of agency, meaning, security and belonging and as a site where inequalities and hierarchies can be reinforced, and where violence can be 'embraced and reproduced'.[30] This recognition is informed by a growing awareness of the diffuse, dispersed, complex and plural ways in which power operates and the extent to which any society is infused by multiple systems of hierarchy.[31] This, in turn, is fostering greater awareness of the ways in which 'individuals can be simultaneously positioned as powerful and powerless' in the context of different relational configurations.[32]

As the fields of critical peacebuilding and transitional justice increasingly intersect, it is not surprising that transitional justice scholars are also engaging with the concept of the everyday. Among the first to use the concept were South African scholars, who deployed the everyday as a critical tool to explore the ways in which discourses and practices of justice and reconciliation had silenced and de-historicised structural violence.[33] Many were inspired by the work of Njabulo Nbebele, whose 1984 series of essays, *The Rediscovery of the Ordinary*, called on South African writers to reorient their focus away from the 'spectacular' and monstrous aspects of life under apartheid to the 'ordinary'.[34] Heeding this call, these scholars began to illustrate the ways in which everyday life in South Africa remains marked by the racism, poverty and inequalities of the apartheid era, despite the Truth and Reconciliation Commission's efforts to mark a definitive break between the past and the present.

---

27 Mac Ginty, 'Everyday Peace', 551.
28 Mitchell, 'Quality/Control', 1630.
29 Ibid., 1630, 1632.
30 Alcala and Baines, 'Editorial Note', 388.
31 Vinthagen and Johansson, '"Everyday Resistance"', 14, 26, 31.
32 Ibid., 31.
33 See Gready, *The Era of Transitional Justice*; Grunebaum, *Memorializing the Past*; Ross, *Bearing Witness*.
34 Nbebele, 'The Rediscovery of the Ordinary'.

Beyond the South African context, an increasing number of transitional justice scholars are calling for more attention to everyday reconciliation or social repair. Among them are Alcala and Baines, who describe everyday social repair as:

> the myriad ways in which people pursue mundane activities and practices to restore the basic fabrics of meaningful social relations, negotiate or recreate protective mechanisms and provide some sense of continuity in their lives and sense of self in relation to others.[35]

In contrast to the conventional way in which the concept of reconciliation is treated in the transitional justice scholarship—to refer to 'resolution, remission or relief'[36]—scholars interested in everyday reconciliation recognise the open-ended, partial and situated nature of this ongoing process.[37] To put this slightly differently, reconciliation is viewed in agonistic terms; it is seen as a 'difficult, restless and unceasing negotiation'[38] rather than as a 'linear movement towards a harmonious end'.[39] This open-ended conception allows for a consideration of the everyday ways in which adversaries interact without necessarily being motivated by a commitment to forgiveness. It also enables attention to the structural inequalities and constraints that impede the ability of those living in so-called 'postconflict' societies to draw a bright line between the past and the present. Collectively, this scholarship helps to capture the dynamic dimensions of reconciliation, and its precarious, nonlinear nature.

Despite this burgeoning interest, the everyday remains a relatively neglected concept in the transitional justice scholarship, even among those scholars interested in hybridity. One of the reasons for this is that transitional justice scholars and practitioners (like their peacebuilding counterparts) remain preoccupied with prescriptive as opposed to descriptive approaches to hybridity.[40] There is, for instance, a tendency for scholars to be concerned with how local practices and rituals with sociocultural significance might be incorporated into—and enhance the legitimacy of—national-level transitional justice processes.[41] While such

---

35   Alcala and Baines, 'Editorial Note', 386.
36   Williams, 'Reproducing Everyday Peace in North India', 233; see also Ring, *Zenana*.
37   Eastmond, 'Introduction: Reconciliation, Reconstruction and Everyday Life', 3.
38   Norval, 'Memory, Identity and the (Im)possibility of Reconciliation', 251.
39   Eastmond, 'Introduction', 5–10.
40   The terms 'descriptive' and 'prescriptive' hybridity were coined by Gearoid Millar. See Millar, 'Disaggregating Hybridity'.
41   Baines, 'Spirits and Social Reconstruction after Mass Violence', 416–417.

efforts are valid, and important, what they tend to miss is close attention to the ways in which local practices and strategies unfold in their own right,[42] may vary markedly across different social and geographic settings and continuously evolve in response to changing contexts, circumstances and dynamics.

Perhaps the key reason for the neglect of the everyday is that the transitional justice field remains dominated by legal and political science scholars who are focused on institutions and are interested in normative questions. This leads to a gravitation towards local practices that are recognisably 'law like', such as customary dispute resolution practices,[43] that appear to be oriented towards the 'resolution' of conflict. What tends to be left out of the analysis is the range of seemingly mundane ongoing everyday practices, negotiations and activities that may seem, at first blush, to have little to do with dispute resolution.

Contributing to this bias is the fact that customary dispute resolution practices are far easier for scholars to 'see' than everyday reconciliation tactics, which are by their nature fluid, shifting and subtle, and as such inherently difficult to study. As Mac Ginty notes, sophisticated methodological tools are required to capture something that 'passes by, passes through'.[44] What is more, accessing the domain of the everyday can be difficult, and requires long-term engagement with research sites and language competence. It can also be ethically fraught, particularly if researchers seek to expose precarious coping strategies to public view. All of this serves to highlight the myriad practical, ethical and methodological challenges to studying the everyday.

Everyday reconciliation in Timor-Leste

The dynamic, social and relational dimensions of everyday reconciliation are starkly apparent in Timor-Leste. While it is now 15 years since the nation gained its formal independence and 10 years since the formal transitional justice mechanisms established by the United Nations (UN) reached the end of their formal mandates, the effects of the Indonesian

---

42 Ibid.
43 Waldorf, 'Local Transitional Justice', 158.
44 Mac Ginty, 'Everyday Peace: Bottom-Up and Local Agency', 550, quoting Seigworth and Gardiner, 'Rethinking Everyday Life', 140.

occupation continue to reverberate in everyday life for many East Timorese. An obvious barrier to 'closure' is the continuing impunity of senior members of the Indonesian military; despite some prosecutions of East Timorese perpetrators, those living in Indonesia were out of the jurisdiction of the UN-sponsored Special Panels for Serious Crimes and remain out of reach of Timor-Leste's fledgling domestic legal system. Compounding these difficulties is the fact that the transitional justice mechanisms had short-term mandates, a limited temporal focus (the post-referendum 1999 violence), and were oriented towards a particular set of identities and relationships (that is, the relationship between 'victims' and 'perpetrators'). This has restricted their ability to address many of the complicated and enduring legacies of distrust and betrayal that have seeped into local communities and families.

These legacies of distrust are a reflection, in part, of the multiple roles many East Timorese played within the coercive context of the 24-year Indonesian occupation, which included, at different times, forms of both resistance and collaboration. It is well known that during the occupation the heavily militarised Indonesian state co-opted individuals into its security and administrative apparatus at all levels and developed an intricate systems of spies and informers, fostering fear and suspicion.[45] In this coercive and corrosive context, neighbours and family members often denounced others as belonging to the resistance in part to protect themselves from being similarly denounced or as part of a dynamic of revenge/settling scores in relation to much older conflicts. Others infiltrated the military in order to assist the resistance.[46] Many 'played both sides', at times working for the resistance and at other times collaborating with the regime, in an effort to 'enhance their own power' or in a desperate attempt to protect themselves and their relatives from harm.[47] Elizabeth Drexler refers to these complex legacies as 'fatal knowledges', 'the particular knowledge that people have of past betrayal and complicity'.[48] Fatal knowledges, she suggests, 'are not inert facts but rather dynamic performances of knowing or not knowing'.[49] They might be seen as embodied knowledge of the past

---

45   See Robinson, '*If You Leave Us Here We Will Die*'; see also Larke '"… And the Truth Shall Set You Free"'.
46   Drexler, 'Fatal Knowledges', 76.
47   Ibid., 75.
48   Ibid., 92.
49   Ibid., 92.

that can, at any time, be re-animated in the present.[50] In this sense, they continue to pose powerful obstacles to peoples' efforts to rebuild ordinary lives and re-establish relationships.

Against this backdrop, people do the best they can to engage in forms of everyday reconciliation that might help to improve their lives, their economic circumstances and their relationships with their extended families and communities. These practices, negotiations, rituals and acts of everyday reconciliation resonate with Mitchell's concepts of 'worldbuilding' and 'threatworks' in that they are indicative of the ways in which individuals, families and communities are seeking to resume patterns of communication, exchange and sociality, as well as resist threats to their existence and exert a degree of control over their lives.

One example of an everyday reconciliation tactic can be seen in the ways in which those living in both rural and urban communities have been slowly reintegrating those who had fled, or were forced, across the border to Indonesian West Timor after the 1999 referendum. Around 200,000 East Timorese people are thought to have been displaced from Timor-Leste at that time, many at the behest of pro-Indonesian East Timorese militia groups. These groups, which had been armed and trained by the Indonesian military, wreaked a trail of destruction after the referendum, looting and burning houses, and killing more than 1,000 people.

During the period of UN administration of the territory, a formal repatriation program was initiated by the United Nations Transitional Authority in East Timor, in coordination with the United Nations High Commissioner for Refugees and the International Organization for Migration, and refugee returns peaked just prior to Timor-Leste gaining formal independence in May 2002.[51] Since then, a 'small but steady stream' of East Timorese continue to informally and voluntarily return to their home.[52] Due to a complex mix of factors, including the state's need to focus on building diplomatic relations with Indonesia, and the fact that these East Timorese are no longer classified as refugees but are recognised as new citizens of Indonesia, those seeking to return receive

---

50   See Das, 'What Does Ordinary Ethics Look Like?', 2.
51   Myat Thu, 'Displacement and Informal Repatriation in a Rural Timorese Village', 255.
52   Ibid.

little or no assistance from the state.[53] As a consequence, many return illegally, offering bribes to border patrol officers or taking risky paths along *jalan tikus* (goat tracks) to avoid the attention of the authorities.[54]

Given their extended absence from their communities, perceptions of their dubious pro-Indonesian associations, and the significant financial, social and political implications[55] that are entailed in uprooting lives once again, it is common for potential returnees to make multiple visits to their communities over a period of years before definitively returning. During these visits, people participate in family rituals such as weddings and funerals, and investigate the status of their land and their prospects for economic survival. Their embodied presence in their communities seems to act as a form of communication in itself—a sign that they have not cut links with their homeland—and as a 'testing of the waters' as to whether their return would be welcomed.

In the small number of communities I have visited where returnees have recently arrived, a number of informal practices are occurring, which are suggestive of the ways in which dispersed families are seeking to re-establish ties. For instance, the participation of families in everyday activities such as church services, and the resumption of farming, appears to be a sign that they are welcomed, or at least tolerated. Other signs of welcome include the donation by village chiefs of rice and other provisions to returnees, and assistance by members of extended families in the rebuilding of the returnees' houses or *uma luliks* (sacred houses). Ritualised practices, involving the slaughter of animals and family feasts, are also taking place at *uma luliks* and at returnees' homes. These practices indicate the significance, for returnees, of remaking ties not only with living kin but with the ancestors, and the land with which they are integrally connected. Collectively, these practices demonstrate how returnees and their extended families seek to re-establish webs of connection and repair frayed kinship networks.

---

53 According to the International Crisis Group, those who chose not to participate in formal repatriation programs by 2002 were registered as Indonesian citizens. International Crisis Group, *Timor-Leste: Reconciliation and Return from Indonesia*, 3.

54 Myat Thu, 'Displacement and Informal Repatriation', 256.

55 For instance, returnees must relinquish their Indonesian citizenship upon returning to Timor-Leste.

Closely related to practices of reintegration are practices of social exclusion and shunning. It is interesting to observe that, just as some families are returning from West Timor, many others are not. While it is difficult to obtain firm figures, some suggest that the population of East Timorese in West Timor currently sits at around 100,000 people.[56] Damaledo refers to members of this group as those who are 'guilty by association' because, while the majority were not members of pro-Indonesian militia groups, the Indonesian police force or the military, they comprise family members and relatives of militias and the Indonesian security forces, and thus are vulnerable to incrimination.[57]

Some East Timorese who do seek to return are not welcomed. A prominent example is the case of Martinus Bere, a former member of a Suai-based militia group who was indicted by UN serious crimes investigators for his role in the Suai Church Massacre in 1999 and charged with crimes against humanity. Bere, who had been living beyond the court's jurisdiction in West Timor since 1999, sought, in 2009, to return to his community to attend a family funeral. Some reports suggested that, after being recognised by members of his local community, he was detained and beaten before being handed over to the East Timorese police. Other, less prominent, examples of eviction have also occurred. For instance, a group of people who sought to return to their village in Same in 2014 was reportedly driven out of their community because of their connections to local militia groups.

These forms of 'rough justice' and social exclusion—which resonate with Mitchell's concept of threatworks—mesh uneasily with Timor-Leste's national legal framework.[58] Yet, in a context in which political decision-makers do not always adhere to the formal law,[59] communities create their own forms of regulation that help to police the boundaries of community and keep perceived threats at bay. These everyday rules remain largely unspoken and are shifting and fluid. They are also imbued with the asymmetrical, hierarchical and gendered power relationships

---

56 International Crisis Group, *Timor-Leste: Reconciliation and Return from Indonesia*, 3.

57 Damaledo, 'From Refugee to Citizen', 24.

58 According to this framework, those who are the subject of an indictment order by UN serious crimes processes for their role in 1999-related serious crimes should be prosecuted by the Timorese courts.

59 In relation to Martinus Bere, for instance, soon after Bere's transfer to Becora prison to await trial, he was released back into Indonesian territory, following the intervention of the prime minister and president. This occurred on 30 August, the day of the tenth anniversary of the referendum. See CIGI, *Security Sector Reform Monitor: Timor-Leste*.

of life in a kinship-based society. For instance, practices of eviction or inclusion appear to be based on a complex blend of factors that includes, among other things, local knowledge of a person's past 'mistakes' (in the form of violent crime or community betrayal), their perceived resistance credentials, and their relationships to others in the community, including their status. Those who are members of powerful families seem to have more community protection than those with less power, while those who are perceived to have played important roles in the resistance movement also appear to have significant social capital (even in cases where they have committed crimes).[60]

Another way in which people are negotiating the legacies of the conflict is through the subtle avoidance of, or silence about, certain conflict-related topics. Two topics remain particularly sensitive and difficult to speak of in public life. One is the issue of East Timorese 'collaboration' with the Indonesian regime. The second is the issue of sexual violence against women. The experiences of women who, during the Indonesian occupation, were coerced into long-term sexual relationships with members of the Indonesian military raise the spectre of both kinds of 'unspeakability'. Not only were these women subjected to sexual violence but they are also perceived as collaborators due to becoming 'military wives'. These women's experiences also bring to the fore complex kinds of 'fatal knowledges'; specifically, they highlight the extent to which local leaders and women's own families were at times complicit in their 'marriages', sacrificing them in exchange for the security of the village or family. For all of these reasons, public discussion of their experiences remains taboo and some of these women have not spoken about this aspect of their pasts even to their own families and children.[61]

Viewing these women's silences through the lens of the everyday allows for a consideration of their multiple meanings. It also enables attention to the ways in which, at different times and in the context of different relational configurations, women might elevate one tactic over another.

---

60 To give two brief examples, I was informed by an observer of the same case that those who had sought to return were not members of a powerful *liurai* (royal) family and, as a consequence, had little community protection or support. By contrast, a community in Los Palos had seemingly reintegrated a militia member who, after having served a small portion of his 33-year jail sentence for crimes against humanity, had been pardoned. Part of the reason for the community's acceptance of this person seems to relate to high status and his resistance credentials; specifically, he had been involved in the FALINTIL resistance (before switching sides) and was also a member of a powerful *liurai* family.

61 See Kent, 'Narratives of Suffering and Endurance'.

For instance, on one reading, it is possible to understand the women's silence as a consequence of ongoing structural violence and discrimination, which makes it difficult for them to speak for fear of shame, humiliation and ostracism. In this sense, it is a reflection of the women's limited social capital in a context where their survival is fundamentally dependent on the maintenance of reciprocal family and kinship relationships. On another reading, the women might be understood to be exercising a constrained form of agency. Their silence in certain social contexts enables them to fulfil their maternal obligations by building better lives for their children. It also helps them to protect their own reputations (and the reputations of other women), carve out a degree of social acceptability, and maintain essential social and political relationships with their extended kin. In this sense, it might be understood, at least in part, as a silence of 'civility' and a silence of 'pragmatism'.[62] It is a form of everyday reconciliation that is partly informed by a shared recognition that speaking about the past might be counterproductive and possibly dangerous to themselves and others.

Towards a more dynamic conception of hybrid transitional justice

As the examples drawn from Timor-Leste suggest, attending to practices of everyday reconciliation might help to enrich scholarship on hybrid transitional justice in a number of ways. In the broadest sense, the value of the concept of the everyday—like the concept of hybridity—lies in its ability to bring about a reorientation of our analytical lens away from elite, institutions and one-size-fits-all formulas towards the ways in which communities are experimenting with ways of living together. While not suggesting that there is no place for prescriptive hybridity, a focus on the everyday helps to reveal that formal, institutional initiatives—with their limited time frames, mandates and geopolitical constraints upon their work—will go only so far towards responding to peoples' everyday needs and concerns. The contours of these concerns often revolve around the complex dynamics of building and sustaining relationships, ensuring economic survival, caring for family, maintaining some form of control over the quality of life and warding off perceived threats.

---

62   Kent, 'Sounds of Silence'.

The lens of the everyday also allows for a shift away from the binary categories that infuse transitional justice discourse and practice, including the categories of victim and perpetrator. By attending to everyday negotiations and interactions, it becomes clear that these static identities break down and a more complex and fluid set of identities and social relationships emerges. I would go so far as to argue that engaging with these complexities is essential given the nature of modern conflict. It is no longer possible, in many conflicts, to disentangle the 'home front' from the 'war front'. Additionally, the impact of conflict is increasingly seen in the form of a low-level, ongoing, chronic form of violence.[63] Because of this, many people are implicated in what Primo Levi has aptly termed a 'gray zone' of mutual betrayal and complicity.[64] All of this means that a focus on the rigid dichotomies of civilians/combatants, victims/ perpetrators—and indeed conflict/peace—is increasingly untenable, and makes it imperative to consider how complex forms of 'fatal knowledge' complicate efforts to rebuild.

Attending to the everyday also highlights that efforts at reconciliation are *ongoing*. What emerges from the Timor-Leste context at least is that there is no straightforward rupture between the conflict and the postconflict period. For many East Timorese, the reality of postconflict life is marked as much by continuity as change, particularly when it comes to questions of structural violence, economic opportunities and 'fatal knowledges' of community betrayal. While tentative forms of closure and resolution may be possible, it seems that people remain engaged in a dialogue with the past rather than making a complete break with it. Through the lens of the everyday it is possible to move beyond a focus on resolution and to contextualise one-off 'events' (such as dispute resolution practices) within a broader context. This is a context in which people deploy a range of fluid, shifting practices and tactics in both formalised and less-formalised settings and within different kinds of relationships, and where an ultimate form of 'resolution' may not be imaginable.

There is of course a danger that the concept of the everyday, like the concept of hybridity, sets up its own set of binaries. For instance, the everyday is often associated with 'local' actors who operate in a different

---

63   See Turcot DiFruscia, 'Listening to Voices', 137–138.
64   Scheper-Hughes and Bourgois describe Levi's 'gray zone' as 'a morally ambiguous space of mutual betrayal and complicity with the enemy'. See Scheper-Hughes and Bourgois, 'Introduction', 10, discussing Primo Levi, *The Drowned and the Saved*.

sphere from the national/international actors. Mitchell reminds us, however, that the everyday is not a 'level of human organization' but rather 'dimension of human experience'.[65] In other words, a range of actors— both 'local' and 'international'—engage in practices of worldbuilding. The spheres of the 'local' and the 'international' are, moreover, overlapping and co-constitutive. In relation to the Timor-Leste context, for instance, the everyday reconciliation tactics of ordinary Timorese are necessarily entangled with, and constrained by, broader structural and geopolitical dynamics. Local tactics of silence and inclusion/exclusion need to be understood as a response, in part, to the impoverished possibilities of the globalised transitional justice template and the power dynamics that often infuse its practices. They speak, in part, to the unwillingness of powerful states to pursue the prosecution of senior members of the Indonesian military and the efforts of the Timorese Government, in this context, to pursue a strong relationship with its former occupier and powerful neighbour.[66]

Moreover, as the examples drawn from Timor-Leste bear out, the everyday is marked by deep ambiguities. It should not be romanticised or viewed as a repository of shared values. While the everyday provides a source of meaning, security and belonging for many people, it is also a site where violence is enacted, and inequalities and hierarchies reinforced. This violence is not only imposed by powerful outside forces, but is reproduced within communities, whose members are inevitably configured in asymmetrical relations of power with one another. All of this means that, just as questions are asked about the normative assumptions of, and power dynamics underpinning, liberal transitional justice discourse, they also need to be asked about the everyday. For instance, whose version of everyday reconciliation is being imagined? Whose interests does it serve? What practices of power does it disguise?[67]

Finally and relatedly, while there is an emphasis in the peacebuilding literature on the everyday as a site of creativity, resistance and potentially, of emancipation, the everyday emerging from the brief examples drawn

---

65   Mitchell, 'Quality/Control', 1625.

66   They also underscore the limitations of a focus on 'victims' and 'perpetrators'. Not only has this focus been unable to attend to complex legacies of betrayal and distrust, but it has neglected the broader injustices of occupation and exploitation that continue to have ramifications in peoples' everyday lives.

67   Williams, 'Reproducing Everyday Peace in North India', 245, puts forward these questions in regard to everyday peace.

from Timor-Leste speaks more to the ways in which those with limited power 'make do' with the resources, tactics and possibilities at hand. De Certeau's distinction between 'strategies' and 'tactics' is salient here, as it is a reminder of the degree to which impoverished communities have limited scope to engage in long-term planning for their lives and, because of this, tend to 'navigate the everyday tactically rather than strategically'.[68] This is not to suggest that agency and creativity is absent, but to recognise that the tactics, actions and practices in which people engage are often immediately responsive to the context at hand. They have a fluid, shifting quality, may not be planned or organised, and cannot necessarily be predicted in advance. All of this seems to call for peacebuilding and transitional justice scholars to develop more nuanced and complex conceptions of human agency that go beyond a focus on creativity and resistance.[69]

Conclusion

Studying the everyday raises thorny methodological, ethical and practical challenges. Without wishing to minimise these, what I hope to have established here is simply that more attention is needed to the range of successful and less successful ways in which people seek to rebuild their everyday lives in the aftermath of protracted conflict. Insufficient attention is currently given to these complexities within analyses of hybridity in the transitional justice literature. What I find useful about the concept of the everyday is that it provides a critical tool with which to examine the unique, diverse and unexpected nature of everyday tactics while also making visible the broader geopolitical context, the power dynamics at different scales and the patterns of inequality that inevitably shape and constrain those tactics. Perhaps more so than the concept of hybridity, the everyday also helps make a shift beyond formal, institutional spheres towards a focus on the ways in which ordinary citizens in conflict-affected societies navigate and negotiate the realities of life.[70] In essence, what I am arguing is for transitional justice scholars to embrace a rich, fluid and relational conception of hybridity, one in which the everyday occupies a central place.

---

68   Ross, *Raw Life, New Hope*, 124.
69   I borrow this idea from Veena Das. See Turcot DiFruscia, 'Listening to Voices', 138.
70   Mac Ginty, 'Everyday Peace', 550.

10

Post-hybridity Bargaining and Embodied Accountability in Communities in Conflict, Mozambique

Victor Igreja

Introduction

Students of anthropologies of Africa would have frequently heard the everyday expression, 'one leg does not dance alone'. Many Africans often like to reiterate the collective nature of their endeavours, even if this is not always the case, so that, to return to the proverb, the origin and durability, type and size, and gender and colour of the second leg does not matter, so long as the dance can be performed. The late Terence Ranger designated this sense of practical reasoning to face diverse life events as 'creative and resilient pluralism', which is embedded in histories of contradiction and contestation through appropriation and innovation. He suggested that such practical sense 'helps to explain the remarkable adaptability of African societies and individuals during changes of colonial capitalism'.[1] The implications of this adaptive capacity should also include how Africans shaped the actions of colonial officials and their policies, to the extent that the exiguous state bureaucracy that the European colonisers

---

1   Ranger, 'The Local and Global in Southern African Religious History', 73.

attempted to implement sometimes emerged out of 'ongoing negotiations and compromises with Africans and among themselves'.[2] The processes of negotiation, notwithstanding colonial violence, led colonial officials to subtly consume powers generated in the marginal worlds of the colonies so that they sometimes acted by violently persecuting and punishing alleged witches, which colonial laws had denied ontological reality.[3] In other contexts, the colonised were instructed to codify their 'customs', yet unlike the colonisers who regarded custom as 'ahistorical, static and to some degree unchangeable', the Malaitans (Solomon Islands), for instance, regarded their own created *kastom* as 'dynamic, flexible, and rapidly changing'.[4]

If I take these ethnohistorical analyses seriously, there are no strong reasons to dwell on hybridity given that the contacts among the colonised and between the colonised and colonial state agents and missionaries was never preceded by a state of being 'pure'.[5] Instead, my focus is on what I term post-hybridity bargaining whereby in Mozambique war survivors, community leaders and spiritual agents sometimes negotiate with state authorities the terms of their relations. Occasionally they ignore, gamble with or manipulate one another and state authorities for securing personal and culturally meaningful forms of accountability. In turn, state authorities also shift between taking diverse community agents seriously to ignoring, manipulating or exerting violence upon them as part of their attempts to shun accountability. The bricolage arrangements that shape these relations are not permanent, neither can they be predicted. Therefore, the focus should be on the politics of rebuilding social life in communities in conflict by analysing the shifting qualities of alliances made by diverse individuals and institutional and non-institutional groups, contingent modes of struggle and various meanings of violence. This type of comprehensive analysis unseats the current focus of hybridity which hastily assumes a permanent state of co-existing and overlapping political orders, predictable in their modus operandi.

My analysis is based on nearly two decades of intermittent research conducted in diverse locations in Mozambique, a country that was involved in a protracted civil war from 1976 to 1992. State authorities

---

2   Spear, 'Neo-traditionalism and the Limits of Invention in British Colonial Africa', 26.
3   Fields, *Revival and Rebellion in Colonial Central Africa*; Luongo, *Witchcraft and Colonial Rule*; Mesaki, 'Witchcraft and the Law'.
4   Akin, *Colonialism, Maasina Rule, and the Origins of Malaitan Kastom*, 6–7.
5   Stockhammer, 'Questioning Hybridity'.

have over time denied justice for serious offences perpetrated during the war. However, my systematic focus is on the centre of the country, which since 2013 has been exposed to a new military conflict between the Frelimo Government and the armed wing of the Renamo party. For almost two decades, I conducted research in Gorongosa, a rural district with a predominantly agriculture-based economy.[6] The majority of people speak 'Chi-Gorongose', and a minority also speak Portuguese. The region features political, legal and religious pluralism through the evolving presence of various local cultural groups, Christian and Muslim denominations, formal civil society organisations and state institutions.

The politics of hybridity in marginal worlds

Contemporary political analysts and policymakers have long attempted to explain the configurations of modern state institutions and political and economic orders in numerous non-Western societies around the world. Given enduring political instability, weak implementation of state institutions in national territories, and state incapacity to generate meaningful order, halt the impacts of cyclical famine and better control the spread of preventable diseases and violence, some analysts have labelled these states as fragile or failed states.[7] These labels have generated further responses among academics that have either reinforced them by exploring the array of causes that sustain state fragility or contested them by advancing alternative explanations to the seeming state failure. Of interest in this analysis is the notion of hybridity, which has taken the form of hybrid political orders,[8] and hybrid state perspectives and the paradigm of the transplanted state.[9]

Proponents of the 'hybrid political orders' concept developed it to counter top-down approaches to statebuilding.[10] At the centre of these approaches are beliefs that statebuilding around the world should be modelled along the discipline of the modern Western state and that prevailing fragile and failed states in marginal worlds constitute obstacles for peace and development. Alternatively, bottom-up approaches are

---

6   Igreja et al., 'Agricultural Cycle and the Prevalence of Posttraumatic Stress Disorder'.
7   François and Sud, 'Promoting Stability and Development in Fragile and Failed States'.
8   Boege et al., 'Hybrid Political Orders, Not Fragile States'; Boege et al., 'Building Peace and Political Community'.
9   Chabal and Daloz, *Africa Works*.
10   Boege et al., 'Building Peace and Political Community'.

highlighted in order to account for local resources, agents and dynamics involved in the production of hybrid political orders.[11] It is suggested that in hybrid political orders, 'diverse and competing claims to power and logics of order coexist, overlap and intertwine, namely the logic of the "formal" state, of traditional "informal" societal order and of globalization and associated social fragmentation (which is present in ethnic, tribal, religious forms)'.[12] This basic application of the notion of hybridity is useful in its attempts to tame the universal modelling and appetites of the proponents of the Weberian state. The problems with, and limits of, hybridity are highlighted by those scholars who have taken a genealogical approach to this concept as well as an ethnohistorical analysis of the encounters of Western European colonial officials and missionaries with social institutions and actors in non-Western worlds. Additionally, the limits are exposed when the concept is used to advance explanations of all peacebuilding and accountability processes around the world. In such attempts, the unpredictability, contradictions and limits of state and non-state actors and approaches and the struggle that traverses the rusting and essentialisation of boundaries tend to be overlooked for the sake of identifying two seemingly clear-cut camps—namely, state institutions and non-state actors—which coalesce to produce a putative state of hybridity.

The late Patrick Chabal and his collaborator Jean-Pascal Daloz acknowledged that Africa experienced major sociopolitical transformations during the colonial expansion, as well as continuities in political practice from the pre- to the postcolonial period.[13] Yet they argued that the European state apparatus that was transplanted to colonial Africa was different from that existing in the metropolis and it had distinct purposes. The historical analysis of colonial investment in most of the colonial worlds did not go 'beyond what was required to maintain order and a steady supply of plantation laborers and to collect taxes'.[14] For example, the institutionalisation of property rights was absent from the colonial projects of statebuilding in much of Africa and Asia.[15] Thus the notion of hybridity, which suggests an encounter between 'genuinely different societal sources that follow different logics'[16] and some subsequent

---

11   Ibid.; Brown et al., 'Challenging Statebuilding as Peacebuilding'.
12   Boege et al., 'Building Peace and Political Community', 606.
13   Chabal and Daloz, *Africa Works*.
14   Akin, *Colonialism, Maasina Rule, and the Origins of Malaitan Kastom*, 5; Chabal and Daloz, *Africa Works*, 12.
15   Doyle, 'Three Pillars of the Liberal Peace', 465.
16   Boege et al., 'Building Peace and Political Community', 606.

transformation evolving out of this encounter and post-encounter dynamics makes little sense. The ideal type of the bureaucratic state 'essentially remained a myth of the colonial mission'[17] and can hardly account for some kind of meaningful hybrid outcome.

Thus, 'the paradigm of the hybrid state cannot be taken at face value since the very colonial state which was re-appropriated and re-shaped after independence hardly qualified as a modern Western institution in the first place. The colonial state was but superficially akin to its Western model.'[18] Colonial officials manipulated local values and organisation logics for maximising the exploitation of the colonies; in their turn, local elites also employed the diffuse colonial ideas of institutionalisation to protect their sources of power and advance their interests.[19] Furthermore, while there has been a major tendency to neglect accounting for the role of women in these colonial and postcolonial political struggles, recent historical reanalysis based on archive materials,[20] and feminist analysis,[21] has contributed to shifting the current imbalances in women's contribution to world history and politics of making and breaking boundaries.[22]

Post-hybridity bargaining

The notion that 'a person is never complete' is a popular saying in Gorongosa as in many parts of Africa. The implications of this recognition is that many people in Gorongosa and around Africa keep inventing new techniques and medicines not to create a sense of completeness. Instead, these new but ephemeral creations are instrumental to reveal the various sources of incompleteness, and women often figure prominently in these revelations.[23] Unfortunately, these cultural realities and historical developments have not figured in the analysis of the advocators of hybridity. Yet it is indisputable that the notion of hybridity has gained popular currency. It has allowed an easy and rapid circulation of

---

17   Chabal and Daloz, *Africa Works*, 12.
18   Ibid., 13.
19   Akin, *Colonialism, Maasina Rule, and the Origins of Malaitan Kastom*; Fields, *Revival and Rebellion*; Luongo, *Witchcraft and Colonial Rule*; Mesaki, 'Witchcraft and the Law in Tanzania'; Pels, *A Politics of Presence*.
20   Thornton, 'Legitimacy and Political Power'; Vilhena, *Gungunhana*.
21   Nye, *Feminism and Modern Philosophy*.
22   Argenti-Pillen, *Masking Terror*; Igreja and Dias-Lambranca, 'The Thursdays as They Live'.
23   Igreja, 'Negotiating Order in Postwar Mozambique'.

knowledge of statecraft in certain sectors of higher academia as well as among policymakers of foreign affairs in industrialised nations interested, perhaps, in finding 'scientific' labels and justifications for taxpayers' money invested in those seemingly hybrid politics in marginal worlds. In this regard, I do not intend to further ruminate about the missed opportunities among scholars of hybridity. Instead, I suggest a move towards post-hybridity bargaining to acknowledge the flash popularity of the hybridity turn, but above all to properly account for the multifaceted outlook of power struggles that have unfolded in the production of embodied accountability for serious offences committed during the civil war in Mozambique.

Plunging in post-hybridity ventures is necessary because none of the various participants that I have analysed make enduring claims of representing distinct and permanent values that clash, conquer and subdue others' values.[24] Instead, the reality of the various participants and structures evolves in a context of floating boundaries, which has been variously acknowledged through the proverbs 'a person is never complete', 'one leg does not dance alone' and by a state police officer, who once told me during a conversation about witchcraft: 'As a police officer I do not believe [in witchcraft], but as a human being I believe'.[25] The notion that in one regime (witchcraft) a person (police) can be immune to submission and exert domination over others as well as be consumed with fear and paralysis (human being) cannot be captured by the notion of hybridity. Human beings mix and enforce boundaries as part of diverse struggles, which depend on what is at stake in each instance. From this perspective, some of the details about the struggles for accountability that I consider here may be specific to Mozambique, yet also demonstrate broader features of global struggles for justice. Internationally, there have been recurrent discussions over how to address culpability in contexts of serious offences. Over the past 30 years, national and international institutions have deployed legal mechanisms to allow witnesses to give testimonies of serious offences committed during repressive dictatorships and wars.[26] However, there is often a sense of incompleteness surrounding these official practices; for many war survivors in Mozambique, and more broadly in

---

24   Igreja, 'Testimonies of Suffering and Recasting the Meanings of Memories of Violence in Post-war Mozambique'.

25   Igreja, 'Memories of Violence, Cultural Transformations of Cannibals, and Indigenous State-Building in Post-conflict Mozambique', 787.

26   Hayner, *Unspeakable Truths*.

sub-Saharan Africa, justice and wellbeing and injustice and illness are related, such that addressing injustice and illness entails confronting not only the visible and quantifiable dimensions of evil but also the mechanisms and agents believed to be involved in its perpetuation.[27]

Imaginaries of violence in colonial and postcolonial Mozambique

The colonisation of Mozambique by the Portuguese colonial regime occurred through military, political-economic, legal and religious means. Portuguese colonial officials manipulated some of the traditional authorities known as *regulo* that led to the deployment of some of them as village collaborators of the colonisers. *Regulo* is the common name for the position of the highest chief in a village. The name *regulo* was created by the Portuguese colonialists but it survived the postcolonial metamorphosis in Mozambique. Yet some local leaders resisted while others were co-opted and still others joined Portuguese officials for their own self-interest, to acquire more power and defeat their local rivals. It is noteworthy that the mother of Ngungunhane, the feared emperor of the Gaza Empire (1824–1895), plotted with Mouzinho de Albuquerque, captain of the Portuguese cavalry in colonial Mozambique, to remove her son from power as he had become erratic and staged violent acts and killed many of his own people without clear imperial purposes.[28]

In central Mozambique, people's memories of colonisation usually focus on some of the actions of the Portuguese administrators and the *cipaios*, who were a group of African men used by the colonial officials as policemen to violently coerce the local populations into paying the hut tax and force them into labour camps.[29] These *cipaios* mimicked some aspects of African magic by adopting nicknames that evoked cultural imagery and ritual violence in order to legitimise colonial power.[30] The *cipaios* instilled fear in people, who were also ambivalent about the *cipaios'* violence. This was partly because of the ritualised nature of some

---

27   Igreja, 'Intersections of Sensorial Perception and Imagination in Divination Practices in Post-war Mozambique'.
28   Vilhena, *Gungunhana*.
29   Carvalho, *A Guerra que Portugal Quis Esquecer*; cf. Akin, *Colonialism, Maasina Rule, and the Origins of Malaitan Kastom*.
30   Igreja and Skaar, '"A Conflict Does Not Rot"'.

of the violence and because of the *cipaios'* determination and sense of responsibility and loyalty to their colonial masters during the fulfilment of their duties. The *cipaios* persecuted individuals who failed to pay the hut tax and fugitives accused of committing serious offences and brought them to the colonial administrator who rendered official justice himself, instead of 'a magistrate sitting in a court of law' as was the case in Europe.[31] In spite of working for the colonisers, the *cipaios'* sense of commitment and courage lured the local populations which culminated in the integration of the figure of the *cipaio* into the category of spirits named *mucipai* (plural of *cipaio* in Chi-Gorongose language) in the apparatus of local healers. *Mucipai* resisted the erosion of time and are the spirits that help healers to search for clients in a rather similar logic of the *cipaio* who used to uncompromisingly hunt his prey.

In 1962 the Mozambique Liberation Front (Frente de Libertação de Moçambique; Frelimo) was founded to wage a war for independence against the Portuguese. The country attained independence in June 1975 at the height of the Cold War. As in other socialist-inspired revolutions, the Mozambican state officials appeared versed in so-called 'scientific socialism'; they banned various religious and cultural practices and arrested and executed individuals believed to be involved in 'obscurantist practices' and regarded as 'enemies of the people'.[32] The legacies of the colonial rivalries among various nationalist groups in tandem with the postcolonial revolutionary excesses and the politics of the Cold War gave birth to a civil war (1976–1992) that pitted the Frelimo Government against the Mozambican National Resistance (Resistência Nacional Moçambicana; Renamo).

It has been estimated that one million people died and four million became internally displaced persons and refugees. Both armies fought for the control of populations in order to sustain the war. People under government control lived in communal villages, whereas people in Renamo areas lived in *madembes* (old residences). Renamo took advantage of the resentment harboured by the local leaders and their people and allowed local leaders, healers and Christian churches to operate in their zones of control. Throughout the country were numerous reports of abductions of men and women, and children were used as soldiers; there were frequent

---

31   Chabal and Daloz, *Africa Works*, 12.
32   Igreja, 'Frelimo's Political Ruling through Violence and Memory in Postcolonial Mozambique'; West, *Kupilikula*.

reports of forced marriage of young girls, and sexual violence against women.[33] Some parents compelled their young children (boys and girls) to hasten marriage as a potential protection against humiliation and loss resulting from rape, while other young girls did *ku toera mabota* ('go after the boots', meaning soldiers, to flirt with them) to survive.[34]

Cultural and religious rituals were as much implicated in the making of war as of peace.[35] During the early years of the civil war, Renamo soldiers used *piça wega* (burn yourself). After assaulting a communal village, the soldiers compelled the people to remove valuable objects (related to magic) from inside their huts and then forced them to set their huts on fire. This was to prevent the soldiers and the villagers from being persecuted and afflicted by magical spells. Burning the huts was a violent act and dispossessed the people, but the burning took into account people's magical and religious traditions. The recognition of magic and the necessity to act accordingly also revealed the soldiers' sense of fear in relation to the power of local traditions. Such a posture conferred a measure of legitimacy to the broader purpose of the war on the side of Renamo.

The civil war was aggravated by periods of severe drought and ensuing famine, particularly in 1987–1988 and 1990–1992, which claimed many lives. At the war's end, war survivors attempted to forgive and forget and move on without accountability. Yet forgetfulness was not always possible as war survivors were compelled through cultural processes to address their deeply unsettled divisions as a basis for a life in common.[36]

Peace agreement: Spaces of autonomy and amnesty law

Following the collapse of the Soviet Union and the end of the Cold War, at the end of the 1980s the Frelimo Government engaged in regime change. It adopted a democratic constitution in 1990, which expanded citizens' rights by recognising cultural and religious pluralism, freedom of expression, economic liberalisation and a multi-party democratic system. Through two years (1990–1992) of brokered negotiations,

---

33   Nordstrom, *A Different Kind of War Story*; Schafer, *Soldiers at Peace*.
34   Igreja, 'Media and Legacies of War'.
35   Lubkemann, *Culture in Chaos*.
36   Igreja, 'Cultural Disruption and the Care of Infants in Post-war Mozambique'.

Renamo was swayed to recognise the legitimacy of state institutions under Frelimo rule and the Acordo Geral de Paz (General Peace Agreement), consisting of seven protocols, was signed in Rome on 4 October 1992. The Frelimo Government agreed to attribute a space of autonomy for the traditional structures of governance, which created a dual ruling regime and was sealed in Protocol V 'On Guarantees' of the peace agreement.

Protocol V of the General Peace Agreement created pluralist and decentralised spaces whereby war survivors could engage in serious, albeit unpredictable, struggles for a whole range of rights including, although not stipulated, accountability for wartime offences. Yet 10 days following the signature of the peace agreement, the Frelimo Government passed an unconditional amnesty law (Law 15/92) exempting everyone involved in the civil war from criminal prosecution.[37] The amnesty law was followed by legal reforms that were publicly intended to create democratic institutions and practices based on scientific methods.[38] Of particular relevance for this analysis was the development of legal provisions that granted further autonomy to community leaders,[39] namely the Decree Law 15/2000 of the Autoridade Comunitária (Community Authority), which legally recognised various community leaders.[40] Within this context various civil society organisations were legally formalised such as one of traditional healers, known as Associação dos Médicos Tradicionais de Moçambique. Yet over time when the Frelimo Government realised that it was no longer harvesting the dividends of decentralised politics through control of politics at community level, the party cadres legally reverted to centralised modes of ruling.[41]

Pluralist social orders and embodied accountability

The state amnesty law did not manage to silence war survivors nor put a lid on struggles for accountability in postconflict Mozambique because of the pluralist nature of perceptions and practices of social orders, disorders, wellbeing and illness, justice and injustice. Ironically,

---

37   Hayner, *Unspeakable Truths*; Igreja, 'Amnesty Law'.
38   Igreja, 'Memories of Violence', 780.
39   Igreja and Skaar, '"A Conflict Does Not Rot"'.
40   Kyed, 'The Politics of Legal Pluralism'; West, *Kupilikula*.
41   Igreja, 'Politics of Memory, Decentralisation and Recentralisation in Mozambique'.

the Frelimo Government and main opposition party, Renamo, were also not successful in their vows to forget the past and focus solely on development. The newly created multi-party parliament was established in 1995 and mirrored a melting pot of diverse and hastily digested institutional influences and practices of the colonial minimalist state structures, Frelimo's postcolonial revolutionary enthusiasm and excesses, and the civil war techniques of psychological warfare. As the new multi-party parliament initiated activities, both parties broke the silence and used memories as weapons that denied one another political legitimacy.[42] Yet when parliamentary discussions focus on salaries and other member privileges, both Frelimo and Renamo parties speak in unison, and regard one another as brothers. This behaviour provides further evidence of how the divisions and symbiosis are not permanent.

At the community level and in war-torn regions such as Gorongosa, struggles for justice were manifested through protracted family conflicts and severe bodily symptoms triggered by the spirits of the dead, which returned to the realm of the living to disturb the alleged perpetrators and their kin.[43] In this regard, accountability is an embodied phenomenon, in the sense that it is inseparable from the lived experiences of war survivors, their relatives and postwar generations. Embodied accountability means that alleged perpetrators and their victims become tied through the suffering that shatters their bodies and everyday lives, thereby compelling both perpetrator and victim and their kin to act in the pursuit of truth and justice.[44] The victim seeks justice in local cultural terms, whereas the alleged perpetrator seeks resolution because he or she lives with a reputation of embodying *tserusso*. *Tserusso* means that the individual is often suspected of being an evil person. Such a reputation amounts to a form of social incarceration. The imprisoned person is known to be enveloped in a world of *tchidimadima* (mystery), which severely limits the person's pursuit of a life of communality and dignity. Since persons are not understood as autonomous individuals, 'but as nodes in systems of relationships',[45] serious violations also affect the wellbeing of the kin group of the alleged perpetrator, so that certain forms of guilt are also collective. Thus, in this sociocultural setting, health and illness is inextricably linked to the sense of justice and injustice, and certain experiences of illness and

---

42 Igreja, 'Memories as Weapons'.
43 Cf. Mueggler, *The Age of Wild Ghosts*.
44 Igreja, 'Legacies of War, Healing, Justice and Social Transformation in Mozambique'.
45 Ferguson, 'Declarations of Dependence', 226.

injustice are expressed in ways that escape the control of the suffering person and kin group. From this perspective, it is useful to think in terms of post-hybridity bargaining because it is not possible to predict when the embodied accountability will be placed *en demarche* for everyone to see and act accordingly. While it is known that embodied accountability can be expressed through the mediation of spirits of the dead in male and female bodies (although more prominently female bodies), still it is impossible to know beforehand which alliances (or no alliances) will be mobilised among community leaders, Christian and Islamic leaders, state police and judicial courts in order to attempt a resolution for war-related unresolved conflicts.[46]

In this region, the spirits are regarded as persons with their own volition,[47] and their rules are regarded as possessing autonomy from and power over the living. This conception evokes forms of personhood, whereby agency and subjectivity are also attributed to spiritual and natural agents, and these are continuously negotiated with the living.[48] The rules of the spirits and the changing customs of the living determine the seriousness of a breach and the type of resolution that should be followed. The most serious offences occur when people die from unjust death triggered by physical violence, extreme negligence or refusal to provide care. Such cases are considered as serious offences and unforgivable unless there is resolution. The rule is *micero ai vundi*—a conflict does not rot or disappear until it has been redressed.[49]

Gamba spirits, embodied accountability and post-hybridity bargaining

In the past two decades, I have had the opportunity to witness diverse struggles for accountability. The majority of accountability cases I came across were related to serious offences perpetrated during the civil war. Following the civil war, *gamba* (plural *magamba*) spirits came to take over processes of war-related accountability. *Gamba* refers to spirits of male

---

46   Igreja, 'Traditional Courts and the Struggle against State Impunity for Civil Wartime Offences in Mozambique'.
47   Boddy, *Wombs and Alien Spirits*; Kwon, *Ghosts of War in Vietnam*; Lambek, *Knowledge and Practice in Mayotte*; Masquelier, *Prayer Has Spoiled Everything*.
48   Igreja, 'The Politics of Peace, Justice and Healing in Post-war Mozambique'.
49   Igreja and Skaar, '"A Conflict Does Not Rot"'.

soldiers who died during the civil war. Following the war, *gamba* spirits became vengeful and demanded justice for wartime violations. These spirits also evolve to use the bodies of some of their hosts, particularly women, to work as *gamba* healers.[50] In this regard, women have become central to processes of coming to terms with the diverse legacies of a modern warfare as it was waged in the country's war theatres. *Gamba* spirits bear witness to some of the grisly events that unfolded in the context of tripartite relations involving soldiers, families and communities. These spirits prefer to speak through the bodies of the alleged wrongdoers or their relatives, and this is manifested through altered state of consciousness, which paves the way for voicing indictments against alleged perpetrators. Following *gamba* spirit possession episodes, the spirit's host gets post-facto amnesia (unable to recall what happened). *Gamba* spirits refuse the attempts of the local people and central government authorities to discreetly appease them; they want accountability through public indictments and deliberations to denounce the culprits of serious offences perpetrated during the civil war. If such performances are not offered, the host is doomed to suffer. The continuity of torment is part of the local ethic of reciprocity, which holds that conflicts stemming from serious injuries leading to death continue unless they are appropriately redressed. Specifically, during possession, *gamba* spirits publicly re-enact war-related events, make indictments and, while doing so, are violent towards the host's patri-kin. To the audience these performances evoke war memories that had been hidden and for the host/patient these performances evince severe suffering.

While it is known that present circumstances, often involving ongoing social suffering and interpersonal conflicts, can trigger serious disputes about violent events from the civil war, these circumstances do not determine whether disputes will escalate into open conflict centred on accusations of wartime offences. The manifestation of open conflicts, often mediated by *gamba* spirits, can mean that the parties involved failed to reach a compromise which could have entailed staging public performances of acknowledgement of wrongdoing.[51] Depending on the severity of the problem and in case one of the parties refuses to collaborate, the plaintiffs can increase their bargaining power by consulting a healer, community court, religious authorities or the offices of the state police and judicial court.[52]

---

50 Igreja, 'Mozambique'.
51 Igreja, '"Why Are There So Many Drums Playing until Dawn?"'.
52 Igreja and Racin, 'The Politics of Spirits, Justice, and Social Transformation in Mozambique'.

It is noteworthy that some litigants take their war-related disputes, albeit often masked in idioms involving spirits or witchcraft, to the police or judicial court when, in principle, these institutions are driven by secular projects and it is known they have no legal mandate to deal with such cases, given the amnesty law. Comparative analysis can shed some light on these conundrums. Peter Pels has suggested that since the earlier days of contact between European administrators and missionaries and the Waluguru people (Tanzania), the former regarded magical acts as religious, whereas the Waluguru regarded spirits and witchcraft as 'something to be countered by secular means and they failed to see why missionaries had to interfere, and government was loath to cooperate, in a secular measure for the common good'.[53]

When war survivors engage with the police and the justice sector in Mozambique, they enshroud their war-related disputes in the language of spirits in order to circumvent the amnesty law. State officials (district level) know that the amnesty law impedes both the police and the people from evoking serious offences of that era. Yet when the conflict appears enshrouded in the 'invisible realm',[54] the police can refer the case to healers. Nevertheless, the ultimate course of action is contingent upon the police officer in charge of the police station when the problem is brought to their loose jurisdiction. Depending on the discretion of the officer in charge, there is a likelihood that a kind of handwritten subpoena is issued to compel one of the defendants to show up, either in the consultation yard of the healer or in the community court.[55] Occasionally, the police officer can wink at the litigants and indicate that he/she is thirsty or lacking credit on his/her mobile phone, which means that, should the plaintiff pay the officer a discreetly negotiated fee on the spot, the officer can accelerate family reunion to try out a resolution by bringing with him/her the weight of the bureaucratic state structure (through wearing the police uniform and carrying the AK-47 weapon) to bear on the defendant who has refused to collaborate with family members. Still, on other occasions, the state official can embody state fragilities and find himself or herself trapped in beliefs of spirits and witchcraft both as a police officer and as a human being, thereby becoming personally interested in the case.

---

53   Pels, *A Politics of Presence*, 245.
54   Stroeken, *Moral Power*; West, *Kupilikula*; Wiegink, 'Why Did the Soldiers Not Go Home?'.
55   Igreja, 'The Politics of Peace'.

Thus, the officer can show up later, out of uniform, at the healing session to gain further knowledge that can be instrumental to allegedly defend himself and the state.[56]

Additionally, depending on the gravity of what is at stake, the police commander can request the services of healers to cleanse the police station and vaccinate willing police officers with magical potions, given the putative pollution left by alleged witches who had been arrested and held in the police prison cells.[57] Occasionally, the activities of state officials can expand to involve the district administrator, as was reported in the Ibo district of Cabo Delgado province in north Mozambique with a predominantly Muslim population. The local administrator granted support to Associação dos Médicos Tradicionais de Moçambique to engage in compulsory homestead surveillance actions to detect alleged witches and punish them appropriately.[58] One of those alleged witches was a *maulana* (a Muslim man revered for his religious learning or piety), who claimed that the healers invaded his house, shaved his hair and grabbed his Koran under the justification that they were searching for witchcraft.

Despite these alliances between state officials and healers, when state officials need a public sacrifice in order to expand broad base support and convey a sense of strength and control of intimate district life, they can arrest healers under the justification that they violate state laws by using excessive force and violence against alleged witches. In turn, healers can initiate a public defamation against the police under the justification that the police do not know what is required to subdue witches and maintain social order in their communities.[59] Lastly, sometimes war survivors approach the police in ways that both acknowledge and rebuff their existence by reverting to a kind of radical metaphysics that seemingly makes it difficult for secular-driven mindsets to break the boundaries of inner logics. For example, I once participated in the resolution of a serious conflict involving a maternal grandfather and grandson, which led to a criminal offence perpetrated by the young man that almost killed his grandfather. After first aid was performed at the district hospital, the nurses referred the case to the police given that in principle only the

---

56 Igreja, 'Justice and Reconciliation in the Aftermath of the Civil War in Gorongosa'.
57 Igreja, 'Memories of Violence'.
58 *Canalmoz* newspaper, Maputo, 15 April 2013.
59 Igreja, 'Memories of Violence'.

police have jurisdiction over serious physical injuries. When the litigants presented the case in the police station, they informed the police officer that the old man had been beaten by a spirit. The officer said 'the spirit might have been very strong to cause such a serious injury'. He transferred the case without enquiring how a spirit could have actually inflicted the physical wounds the victim had in one of his ribs. Given the gravity of the case, which the police have sole prerogative to deal with, it is seemingly incomprehensible why the police officer gave full autonomy to the people involved by not raising questions to clarify how a spirit could have caused those bleeding wounds. The victim, who could hardly speak to present his version of the events, saw his grandson walking free from the police station, and they headed to the healer's association for follow-ups.

This example elucidates that, in the relations between state agents and the people and among the people themselves, there are no permanent boundaries nor stable bricolages. These relations can be better understood when viewed through the lens of bargaining practices for a convenient order. This means that in these power contests, sometimes each side interpenetrates whereas at other times they raise their boundaries to cogently claim spaces of differentiation and autonomy, so that neither the interpenetration nor the sense of differentiation become a permanent state of affairs. Sometimes the people bond to increase their bargaining power. This was the case with the *gamba* spirits, which allowed many war survivors to attain personal and culturally inspired forms of justice.[60] Other times, the same people manipulate one another while establishing alliances with state actors (administrator, police and judiciary) to pursue personal interests. In turn, state actors also selectively make and break alliances to pursue personal and alleged state plans.

Conclusion

In closing, the notion of post-hybridity bargaining draws attention to the analysis of a more complex set of relations involving spirits, people and various state institutions and actors. These relations are not unidimensional given that the various participants acknowledge their multiple identities as in the case of the police officer who is also

---

60 Igreja et al., '*Gamba* Spirits, Gender Relations, and Healing in Post-Civil War Gorongosa, Mozambique'.

a human being; a leg that cannot dance alone therefore always searches for a complementary one; a person who is never complete thus always reverts to other persons, animals and nature more broadly, not to capture some sense of completeness but to reveal the sources of this incompleteness. In this regard, these notions and the practices they entail cannot be bounded by the notion of hybridity and the sense of stability that hybridity evokes. Post-hybridity focuses on the ongoing fashion and refashion of social life according to what really matters for the people in a given predicament.

From a policy perspective there is little doubt that the implications of the processes I have described and analysed here are marred with complexities. While acknowledging the intricate role played by diverse local structures, agents and resources is an important step, it is nevertheless not simply a matter of hastily financing them with the expectation that these agents and processes can become formalised and predictable. The conundrum is that unpredictability and malleability are key sources of innovation and social change. In this way, policymaking initiatives should include ways of empowering existing resources and agents without attempting to block their creative drive. From the perspective of post-hybridity bargaining, policy initiatives need to be experimental in most communities in conflict. For example, one experimental policy area could focus on specifically acknowledging the central role played by women in accountability processes for some of the serious offences committed during the civil war in Mozambique;[61] another policy area could promote the organisation of women in ways that boost and spread accountability practices to other areas of social and political life such as marital practices, domestic violence, corruption in community and state institutions, and educational sector and economic entrepreneurship.

---

61   Igreja, 'Traditional Courts'.

11

Hybrid Peacebuilding in Hybrid Communities: A Case Study of East Timor

James Scambary and Todd Wassel

Introduction

East Timor achieved independence in 1999 after 24 years of brutal Indonesian military occupation and more than 400 years of Portuguese colonial rule. With the aid of an international peacekeeping force, a United Nations (UN) mission installed an interim administration that set about preparing East Timor for self-governance. However, while its new-found freedom was much celebrated, persistent tensions, rather than unity and peace, came to characterise East Timor's society in the post-independence period. These tensions reached a peak in what is now popularly referred to as the 'Crisis'. From April to June 2006, a rapid series of events resulted in the unravelling of the six-year UN statebuilding project. National-level political tensions and divisions within the security services served as a catalyst for a wider communal conflict on a national scale, which was to last for nearly two years.

In response, a comprehensive, national-level donor and government effort was rolled out to address the perceived causes of this conflict, and get internally displaced people back into their communities. These largely generic, top-down responses included an intensive community mediation campaign and a raft of programs to improve educational and employment opportunities. Nonetheless, sporadic communal conflict persisted and, by early 2009, began to increase in both urban and rural areas. Clearly, the sources of violence were more complex and deeply rooted than thought. Longer-term approaches were needed with more local ownership, which would in turn require more hybrid strategies to engage with traditional social structures. As Leonardsson and Rudd,[1] and others in this publication contend, there is, however, considerable conceptual ambiguity around the concepts of both hybridity and local ownership, with the term 'local', for example, being employed to denote an entire country. This ambiguity is reflected in both theory and practice on peacebuilding in East Timor, where the understanding and use of hybridity has only slowly evolved with a latent appreciation of the highly localised scale and complex nature of conflict.

Hybridity is not new to the East Timor context. A range of government and international non-government organisation (INGO) and donor-driven initiatives have engaged some aspect of hybridity in order to secure local ownership since the early independence era.[2] In addition, the role of traditional authorities in community mediation and security is enshrined by Law No. 3/2009, which sets out the responsibilities of *suku* (village) councils.[3] Since 2006, however, hybridity has become a standard component of the mix of approaches to development and peacebuilding by government and international development agencies. Much of this is, though, as described by Millar, top-down and internationally created and administered hybridity.[4] How hybridity is used by external actors rests on an often idealised, or misconstrued understanding of what constitutes traditional, and what is local. As de Coning notes, the ability of external agents to gain knowledge of the complex and nonlinear social systems often involved in the peacebuilding context is inherently limited.[5] In East Timor, attempts at hybrid peacebuilding by both international and government agencies have frequently failed to reflect the heterogeneous and dynamic nature of East Timor's society, and the changes it has undergone during the past three decades. These attempts have also, until quite recently, failed to understand the very localised scale and endemic nature of conflict in East Timor. As a consequence, outcomes have been often temporary at best.

---

1   Leonardsson and Rudd, 'The "Local Turn" in Peacebuilding'.
2   See, for example, Hohe, 'Local Governance after Conflict'.
3   See Asia Foundation, *Reflections on Law No. 3/2009*.
4   Millar, 'Disaggregating Hybridity'.
5   de Coning, 'Understanding Peacebuilding as Essentially Local'.

This chapter adopts a case-study approach, drawing on the practical field experiences of both authors over the past decade, to trace the evolution of peacebuilding approaches in East Timor from 2006. It will analyse how both the state and international actors have used hybridity in tandem with changing and more complex understandings of both the nature of conflict and of communities. We argue that to be successful and sustainable in the long term, peacebuilding approaches need a much deeper understanding of societal dynamics, but also need to adopt a more flexible, nuanced and contemporary view of what constitutes 'traditional' and 'local', and recognise that there is more than one variety of hybridity.

This chapter is divided into four sections. The first section addresses the changing nature and understandings of conflict in East Timor, and early attempts at peacebuilding. The next section questions some of the underlying assumptions of these attempts by describing the impact of the Indonesian occupation on traditional social structures and some of the fundamental changes East Timor's society has undergone since independence. We then proceed to analyse the implications of these changes for current peacebuilding approaches. We conclude with a discussion of how more recent and more innovative peacebuilding and policing initiatives, both local and international, have acknowledged some of these complexities and attempted to engage with them.

The post-independence period

East Timor voted for independence from Indonesia in a UN-sponsored referendum on 30 August 1999. By this time, the violence of the Indonesian-occupation era and the struggle for independence had claimed the lives of approximately 205,000 people.[6] The violence did not end there. Almost immediately after the vote, Indonesian troops and their proxy militias began a nationwide campaign of murder, violence and systematic destruction of property leading to around 1,200–1,500 deaths and the loss of as much as 85 per cent of East Timor's infrastructure.[7]

Following the restoration of order, the UN Security Council mandated the establishment of the United Nations Transitional Administration of East Timor (UNTAET) to manage East Timor's transition to independence. UNTAET's responsibilities were comprehensive, ranging

6   CAVR, *Chega!*, 2.
7   Robinson, *East Timor 1999*, 4.

from humanitarian assistance through to building the foundations of a new democratic state, including setting up administrative and judicial institutions and the various functions of government.

Despite the euphoria of independence, tensions soon began to surface. One major source of instability arose from the demobilisation process for the former resistance force, Forças Armadas de Libertação Nacional de Timor-Leste (Armed Forces for the National Liberation of East Timor; FALINTIL), and the subsequent recruitment process for the national army, the FALINTIL-Forças de Defesa de Timor-Leste (F-FDTL) and the national police, the Polícia Nacional Timor-Leste (PNTL). Many resistance veterans missed out on jobs in what they regarded as a flawed and secretive process. Angered by their exclusion, and by the fact that 300 former East Timorese members of the Indonesian police force had been recruited into the PNTL, they began to mobilise and engage in often violent demonstrations and attacks on police posts.[8]

Another source of instability, with no apparent relation to any of these issues, was outbursts of communal conflict involving martial arts groups—there are between 15 and 20 of these groups in East Timor. While there are few reliable statistics kept on this period, data from the Ministry of Interior indicate that, between 2002 and 2004, registered cases increased from seven to 37, spreading from four districts in 2002 to 11 of 13 districts in 2004.[9] The figures also give no indication of the seriousness of the clashes. A riot in March 2001, for example, ostensibly between rival martial arts groups, almost entirely destroyed two villages in Viqueque District in the east of the country.[10]

While generally glossed as martial arts group violence, there are close symmetries between membership of these groups and of descent groups, village boundaries and political-party allegiances. Therefore, martial arts group violence is more often than not a manifestation of deeper communal tensions driven by a range of factors, particularly land disputes, but often of a longstanding historical nature.[11] Despite the alarming frequency and scale of this subnational conflict, however, any mention of such conflict was largely confined to a few press articles, or buried in donor reports.[12]

---

8   Shoesmith, 'Timor-Leste', 250.
9   Ostergaard, *East Timor Youth Social Analysis Mapping and Youth Institutional Assessment*, 23.
10   United Nations Integrated Mission in Timor-Leste, Media Monitoring, Dili, 17 March 2001.
11   Scambary, 'Anatomy of a Conflict'.
12   See, for example, Brown et al., *Conflict Assessment: East Timor*.

Peacebuilding approaches in East Timor have until recently been largely reactive, and shaped by changing understandings—or misunderstandings—of the nature of conflict. Conflict was largely understood in the immediate post-independence period in terms of the war of resistance against Indonesian occupation—as something that happened in the past. Beyond the Comissão de Acolhimento, Verdade e Reconciliação de Timor-Leste (Commission for Reception, Truth and Reconciliation in East Timor; CAVR),[13] which focused on investigating crimes committed from 1974 to 1999 and resolving resultant communal tensions, there were few, if any, government or donor programs or institutions tasked with conflict resolution or mediation, or even major programs specifically addressing youth needs. This all changed after 2006.

On 28 April 2006, a protest by a group of sacked soldiers—known as the 'Petitioners' for their list of demands presented to the government—descended into a riot leading to a series of confrontations between the police and army. These confrontations sparked a wider communal conflict which initially assumed the appearance of a regional east versus west divide.[14] Most accounts of this period have focused on events from April to June 2006,[15] yet the conflict lasted for another 18 months. Once the politically driven east–west nature of the conflict ended in October 2006, the violence took on a very different, and seemingly random dynamic. Conflict continued in the capital, Dili, but erupted in a number of rural areas, particularly in regions that had suffered from endemic violence since independence, and in many cases, long before. There was no discernible overarching political or ethnic narrative for this violence; it now had a distinctly local nature, pitting family against family and village against village, driven by a host of factors including disputed land claims, payback killings and other historical grievances. This type of sporadic, low-level, highly localised conflict has continued to characterise post-Crisis violence.

---

13   The commission was set up under UNTAET Regulation No. 2001/10 (www.un.org/en/peace keeping/missions/past/etimor/untaetR/Reg10e.pdf). CAVR provides an early example of an interesting mix of hybridity. It was run by an all-Timorese commission, with assistance from international staff, but also dealt with customary village-based systems, supporting over 1,400 community reconciliation processes (Braithwaite, 'Evaluating the Timor-Leste Peace Operation', 292).

14   The west in East Timor is considered to be the 10 districts to the west of Dili and the east is the three districts to the east of Dili. See Kammen, 'Subordinating Timor', for a detailed discussion of this cleavage.

15   See, for example, Kingsbury, 'East Timor's Political Crisis'; Sahin, 'Building the State in Timor-Leste'.

Nonetheless, informed by the dubious twin assumptions of this four-month time line and that the violence was due to ethnic tensions and youth alienation—a product of rural–urban drift—the government and international donors rolled out a range of national-level vocational training and employment schemes. These initiatives were based on a rather optimistic faith in the redemptive influence of work and education on 'delinquent' youth. At the same time, the United Nations Development Programme and the International Organization for Migration supported government efforts to return internally displaced people to their communities through a process of community mediation and compensation to victims, in order to rebuild community trust and cohesion.[16]

Despite all these efforts, conflict persisted and began to recur with increasing frequency and scale. In the latter half of 2011, a series of highly publicised outbreaks resulted in about six deaths and over 100 houses being burned down, leading to the rather futile banning by the government of martial arts group training, on 22 December 2011.[17] Alarmed by this upsurge in violence, the government embarked on an intensive community reconciliation program, coordinated by the Ministry of Social Solidarity, which sent mediation teams out to conflict hotspots in Dili and rural areas. A number of INGO programs were also implemented in urban areas of Dili from 2006 to 2010 to engage with the different antagonists such as martials arts groups and violence-afflicted communities.

While some used prescriptive methods simply pulled off the rack from a completely different international context such as Bosnia, many used what could be broadly described as a hybrid approach. They enlisted village chiefs to mobilise communities to attend meetings and to represent their communities in mediation sessions. Traditional rituals such as *tara bandu* were used to encourage communities to foreswear violence and commit to peace.[18] These different programs met with mixed success at best. Quite frequently, conflict broke out only a week or two after a supposedly binding *tara bandu* ceremony took place. In some cases, no community members at all showed up to mediation sessions.

16 RDTL, '*Simu Malu* and *Fila Fali*'.
17 *East Timor Subscriber News*, 13 January 2012.
18 *Tara bandu* ceremonies are traditionally employed in natural resource preservation, whereby communities swear under a sacred oath—often accompanied by animal sacrifice—not to eat particular foods or cut down particular plants or trees.

Hybrid communities

As Mac Ginty and Richmond claim, some policy approaches to hybridity can be described as 'a shallow latching onto an apparently "trendy" concept'.[19] As they argue, artificially created hybrids, manufactured as part of a top-down peacebuilding intervention, can lead to sham processes.[20] Hybrid approaches to peacebuilding—as stated—are not new in East Timor, although their implementation has been somewhat ad hoc. According to McWilliam et al., *tara bandu* ceremonies have been employed by international agencies such as the World Bank since 2003.[21] But while government and INGO willingness to engage with traditional forms of authority is encouraging, these approaches are too often marred by inadequate understandings of the heterogeneous and fluid nature of many communities and local conflicts, and so are rarely more than temporarily effective. Part of the reason for this is that they are often premised on an idealised notion of 'tradition', a common set of assumptions about the legitimacy of traditional authority, and the demographic and territorial integrity and cohesiveness of Timorese society.

As Boege argues, tradition, or 'custom', is in a constant flux. It changes over time and adapts to new circumstances, particularly when exposed to external modernising influences.[22] East Timor has undergone major demographic changes since independence, with significant implications for traditional social structures. The country is divided into districts, subdistricts, *sukus* (villages) and *aldeias* (hamlets)—*aldeias* being the more traditional of the two latter entities. According to Traube, the Portuguese imposed the territorial-based administrative system of *sukus* over a genealogically based system, so that many Timorese do not recognise *sukus*, or at least only relate to them as a purely geographic distinction.[23] Each *aldeia* and *suku* is headed by a *chefe* or chief, and a *suku* council composed of the *chefe aldeias* and the *chefe suku*, together with five other members. While these roles are now elected, in many cases the positions are filled by traditional leaders who therefore bear both modern administrative and traditional authority.

---

19   Mac Ginty and Richmond, 'The Fallacy of Constructing Hybrid Political Orders', 225.
20   Ibid., 233.
21   McWilliam et al., '*Lulik* Encounters and Cultural Frictions in East Timor', 314.
22   Boege, 'Potential and Limits of Traditional Approaches in Peacebuilding', 437.
23   Traube, 'Unpaid Wages', 20.

Descent groups are geographically centred on the physical structure of a sacred house, or *uma lulik*, a term that is also synonymous with descent group and ancestral landholdings. The kinship system, as embodied by descent group, is the cornerstone of the Timorese social order. Traditional leaders at the head of such families are still the main source of mediation and local justice. They also act as a conduit between the government and their communities, facilitating government programs and projects at a *suku* level. This role is also enshrined in law and the constitution.[24] It is a reasonable assumption, then, to believe that if you engage with a traditional leader, you are also engaging with the wider community delineated by *suku* or *aldeia* boundaries.

Even in rural areas, such assumptions are problematic. The legacy of displacement and forced resettlement under the Indonesian occupation has led to an often tense co-existence between original inhabitants and family groups resettled on their land. In many cases this has led to conflict. As described by Fitzpatrick et al. in their case study of land disputes in Ainaro Municipality in the central mountains of the country, for example, there are about six significant former 'transit' or 'concentration' centres for displaced persons from Ainaro and surrounding areas.[25] These are also regular conflict flashpoints as the original occupants reassert their claim to the land and attempt to force the settlers back to their original landholdings, in a pattern common to a number of conflicts around the country.

The issue of demographic fragmentation is particularly pronounced in urban contexts. Dili has experienced exponential growth since independence. Forced resettlement and displacement under the Indonesian occupation and post-independence in-migration from rural districts has boosted Dili's population to more than eight times its 1974 pre-Indonesian invasion size of less than 30,000.[26] While there have been a number of waves of migration, following different phases of the armed resistance against the Indonesian occupation, most of the growth has been since independence. According to the 2010 census, from 1999, Dili's population grew from 100,715 to around 252,884 and as much as half of this growth is due to migration from rural areas.[27]

24 Everett, *Law and Justice in Timor-Leste*.
25 Fitzpatrick et al., *Property and Social Resilience in Times of Conflict*, 227.
26 Ranck, 'Recent Rural–Urban Migration to Dili, Portuguese Timor'.
27 RDTL, *2010 Population Census*.

Then there is circular migration, which considerably swells the population of Dili in regular annual cycles. There are five to six significant temporary population movements per year in East Timor. In addition to population movements out of Dili, in August and September students arrive in Dili from the districts to register for school and university. There are other seasonal movements too, such as people coming in to Dili to sell agricultural produce—which many do on a daily basis.[28]

Migration patterns into Dili follow global chain migration patterns,[29] whereby one family establishes a base and then 'sponsors' others from the extended family and home *aldeia*, helping them find housing and even employment. This means that enclaves of the rural *aldeia* of origin and extended family are established alongside enclaves of other migrant groups, creating a patchwork of different descent groups. In rural areas, an *aldeia* is essentially a family unit, but this principle largely holds true for established urban *aldeias* (although there is considerable variation), with one larger family dominating but with a number of smaller enclaves of other descent groups from other *sukus* or districts.[30]

Those areas composed of former Indonesian housing are different again. These new neighbourhoods were created almost overnight, when rural migrants rushed to occupy vacant Indonesian civil service and military housing. They are essentially squatter communities, or informal settlements, although many residents have formal or semi-formal claims to ownership. The cosmopolitan nature of these *aldeias* gives them a very different dynamic to the clan-centric traditional *aldeias* of the rural hinterland, or the still somewhat heterogeneous but older, more established *aldeias* in Dili.[31]

These informal settlements also have a highly transitory nature. A 2010 World Bank study found that at least 36 per cent of the inhabitants of one such neighbourhood had been there five years or less, and about 18 per cent had been there two years or less.[32] Such frequent population movements make this a highly fluid social environment. Social dynamics therefore vary from *aldeia* to *aldeia*.

---

28   Scambary, 'Conflict and Resilience', 1942.
29   Choldin, 'Kinship Networks in the Migration Process', 164.
30   Scambary, 'Conflict and Resilience', 1938.
31   Ibid., 1940.
32   World Bank, *Violence in the City*.

A recent World Bank report also described informal *bairros* or clusters of settlements within each *aldeia*, or within a suku.[33] One of these, for example, was centred on the *chefe suku's* residence, comprising almost half of all the settlements in that *aldeia*, while others were situated along the main road. Some areas were more spread out or even uninhabited; some were well served by roads and public transport, while others were more isolated or even completely cut off. The report also described a number of different communities within different *aldeias* within this *suku*, including political, clandestine and religious groupings.[34] Each of these groupings will have leaders who constitute alternatives to formal authority and structures such as *chefe sukus* or *suku* councils.

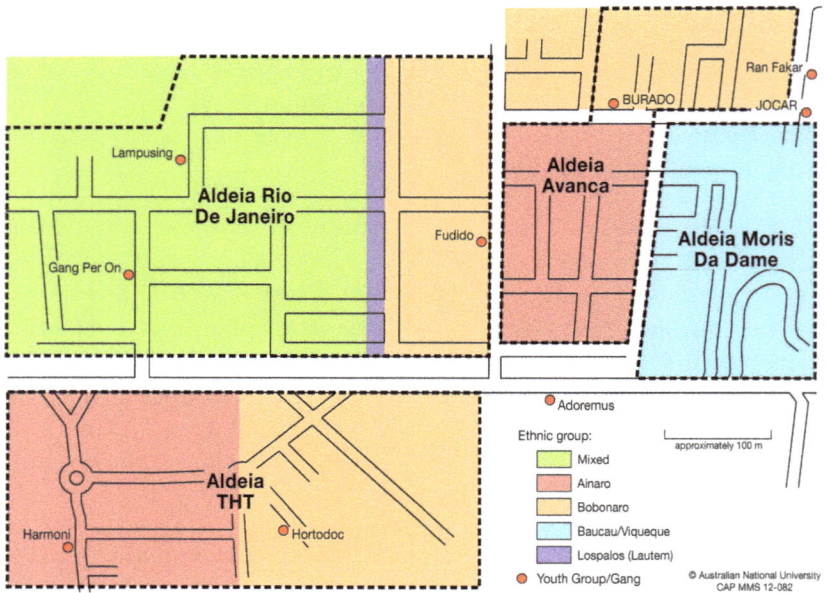

Figure 11.1: Linguistic group distribution per aldeia in Perumnas informal settlement, Dili

Source: The Australian National University, College of Asia & the Pacific.

Apart from varying population density and a diversity of ethnolinguistic and descent groups (Figure 11.1), there are also contrasting class and occupational differences. Some suburbs are predominantly composed of civil servants, while others may be dominated by highly transient market

33   Muizarajs et al., *Programa Nasional Dezenvolvimentu Suku Research and Evaluation Program*.
34   Ibid.

traders or shopkeepers—who in some cases are predominantly foreigners, such as Indonesians and mainland Chinese. Each of these constitute communities in themselves.

Questions of legitimacy, localism and contested hybridity

These factors have significant implications for hybrid approaches as well as more conventional approaches to peacebuilding. As a 2010 World Bank survey found, while traditional authorities were the main sources of security, there were often highly ambivalent attitudes towards them among their residents, varying considerably with each village.[35] There are a number of reasons for this.

One reason is that during the communal violence of 2006–2007, village chiefs alienated sections of their communities in many cases through sectarian behaviour such as involvement in or endorsement of arson, looting and intimidation (there are numerous cases around Dili and nationally of traditional leaders also being martial arts group or gang leaders). Conversely, traditional leaders have sometimes gained respect across kinship and linguistic boundaries, either through neutrality, protecting victims or through playing a mediation role.

Another reason, however, is that as settlement patterns in hybrid urban neighbourhoods are highly fragmented, these can also be reflected in the dynamics of traditional leadership. Given that traditional authority stems from family lineage, the ad hoc, patchwork nature of these neighbourhoods makes it highly unlikely that any of the village chiefs represent their whole village in the way that they might in a conventional, rural village. Even when a leader comes from the same district and speaks the same language as their community, this does not guarantee authority. While in many more established *aldeias*, residents have accepted the authority of leaders from other descent groups over time, in the newer *aldeias*, it is unlikely that a *chefe aldeia* will have authority over any group other than their own descent group. In some *aldeias*, where one descent group predominates, for example, the *chefe aldeia* will have more authority, but some *chefe de aldeias* may only represent an enclave of their *aldeia*—a cluster of a dozen

---

35   World Bank, *Violence in the City*.

houses in one case. As stated earlier, cyclical and permanent rural–urban migration can also change the demographic status over time, so that one group may decline in numbers while another grows, which may lead to the undermining of *chefe de aldeia* authority.

In some instances, particular linguistic groups may be more scattered than others and may have no formal or traditional leadership at all. In the Dili *suku* of Bairro Pite, an area particularly hard hit by violence in 2006–2007, one resident from the Lospalos subdistrict in the eastern part of East Timor reported that despite being violently evicted from their houses in 2006 by many of their neighbours, because her community is scattered in pockets over four *aldeias*, they had never been involved in any peace process, as they do not have a formal leader. To further underscore the pitfalls of crudely employing hybrid approaches to peacebuilding, the same resident claimed that initially her community was represented at an INGO-sponsored peace process by the same *chefe de aldeia* who had looted her house during the 2006 violence.[36]

In such a heterogeneous environment then, the use of 'traditional' rituals like *tara bandu* is also highly problematic. The Lospalos resident cited above, for example, claimed that while she and her community voted for a widely respected *chefe de aldeia* from the western part of the country and allowed him to represent them in civil matters, this *chefe de aldeia* could not represent them in the case of a *tara bandu* ceremony, given that this ceremony draws on ancestral sanctions to enforce obedience. Only traditional leaders at the head of descent groups can conduct these ceremonies and they are only applicable to people from these descent groups.

In addition, as well as extended family groups, there are more than 35 language groups in East Timor. While these language groups may share many traits in common with other groups, as Hohe points out, there are a variety of complex traditional dispute resolution and justice mechanisms in East Timor, varying with each linguistic group and with the nature of the dispute or crime.[37] As such, *tara bandu* is not common to all linguistic groups. According to McWilliam et al., the post-independence appropriation of the concept of *tara bandu* has effectively

---

36   Interview with Lospalos-born resident of Bairro Pite, Melbourne, 16 March 2010.
37   Hohe, 'The Clash of Paradigms'.

hijacked a diverse range of traditions and reformed them into a different and more homogenous regulatory practice, in which the state is centrally involved. As they contend:

> With this newly confected tara bandu, international development organisations as well as the government could press their conservationism and 'rule of law' upon the rural people. National NGOs, beholden to donors, followed suit. All development stakeholders participated in the idea that tara bandu was the essence of Timorese law.[38]

The constant process of rural–urban migration, as described earlier, poses significant problems for ceremonies based on assumptions of static, settled communities. People from outside who enter the area regulated by a *tara bandu* are not bound by its sanctions. Indeed, communities interviewed for a 2011 report on an urban peacebuilding project complained about newcomers from the districts entering their *aldeias* and fracturing painstakingly negotiated reconciliation processes.[39]

Such heterogeneity and the fluid nature of conflict also means that the source of conflict or tensions can be misidentified, such as through attempts to mediate long-extinct 2006 east versus west tensions instead of a more recent 2007 murder, or mediation efforts directed at the wrong communities.[40] As Boege notes, in segmentary societies, the legitimacy of the recourse to violence and the capacity to use it is vested in every segmentary unit of the society, which means that the potential for violence is widely dispersed.[41] As described earlier, symmetries or interlinkages between descent groups, martial arts groups and political-party allegiance mean that tensions between any of these entities can become mutually generative. In a sense, these can be described as hybrid conflicts—they can be generated by many different causes at the same time, and take multiple forms. Many disputes in 2006 glossed as martial arts violence, or as electoral/political violence in 2007, had a purely local aspect to them. Sometimes it was about pre-marital pregnancies, fights over perceived slights at wedding parties, disputes over a girl or, in one case, an extortion attempt on a bus driver.[42] Sometimes the dispute was related to a conflict originating in a rural village. Given overlapping patterns of circular rural–

38 McWilliam et al., '*Lulik* Encounters and Cultural Frictions'.
39 Catholic Relief Services, '*Laletek* Program Final Evaluation'.
40 Interview with resident of Moris Ba Dame village, Bairro Pite, 16 March 2010.
41 Boege, 'Potential and Limits of Traditional Approaches in Peacebuilding', 438.
42 Interviews with UN Political Affairs, Dili, 24 July 2006; Belun conflict resolution team member, Dili, 24 October 2006; INGO conflict monitoring team member, Dili, 21 January 2008.

urban migration, martial arts group, gang, family and political affiliations, these personal disputes erupted into much wider conflagrations that transcended static notions of localism.

This, in turn, has implications for scale—an important factor to consider in conflict resolution and peacebuilding. Nearly all the conflict of 2007, and since then, has been at the *aldeia* level, and yet most peace processes in the aftermath of the 2007 violence were aimed at the *suku* level. In one 2009 peace process, for example, the putatively opposing *suku* leaders gathered together were actually close friends or relatives.[43] The conflict was between sections of each community, not the entire *suku*. As mentioned previously, the violence was sometimes perpetrated by community leaders against sections of their own community. Also, conflict maps completed for a 2010–2011 Catholic Relief Services urban conflict resolution project found that conflict tended to recur at particular crossroads or junctures, indicating the highly localised scale of most conflict and providing important clues as to who the antagonist groups were.[44]

Equally importantly, given that communal tensions may manifest in different forms at different times and places, thereby masking the original root of the conflict, the history of these conflicts needs to be more thoroughly investigated. Therefore, even if all the antagonist groups shared the same rituals and all appropriate traditional leaders were present to sanction the ceremony, it might still be a futile exercise if the underlying dynamics are ignored.

Recent developments

Such complexities are, however, beginning to be acknowledged in donor and INGO discourse. It is now increasingly recognised that more care must be taken in the use of rituals such as *tara bandu*, and that incorrect application of the procedures, such as not having the appropriate traditional authorities present, can seriously undermine the legitimacy of the process. As a report by Belun and the Asia Foundation noted, for *tara bandu* to be successful in an urban context, it was vital to 'know the map

---

43   Interview with Bairro Pite mediation ceremony participant, Dili, 16 March 2010.
44   Catholic Relief Services, '*Laletek* Program Final Evaluation'.

of Dili', including knowing which communities are based in which areas and the nature of their historical and present-day interactions.[45] The same could be said for rural areas too.

With the realisation that conflict is more complex and entrenched than previously thought, and equally as problematic in rural as urban areas, two parallel government departments were set up with donor assistance. One of these is the Department of Peacebuilding and Social Cohesion, within the Ministry of Social Solidarity, and the other is the Department of Community Conflict Prevention, located within the Ministry of the Interior (formerly the Secretariat of State for Security). With representatives placed at a district level, the main remit of these two agencies is the strengthening of conflict resolution capacity and mechanisms at the community level. While there are many problems with these bodies—which face challenges similar to all government departments such as resourcing and coordination with Dili-based management—nonetheless, their creation is an important recognition that communal conflict requires a longer-term, community-based approach.

Between 2010 and 2011, Catholic Relief Services ran a two-year peacebuilding project in 22 conflict-prone *aldeias* in Dili.[46] At the very beginning of the project were two key departures from past practice. The first was that they did their homework on each community. They conducted an in-depth three-month baseline survey to identify not just the key fault lines in each community, but also the power dynamics among local leaders that prevented effective resolution. A common practice in donor and government programs is to work through *chefe de aldeias* and *chefe de sukus*. Apart from reinforcing patriarchal power structures, these predominantly male leaders frequently contact or include only their own family members in projects, effectively disenfranchising large sectors of the community. Recognising that these leaders were often the problem rather than the solution, Catholic Relief Services also used alternative actors such as local youth groups and even gang leaders to engage and mobilise their communities. The second departure was that participation was voluntary. Only communities requesting assistance would participate, and they had to demonstrate a willingness to resolve conflict themselves. Moreover, nobody was paid to attend meetings, as had been the previous

---

45   Belun and The Asia Foundation, *Tara Bandu*, 24.
46   Co-author James Scambary conducted the mid-term and final evaluations of this project.

pattern by donors and also government departments—the notorious per diem payments that are now widely regarded as an entitlement for participation in any project.

Implementation of the project also differed from previous approaches in a number of other important ways. Recognising that conflict was hybrid and multi-level, the project itself rolled out multiple and sequenced activities to target these different levels and gradually shift people's attitudes towards reconciliation. Rather than treat gang leaders or members as 'spoilers', as they are so often referred to, it recognised that they are often just the vectors of community tensions and included them in the process, even giving them leadership roles.[47] The project was run in partnership with the Catholic Church Dili Diocese Justice and Peace Commission, which lent further legitimacy to the project in a country where Catholicism is practised in tandem with traditional animist belief systems. In the case of one particularly intractable dispute, nuns accompanied Catholic Relief Services project workers in visits to the homes of the key antagonists, breaking the deadlock as a result. Five years later, approximately 18 out of the 22 communities continue to be largely free from conflict.[48]

After the divisions of 2006, substantial attention and funding has also been directed at policing, particularly in the area of formal institutional reform. While some gains have been made, there has been a gradual realisation that with ongoing management and resourcing problems, as per many government public services, and with the remote and difficult terrain of many rural areas, the police will always struggle to fulfil their mandate without the cooperation of the community. The Asia Foundation[49] has been running a community policing project focused on the intersection between state security and community practices as a means to increase community safety and security. The main aspects of the program focused on setting up 123 community policing councils (CPCs) in 11 of 13 municipalities between 2012 and 2016. The CPCs bring together elected community members drawn from local and traditional authorities and *ofisial polisia suku*, or village police officers, in regular meetings to discuss and resolve *suku* security issues. The community members are typically from former clandestine resistance structures such as women's, veterans' and youth groups. Of equal importance, the CPCs aim to help community

---

47   Catholic Relief Services, '*Laletek* Program Final Evaluation'.
48   Based on analysis of press reports and a field visit in 2015.
49   Co-author Todd Wassel was director, Security and Safety Program, and now deputy country representative, of the Asia Foundation, East Timor.

members know and trust police officers, in a historical context where the state has been largely absent from community life and where the formal police have often been associated with domination, and therefore regarded with suspicion.

With enthusiastic support at senior levels of the PNTL command, indications so far are that the program has been a qualified success. Compared with 2008, data show there has been a significant change in justice-seeking behaviours by the population during the period CPCs have started. The 2015 Asia Foundation survey found that three out of four victims of crimes ended up at the police for assistance in 2015. The key difference in the recent survey is that the police are present in the majority of all successful resolutions at the community level, providing a wide variety of functions. These include ensuring security and adding legitimacy, to directly participating in the mediations and negotiations. The police are now just one stop along the justice-seeking path, with 76 per cent of all victims ending up at the community for conflict resolution.[50]

A local non-government organisation, Belun, with international support, has also been running a quietly effective peacebuilding project. The Conflict Prevention and Referral Network, through a district-based network of trained volunteers, compiles information on violent incidents—which are published in Belun's 'Early Warning, Early Response' monthly reports—and conducts mediation. Network members are drawn from traditional and local authorities, women's groups, veterans and members of the PNTL.

Some of these creations emanate from the PNTL itself. One of these is a hybrid form of auxiliary policing known as security volunteers, which are part of a government-led initiative to embed police within communities. The security-volunteer initiative, driven by two district PNTL commanders, has been trialled in two particularly conflict-prone regions in East Timor—Viqueque and Liquisa. The security volunteers are intended to link the PNTL to remote rural areas, enhancing PNTL responsiveness to conflict, crime and accidents, and also to enhance local-level ownership of community security. These security volunteers are tasked with monitoring local-level crime and violence, which includes both communal conflict and gender-based violence. Their actual terms of reference are somewhat improvised and are an uncomfortable fit with more conventional ideas

---

50   Wassel and Rajalingam, *A Survey of Community-Police Perceptions.*

of human rights and policing—security volunteers have been known to physically 'arrest' people, tie them up and wait for the police or in other cases take them to the police station themselves.[51] Nonetheless, while there is a range of other contributing factors, according to interviews with local peacebuilding actors,[52] and judging by the considerable reduction of violent incidents in these two regions in press reports, these pilot programs have almost certainly contributed to a reduction in the intensity and frequency of violent incidents in Viqueque and Liquisa, as well as increased engagement by the police with communities.[53]

Some initiatives are driven by particular communities, and this is an increasing occurrence. In the district of Ermera in 2012, a district-wide *tara bandu* was held which set out regulations governing a wide set of public behaviours. This was in response to widespread community concern over the cost of lavish ceremonies including weddings and funerals and a variety of rituals, and a recognition that such occasions were also a common source of violence. Consequently, parents sometimes had difficulty with school expenses and even experienced food shortages. The local police commander has also trialled the use of traditional elders, known as *kablehan*, in a peacebuilding and community policing role. *Kablehan* traditionally mediate *tara bandu* ceremonies related to environmental conservation, and enforce sanctions. This role appears to be evolving, however, to include community mediation or conflict resolution, and even to resolve paternity suits and theft cases.[54]

A number of other highly localised community initiatives have also sprung up. One of these, for example, also based in Ermera District, is composed of about 21 members of the millenarian group Colimau 2000. Colimau 2000 was a key actor in the 2006–2007 violence, and although little understood, it is widely feared. With some training from the Catholic Church–run Justice and Peace Commission in Dili, this group has conducted conflict resolution sessions between local informal security groups, including Colimau 2000 and local martial arts groups. They also claim to play a preventive role by countering rumours that lead to conflict.[55]

---

51   Asia Foundation, *The Proliferation of Security Providers*.
52   As part of research for the report by the Asia Foundation, *The Proliferation of Security Providers*.
53   Both commanders have since been transferred, so it remains to be seen if the new commanders will continue to drive these programs. Belo and Rajalingam, *Local Leadership of Community Policing Practices*; Wassel and Rajalingam, *A Survey of Community-Police Perceptions*; Asia Foundation, *The Proliferation of Security Providers*.
54   Asia Foundation, *The Proliferation of Security Providers*.
55   Ibid.

Conclusion

As Mac Ginty and Richmond contend:

> hybridity is a condition that occurs, in large part, contextually; it is a constant process of negotiation as multiple sources of power in a society compete, coalesce, seep into each other and engage in mimicry, domination or accommodation.
>
> …
>
> It is from contextual and mediated, local, state and international legitimacy that a localized process of 'peace formation' arises. This means bottom-up rather than merely top-down empowerment [of] local and marginal actors, communities and individuals.[56]

These more recent donor-driven and locally initiated programs are not new in incorporating hybrid approaches. But as described above, many earlier efforts foundered on idealised notions of the value of traditional forms of leadership, locality, social organisation and structure. As we have seen, traditional community leaders have been politicised and mobilised in the name of sectarian violence in many areas. In localities suffering from endemic conflict over the past decade or so, these leaders and community structures clearly have been unable, or unwilling, to play an effective mediation role.

More recent initiatives have, however, sought to reinvigorate these community networks and, for the moment at least, have resulted in peace returning for a prolonged period to areas that had previously suffered from chronic conflict. Part of the reason for their success is improved local ownership, but also testifies to the more nuanced approach adopted to working with hybridity that acknowledges that times have changed. This approach recognises that there are a variety of other actors such as former clandestine networks, youth groups and even the church that are equally integral to engaging communities—that there is more than one type of hybridity. This does not mean that everything is perfect—there have been a number of violent confrontations between the police and communities in the past two to three years, and communal conflict continues to occur—but, overall, these developments provide hope for the future.

---

56   Mac Ginty and Richmond, 'The Fallacy of Constructing Hybrid Political Orders', 220, 231.

Section Three — Hybridity, Security and Politics

12

Hybrid Peace/War

Gavin Mount

We are all hybrids. Our polities, societies, and economies are the result of a long process of hybridisation.[1]

Introduction

It is intuitive to view peace and war as inherently opposite categories. Peace is routinely defined as the freedom from organised collective violence, or as the 'absence of war'. Conversely, war is generally conceived either in Clausewitzian terms as organised violence to achieve political ends or as a moral or legal condition defining the permissible limits of organised violence.[2] And yet, one of the founding tenets of contemporary peace and conflict studies has been to reject this binary 'negative' concept of peace as merely the 'absence of war' by asserting a positive concept of peace that refers to consensual values and the 'integration of human society'.[3] The enduring aspiration of how to achieve peace can be summed up with the phrase 'peace through peaceful means'. While the field has remained normatively grounded on sustaining a prohibition on the resort to violence—*peace through peaceful means*—it has also grappled with

---

1   Mac Ginty, *International Peacebuilding and Local Resistance*.
2   See Metz and Cuccia, *Defining War for the 21st Century*.
3   Galtung, 'An Editorial', 2. For an extensive analysis of modern peace studies, see Galtung, *Theories of Peace*.

questions of how, how much or in what way, military force ought to be deployed in contemporary challenges such as humanitarian interventions, complex emergencies and stabilising postconflict societies.[4] Strategic and security studies have also been grappling with a widening (issues) and deepening (agency) security agenda which has opened up questions about the utility of force to respond to so-called non-conventional threats and in responding to non-state actors. Both fields of scholarship have utilised the concept of *hybridity* in their efforts to understand the blurred lines between peace, war and across a range of challenges in contemporary world politics.

In trying to frame different notions of hybridity, contributors to this volume have differentiated between descriptive, prescriptive, analytical, normative and instrumental understandings or uses of hybridity.[5] In broad terms, hybridity has been characterised as arising from a process of mixing or blending, 'an integration of two or more systems producing something different ... where the whole is greater than the sum of its parts'.[6] Both its etymological origins (Greek, *Hybris*: violation of nature; Latin, *Hybrida*: offspring, mongrel) and links with 'controversial pseudoscientific theories' have been problematically associated with imperialism and racialism. Notably, in the contemporary vernacular, the term has acquired more positive overtones (such as the environmentally friendly 'hybrid car'). These positive uses of the term have also had a longstanding usage in botany ('hybrid rose') or animal husbandry ('the mating of a wild boar with a tame sow'). The notion of hybridity used here retains some of this lineage and acknowledges the concept has elements of *enhancement* built into it, but still recalls less savoury meanings of the term. I also want to cautiously retain the idea that hybrid outcomes can be viewed as an offspring because it serves a purpose of revealing concepts that have been discarded or neglected. Two things should be obvious here: even 'descriptive' uses of the term are likely to have some normative agency seeking to manipulate, observe or evaluate the hybrid output, and we should not imagine that modern uses of the term are any less positional.

4   Lawler, 'Peace Research, War, and the Problem of Focus'.
5   Brown, this volume; Forsyth, this volume.
6   From the initial brief sent to participants of the 2015 workshop.

One of the six themes identified by the editors of this volume[7] was the notion that hybridity has been used to reinscribe binaries of spatiality (local/global), temporality (traditional/modern) and governance (coloniser/colonised, state/tribal). Hybridity opens up space to recognise how the interactions between these categories are themselves bound up with the 'dynamics of power, agency and identity'.[8] Seeking to understand how these (already) hybrid interactions are continuously renegotiated has been viewed as being central to the human condition; one that negotiates subject–object relations and is manifested 'through crises of identity or changing relationships'.[9] While analysis of violence and violent practices are inherent throughout peacebuilding scholarship, it would appear that questions relating to the blurred boundaries between war and peace require further consideration.

The following analysis will apply a 'hybrid sensibility' as a heuristic tool to consider how the peace/war binary might be reinscribed. It begins with a review of canonical texts that inform peace and war studies and asks two questions: 'how has *war* been understood in peace theory?' and 'how has *peace* been understood in war studies?' It then considers contemporary peace and conflict empirical research to show how a focus on hybridity helps to understand how the major trend of conflict recurrence is related to the interstitial period between the ending of war and the negotiations of peace.

Hybrid concepts of war in foundational peace texts

Augustine is widely regarded as a founding figure of the just war tradition, but he also made important contributions by introducing the concept of *jus post bellum* and was an early proponent of a universal peace understood as the 'harmonic interaction of individuals with each other'.[10] The central focus of Augustine's work was to understand the conditions through which Christians could endure their existence in the City of Man in such

---

7   Kent et al., 'Introduction', this volume.
8   Richmond, 'The Dilemmas of a Hybrid Peace', 52.
9   Bassetti, 'Hybridity'.
10   Recent reflections on St Augustine by Zwitter and Hoelzl have argued that he should not be thought of as a founding just war theorist but a founding figure of the just peace tradition. Zwitter and Hoelzl, 'Augustine on War and Peace'.

a way that might prepare them for their ascendency to the City of God. This meant pursuing a life that was moral and just, even when engaging in practices as transgressive as fighting a war. From his theological perspective, the profane world was full of strife and disappointment. Even in a condition of relative peace, Augustine warned of the dangers of sin and political manoeuvring:

> For every man seeks peace by waging war, but no man seeks war by making peace. For even they who intentionally interrupt the peace in which they are living have no hatred of peace, but only wish it changed into a peace that suits them better ... even robbers take care to maintain peace with their comrades, that they may with greater effect and greater *safety invade the peace of other men* [emphasis added].[11]

The notion that war is waged for peace illustrates a form of conceptual hybridity, but Augustine's observations about agency and interest in the peace that follows is an inherently political insight demonstrating how he can be read as a key influence for contemporary hybrid postconflict analysis.

Contemporary just war theorists such as Michael Walzer have recalled and restated *jus post bellum* to remind military planners of the moral obligations that come with the transitional period from war to peace.[12] In his *Law of Peoples*, John Rawls also insists that at the end of a war, 'the enemy society is to be granted an autonomous well-ordered regime of its own'.[13] More astutely, he recognised how 'statesmen' must take into account the way that the dispositions and grievances of a war can generate resentment in the host community:

> The way a war is fought and the deeds done in ending it live on in the historical memory of societies and may or may not set the stage for future war. It is always the duty of statesmanship to take this longer view.[14]

If we now turn to Immanuel Kant as a foundational thinker of universal peace, we might also explore how, if at all, he conceived of war. Kant is most famous in modern peace studies for arguing that peace should not merely be understood negatively as the 'absence of war' but as a positive conceptual category. In *Perpetual Peace*, he developed the philosophical

---

11   Augustine, *De Civitate Dei Contra Paganos*.
12   Walzer, *Arguing about War*.
13   Rawls, *The Law of Peoples*, 122.
14   Ibid., 96.

case for the republic (or democratic) peace thesis and for a cosmopolitan world order. At his most utopian, Kant envisaged the abolition of standing armies and spies. Nevertheless, even in such a profoundly 'categorical' and normative work, there are signs of hybridity. We need look no further than the 'First Preliminary Article', which states:

> No peace treaty is valid if it was made with mental reservations that could lead to a future war.[15]

Kant's 'mental reservations' reveal how the formal process of making peace can itself be a potential cause of future war. In the modern era, one need only think of the ruptures and resentment encoded in famous peace treaties from Versailles, the Arusha Accords or the Dayton Agreement to see how formal conflict resolution structures can serve to calcify grievances and resentment which may be at least partly used to rationalise the next wave of violence.

Brian Orend has recently applied a Kantian cosmopolitan framework to the question of justice after conflict and arrived at a number of principles that he feels ought to peacefully guide the transition from war to peace.[16] More controversially, Roger Scruton asserted there were 'good Kantian reasons' for the 'civilised world' to 'take pre-emptive measures' in the Iraq war.[17] A decade later, Scruton declared that Iraq was a 'write-off' because liberal principles had not, and perhaps would never, take hold. He argued that the 2003 Iraq war failed because it was formed on two fundamentally naive assumptions:

> First, that democracy is the default position in politics, and secondly that you can achieve democracy even where there is no genuine nation state … What makes a democrat possible? The answer is: the nation. When you and I define our loyalty in national terms, we can put aside all differences of religion, tribe and ethnicity, and submit to a shared system of law.[18]

Dynamics of power, legitimacy and identity are revealed in this hybrid reading of Kant's moral philosophy. Kantian observation about peace treaties forewarns about how failing to apply moral philosophy to formal peace negotiations can become the seeds of grievance for future war and

---

15 Kant, *Perpetual Peace and Other Essays on Politics, History, and Morals.*
16 The principles are: proportionality and publicity; rights vindication; discrimination; punishment #1 (leaders), #2 (soldiers); compensation; and rehabilitation (Orend, 'Justice after War', 55–56; see also Orend, *War and International Justice*).
17 Scruton, 'Immanuel Kant and the Iraq War'.
18 Scruton, 'Why Iraq Is a Write-Off'. See also Schmidt, *Rethinking Democracy Promotion.*

organised violence. It highlights how interstitial periods of transition from war to peace are often the most challenging and volatile. While Kantian cosmopolitanism (especially in Scruton's interpretation) can be accused of imposing ethnocentric 'civilising' liberal state structures in interventions such as Iraq, what is revealed through the application of Kantian philosophy is the renegotiation of cultural identity during periods of conflict transformation. As James Gow observed in his analysis of the Balkan wars:

> A critical challenge to legitimacy at a governmental level is not so serious as a challenge at the community level where the very existence of a political community, such as the Yugoslav state, is brought into question.[19]

The above analysis has brought us to a curious twist. At the cosmopolitan 'international' level, the tacit conditions for war following a peace settlement reside in the neglect of, or failure to implement, core liberal principles. But, the 'mental reservations' that appear to be most responsible for perpetual conflict reside in the stubbornness of tribal or ethnic loyalties and authority. For Scruton, the failure to form a national identity lies at the heart of naive liberal interventions. It follows that externally imposed coercive liberal 'nation-building' projects have been the central target of criticism in the current hybrid peacekeeping literature.

Hybrid notions of peace in foundational war texts

Turning now to foundational texts on war, we may begin with Thomas Hobbes as the pre-eminent theorist on the state of nature being a condition of war of all against all. Hobbes's philosophy asserts that the human condition is governed by a restless desire for power in us all and the condition of fear that this creates in others. The purpose of a commonwealth (or *leviathan*) is to assuage these fears among its citizens. Hobbes's views on the state of nature need not be recited except that we appear to have persistently forgotten how the passage ends:

> Hereby it is manifest that during the time men live without a common power to keep them all in awe, they are in that condition which is called war; and such a war as is of every man against every man ... so the nature

---

19   Gow, *Legitimacy and the Military*.

of war consisteth not in actual fighting, but in the known disposition thereto during all the time there is no assurance to the contrary. *All other time is PEACE* [emphasis added].[20]

Even though Hobbes was writing amid a protracted civil war, his notion of war of every man against every man was hypothetical and, most intriguingly, understood as an ontological 'disposition thereto' or a state of mind. The commonwealth is assigned the responsibility to provide the normal condition of peace at all other times and it would appear that Hobbes also understood that the process of reconstituting a commonwealth required complex negotiations of power, legitimacy and identity. Central to this task was the ability for the state to command a historical narrative of possession and belonging. In this regard, his analysis concerning the dissolution of commonwealths is astonishingly prescient and relevant for contemporary postconflict analysis.

> That they [states] will all of them justifie the War, by which their power was first gotten, and whereon (as they think) their Right dependeth … Therefore I put down for one of the most effectuall seeds of the Death of any State, that the Conquerers require not onely a Submission of mens actions to them for the future, but also an approbation of their actions past; when there is scarce a Common-wealth in the world, whose beginnings can be justified.[21]

While the above emphasis on Hobbes's vision of peace may seem tenuous for some, our neglect of his theory of the peaceful condition of normal political life means that we have also tended to overlook other nuances in his philosophy that have attracted considerable critical attention in recent international political theory.

In *The Empire of Security*,[22] William Bain reminded us that Hobbes provided one of the most succinct and pertinent conceptions of security when he declared: *the safety of the people is the supreme law.*[23] Bain goes on to explain that the term 'safety' has critical and contemporary relevance and should be differentiated from cruder notions of mere survival: 'not the sole preservation of life in what condition soever, but in order to its

20   Hobbes, *Leviathan or the Matter, Forme, and Power of a Common-Wealth Ecclesiasticall and Civill*, ch. 13.
21   Ibid., bk 29.
22   Bain, *The Empire of Security and the Safety of the People*.
23   Hobbes, *De Cive (The Citizen)*, bk 13.2.

happiness'.[24] More interestingly for our purposes of searching for a hybrid sensibility is how Hobbes conceives of 'the people' as 'not one civill Person, namely the City it selfe which governs, but the multitude of subjects which are governed'.[25] In part, Hobbes is distinguishing the citizenry from his notion of the leviathan as an embodied political actor. But the above statement may also refer to a wider sense of the 'people' which includes all of those who reside under the aegis of the commonwealth. We might, for instance, imagine he is contemplating the challenge of living together after the experience of a civil war.

Another major re-examination of the Hobbesian legacy asserts that the persistent misrepresentation of Hobbes has created a significant distortion in how international relations understands itself. Reassessing Hobbes is a necessary step in helping international relations move past crude notions of state centrism.

> International theory can be understood as a field of *politics* rather than just the study of the *inter-state* clash of national interests in a balance of power. Hobbes is self-consciously aware of the intimate connection between sovereignty and what we would now call politics ... He establishes his conception of sovereignty—the greatest accomplishment of the artifice of men—precisely as a solution to politics.[26]

Recent reinterpretations of Hobbes provide an opportunity to view this profoundly influential work in new ways. One aspect that must be borne out when viewing Hobbes as a theorist advocating the 'safety of the people' is that he was writing amid such violence. This is perhaps symptomatic of Western liberal philosophy whereby 'modern liberalism begins by forgetting the English revolution'.[27] Hobbes's aspiration to find a solution to the problem of human nature, as he saw it, was precisely to understand the dynamics of power, agency and identity during a tumultuous period of civil war and postconflict transformation.

At first glance, it may seem ambitious to search for a theory of peace in Clausewitz's seminal work, *On War*.[28] In addition to his most famous aphorisms considered below, he also stated 'to secure peace is to prepare for war'. Basil Liddel Hart also accused Clausewitz of making policy

---

24 Ibid., bk 8.4.
25 Ibid., bk 13.3.
26 Prokhovnik and Slomp, *International Political Theory after Hobbes*, 189.
27 Feltham, *Anatomy of Failure*.
28 Clausewitz, *On War*.

the slave of strategy and in doing so 'looked only to the end of war, not beyond war to the subsequent peace'.[29] More recently, Gideon Rose has taken a different view, perhaps not of Clausewitz, but of how his work might inform analyses of these transitional periods. In *How Wars End*, Rose documented the failure of successive United States administrations to satisfactorily manage the conclusion of six wars spanning the twentieth and early twenty-first century.[30] Central to his argument is what he calls the 'Clausewitzian challenge':

> Wars actually have two equally important aspects. One is negative, or coercive; this is the part about fighting, about beating up the bad guys. The other is positive, and is all about politics. And this is the part that, as in Iraq, is usually overlooked or misunderstood.[31]

When we think about this notion of the 'other means' in Clausewitz, we can discern that he has firm ideas about the nature of what might constitute normal political life. Like Hobbes, Clausewitz concludes his aphorism with an indication that we might all share a consensual understanding of the everyday or the 'normal' means of political life.[32] What Rose found in his application of the political meaning of war in Clausewitz was a fixation in United States military and political leadership to win the war combined with a persistent failure to build the peace. The mindset and institutional momentum were entirely oriented towards the former at the expense of the latter:

> Both the planners and the commander had been schooled to see fighting as the realm of war and thus attached lesser importance to post-war issues. No officer in the headquarters was prepared to argue for actions that would siphon resources from the war fighting effort, when the fighting had not yet begun ... Who could blame them? The business of the military is war and war is fighting ... Only a fool would propose hurting the war fighting effort to address post-war conditions that might or might not occur.[33]

---

29   Howard, 'The Influence of Clausewitz', 39–40.
30   Rose, *How Wars End*.
31   Ibid. Clausewitz's two concepts of war were: (1) an act of force to compel our enemy to do our will and (2) nothing but a continuation of policy by other means. Clausewitz, *On War*, bk 1.1, 24.
32   This is not to say that we find a pluralist and vernacular understanding of everyday experience of security and politics in Clausewitz. For a contemporary hybrid analysis of this see Luckman and Kirk, 'Understanding Security in the Vernacular'.
33   United States military planner Lieutenant Colonel Steven Petersen. Cited in Rose, *How Wars End*, ch. 1.

It is routinely observed that strategic failures are often attributable to the phenomenon of commanders still trying to 'fight the last war'. What Rose showed was that successive United States administrations failed to win the last peace. Clausewitz continues to exert enormous influence over contemporary war studies. Contemporary Clausewitzians acknowledge that while the character of war will always be susceptible to change with political, economic, social and technological shifts, the essential nature of war as violent, instrumental and political remains constant.[34] Even within this traditionalist mode of war studies, we can discern profoundly constitutive, dynamic and hybrid understandings of the relationship between war and political legitimacy. For instance, postcolonial theorists Tarak Barkawi and Shane Brighton call for the *decentring* of war, describing how:

> the changing character of war concerns relations between the transformation of polities and societies through war and the effects of those transformations on war itself ... war disrupts knowledge (and thereby generates the need for new knowledge) and how this process of disruption and generation has direct consequence for political authority ... the formulation 'war *in* society' ... attending to the co-constitutive character of war and society relations in world politics.[35]

More radical scholars have also returned to war studies to reclaim the ground, especially as an embodied and deeply social experience. Acknowledging that she has 'no stomach for war', postmodern feminist Christine Sylvester nevertheless insists that it should be examined from a critical perspective because:

> war cannot be fully apprehended unless it is studied up from people's physical, emotional, and social experiences, not only down from 'high politics' ... [and] bodies, always contested identities, can become bewildering in their multiplicities and overlapping identities during war.[36]

In using Clausewitz's enduring notion of war as a continuation of policy or politics, we arrive at a point on our hybrid journey where the most famous theorist of war has provided one of the most enduring insights into the possibilities of peace. Following Rose's analysis, Clausewitz reminds us that the failure to think through the implications of rebuilding consensual and pluralist political communities is likely to lead to conflict recurrence. Contemporary war studies is extending this notion of politics by other

---

34 Strachan and Scheipers, *The Changing Character of War*.
35 Barkawi and Brighton, 'Conclusion: Absent War Studies?', 525f.
36 Sylvester, *War as Experience*, 2, 117.

means into co-constitutive epistemological and social understandings of war (and peace). The 'experiential turn' in international relations has set its sights on the conventional intellectual terrain of war studies precisely because it seeks to reveal the emotional and embodied experiences of people, especially those who are most seriously affected and marginalised, by the practices of modern warfare.

Conflict dynamics and recurrence

The above ruminations on philosophical arguments suggest that binary categories of 'war' and 'peace' have always been viewed critically and that notions of hybridity are quite discernible in formulations such as Augustine's caution about the 'invasion of peace' or Kant's 'tacit conditions' of war. Hybridity encourages a focus on the dynamics of power, legitimacy and identity in 'conflict affected' societies. Whereas Clausewitz had established the idea that war was a continuation of politics by other means, hybrid approaches to peace recalibrate that aphorism to reveal how the interstitial space between war and peace is also inherently anchored to the 'political'.

Current empirical research on the trends of armed conflict also reveals that the dominant trend over the past decade especially has been the high rate of recurrence of armed conflict. Leading providers of armed conflict data such as the Uppsala Conflict Data Program confirm that the dominant trend over the past few decades has been that most conflicts are not new but recurring.[37] In other words, the empirical evidence of conflict recurrence demonstrates that wars are not only the continuation of policy by other means, but are tending to occur because peace processes are regularly breaking down.

Analysing this data through the lens of hybridity encourages us to think more critically about the limitations of top-down approaches to conflict resolution and management. Conflict transformation theory has explored the idea of *negative* transformations understood as the potentially violent outcomes of peace resolution, settlement or management processes.[38] Notions of critical realism or what we might call a strategic understanding

---

37   See Gates et al., 'Conflict Recurrence'; Hewitt, 'Trends in Global Conflict' and Melander et al., 'Organized Violence'.

38   See Ramsbotham et al., *Contemporary Conflict Resolution*; Ryan, *The Transformation of Violent Intercommunal Conflict*.

of peace have also challenged the rigid categorical binary between war and peace.[39] Critical peacebuilding scholars have also examined notions of negative and positive hybridity and shown how these generate significant dilemmas.[40] Empirically, this intellectual movement in hybrid peace has encouraged more research from the point of view of localised people caught up in the everyday challenges of transformation. Mac Ginty and Richmond observe that internationally prescribed peace agreements fail because they do not engage with 'the local':

> Attempts at making peace agreements around the world are normally negotiated in Western bubbles (geographically in the West or within a 'green zone' in the conflict environment), according to Northern rationalities, with few local elites involved who have a controversial claim to represent local constituencies.[41]

To understand the emotional and social dynamics of conflict recurrence, qualitative research that documents feelings of frustration and grievance has produced powerful insights into the dilemmas of transformation.[42] Conceptually, new arguments are emerging through this analysis. One example is Mary Kaldor and Sabine Selchow's *Subterranean Politics in Europe*, which documented 'ripples of discomfort in established institutions, challenging dominant ways of thinking and unsettling normal assumptions about how politics is done'.[43] Kaldor's recent commentary on identity and war has also lead to an incisive observation about 'sectarian' identity:

> Sectarian identity is an outcome of war rather than being a deep-rooted legacy of the past that can lead to war, even though such identities build on (selective) memory and culture. The implication of this proposition is that war should be interpreted less as an external contest of will between two sides but rather as a one-sided and/or parallel effort to construct unidimensional political identities as a basis for power. Power derived from identity so constructed is likely to be authoritarian and repressive.[44]

Empirical research deploying notions of hybrid peace is often strongly focused on the operational and agency level. As Richmond puts it, hybrid peace refers to 'the politics of peacemaking and the dynamics of power,

---

39   Piiparinen, *The Transformation of UN Conflict Management*.
40   Richmond, 'The Dilemmas of a Hybrid Peace'.
41   Mac Ginty and Richmond, 'The Local Turn in Peace Building', 763–764.
42   Brown and Gusmao, 'Peacebuilding and Political Hybridity'; Wallis, 'A Liberal–Local Hybrid Peace Project'.
43   Kaldor and Selchow, *Subterranean Politics in Europe*, 8.
44   Kaldor, 'Identity and War', 345.

agency and identity'.[45] This has produced important analysis challenging the effectiveness of peacebuilding operations and seeking to understand conflict transformation from the ground up. Some of the more interesting conceptual arguments to emerge from these studies return to the central themes identified in the earlier discussion of the canon. It has a future-oriented goal and seeks to grapple with the challenges of negotiating legitimacy under stressful conditions of political community reformation. As Brown and Gusmao put it:

> peacebuilding works toward the *restoration or reconstitution of political community*, in the most fundamental and inclusive sense, in the face of a legacy or the ongoing reality of violent conflict … Political hybridity is the co-existence of introduced Western (generally liberal institutional) models of governance and local governance practices, rooted in place and culture, and enjoying widespread social legitimacy [emphasis added].[46]

Trying to make sense of the interaction between international ideas, agendas and practices and various forms of local response, resistance and reinterpretation is a major empirical challenge for analysts of hybridity in postconflict societies. Normative assumptions about 'restoration', for example, need to be carefully scrutinised because they may provide political support for conditions that caused earlier conflicts. As the problem of conflict recurrence continues to bedevil policymakers at the global level, more careful consideration and dialogue with a wider array of local actors have been demonstrably successful.[47] It will not be the case that all local responses are viewed favourably. Indeed, as Kaldor and others have shown, the international community is liable to grow increasingly anxious about local practices of resistance, especially those that are deemed to pose serious threats to global security.

Conclusion

Projects of making or building peace are not merely concerned with settlement or restoration of previous power relations. They are also crucially about more dynamic practices such as reconstitution and many other things. In order for 'normal' political life to return, decisions must be

---

45 Richmond, 'The Dilemmas of a Hybrid Peace', 52.
46 Brown and Gusmao, 'Peacebuilding and Political Hybridity', 61, 62.
47 See Boege, 'Vying for Legitimacy in Post-conflict Situations'; Regan, 'Lessons from a Successful Peace Process in Bougainville, Papua New Guinea'.

made to support 'everyday' life. People need to eat, be housed, hopefully get to school and find employment. Postconflict societies are in this sense anything but 'still'; they are busy and complicated. Political decisions must also address issues of opportunity and equality. Perceived or real biases, resentment, grievances and rights must be managed in the political space. Many of these decisions do not occur at the level of government, but at the level of the home or the village. Some disputes may be addressed through traditional mechanisms such as tribal councils. Goods and services may be more readily available through illicit entrepreneurs.

Observers of postconflict societies have sought a new lexicon to make sense of these complex transitional forms of political and social life. Hybrid analysis is drawn towards these alternative governance and agency stories and is likely to rebound critically on top-down, static, linear structures often attributed to 'international' institutions or the 'governmental' viewpoint. Hybridity should also be alert to the way that empowering local agency dynamics might generate pernicious outcomes.

Questions of legitimacy are all the more important and acute in postconflict societies because political life is being remade. A postconflict scenario is tumultuous not only because it is a statebuilding activity, but crucially a nation-building one. Conflict may reignite because questions of power, agency and identity are unresolved. Perhaps there were portions of the community that sought advantage or opportunities to invade the peace of others? Perhaps the formal agreements incorporated elements that systematically disadvantaged some members of the community? Perhaps the hybrid political order had not adhered to the supreme law of ensuring the safety of all the people (not just the citizens and elite)? Or maybe the elite were focused only on winning the war and failed to fulfil their responsibilities to continue and restore normal political life?

As a conceptual or heuristic tool, hybridity allows analysts to reinscribe rigid binaries to reveal nuances and overlapping understandings. Peace and war are difficult to define but they are not static and perhaps not usefully understood as pure categorical opposites. A brief review of the canon reveals that peace/war exist on a continuum that is conceptually anchored to the 'political'.

13

(In)Security and Hybrid Justice Systems in Mindanao, Philippines

Imelda Deinla

Introduction

Hybridity is often conflated with the fragile state or the 'absence' of the state in a conflict environment.[1] The emergence of hybrid institutions is also explained primarily in terms of the lack of capacity and legitimacy of state organs and its personnel or in the condition of a power vacuum.[2] A sense of power disequilibrium or societal imbalance and disarray inheres from this presumption. Hybridity, however, serves a function that sustains conflict resilience and at the same time address immediate justice needs. Hybrids arise to provide a state of equilibrium and to provide order in an otherwise messy condition—while also contributing to the messiness. My study of the Autonomous Region of Muslim Mindanao (ARMM), Philippines, points to how hybrid justice mechanisms have developed to cope with insecurity arising from actual and perceived injustices in the community.[3]

---

1   Boege et al., 'Hybrid Political Orders, Not Fragile States'; Boege et al., *On Hybrid Political Orders*; Clements et al., 'State Building Reconsidered'.
2   Ibid.
3   This article is part of a broader study on plural justice, women and peacebuilding in ARMM through an Australian Development Research Award Scheme grant. Data collection was undertaken from 2014 to 2016 by conducting a justice provider survey (using qualitative methods of interviews and focus group discussions) and a justice user survey (using more quantitative, face-to-face survey

In this region where almost 90 per cent of the population are Muslims with a long history of resistance to colonialism and central state authority, hybrid justice mechanisms are drawn from a panoply of customary, Islamic and state legal practices and personnel.[4] Hybrid mechanisms operate through informal and formal networks to deliver 'justice' and secure the community from further escalation of violence arising from retribution. While most hybrids are local innovations and assured by the predominance of, or coalition of, local power holders, local–national innovation has also emerged in responding to local demands for speed, flexibility and adequacy of remedies and outcomes. Some form of state-led hybridity has also emerged and offers some insights on enhancing the delivery of effective and relevant justice services through professional and culturally attuned justice personnel. This may provide a counterbalance to other forms of hybrids that capitalise on power asymmetry and discriminatory practices.

Statebuilding, hybrid legal order and justice

The term 'hybrid political order' is a fairly recent conceptual tool to describe a condition where 'diverse and competing authority structures, sets of rules, logics of order, and claims of power co-exist, overlap, interact, and intertwine'.[5] Hybridity can be observed in many plural and multi-ethnic environments but it is in conflict and postconflict regimes that hybrid political orders are expressed more concretely. This has given academics, policymakers and development workers a better understanding of the complex and multilayered nature of rules and norms that operate in conflict-affected environments. An appreciation of hybridity has increasingly become relevant in peacebuilding and development programming by a range of actors. It has become a useful approach to describe a state of flux, nonlinear movement of change and

---

instruments in selected areas in Mindanao). All interviews and focus group discussions are anonymised to protect the identity of respondents. Special thanks to Professor Veronica Taylor, co-investigator in this project, and local partners: Dr Acram Latiph, Araceli Habaradas, Amanah Busran Lao, Alamira Alonto, National Commission for Muslim Filipinos, Office of the Court Administrator Supreme Court of the Philippines, Nisa ul Haq Bangsamoro, Teduray Lambiangan Women's Organization and Public Attorney's Office for support in data collection. Opinions expressed in this article are the sole responsibility of the author.

4   See Deinla and Taylor, 'Towards Peace'.
5   Boege et al., 'Hybrid Political Orders, Not Fragile States', 17.

spheres of influence, the crisscrossing of actors in various domains aside from highlighting the non-exclusivity and non-privilege of state authority as a source of law, order and security.[6]

Hybridity has also challenged conventional views about the process of statebuilding, particularly in conflict-affected regions. The conventional perspective makes an association between hybridity and a weak or fragile state. It follows from this assumption that dispersion of authority or power structures may not be conducive to building sustainable peace and development. This view takes an opposite or less enthusiastic appreciation for the role of hybrid and other informal institutions in building sustainable peace and strengthening state institutions.[7] Objections are centred on their ad hoc flexible nature, persistence of discriminatory practices and the tendency of certain arrangements to privilege, and thus exclude, a particular class of people over other groups. For instance, an 'exclusive' hybrid political order limits key political functions to a small group of elites who have control or monopoly of power. On the other hand, and showing case studies of different hybrid sites, several authors put forward an argument that makes the case for hybrid structures. They argue that being derived from or being mediated by historically and organically grown institutions such as kinship-based and traditional informal institutions, hybrids are in fact valuable owing to their strong social embeddedness and local legitimacy.[8]

The main enquiry for this chapter is to re-examine statebuilding processes and hybridity, and their relationship with the provision of justice in a conflict-affected area. The World Bank Development Report 2011 points to 'injustice' as one of the major causes of conflict and vulnerability of the state system.[9] Why has conflict, particularly what is termed 'low-intensity' conflict, endured for decades? In this condition, the state remains—though obscurely—and state institutions continue to provide a modicum of public goods to the people. In areas where conflict and the cycle of violence have persisted, the terms 'justice' and 'injustice'

---

6   Boege et al., 'Hybrid Political Orders, Not Fragile States'; Boege et al., *On Hybrid Political Orders*; Boege et al., 'States Emerging from Hybrid Political Orders'; Kraushaar and Lambach, 'Hybrid Political Orders'; Mac Ginty, 'Hybrid Peace'.
7   See, for example, Fritz and Rocha Menocal '(Re)building Developmental States'; Ghani et al., 'An Agenda for State Building in the Twenty-First Century'.
8   See, for example, Boege et al., *States Emerging from Hybrid Political Orders*; Clements et al., 'State Building Reconsidered'; Höglund and Orjuela, 'Hybrid Peace Governance and Illiberal Peacebuilding in Sri Lanka'; Wiuff Moe, 'Hybrid and "Everyday" Political Ordering'.
9   World Bank, *World Development Report 2011*, 7, 82.

may not be mutually exclusive, while a dichotomy between a weak and strong state may be an oversimplification. By examining the nature and operation of a hybrid justice system in Mindanao, I will show the high degree of entanglement between society and the state that has allowed for a condition of 'stability' and sustained and reinforced both traditional and modern bases of authority. This is the condition of equilibrium among different competing authorities in state and non-state sectors that is also reflected in the development of a hybrid legal order—and justice system—in Mindanao.

A corollary question in this chapter is: how viable are hybrid justice mechanisms in securing sustainable justice? Inherent in hybrids is their ability to manage or cope with instability, stress or break in social relations.[10] While hybrids provide 'solutions', they also have a propensity to 'normalise' relations between opposing authorities and in the day-to-day interactions of communities. Using local traditions and available resources—but often underpinned by local drivers, primarily the local elites—hybrids rebalance the stresses and disequilibrium caused by disruptions, breaks, tensions and threats to 'social order'. In tackling this issue, I will show the paradox of justice in Mindanao and why the cycle of violence and injustice prevails despite an explosion of various justice mechanisms that all claim to respond effectively to the justice needs of the people. This research has identified a proliferation of avenues where people in the community run to in order to seek redress for their justice issues. In varying ways and means, different justice providers render services that seek to satisfy the justice needs of individuals and families affected by disputes. What 'justice' means in Mindanao, and other contexts, may differ from Western liberal values that are centred on a fair and public trial being presided over by an impartial and impersonal judge rendering decisions backed by the state's coercive mechanisms. In this region, the participation of the affected parties and their families in discussing the offences and remedies, provision of security, payment of blood money and reconciliation are desired justice outcomes that are highly preferable over public trial and court judgement. And yet, many forms of injustice recur as frequently as they are resolved or adjudicated in many forums.

---

10   Boege et al., 'Hybrid Political Orders, Not Fragile States', 18.

A key point here is that the issue is not so much whether hybrid reality needs to be taken account of but on how much or how far existing hybrid arrangements are to be part of future institutional and legal order. How do we use our knowledge of hybrid justice orders in informing or shaping a justice architecture that responds effectively to the cycle of injustice?

(In)security, conflict and hybridity

A starting point for this chapter is to see injustice as a by-product of unresolved or recurring conflicts in society. Systemic issues in the political, economic and cultural spheres—all interlinked—shape the forms and dynamics of conflicts. As many studies in Mindanao have shown, disputes have many dimensions, new forms of conflicts are created and existing ones become even more complex.[11] The recurrence of conflicts further influences structural issues and the way conflicts are addressed. The escalation of conflict—particularly the intensified use of violence—drives rapid hybridisation especially in dealing with the most destructive consequences of violent conflict and in providing security and stability. Figure 13.1 illustrates the enduring relationship of conflicts and hybrid justice mechanisms.

In this research, I see the role of a hybrid justice system in performing this rebalancing role by providing 'immediate justice needs' (primarily compensation in the form of blood money) and security (often in the form of counter/contra violence against perpetrators) to 'justice seekers'. Thus the state has much to owe hybridisation for its survival in the same (or similar) manner as traditional forms of authority. Hybridisation, however, often involves compromise and convenience in a situation of dispersed authority and conflict. The lack of a critical and more deliberative form of hybridisation results in entrenching an 'exclusivist' hybrid political order of local powerful families or clans. It fosters the emergence of alternative forms of justice mechanisms that promise 'more effective and swift' delivery of justice but run counter to fundamental human rights standards. Hybridisation has also shown disproportionate or inconsistent treatment of offences or issues involving women.

---

11   See, for example, Abinales, *Making Mindanao*; Lara and Schoofs, *Out of the Shadows*; Quimpo, 'Back to War in Mindanao'; Torres, *Rido*.

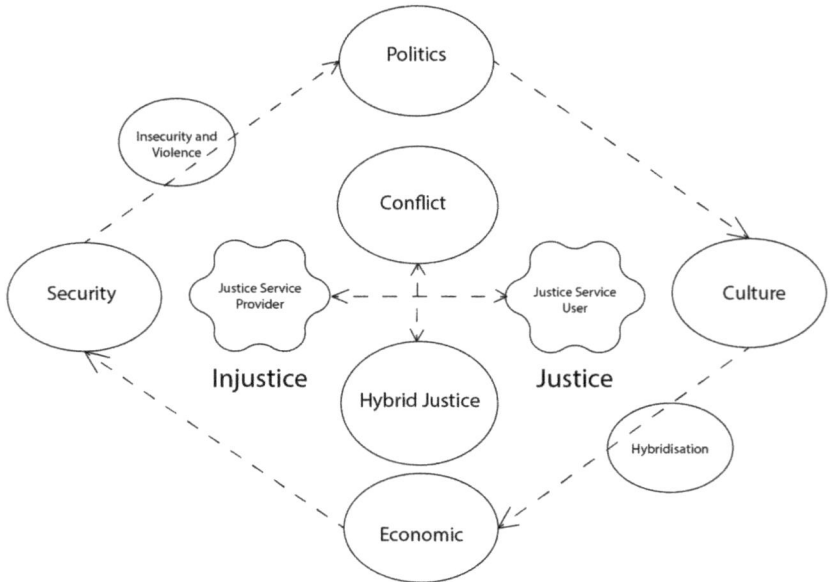

Figure 13.1: The relationship of conflict and hybrid justice mechanisms
Source: Author's work.

In this chapter, I show how the interaction of conflict and local power dynamics has become the main trigger for hybridisation—on state, non-state and often the coalescing of the two sites that results in the dissolution of the binaries. Local actors perform a range of roles that do not distinguish between private, public, state and non-state functions, although these binaries or categories are often used by the actors themselves. In my research I deploy the term 'justice providers'—those who perform justice services such as by adjudication, mediation, negotiation and provision of remedies to parties, although they themselves can be both providers and users, even at the same time. In ways, these hybrid entities identify themselves as 'non-state, informal, or traditional' to differentiate themselves from entities created by the state or those that are not expressly, but in many ways, tacitly, recognised by the state. Users also recognise these binaries, and do so without realising or acknowledging that these 'informal, traditional mechanisms' are highly formalised and have appropriated elements of what they call the state formal system.

By engaging in a critical examination of how hybrids evolve, this may also allow us to determine the occurrence of 'hybrid capture'. This is a condition where particular interests dominate both process and outcomes for their own advantage or gain, to exclude some groups, or pursue their agenda. But even with this 'capture' we cannot also deny the agency of the users—or simply those who avail themselves of the remedies or outcomes offered by these service providers. Forum shopping has long been recognised as a feature of the existence and co-existence of different legal orders and norms, and is, if not equally, a main driving force for innovation and competition, or the process of continuous hybridisation.[12]

Hybrid justice and security in Mindanao

The Autonomous Region of Muslim Mindanao (ARMM) is a multi-ethnic region that easily lends to a highly plural and hybrid, legal order. There are at least 13 identified Muslim and non-Muslim ethnolinguistic groups.[13] The largest ethnic groupings in terms of their population size are the Maguindanaoan (Maguindanao), Maranao (Lanao del Sur) and Tausug (island provinces of Basilan, Sulu and Tawi-Tawi).[14] The Muslim population is estimated to be 90 per cent of the total population of 3,256,123 million people, while the rest comprise Christians and other smaller Islamised and non-Islamised ethnic groups.[15] The region is composed of five provinces (Maguindanao, Lanao del Sur, Basilan, Sulu and Tawi-Tawi), formed out of a plebiscite conducted in 1989 and later in 2001 after Republic Act No. 9054 (RA 9054) was passed into law. RA 9054 incorporated the agreement in the 1996 Final Peace Agreement between the Philippine Government and the then-dominant Muslim insurgency group, the Moro National Liberation Front (MNLF), which called for the expansion of areas covered by autonomy.

Understanding the term 'justice' in Mindanao has to start from an understanding of the multilayered nature of conflict in the region and what is being demanded for the resolution of these conflicts. First, there is conflict between the state and the Moros arising from 'historical injustice' of colonisation, the formation of the Philippine state that deprived them of their claim for self-determination, and their marginalisation from

---

12   See Deinla and Taylor, 'Towards Peace', 27; Holbrook, 'Legal Hybridity in the Philippines', 449; Tamanaha, 'Understanding Legal Pluralism', 389.
13   Asian Development Bank, *Indigenous and Ethnic Minorities and Poverty Reduction*, 4.
14   See Gowing, *Muslim Filipinos*, 59–61; Hooker, 'Muhammadan Law and Islamic Law', 163; Jundam, *Tunggal Hulah-Duwa Sarah*, 10; Tan, *Decolonization and Filipino Muslim Identity*, 2–4.
15   Based on population census as of 1 May 2010, Philippine Statistics Authority, Philippine Standard Geographic Code, nap.psa.gov.ph/activestats/psgc/regview.asp?region=15

central authority in terms of participation in political and economic affairs.[16] Justice in this light is seen to require a recognition of the Muslim peoples' right to self-determination including their way of life and justice. Thus the first peace negotiation involving the MNLF heralded the establishment of the Shari'ah court system in Mindanao with the passage of the Code of Muslim Personal Laws of the Philippines.[17]

Since the formation of the Philippine state, the region has been plagued with an unabated cycle of violence that was heightened with the declaration of martial law in 1972.[18] Peace negotiations have been carried out by successive governments, with the exception of the administration of Joseph Estrada that waged an 'all-out' war in Mindanao in the early 2000s. In this period, more than half a million people were displaced from their homes. Since the 1970s, it is estimated that more than 120,000 people have died resulting from or as an incidence of conflict.[19] Peace agreements were signed first with the MNLF and recently with the Moro Islamic Liberation Front (MILF), a splinter group that was established in the late 1970s to fight for secessionism. The MILF negotiated with the Philippine Government for greater autonomy during Gloria Macapagal-Arroyo's administration but it was during the outgoing presidency of Benigno Aquino Jr that produced a near-culminating comprehensive peace settlement.[20] In this latter peace agreement, a Comprehensive Agreement on the Bangsamoro was forged between the government and MILF that would have paved the way for the creation of the Bangsamoro entity that will exercise greater autonomy.

However, subnational conflicts are endemic in the region and are causing as much violence and crime as the insurgency war. The five provinces in ARMM have one of the highest incidences of crime in the country on a per population basis.[21] The impact of this enduring conflict is seen

---

16   See Abinales, *Making Mindanao*; Bertrand, 'Peace and Conflict in the Southern Philippines'; Quimpo, 'Back to War'; Quimpo, 'Mindanao'.

17   Embodied in Presidential Decree No. 1083 (1977); see also Mastura, 'Legal Pluralism in the Philippines', 463–465.

18   Abinales, *Making Mindanao*; Kreuzer, *Violence as a Means of Control and Domination in the Southern Philippines*; Quimpo, 'Back to War'.

19   Schiavo-Campo and Judd, 'The Mindanao Conflict in the Philippines', 5.

20   The peace settlement, in particular the passage of the bill on the Bangsamoro Basic Law, was halted and derailed in the aftermath of the Mamasapano massacre on 25 January 2015 that resulted in the deaths of 44 policemen.

21   International Alert, 'Violence in the Bangsamoro and Southern Mindanao'; data for 2008–2013 gathered in this research from the Philippine National Police.

in the deprivation and marginalisation in the social and economic life of the people in the region. All of the ARMM provinces are consistently in the bottom 10 of the poorest provinces in the Philippines.[22] Insurgency and subnational conflicts also have a reciprocal relationship which fuels and sustains all types of violence and conflict.[23] Inadequate state security, proliferation of firearms, the presence of different armed groups including private armies and terror and crime groups, and the weak functioning of the state justice system all contribute to a climate of violence and impunity.[24]

Underlying conflicts in Mindanao is the phenomenon of *rido*, a form of clan feuding that is rooted in the sociocultural fabric of society.[25] Honour or *maratabat*—and its reverse, shame—is a paramount value in traditional societies in Mindanao; putting a clan's honour on the line has dire consequences for those who tarnish or undermine it.[26] Individual honour, or shame, is a collective trait and responsibility such that an infraction against a person is treated as one against their family and clan. *Rido* can be triggered by major disputes such as political and economic competition, land disputes and violence committed to a person.[27] It can also be precipitated by minor or petty issues. Interviews conducted reveal that all forms of issues are susceptible to *rido*. Some of the stories narrated were over disagreements on dowry and guardianship, offending family members by showing affection to a woman, and non-payment of debts. *Rido* is a form of dispute settlement where disputes are settled by exacting a 'score' against the opposing family or clan. Until the number of hits or fatalities are almost parity, the dispute is not considered ripe for settlement. While *rido* is generally seen as negative and destructive, it is widely exercised across Muslim, indigenous and Christian populations in Mindanao. My research also reveals that many favour *rido* as essential in order to settle disputes despite its destructive impact on the family and the community.[28] As the following discussion demonstrates, *rido* is the force behind the dynamic hybridisation of the justice architecture in Mindanao.

---

22   UNDP, 'Human Development Index Highlights Inequality'.
23   On conflict morphing see International Alert, *Rebellion, Political Violence and Shadow Crimes in the Bangsamoro*, 28.
24   See Lara and Schoofs, *Out of the Shadows*.
25   Torres, *Rido: Clan Feuding*, 11–13.
26   Durante et al., 'Management of Clan Conflict and Rido amoung the Tausug, Magindanao, Maranao, Sama, and Yakan Tribes', 105; Torres, *Rido*, 20–22.
27   Torres, *Rido*, 16–17; also interviews conducted among justice providers; there is increasing competition over illegal economic activities such as drugs trade.
28   Justice user survey, Marawi City, Lanao del Sur province, September 2015.

Hybrid justice and security in ARMM

The plural and hybrid justice architecture in ARMM is a by-product of its own historical development, the process of state–society formation and interaction, and of the persistence of conflicts. These three forces developed and continue to shape laws, norms and mechanisms that respond to problems or issues that community members face in their day-to-day lives. The 'everyday life' of residents in a conflict or postconflict area differs, however, from those living away from a condition of daily threats of violence and armed conflict. Often, broader social justice issues such as political exclusion and competition, economic inequality, poverty, access to education and health services, and land conflicts underlie many crimes or socially unacceptable behaviour that disrupt peace and drive further conflict in the community. For example, small crimes handled in secular courts in conflict-ridden areas involve thefts in shopping centres, money scams and non-payment of debts or loans that reflect on the dire economic condition of many people. In the aftermath of the siege of Zamboanga City by a faction of MNLF combatants, civil court judges reported high incidences of shoplifting of infant formula milk.[29] These types of cases impose a heavy burden on women, who not only face the challenge of providing for the basic needs of their families but are also subject to various suits in civil courts.[30]

The continuation of traditional authority and norms that survived waves of Western colonisation has ensured that state formation in this region is uneven, complex and fraught with difficulties. While the process of statebuilding disrupted the further evolution of nascent state-like authority which had been based on the authority of the sultan and *datu* (village chief), traditional authority, through cooperation, negotiation or co-optation, ensured that the Philippine state is a constant presence in the region. The state, and its structures, has created winners and losers in the process, including by introducing a new arena for competition among families or clans. The state as a source of formal-legal power, patronage and of economic and resource opportunities provides incentives for fierce and often coercive contestation among contending elites and other authorities vying for power.[31] In return, local state officials ensure the omnipresence of the

---

29   Interview with civil court judges, April 2014.
30   Interview with civil court judges, April 2014. According to interviews, breaches of contracts and non-payment of loans are usually the responsibility of women in the household.
31   Abinales, *Making Mindanao*, 188; Caballero-Anthony, 'The Philippines in Southeast Asia', 7–13; McCoy, *An Anarchy of Families*.

state and provide local 'stability'. Results of the justice user survey reveal that 73 per cent of respondents feel 'secure' in their community.[32] Local state elites in Mindanao, as elsewhere in the Philippines, have enjoyed autonomy from the state and even from the insurgency groups given their possession of state authority, resources and means of coercion.[33]

The most violent and destructive forms of *rido*—and the most difficult to resolve—have been fought over electoral contests and economic competition or rivalry.[34] *Rido*, which usually happens between ethnic groups, has also become more vicious with this new layer of contestation. While women and children are generally spared from reprisals, spates of *rido* involving electoral competition in recent years have seen several children, elderly and women killed or brutalised.[35] For these types of *rido*, the cycle of violence continues for years or decades even if there is cessation of hostilities and settlement of the dispute.[36] It needs to be stressed that violence involving women—whether Muslim, indigenous or Christian—is borne out of this complex relationship of tradition, politics, economics and conflict that make women more vulnerable to physical, sexual, economic and emotional violence. For example, women public schoolteachers, regardless of their ethnicity, have become targets of *panggoyod* (forcible abduction for marriage) in the island province of Sulu due to the income they can bring to the family, or targets of physical violence for fulfilling their duties as election officials.[37]

The interlocking nature of conflicts in Mindanao therefore lends itself to multiple and complex processes of dispute resolution and justice outcomes. A hybrid justice system is a necessary consequence of the complex dynamics of history, politics and conflict that serves to provide

---

32   The justice user survey, conducted in July 2016 in ARMM, had 544 respondents: 39.5 per cent male, 57 per cent female and 3.5 per cent 'no response'. The survey was conducted in collaboration with the National Commission of Muslim Filipinos.

33   Abinales, *Making Mindanao*, 18; Caballero-Anthony, 'The Philippines in Southeast Asia', 11; Kreuzer, *Philippine Governance*'; Lara and Champain, *Inclusive Peace in Muslim Mindanao*, 22.

34   Durante et al., 'Management of Clan Conflict', 106–109; Lara and Champain, *Inclusive Peace*, 15; Lara and Schoofs, *Out of the Shadows*, 29–30; Torres, *Rido*, 16–17; qualitative interviews with justice providers. Economic competition happens in either legitimate or illicit businesses such as drugs, trafficking and gun smuggling.

35   The Ampatuan massacre in 2010 had women raped before being killed and mutilated while the *rido* ambush on 28 July 2014 in Sulu happened on the occasion of Eid-al-Fitr.

36   Based on interviews, some descendants would re-open *rido* to exact revenge. One story involved the son of a murdered man who killed his father's killer years later after settlement of *rido*.

37   Based on interview from respondents from Sulu; see also Alipala, 'Abducted Teacher Rescued by Soldiers in Sulu'; Fernandez, '2 Teachers Killed, 2 Hurt in Cotabato City'.

a stabilising platform for contending authorities in the region. There are at least three layers of authority in ARMM: the state, the local or village authority, and the family or clan.[38] All three have their own laws, rules and norms; each claiming their boundaries, competing to expand their power and authority, but also in the process of cooperating and deploying resources from each other. This is the state of equilibrium in the region that maintains order but also sustains the cycle of violence. This hybridity is fluid, ad hoc and composed of multiple actors who crisscross and penetrate various domains of justice provision.

My research has identified at least 16 mechanisms where people can bring their problems or issues for resolution and seek redress for the wrongs— actual or perceived—they suffer from (Table 13.1). For the purpose of ease in categorisation, although this is by no means a strict classification, I outline four categories of justice provider in the region. It needs to be clarified that justice services or justice needs are the preferred terms to how people understand and describe 'justice' rather than the normative ideas of fairness and due process that are usually associated with formal-legal justice. Hence, the term 'justice provider' is used to denote a more expansive list of actors and mechanisms that deliver justice services to those who need them.

Table 13.1 shows the existence of a hybrid justice system, the creation of new hybrid mechanisms and the hybridisation of existing mechanisms of justice. The four categories listed are a combination of actor-based classification and where the service provision is taking place. The state court system covers state-provided civil courts, Shari'ah courts, public prosecutors and public defenders. Its proceedings are mostly done within court or official premises and follow prescribed procedures and formalities. Non–state based courts are organised by non-state groups, in particular the insurgent groups within their areas of control or influence (that is, the MILF, MNLF and People's Court); the proceedings in these courts are also conducted in a formalised manner and in accordance with some rules to ensure due process for the parties and to gather evidence.[39]

---

38   Kreuzer, *Political Clans and Violence*; Adam et al., 'Hybrid Systems of Conflict Management and Community-Level Efforts to Improve Local Security in Mindanao'.
39   See Stephens, 'Islamic Law in the Philippines', 22–23; author's interviews with MILF Shari'ah court judges and People's Court cadres.

Table 13.1: Categories and mechanisms of justice provision in the Autonomous Region of Muslim Mindanao

Level	State court system	Local state-based and civil society hybrids	Traditional and religious mechanisms	Non-state based courts
National	Supreme Court			
	Court of Appeals			
	Sandiganbayan			
	Ombudsman			
	Department of Justice			
Regional/ Provincial	Regional trial courts	Regional Reconciliation and Unification Commission		MILF Supreme Court and Court of Appeal (Shari'ah)
	Public prosecutors – Department of Justice	Provincial Peace and Order Council		
	Public Attorney's Office – Department of Justice	Municipal Peace and Order Council		
	Municipal and city courts	Governors		
	Shari'ah district and municipal courts			
Village		Katarungang pambarangay	Muslim religious leaders	MILF Shari'ah
		Police force	Traditional Muslim leaders and elders	MNLF Shari'ah
		Military	Indigenous justice system	Abbu Sayyaf Group Shari'ah
		Quick Response Team, The Asia Foundation	Family/clan leaders	Other rebel groups' Shari'ah*
		Mayors	Christian church leaders	People's Court (CPP-NPA)
		Other local executives	Community Shari'ah	
		Teachers		

MILF = Moro Islamic Liberation Front; MNLF = Moro National Liberation Front.

* A prominent example is the group of an 'autonomous' MILF commander in Lanao del Sur which operates a 'Shari'ah Court' separate from the one run by the MILF.

Local state-based and civil society hybrids are those established by local executives and operated mainly through local state structures as well as those developed by local non-government organisations with the support of international development organisations.[40] Similar to non-state courts, this type of justice mechanism, with the exception of the *katarungang pambarangay*, is a recent phenomenon that developed from local initiatives to cope with difficulties in dispensing justice in a multi-ethnic community mired in conflict.[41] The formation of the Provincial Peace and Order Council and the Municipal Peace and Order Council in various places in ARMM has coincided with the increasing power of local executives as they started to receive automatic revenue appropriations from the central government in the late 1990s when the Local Government Code was passed to provide fiscal autonomy to local government units. Known as internal revenue allocation or 'IRA', this fund is intended for the delivery of basic government services but has been a source of corruption, patronage and dependence of local government units on central government authority.[42] This fund has also been used by local executives in the region in dispensing their roles as justice providers, whether in the *katarungang pambarangay*, Municipal Peace and Order Council or Provincial Peace and Order Council, in raising funds for blood money and in defraying costs and remuneration for some personnel involved in settling disputes.[43] Local executives have given 'allowances' to state civil court judges assigned in their areas.[44] As local executives also gain more control over police in their areas of authority, they are able to deploy 'coercive power' of arrest and enforcement of decisions or settlement. The combination of state authority and resources, traditional authority or indigenous means of settling disputes, and flexibility in the process of dispute settlement has made this 'hybrid group' increasingly popular among the population.

The need for security, as an immediate justice outcome, shows the power dimension in the delivery of what constitutes an 'effective' justice service in a conflict environment. Almost all providers of justice interviewed were unanimous in pointing to the provision of security—for themselves, for

---

40 Such as the Asia Foundation's support for the Quick Response Teams.
41 Interviews with local community-based justice providers, November 2015.
42 See Santos, 'Not a Lot to Allot'.
43 Interviews with community-based justice providers.
44 Interviews with civil court judges and state Shari'ah court judges. It appears that civil court judges receive more support from local executives than their Shari'ah counterparts and that Shari'ah judges assigned in Christian-dominated local councils receive more support than those in Muslim-dominated local councils.

the parties and their families—during the process of conflict settlement as indispensable in settling disputes.[45] As practically all issues, rivalry and misunderstanding can precipitate a *rido*, the first task for the justice provider is to ensure that no violence ensues or if it did occur that a 'ceasefire' is worked out among the clans.[46] Speed in resolving the conflict is thus a necessary complement to security provision. Bringing the parties to agree to settle the dispute is a complex process that requires the justice provider to trace common lineages or relationship between the disputing clans.[47] Security, speed, flexibility and participation of the parties are identified as essential in the process of justice delivery in ARMM and are synonymous with justice itself. The payment of blood money is the culmination of the process of mediation and negotiation that takes place among the justice provider, the disputing parties and their families or clans. In most cases, the justice provider is also asked to help in raising blood money and oftentimes ends up contributing their own resources for this purpose.[48] A feast, called *kanduli* in some areas, is often held to celebrate the reconciliation of clans involved in the dispute.

Hybridisation takes place in all four categories and levels of justice services, driven by the necessity for the 'justice essentials' described above. Even in the state court system, hybridisation is taking place, albeit informally and sometimes with or without official sanction. For instance, state Shari'ah court judges have resorted to the 'traditional method' of settling disputes or run the risk of becoming 'irrelevant'.[49] This mediation effort, which takes place outside the court, is not recognised as 'judicial duties' by the Supreme Court. In fact it is prohibited. Out-of-court settlement is the preferred option among justice users and this is shown in the declining number of cases being adjudicated in both civil and state Shari'ah court systems.[50] On the other hand, the public defender's office, the Public Attorney's Office (PAO), has formally instituted a 'pre-litigation conference' process to allow PAO lawyers to mediate or settle disputes among the parties. The PAO in ARMM, which has many young Muslim

---

45   Various interviews with justice providers in ARMM, conducted from 2013 to 2015.
46   Various interviews with justice providers involved with settling *rido*, conducted from 2014 to 2015.
47   See, for example, Menkhaus, 'Traditional Conflict Management in Contemporary Somalia', 186–187.
48   Many of those interviewed who have had experience in resolving a *rido* revealed this has become a huge responsibility for them to ensure that adequate blood money is raised and often contribute their own money, animals and property for the settlement and *kanduli*.
49   Interview with state Shari'ah judges.
50   Court data obtained from the Supreme Court for 2008–2013.

women lawyers as personnel, is also conducting information and outreach programs to communities. During interviews, some lawyers revealed that they combine traditional knowledge and secular rules in arriving at solutions to problems.[51] Surveys conducted in this research found that, among users in ARMM, PAO lawyers are trusted and well respected by the community and the courts.[52]

Hybridity also reflects the rise of non-traditional actors involved and the methods by which disputes are resolved. Trust is a vital attribute that the justice user looks for in a justice provider.[53] This means trust that the justice provider can provide security and deliver the best outcomes for the party and their family in the most expeditious manner. A high degree of enforcement is also correlated with trust of the person delivering the service. It is not surprising therefore that users of the hybrid justice system overwhelmingly chose 'family/clans' as the most sought after provider of justice and also with the highest trust preference.[54] Elders or leaders of the clan are constituted, individually or as a group, to approach the disputing parties and their families and conduct informal mediation. A high degree of enforcement is also an attribute of rebel Shari'ah courts, which possess the ability to dispatch armed personnel for enforcement. For instance, in Lanao del Sur, a commander's court boasts of an effective justice service through its uncompromising approach in seeking out the perpetrators and rehabilitation approach combined with physical punishment and learning Qur'anic teachings and virtues. It claims that families have even voluntarily entrusted their children for drug rehabilitation.[55]

An increasing trend towards dispute resolution by local state executives such as elected village head chiefs and municipal, provincial and regional state officials shows how power is harnessed in delivering justice to the community. Next to clan-based justice, the second-most preferred groups of justice providers are the *katarungang pambarangay*, or village council mediation, composed of elected local village chiefs and the mayors. *Katarungang pambarangay* is a creation by law that is based on

---

51   Interview with PAO lawyers, Community Legal Aid providers survey.
52   Justice user survey conducted in selected areas in the five provinces of ARMM in October 2015 and June 2016.
53   Results of qualitative interviews and of the user survey.
54   Result of survey in Marawi City, Lanao del Sur and interviews with government employees in ARMM.
55   Interview with rebel Shari'ah court personnel, February 2015. This group operates a prison dug out from the ground where 'offenders' and drug users are held for some time until rehabilitation is completed.

traditional methods of mediation and dispenses the need for lawyers.[56] It is mandated to conduct mediation and to provide the avenue for an 'amicable settlement' between the parties to the conflict; its jurisdiction is limited to small criminal or civil matters. In ARMM, *katarungang pambarangays* have evolved into solving serious crimes or issues in the community such as murder, *rido* and rape. Village officials have become involved in providing security for the parties and in raising blood money. Some of them use state court methods such as issuing a 'warrant of arrest' or 'subpoena'. One account also mentions that it provides a facility for temporary detention of the parties involved in the dispute in order to prevent the escalation of further violence or to keep the person safe from retribution from the other party or clan.[57]

Conclusion: Towards a sustainable justice?

The existence of a hybrid justice system operating within and outside the state system reflects the complexity of conflict and power dynamics in Muslim Mindanao. It shows how the development of hybrid political order—and that of hybrid justice mechanisms—parallels the process of statebuilding in the region. This is characterised by a state highly dependent on local power structures and dispersion of power among local power holders. The state—and corresponding legal hybridity—has ensured a fluid co-existence of traditional and state authorities. This means that the state has not disappeared but functions through clan-based authority. This is demonstrated in how justice provision works through clans and the development of new hybrids that harness the resources and power of both state and traditional authorities.

The delivery of holistic or comprehensive justice services has become an important attribute of newly developed hybrid mechanisms in Mindanao. The segmentation of different pillars of justice, each working separately and with their own set of personnel, works to disadvantage state formal mechanisms of justice which need to observe pre-agreed rules and separation of justice functions from apprehension of wrongdoers, to prosecution, judicial determination and enforcement. Hybrid justice providers fill a crucial role in delivering prompt and effective justice to an

---

56　Provided under Presidential Decree No. 1508 and later amended by Republic Act No. 7160 (Local Government Code of 1991).

57　Interview with justice provider, Community Legal Aid.

environment where conflict dynamics are complex. The delivery of justice and security provision are intertwined functions that require flexibility of rules, coordination of multiple actors and authoritative capacity of the justice provider. As shown in this chapter, an effective justice provider is one who possesses multiple authorities and can deploy adequate resources to meet the justice demands of parties. While justice provision is a demonstration and source of power by local elites, and susceptible to hybrid capture, it needs to be recognised that the delivery of justice is an essential public service to which hybrid and non-state justice mechanisms provide a significant contribution.

Do hybrid justice mechanisms better serve the justice interests of people in multi-ethnic and conflicted areas? We have seen in Mindanao that hybrid justice mechanisms are providing security and a more holistic approach to justice which the state court system is unable to provide. The case in ARMM shows that these mechanisms are, however, power dependent and their legitimacy is based primarily on the resources and coercive power that can be deployed to be effective. Their seats of authority are also highly contested and a source of violent conflict among competing clans, and the rules may not be applied to all, especially when the conflict involves more powerful parties. We have also seen that the state court system is undergoing hybridisation in the way it responds to demands for flexibility and speed in resolving issues by undertaking mediation and settlement functions.

Except for the Public Attorney's Office, there is reticence on the part of state authorities to officially sanction a more flexible approach to dispute settlement. As non-court state hybrids and non-state adjudication become more popular, there is a danger that state court processes may be rendered irrelevant, as they are now underutilised. The uncoordinated process of hybridisation and lack of deliberation may also serve to foster competition among various justice providers and deliver disparate and competing outcomes. This engenders heightened forum shopping and for parties to dictate the terms and process of proceedings, as is already happening.[58] A hybrid justice system that is ruled by the dynamics of conflict, rather than normative ideas of justice, can deliver only palliative outcomes and does not work to deter crimes and conflicts. The complex dynamics of conflict in ARMM also show the need for sustainable hybrid justice mechanisms to connect to the realisation of social justice.

---

58   Interviews with various justice providers and justice users in ARMM.

Section Four — Hybridity and Gender

14

Inside and Out: Violence against Women and Spatiality in Timor-Leste

Damian Grenfell[1]

Introduction

Violence in Timor-Leste has been a continuous point of analytical inquiry, not least given the consequences of Portuguese colonialism, Indonesian occupation and the civil strife that ebbed and flowed in the new republic from 2006 to 2008. Since independence, efforts to reduce violence against women have been constant, even if much of this has been in the form of advocacy competing with other post-independence agendas. Despite innumerable programs and associated research, all available evidence suggests that violence against women is not abating. According to the *Timor-Leste Demographic and Health Survey* published in 2010, 38 per cent of women in Timor-Leste aged 15 to 49 have experienced physical violence.[2] The 2016 study *Understanding Violence against Women and Children in Timor-Leste* found that 59 per cent of ever-married women aged 15 to 49 had experienced physical and/or

---

1   My appreciation to colleagues both in Timor-Leste and Australia, not least those who contributed to research for the 'Beyond Fragility and Inequity, The Economic Dimensions of Domestic Violence in Timor-Leste' project, which provided several ideas further developed here.
2   National Statistics Directorate, *Timor-Leste Demographic and Health Survey*, 229.

sexual violence by a male intimate partner at least once, though a large majority (81 per cent) had experienced intimate partner violence many times.[3] Entrenched patriarchies and gender inequity remain central to this problem, and responding to these in the context of what is referred to here as a 'hybrid order' adds variously to the challenges of addressing this violence.

The key argument of this chapter is that violence against women and the interventions to prevent it shape and are shaped by different forms of space within a hybrid order. This is just one of the possible conceptual deployments of hybridity in a site such as Timor-Leste where customary social relations have continued to play a significant role in patterns of social integration and political life.[4] As a concept, hybridity creates space for analysis of different forms of sociality that do not clearly sit within the domain of what may be described as 'modern'. Rather than seeing the world through the narrow and flat lens of modernity—for instance, via state-centric approaches—it draws analysis towards an examination of constituent elements that in turn contribute to understanding the character and complexity of everyday sociality.

The first two sections of this chapter provide an initial discussion of hybridity, setting out the constituent elements focused on here as the modern and the customary, and in turn discussing how these relate to spatiality. Building on this, the third section argues there is a tendency for exogenous forces—such as donors, non-government organisations, aid agencies and academics—to 'render' East Timorese society as patriarchal, establishing a point of difference that in turn justifies the shape of interventions. The fourth and fifth sections shift the focus to the control of space where women are subjected to a kind of 'double sovereignty'. In the context of Timor-Leste, the 'double' refers to the fact that women are constrained across both modern and customary spatialities, with sovereignty used to denote the control over space, in this instance masculine control expressed through patriarchal power that effectively limits the mobility of women. This approach to sovereignty is not to be confused with liberal notions of popular or individual sovereignty but, rather, is an adaptation of a Weberian notion of control over a particular territorial formation and the relationship to violence. While this form of sovereignty is often discussed as part of debates on globalisation where it is understood

3   Asia Foundation, *Understanding Violence against Women and Children in Timor-Leste*.
4   Wallis, 'A Liberal–Local Hybrid Peace Project in Action?'.

as 'the extension and institutionalization of control and authority within a spatial field', here sovereignty is used to describe the control of space within 'petit polities' that exist quite apart from the nation-state system.[5] As power is concentrated in masculine identities, sovereign control is expressed via men over different kinds of space, limiting pathways for help and support for women who are experiencing abuse. Underpinning each of the arguments in this chapter is a concern that modernity, especially in the context of a hybrid order, does not necessarily provide a pathway for women to reduce the risk and experience of abuse.

Hybridity and Timor-Leste

Not without some irony the concept of 'hybridity' has largely shed its association with its racist heritage.[6] Having in recent decades become more prominent in the social sciences and humanities, hybridity allows for a greater identification of sources of power and identity that are distinct from modern political and social domains. It has largely gained traction as a way to counter depictions of 'state-failure' and of 'ungovernable' populations, particularly in postcolonial states that have experienced large-scale violence including contexts where the modern state is unevenly constituted.[7]

Hybridity in this chapter is taken as a way of explaining contexts where multiple patterns of social integration—or 'life-worlds' as they will be referred to in shorthand—are in evidence to the extent that it is difficult to claim that one has a clear dominance over another. Instead, it is taken that there are multiple forms of sociality of significance; 'life-worlds' that speak to the embedded assumptions that shape patterns of practice. Cohen and Arato describe a 'life-world' as 'the reservoir of implicitly known traditions, the background of assumptions that are embedded in language and culture and drawn upon by individuals in everyday life'.[8] This chapter follows in similar sense, with the emphasis on the relationships between people (social integration) as manifest in the patterns of everyday practice. Extending further than the domains

---

5   Agnew, *Globalization and Sovereignty*, 2.
6   Dinnen and Kent, 'Hybridity in Peacebuilding and Development'.
7   Boege et al., 'Hybrid Political Orders, Not Fragile States'; Mac Ginty, *International Peacebuilding and Local Resistance*; Mac Ginty and Richmond, 'The Fallacy of Constructing Hybrid Political Orders'; Mallet, 'Beyond Failed States'; Richmond, 'Post-colonial Hybridity'.
8   Cohen and Arato, *Civil Society and Political Theory*, 427.

of language and culture, however, these include socioeconomic and sociopolitical practices, and in turn encompass what these 'assumptions' are across space, time and epistemology.

A hybrid order refers to contexts where differing life-worlds are each co-present to significant extents, with the focus here on the 'customary' and 'modern'. The customary reaches beyond culture, and in Timor-Leste is a way of describing a world view that reverberates through forms of exchange, production, organisation, communication and so on, framed by a cosmological view of the world bound very strongly to a sense of origin. The modern, however, is grounded in different forms of practice (for instance, the dominance of mass digital communication over the oral, technocratic leadership over genealogical authority), and where secular logic and rationality are the dominant ways in which society is integrated and ordered. This pushes the analytical lens past ideology for instance, which is itself a manifestation of modernity, and thus debates about the liberal peace are understood here as one possible manifestation of a modernity in which the individual and a particular form of state (largely Weberian) come to the fore.[9]

It is difficult to claim that either the customary or the modern has a particular dominance in Timor-Leste. While speaking of 'Timor-Leste' is an immediate reference to a modern political formation, other ways of organising social life remain vitally important across the territory. The customary—often cast discursively as traditional, indigenous, local or even 'culture'—on one hand, and the modern on the other, give an account of important moments in the texture and contours of social life. These terms are nevertheless heuristic devices used here to allow for analysis that distinguishes an ontological basis for patterns of practice. Analysis is an abstracting process and the separation of social life into categories (these, or others such as the state and civil society, or the local and the global) does not tend to exist *in the same way* in terms of how people see their own actions in an everyday sense. As such, these categories allow for analysis to occur, but are not necessarily representative of the ways people would readily see themselves or categorise their practice in the first instance (which can begin to occur when people are asked questions by researchers). In turn such categories do not *necessarily* create binaries, though analysis that assumes, for instance, there is a tension between

---

9   Steger, *The Rise of the Global Imaginary*, Chapters 1–3.

the two tends in that direction, and similarly where analysis implicitly or explicitly claims there are only two social possibilities: the modern and the otherwise (however categorised). As such, while drawing to these two categories of social integration, they do not present an overall unity nor claim to explain all the different dimensions of sociality. These are merely two points of emphasis that are relevant in Timor-Leste.

Customary and modern spatiality

The endogenously and exogenously driven modernising efforts that occur in Timor-Leste have not resulted in a demise of customary social relations.[10] The customary and modern are often seen to create points of friction, or entanglement, in forms of governance, systems of exchange and—as per the following quote from a 2003 report—at the intersection of justice processes and gender relations:

> Women leaders feel that the use of local justice systems is 'not better than [*sic* than] nothing' as it undermines attempts to implement standards of law which might combat factors preventing women from accessing it, such as powerlessness and shame. However, inherent cultural practices, beliefs and norms are so powerful that even with education in the era since Independence, standards of human rights and other modern concepts are being both misunderstood and completely lost due to the massive gap between these concepts and the realities on the ground.[11]

While the quote suggests tension between two life-worlds, it also gives rise to a sense of one being drawn into and reframed by the other (in this instance as modern concepts are 'misunderstood'). More than a decade after this was written, women continue to navigate narrow possibilities across two forms of justice to the extent that some have called for a formalised negotiation between different legal systems.[12] Rather than examine the process of justice itself, this chapter takes a different route and argues that each 'system' is situated in a life-world and in analytical terms underpinned by different forms of epistemology, temporality and, as the focus here, spatiality.

---

10   Carroll-Bell, 'Development Alternatives in Timor-Leste'; Hohe, 'The Clash of Paradigms'; McWilliam, 'Houses of Resistance in East Timor'.
11   Swaine, *Traditional Justice and Gender Based Violence*, 14.
12   Kovar and Harrington, *Breaking the Cycle of Domestic Violence in Timor-Leste*.

Space is an abstraction that enables humans to order their relationship to both the material world and to one another. Space is distinguished by bounded areas that mark that which is inside and outside, and can be materially defined—for instance, the marked boundaries to land—to that which is seemingly immaterial: an online community, a network, a national space, a public sphere. As the existence of boundaries suggests, there are always multiple spaces; these layers cut across one another and, following Massey, are in a constant state of reproduction:

> First, that we recognise space as the product of interrelations; as constituted through interactions, from the immensity of the global to the intimately tiny … Second, that we understand space as the sphere of the possibility of the existence of multiplicity in the sense of contemporaneous plurality; as the sphere in which distinct trajectories coexist; as the sphere therefore of coexisting heterogeneity … Third, that we recognise space as always under construction. Precisely because space on this reading is a product of relations-between, relations which are necessarily embedded material practices which have to be carried out, it is always in the process of being made. It is never finished; never closed.[13]

In turn, 'spatiality' is taken here as referring to the relationship between social life and space. It is more than the domain itself in a dimensional sense, referring to the social relations that constitute that space. Its use here is similar to Silva's approach to place in her work on Dili and the 'mountains' in Timor-Leste, where she uses 'the category place as a morally meaningful space to which certain actors and agencies are associated'.[14] While place here is understood as a fixed and identified geographic location, spatiality takes on the moral dimensions that Silva speaks to as well as other elements of social life, such as knowledge, rights and history.

One way of thinking about a hybrid order is conceiving it as a multitude of spatialities composed both across and within different patterns of practice that are in a constant state of reproduction and change. Here, then, to speak of customary and modern forms of spatialities is to draw back to a metatype that allows for generalised analysis, though as any inquiry becomes more specific the more immediate context would shape and contour any description, adding nuance and variation.

---

13   Massey, *For Space*, 9.
14   Silva, 'Foho versus Dili', 146.

Customary space in an East Timorese context could be characterised by interrelationships in two ways: the genealogical and kinship connections between living people, and in turn their relationship with the ancestral domain. Space and place—the latter being the specific identified geographic location—tend to be closely proximate, their boundaries may not be contiguous, they tend to incorporate sacred sites that are exclusive to a specific group, and they are often associated with a powerful sense of origin. The ground, or land in a more generalised sense, tends to be of intense importance in this form of space.

Modern space, in the alternative, is treated as secular, empty, commodifiable, transferrable, unifiable and homogenous, and tends to be sharply delineated. To return to 'Timor-Leste', 'territory' is a form of modern space where what might have been fairly open frontiers are now hard borders measured to the centimetre by satellite systems.

In the remainder of this chapter I argue that in the context of a hybrid order different spatialities inform the patterns of violence against women. Challenges lie with external agencies and how they approach gender more broadly in Timor-Leste and, as discussed in the next section, different forms of spatiality may be transgressed in ways that could undermine the broader objectives of ending violence against women.

Rendering Timor-Leste

A recently published article opened with the explanation that 'patriarchal traditions and a history of armed conflict in Timor-Leste provide a context that facilitates violence against women'.[15] The sentence is ambiguous enough to avoid the claim of direct causality, though the reader is left very much with the impression that violence against women is inextricably linked to two localised characteristics, namely 'tradition' and 'history'. Such a claim is hardly exceptional as Timor-Leste is frequently described as a 'patriarchal society', referring to the fact there is a clear power inequity between women and men that transpires in a myriad of ways. While the participation of women is regulated on local governing councils

---

15   Meiksin et al., 'Domestic Violence, Marital Control, and Family Planning, Maternal, and Birth Outcomes in Timor-Leste', 1338.

(*konsellu suku*), and Timor-Leste leads the way in terms of participation of women in parliament, this has not translated into shifting power imbalances more generally.[16]

The key concern here is that while it is possible to classify Timor-Leste as patriarchal, when it is done as a broad descriptor—and as an implicit differentiator from other societies—then the effect is a powerful one. If it is accepted that virtually all societies reflect significant patterns of patriarchy, then differentiating on these grounds appears, when undertaken by outsiders, to establish points of separation rather than creating opportunities that allow for meaningful connections to be made. This is a kind of 'rendering' that labels a population negatively and as a consequence approaches it as if it is in need of treatment.[17] To turn this around and speak of 'patriarchy in an East Timorese context' may appear only to make a minor discursive alteration, though here it is argued otherwise.

In the first instance, assertions of Timor-Leste as patriarchal per se and as an all-encompassing categorisation risk missing the agency of those who struggle against it, and in turn the identification of subsequent counter-spaces. Such an approach also closes rather than opens pathways to build spaces for solidarities and mutual learning across societies. By contrast, rather than concentrating only on points of difference, acknowledging similarities may promote esteem and disable shame or self-blame if survivors of violence come to understand that they are not an exception, either individually or as a defined group.

Second, rendering Timor-Leste as patriarchal provides a kind of legitimating logic for a particular form of intervention into spaces that would otherwise be largely inaccessible to outsiders. Naming patriarchy—or the less confronting surrogate 'gender inequity'—as a societal designator provides the raison d'être for foreign-funded programs to justify interventions. One of the challenges of working on violence against women is that it confronts entrenched forms of power and control in very embodied ways that call an intimate sense of self into question: sex and sexuality, fertility and procreation, household economies, spirituality and faith, the regulation of the body. These are not necessarily based in a customary 'life-world', but in Timor-Leste they often are. Establishing points of

---

16 Cummins, 'The Problem of Gender Quotas'.
17 Pupavac, 'Therapeutic Governance'.

difference then equips the outsider with a rationale for challenging the very body and how it is understood, not least as they become focused at the same points of intimate life; into health and reproduction, or gender norms and behaviours, relationships and so on. These may or may not be helpful in and of themselves, but the point here is the danger in the assumed legitimacy of doing so and the onward effects.

To come back to the hybrid order discussed above, such a form of intervention in Timor-Leste can be seen as occurring across two forms of spatiality. In one way, the modernity of interveners—non-government organisations, aid and humanitarian workers, state agencies—often correlates to the way that practice is matched to conceptions of space. That is, programs are planned to forge social change within a modern space. As a result, activities are directed at the public sphere, into a civil society, through the state, into localised public spaces, school curriculums and so on. Despite the limited reach of television in Timor-Leste, TV commercials are made depicting 'Feto Fantastiku', a superhero woman dressed in a cape made of local weaving. Banners are hung across busy streets, posters placed at the offices of local leaders, T-shirts printed. Existing norms are contested as spatiality is imagined as the modernist either sees it or wills it to be: open, accessible, contestable via evidence and arguments of universal rights, and with the potential of carrying an authoritative voice via disembodied means.

Modern spatiality has remained the preoccupation of foreign-led interventions, though the justification of patriarchy also allows for a transgression of customary spatiality. By this it is meant there is a sense of a legitimate claim to penetrate social relations where access would otherwise be unlikely, such as challenging the role of customary leaders or social priorities (such as spiritual over material). This may be the case as 'culture' is seen as something that must change or simply because there is expatriate blindness to the existence of such a life-world at all. This is, in many respects, where the intervention is at its most powerful and helps us understand why discussions of violence in Timor-Leste often orient towards 'culture' and 'tradition'. The exchange process at the time of marriage, commonly termed *barlake* in Tetun, is an example of a discursive signifier that carries a sense of oppression in spite of counter-evidence. With the origins of violence against women then localised (doubly so when history of warfare is included), the conditions are set in place where demands for change are focused inwards and across space that would otherwise be untraversable by the foreigner. The article quoted at the opening of this section ends up calling for exactly this outcome:

> Our findings suggest that in the short-term, targeted interventions addressing family planning, maternal healthcare, and birth outcome vulnerabilities for Timorese women who have experienced DV or marital control would be a good use of public health resources, due to their elevated risk.[18]

There is a need here to be unequivocal about what is being argued. It is entirely appropriate that there are aid-funded programs that work to support survivors of domestic violence, both specifically in terms of support services and prevention, as well as in health, justice, policing and so on. The challenge then is that this needs to be positioned as emancipatory rather than as a form of societal control, and this is far more difficult to achieve if the broad logic is shaped by differentiation rather than mutuality.

Over the decade or more since independence, it is possible to see, for instance, that resistance to the idea of gender, and gender equity, has developed within local populations and targeted as an 'outside' or foreign idea.[19] Contestation is to be expected, and in some instances suggests a more rigid application of culture as men attempt to maintain control.[20] However, that 'gender' is often deemed a foreign concept that came after independence and is contrary to 'local culture' is also in part a dynamic generated by the way programs have been framed.[21] Carrying a thread of the colonial encounter, power rests on maintaining differentiation and the demands for change cut into spheres of life without generating the inside legitimacy that enable traction. Simultaneously this dynamic demands virtually no reflexivity on the part of the intervener, for instance, in terms of exploring the reasons why violence against women remains so deeply intractable in societies typically designated as 'modern'. In such circumstances, differentiation in this form will more likely lead either to internalisation or resistance, neither productive in terms of ending violence against women and providing support to those who experience it.

---

18   Meiksin et al., 'Domestic Violence, Marital Control, and Family Planning', 1346.
19   UNFPA, *Gender-Based Violence in Timor-Leste*.
20   Niner, '*Hakat Klot*, Narrow Steps'.
21   Smith, 'When "Gender" Started', 56.

Customary spatiality and double sovereignty

A recently published Asia Foundation report found that women were often contained to a 'domestic sphere' where, for a combination of economic and political reasons, it was difficult for them to leave or seek assistance when experiencing abuse.[22] Extending this analysis, the argument across the last two sections of this chapter is that while economic factors are central, they are one part in a pattern of control that is referred to as 'double sovereignty', a term used to explain how a woman's mobility is contained and controlled across both customary and modern spaces. Sovereignty, as discussed in the Introduction, denotes a control over space, and while typically applied in the context of nation-states, here it refers to localised forms of spatiality that set the perimeters for the possibilities of everyday life.[23]

To turn to a discussion of the first element of this double sovereignty, a key aspect of customary spatiality in Timor-Leste is that access to space is based on genealogical and kinship ties. Legitimacy to participate in social life is dependent on how one claims a place in relation to extended familial networks and in turn access to space that is connected to production (the home, land, water, forests, people), spirituality (land, *lulik* sites, graves, ancestors), knowledge (elders, sacred houses), exchange of commodities (extended family, including ritual belongings) and communication (people, embodied communal space).

Forms of customary spatiality are reproduced in a myriad of localised ways, both through designated sacred sites and at moments of ritual, as well as in terms of cosmological understandings of land and ancestors and conceptions of agency, power and control. As such it is also manifest in an unannounced way in how patterns of social life are constantly re-created. These come to the fore at the point of intersection between familial groupings (*uma kains*, as extended clans defined by genealogical and kinship connection). For instance, people announce their sacred house as they arrive at funerals, name sacred houses to denote precedence in relation to land, and terms such as *kaben tama* (the male enters the wife's family on marriage) and *kaben sai* (the female leaves her family at marriage) are used to map the boundaries of inclusion and exclusion of families.

---

22 Grenfell et al., *Beyond Fragility and Inequity*.
23 Agnew, *Globalization and Sovereignty*.

This form of spatiality operates as a series of petit polities that—as discussed in the Introduction—are formed around a kind of spatial sovereignty. Outsiders rarely transgress these in any kind of permanent way (and even a temporary transgression would often require some kind of negotiation). In Timor-Leste, migration without existing connections is uncommon where customary spatialities remain dominant. Customary regulations (*lisan* or *adat*) are seen to regulate households in ways that separate one extended familial unit from another. 'According to our *adat*' is a common preface to sentences. Moreover, there is a constant reference to matters being kept 'within the household', generally meaning either an immediate family (*familia rasik*) or a more extended familial unit bound by genealogy and affinal relations, and ordered through association to sacred houses. Hence, familial units are bound into different forms of sovereignty that are exclusive from one another.

There is a range of ways that customary forms of spatiality can be seen as reproducing patriarchal social relations. These can be seen as most clearly manifest in the overwhelming dominance of males in leadership positions (across the spectrum of spiritual and political), divisions of labour, control over the body, norms around procreation and mobility. The counter-examples of matrilineal systems in Timor-Leste are both exceptional and shift the texture of power but not the power itself.[24]

In this context, sovereign control embedded in masculine identities, and manifest in the relationship between women and men, is exercised to control a women's mobility through economic dependence, divisions of labour, patterns of procreation and forms of coercion. However, the sovereignty also means a resistance to external intervention because 'outsiders'—whether other East Timorese or foreigners—have no legitimacy to reach into the particularities of customary space. The outside world has restricted access, and, when it does enter, it does so frequently as negotiated by males such as where domestic violence cases are referred out to police and then back to the families. The 2010 Law Against Domestic Violence is designed to interrupt this space by mandating that all reported cases are investigated by the police, effectively pulling the inside-customary into the outside-modern space of the nation. However, this only works to a certain extent, not just because of resources but also because the police, health workers and others at the interface of intervention straddle the customary and modern themselves.

---

24   Grenfell et al., *Beyond Fragility and Inequity*, 56–68.

Modern sovereignty and urban violence

The unevenness between the co-existing forms of spatiality in Timor-Leste does not necessarily shift the possibilities for women who are experiencing violent abuse. Despite the concentrations of law enforcement, support agencies, communication systems and transportation, rates of violence against women remain high in urban centres such as Dili.

> The results show that intimate partner violence is a significant problem in all sites across Timor-Leste. However, rates of physical and sexual intimate partner violence were consistently higher in Dili than in other municipality sites, and higher in urban areas compared with rural areas. For example, in Dili 64 percent of ever-partnered women had ever experienced physical and/or sexual intimate partner violence in their lifetimes, compared with 57 percent in other sites.[25]

In part to account for this, I argue here that modern forms of spatiality remain patriarchal and represent the second element or tier of a 'double sovereignty' that results in the control over women's mobility. Critical to this is the way a sharp distinction emerges between public and private spaces as different articulations of modern spatiality.

In a predominantly urban site such as the capital, Dili, a modern spatiality comes to the fore via public spaces that are no longer genealogically determined: roads and pathways, transport, institutional formations such as universities, the public service and hospitals, public parks and soccer fields, commercial enterprises and, more abstractly, a public sphere via digital and print media. The non-contiguous boundaries of community often found in rural areas change for the more rigid boundaries dividing urban *suku* from each other.[26] At the same time, the notion of a private sphere becomes grounded in the intimate family, and family size tends to diminish as does the ability to co-locate extended families. 'Property rights' designate access to bounded land while emergent 'liberal rights' defend against an intrusive state.

A commonality between customary and modern spatialities is found via the way that women remain contained overwhelmingly to the domestic sphere, albeit for different reasons. The allure of cash income within modern modes of production is sustained by unpaid labour at home

---

25 Asia Foundation, *Understanding Violence against Women and Children*, 51–52.
26 Grenfell et al., *Understanding Community*.

including care for children. Such activities are consistently mapped via essentialised notions of gender, and the private sphere becomes a new domain of containment. The result can be both a lack of access to the means of economic production (especially as women become disengaged from land) and a continued if not accelerated dependency on intimate partners, with an effect on gendered identity formations.

> The significantly lower number of income-generating activities carried out by women in Dili, alongside the shift in perceptions that women's role is solely that of 'housewife' rather than 'farmer,' could suggest an increase in women's dependency as urbanisation increases. During participatory rural appraisals and focus group discussions in Dili, women tended to emphasise women's role as primary caregiver and were more likely to state that the woman's role was in the home whereas the man's role was to generate income. This type of statement was rarely heard in the more rural settings.[27]

In speaking of the containment of women's mobility, True points to the way some women in the global North offset their own risk of intimate partner violence by employing women from the global South:

> In a mutually constitutive way, the strict division of roles in the domestic sphere constrains women's public participation and their access to economic opportunities in the market, in turn creating inequalities in household bargaining power between men and women and entrapping women into potentially violent environments at home and at work. Some women, especially those in developed countries, avoid patriarchal, and potentially violent, situations in the family/private sphere by contracting out care work to poor women, including migrant women from the global South.[28]

Even without crossing national borders, a similar dynamic can often be seen in sites such as Dili. In cases where women find work and increase their economic independence, the need for unpaid labour as a carer for the home and children remains with them. In such cases young women, very often at some point of familial connection, are moved from rural communities to Dili and work at very low rates (or even just for board and meals). Where a male is employed but unmarried, then a female from the extended family will often live with him in order to cook and clean. Either way, there is a constant reproduction of modern private spheres being gendered as the essential domain for women.

---

27 Grenfell et al., *Beyond Fragility and Inequity*, 54.
28 True, 'The Political Economy of Violence against Women', 45.

One of the features of modernity is the hard distinction that tends to emerge between public and private. In addition to the private sphere then, the public sphere is a second form of modern spatiality where patriarchal norms are consolidated. In the independence period in Timor-Leste, militaristic masculinities have become vaunted and celebrated via the heroic warrior image associated with the republic's veteran leadership.[29] The creation of ideal forms emerge as marketing becomes more important, as seen at the icon of high modernity, the 'Timor Plaza' shopping centre parades of young women in 'Little Miss Timor' competitions. Nation and gender are connected via abstracted norms of the ideal woman.

While there are always exceptions and degrees of variation, the argument is that men often maintain a kind of sovereign control over modern forms of spatiality. Women remain overwhelmingly contained to the domestic sphere, redoubled by the essentialising symbolic trajectories in the public sphere. Mobility for women may of course be possible, but it is regulated, granted permission and 'chaperoned'. Women might well, for instance, gain an education, but there will be immense pressure for children at some point regardless, and even in the event of professional work they will remain responsible for the home sphere. This creates an environment where women often remain financially dependent and, in periods of abuse, with restricted ability to leave. At the same time in this scenario it can be even more difficult to know where abuse is occurring, especially if the familial networks that can provide support within a customary polity have largely dissolved in the modern urban sphere.

Concluding hybridity

The effect of this form of 'double sovereignty' is profound in that it multiplies the range of inequities and challenges faced when violence against women occurs. Moreover, here two forms of spatiality have been discussed as separate categories that allow for an analysis as they delineate different ways people engage with space. For instance, a woman who migrates to an urban centre for work or marriage may be subject to new forms of containment and yet remain bound into customary socialities in her origin community. Albeit in different ways then, these forms

---

29   Kent, 'Remembering the Past, Shaping the Future'; Kent and Kinsella, 'A Luta Kontinua'; Niner, 'Hakat Klot, Narrow Steps'.

of spatiality can overlap in order to compound the challenges faced, rather than provide pathways out of abuse, and be seen as sovereignty as control over women.

In summary then, I have drawn on the notion of hybridity—and more specifically a hybrid order—to consider how spatialities across different life-worlds exacerbate the experience of violence by women. The complexity of the hybrid order may allow for moments of navigation away from violence, though here the argument has been that—at least in terms of spatiality—neither modernity nor the customary necessarily provide a significant point of alleviation from violence. At a programming level, efforts to reduce levels of abuse that rest on designating populations as patriarchal and singularly localising, risk reducing longer-term efforts to prevent violence. These may allow for a form of justification for intervention, but may do so in a way that builds resistance as a kind of colonial encounter while failing to create a legitimate counterpoint to patriarchy locally. This is not to call for an end to interventions, rather it is an argument for them that is framed with a greater reflexivity on the part of outsiders with regard to their own modernity, and the role of violence and power within it.

15

Hybridity and Regulatory Authority in Fiji: Vernacular Perspectives on Gender and Security

Nicole George

A bicameral parliament with a grass skirt, or some other sort of tokenistic nod to 'the local', does not amount to a hybrid polity. Instead, we see hybridity as a more local but scalar mixing of ideas, norms and personnel, with power in full view.[1]

Introduction

In this chapter, I examine the function of hybridised regulatory authority as it is configured in Fiji and focus specifically on the implications this has for the policing of gender in this Pacific island country. The quote that leads this chapter, from a recent article by Roger Mac Ginty and Oliver Richmond, prompted me to reflect on the symbolism of the dress uniforms that are worn by the Fiji Police Force. In particular, I was reminded of a photograph taken by Ali Rae, an accomplished photojournalist who accompanied me on a fieldwork trip to Suva in 2013. This photograph shows the police force band at the launch of a new communal policing campaign in Suva, resplendent in parade uniforms

---

1   Mac Ginty and Richmond, 'The Fallacy of Constructing Hybrid Political Orders'.

consisting of a navy dress shirt and dazzling tailored white formal wraparound *sulu* (Figure 15.1). But contrary to the more conventional even-hemmed cut of this garment, the hem of the police *sulu* is styled in a way that references more traditional dress — that is, the pandanus or 'grass skirts' of the region.

Figure 15.1: The Fiji Police Force band at the launch of a new communal policing campaign, Suva, 2013
Source: Photo by Ali Rae.

As this chapter will demonstrate, this 'nod' to the 'local' should not simply be read only as a tokenistic incorporation of islands 'fashion' in formal police dress. My contention is that this uniform is also more deeply symbolic of the hybridised 'fashioning' of regulatory enforcement in Fiji and the extent to which the everyday operations of the state security agencies in Fiji are shaped by, and intertwined with, powerful institutions of customary and religious authority. At first glance, this scenario may be taken to suggest that state policing authority, fashioned in this way, is brought 'closer to the people',[2] resonating with the values, practices and protocols that lie at the heart of Fijian identity.[3] What is less sure is the extent to which this system of authority makes 'everyday emancipatory

---

2   Baker and Scheye, 'Multi-layered Justice and Security Delivery', 512.
3   Brown et al., 'Challenging Statebuilding as Peacebuilding', 101.

forms of peace'[4] more achievable or more accessible to all who live within its jurisdiction. This question comes into sharp relief if we ask about the ways gender and sexuality are policed within this hybridised system of regulatory authority.

This question has critical implications for the study of hybridity and hybrid regulatory authority more generally. The concept of hybridity has been invoked by those aiming to understand where and how localised authority functions in ways that may potentially complement 'top-down' sites of regulatory authority, helping to consolidate order through stronger recognition of 'local strengths and resilience'.[5]

But there are more sceptical appraisals of this concept, too. Some have illustrated the co-constitutive nature of the relationship between 'top-down' and 'bottom-up' sites of regulatory authority, and the extent to which formalised sites of authority may construct their own 'local' according to what they are able to 'find, initiate or are willing to support financially'.[6] Others have given close consideration to the ways cultural practices may be appropriated by particular groups to serve sectional interests in ways that potentially subvert the original aims, symbolism or meaning of that activity; a scenario which, in certain contexts, explains the increasing commercialisation of traditional gift giving as part of customary reconciliation practices, for example.[7] A further critical contention, pertinent to debate on hybridity and enforcement, is that the recent hybrid turn aligns with a global neoliberal orthodoxy which encourages public sector retreat from security provision and the outsourcing of security agency work to privatised military and security companies with attendant problems of accountability.[8]

It is only recently that the concept of hybridity has been subject to gendered critique, work which has been pioneered by the likes of Annika Björkdahl,[9] writing with Kristine Höglund[10] and Johanna Selimovic.[11] Drawing on Anna Tsing's foundational work in globalisation and

4   Mac Ginty and Richmond, 'The Fallacy of Constructing Hybrid Political Orders', 220.
5   Brown et al., 'Challenging Statebuilding as Peacebuilding', 101; Mac Ginty, 'Indigenous Peace-Making'.
6   Heathershaw, 'Towards Better Theories of Peacebuilding', 280.
7   Wallis et al., 'Political Reconciliation in Timor Leste'.
8   Abrahamsen and Williams, *Security beyond the State*.
9   Björkdahl, 'A Gender-Just Peace?'.
10   Björkdahl and Höglund, 'Precarious Peacebuilding'.
11   Björkdahl and Selimovic, 'Gendering Agency in Transitional Justice'.

friction,[12] Björkdahl, writing with her various co-authors, has emphasised the 'frictions' that occur when there is an interplay between 'bottom-up' and 'top-down' sites of authority and the extent to which sites of 'local agency' working in cooperation with more formalised sites of authority can be generative of their own gendered exclusions and restrictions.[13] These studies pose important questions about the forms of social control that are legitimated within hybridised environments and how these may compound rather than alleviate gendered insecurity.

How might this frictional interplay between state and non-state sites of regulatory authority be explained in Fiji and what are the frictional gendered outcomes that are produced in this process? Scholarly enquiry into the indigenisation of state agencies of regulatory authority in Fiji provides an important context for this question. This 'indigenisation' has been explained as a contemporary extension of the paternalistic system of colonial authority, devised by the British in Fiji, which enabled them to manage, and keep distinct, the spaces in which indigenous Fijians and, with the beginning of indenture, the imported population of Indian labourers were able to move.[14] Through a system of indirect rule, indigenous sites of authority were rearticulated into the formal system of state regulation. This strategy assisted the penetration of colonial authority into indigenous communities, and endowed the standing of Fijian populations with a particular sort of legitimacy in the eyes of the state. At the same time, this system of indigenised authority emphasised the distinctiveness of the Indian population and undermined the legitimacy of Indians' demands for similar sorts of protective recognition within state structures of regulatory authority.[15]

Much has been written on the contemporary legacies of this scenario in Fiji and the implications this has for the operations of state agencies of security and enforcement.[16] But, beyond the important work done by local gender advocates, very little attention has been focused on the various ways that this fusing of state and indigenous authority structures shapes the policing of gender and sexuality in Fiji in the contemporary context. In this chapter, I squarely address this issue. My contention

---

12   Tsing, *Friction*.
13   Björkdahl and Selimovic, 'Gendering Agency in Transitional Justice', 167.
14   Firth, 'Colonial Administration'.
15   Kelly and Kaplan, *Represented Communities*.
16   Halapua, *Tradition, Lotu and Militarism in Fiji*; Newland, 'New Methodism and Old'; Trnka, 'Remythologizing the State'.

is that even when policy reforms advocating a more liberal policing of gender, or race, have been adopted, the particular configuration of regulatory authority that operates in Fiji tends to result in everyday policing practice which punishes expressions of gender or sexuality that do not adhere to heterosexual conjugal norms. However, this defence of what I term 'conjugal order'[17] is undertaken by police, not simply because to do otherwise is understood by Fiji Police Force officers as a violation of cultural or religious values or protocols that lie at the heart of expressions of indigenous identity, but also because it is understood to pose a threat to widely and deeply held notions of community order and security.

I develop these claims more fully in the following sections of this chapter. First, I briefly establish an intellectual context for the arguments I make here, situating this particular enquiry within a broader debate on gender, rights and culture in the Pacific islands. Second, I draw on feminist contributions to debate on the concept of hybridity to develop a conceptual framework for my examination of gender and hybridised authority in Fiji. Third, I examine the way in which security as a concept is locally defined or 'vernacularised'[18] and why this is relevant to the policing of gender in Fiji. In the fourth section of this chapter, I discuss everyday examples of policing practice to substantiate my claims about state security agencies' active defence of conjugal order, showing how this activity is understood to protect the foundations of communal and national order. I conclude with some reflections on the ways that gendered analysis of regulatory authority can contribute to debate on hybridised systems of governance and security into the future.

Gender and hybridity: A context for critique

Before I progress this discussion further, it is important to establish an intellectual context for the argument I defend here. My effort to uncover the gender-restrictive consequences that accrue when policing is shaped by intertwined sources of customary, religious and state security agency authority in Fiji may be taken by some to suggest that I view the relationship between gender, custom and faith, as this operates more generally in Pacific islands societies, with a feminist scepticism or that I see this relationship as solely disempowering for women.

---

17   MacKenzie, *Female Soldiers in Sierra Leone*, 4.
18   Bubandt, 'Vernacular Security'.

This chapter is not written with the aim of defending this view. It is important to research the relationship between gender, rights and culture in the Pacific islands region with caution, sensitivity and in ways that accommodate nuance and contingency. In this vein, my past research on these questions has examined how women's rights activists in Pacific island countries have advanced demands for increased political participation, or improved responses to high rates of gendered violence, in ways that also draw from local religious and cultural discourses.[19] These acts of 'translation' have yoked universalistic political formulations which establish women's 'rights' to participation and security with customary protocols and biblical teachings which promote respect for women or women's matrilineal authority in familial or clan contexts. I have shown that for women activists in the Pacific islands, these hybridised political claims have been integral to challenging the idea that resistance to women's disadvantage amounts to an acceptance of foreign or inauthentic values that have little resonance with local ways of thinking.[20]

One particularly powerful articulation of this bridging discourse, as it has been formulated in Fiji, has emphasised the significance of the *i tatau* in the context of debates on high rates of physical violence perpetrated against women in conjugal and family settings in Fiji. This indigenous customary practice requires new husbands to make a formal vow, on presentation of a *tabua* or whale's tooth to their wife's family, to care for and protect their daughter. Failure to uphold this vow makes the husband answerable to his in-laws, and has often been severely punished.[21] This customary practice has been invoked by activists seeking to challenge the idea that assertions of women's right to physical security in intimate conjugal or familial settings is a *palagi* or foreign practice that has no place in Fijian society.[22] The *i tatau* example operates here to remind those who are suspicious of 'rights-based' political claims and equate them with 'heartless globalization and irreligion'[23] that similar principles about the standing of women are upheld in Fijian cultural practice.

However, while my research has demonstrated the political significance of processes of rights translation, I have also drawn attention to the enabling *and* constraining aspect of this political activity. This question

---

19 George, '"Starting with a Prayer"'; George, '"Just Like Your Mother?"'.
20 See also Douglas, 'Christian Citizens'; Jolly, 'Woman Ikat Raet Long Human Raet o No?'.
21 Daurewa, 'The Power of Fiji's Women'.
22 Ibid.
23 Douglas, 'Christian Citizens', 21.

gained prominence for me as a new researcher working in Fiji in the early 2000s. At this time, Fiji was recovering from a civilian-led rebel incursion that ultimately resulted in the dismissal of the elected government of the day. This forceful reassertion of indigenous political authority put a brake on the gradual process of liberal reform that had been underway in the country since 1997 when a new constitution allowed Fiji's first Indian-led government to rise to power. The 2000 civilian coup was an event that quickly resharpened and politicised lines of communal and ethnic difference in the country.[24] Self-installed Fijian nationalists sat at the head of government and an authoritarian state. They were quick to legitimate their power grab through appeals to faith and custom and equally prompt to voice criticism of, and sometimes direct threats against, those who did not share their convictions. In this climate, women activists certainly reflected on the value of careful translation strategies when talking about women's rights.[25] But in the same breath, many also voiced misgivings over the necessity of delivering their message in this way. They sometimes expressed this frustration by stating that they felt 'boxed in by culture', or at least by the narrow and highly politicised interpretations of culture that were being promoted by sections of the political elite at the time.[26]

For better or worse, the idea that nationalist invocations of culture or faith can be used to justify gender-restrictive practice (across a range of contexts) has shaped the way I come to the debate on hybridity. It is certainly important to recognise, document and celebrate hybridised forms of rights advocacy as they are developed by women activists in this context as evidence of political creativity and resourcefulness. But, as I will demonstrate, it is equally important to ask about the gendered relations of power that have been configured through interplaying systems of church and customary authority such as we find in Fiji, and to ask if or how this interplay or hybridity shapes the everyday delivery of regulatory authority. It is my contention that these things come together in Fiji in ways that compound the insecurity of particular groups of women in Fiji in significant ways.

---

24   Robertson and Sutherland, *Government by the Gun*.
25   George, *Situating Women*.
26   George, '"Just Like Your Mother?"'; George, *Situating Women*; George, '"Starting with a Prayer"'.

Hybridity and the everyday policing of conjugal order in Fiji

It might seem odd to observers of Fiji's politics that my study of gender and policing in Fiji is framed in terms that suggest a restrictive and indeed punitive security environment. After the military took power in Fiji in 2006 (a coup which was justified, on the surface at least, as necessary to curbing the excesses of indigenous nationalism), a number of legal reforms were introduced to improve the way police responded to the crimes of gendered violence, for example, or the way it treated homosexual citizens. The development of the 2009 Domestic Violence Decree, which aimed to reclassify a range of offences occurring in the 'family situation' as criminal acts, is one example of this shift.[27] Another is the Zero Tolerance Violence Free Community campaign, also launched in 2009, which aims to encourage a rejection of gendered forms of violence at the village level.[28] The 2013 constitution, replicating clauses present in the 1997 Fiji constitution that was overturned by the government in 2009, also protects Fiji's homosexual citizens from discrimination on the basis of their sexuality. This document also builds on a 2010 decree issued by the military government to decriminalise homosexuality, overturning a colonial-era legal statute making homosexuality a criminal offence. When considered together, these developments suggest that Fiji's political elite, who were later democratically elected in 2014, have been keen to present their credentials as gender reformers. Nonetheless, government rhetoric on this subject is soundly contradicted by the everyday operation of state security agencies whose policing of gender seems to frequently operate as if this reform agenda does not exist.

To understand where and, more particularly, how this gap between policy and policing practice is present, it is important to examine how understandings of security are vernacularised in Fiji within a 'hybridised' system of regulatory authority and how this gives a particular shape to the policing of gender in Fiji. To develop this aspect of my argument I draw on Nils Bubandt's ethnographic approach to security.

---

27   Radio New Zealand, 'Decree in Fiji Aimed at Tackling Domestic Violence'.
28   ABC Radio Australia, 'Fiji Women's Minister Defends Domestic Violence Decree'.

Bubandt's work calls attention to the way longstanding vernacular influences inflect prevailing 'idioms of uncertainty, order and fear' and help to legitimate specific 'forms of social control'.[29]

Bubandt asks how localised factors shape ideas about 'safe community'.[30] To do this he investigates how perceived threats to insecurity are framed or, in his words, generate an 'ontological uncertainty'.[31] From his perspective, efforts to come to grips with the 'problem of security' should pay attention to the 'socially constructed anxiety that shapes pertinent kinds of danger, fears and concerns for a particular community at a particular time'.[32] As he goes on to argue, this opens the way for investigating how different societies have different ways of 'socially producing … discursively portraying … symbolically representing … and politically managing ontological uncertainty'.[33] Against this backdrop, he suggests the concept of vernacular security as a 'convenient shorthand' to capture the connection that exists between 'the political rhetoric of safety and an ontology of uncertainty' and also how this connection is managed through the 'relationship that exists between the 'state and the community'.[34]

Following on from this, if we are to understand the gendered impacts of hybridised security environments in Fiji, or elsewhere, it seems important to first consider how multiple sites of regulatory authority operate in relation to one another to build social order and, second, to consider how threats to security are framed and legitimised in these contexts. Consequently, we might better understand how gendered forms of order and security are framed and managed by sites of regulatory enforcement but also how these framing and management strategies are reflective of the broader ontology of uncertainty that is generated within the hybridised security environment.

So what form does an ontology of insecurity take within Fiji's hybridised security environment and what are its gendered dimensions? To give some texture to this idea I draw on reflections and observations on the links between indigenous nationalism in Fiji and indigenous insecurity from

---

29   Bubandt, 'Vernacular Security', 277.
30   Ibid., 290.
31   Ibid., 277.
32   Ibid., 277.
33   Ibid., 277.
34   Ibid., 281.

one of Fiji's leading indigenous statesmen: customary leader, former vice president of Fiji and High Court judge, Ratu Joni Madraiwiwi. According to Madraiwiwi, since the late nineteenth century, Fijians have feared that their culture, their land, their way of life, perhaps their very survival as a people, is threatened by 'forces of change'.[35] These changes included those wrought by colonialism, most starkly the arrival of indentured Indian labourers to work in the colonial economy and whose descendants remain in Fiji and at one time outnumbered indigenous citizens.[36] Colonisation also brought Wesleyan Methodist missionaries to Fiji's shores. This latter group successfully converted large sections of the indigenous population to its church. Where religious conversion was not achieved voluntarily, the colonial state imposed its faith upon indigenous populations through militarised means.[37]

This early fusing of the state and Methodist church regulatory authority has survived Fiji's transition to independence and continued to influence military and policing activity in Fiji's highly communalised, postcolonial political environment. In this context, faith and custom function in an intertwined way as Janus-faced signifiers of order and disorder for Fiji's indigenous and predominantly Methodist population. Faith and custom sustain a sense of distinctive Fijian unity and identity but, conversely, also stoke an insistent ontological uncertainty, giving rise to fears about Fijians' ultimate survival and the need for vigorous state protection of indigenous custom and the centrality of their church.[38] Some Methodist church leaders fuel these fears from the pulpit, encouraging their congregations to reflect upon the dangers posed to Fijian unity by urbanism, individualism, consumerism and sometimes even indigenous customs.[39] For assisting this sense of unease, Fijian Methodism has been described as 'not quite the opium of the masses', but rather 'the caffeine of the masses' which 'energises people while intensifying their anxieties'.[40]

In this sense, to explain the function of hybridised regulatory authority in Fiji, it is important to consider how the exercise of state security and authority is actively shaped and influenced by religious and customary

---

35   Madraiwiwi, 'On Understanding the Fijian People', 23.
36   Firth, 'Colonial Administration and the Invention of the Native'.
37   Nicole, *Disturbing History*, 17.
38   Robertson and Sutherland, *Government by the Gun*, 50–74; Tomlinson, *In God's Image*, 168.
39   Tomlinson, *In God's Image*, 168.
40   Ibid., 25.

institutions. But beyond this, we need to also examine the vernacularised (and gendered) understandings of security and order that circulate and are privileged within this regulatory system.

Feminist security studies provide an important backdrop for this type of enquiry, showing the anti-emancipatory, and indeed gender-restrictive, discourses that emerge when societies are perceived to be under threat. In these contexts, gendered tropes of protection come powerfully to the fore.[41] In the process of holding off these threats, women are frequently identified by community leaders as the bearers of 'distinctive' feminised cultural norms which may be articulated in an idealised, restrictive and subordinating form.[42] Nonetheless, these norms also establish a foundation for notions of gender security, emphasising dutiful and dependent women as those most worthy of protection.[43] In these contexts, there may be a vigorous policing of women's identity and behaviour to ensure those gendered norms predominate. The aim here is not simply to regulate (women's) individual behaviour, but to police these norms because they are understood to provide the foundation for a more generalised sense of community order that is perceived to be under threat.[44]

Megan MacKenzie develops the term 'conjugal order' to capture the idea that there is frequently a link to be drawn between the 'laws and social norms that serve to regulate sexuality' and broader notions of order and stability.[45] Hence she considers how campaigns to protect strongly feminised ideals of domesticity, obedience and conjugal propriety become integral to the broader efforts to maintain forms of order. These broad trends may help to generate ideals of femininity that are upheld in a narrow, 'ethnicised' form[46] that may deny women's capacity for agency and casts activity that does not conform to the feminine ideal as gendered dissidence.

41   Cohn and Jacobson, 'Women and Political Activism', 114; Enloe, *Bananas, Beaches and Bases*; Enloe, *The Curious Feminist*; Young, 'The Logic of Masculinist Protection'.
42   de Alwis et al., 'Women and Peace Processes', 178; Young, 'The Logic of Masculinist Protection', 14.
43   McLeod, 'A Feminist Approach to Hybridity', 54; Young, 'The Logic of Masculinist Protection', 14.
44   Pettman, 'Boundary Politics', 196–197.
45   MacKenzie, *Female Soldiers in Sierra Leone*, 4.
46   Björkdahl and Selimovic, 'Gendering Agency in Transitional Justice', 167.

To understand the ways in which gender and hybridised regulatory authority in Fiji intersect it is important to consider the particular kinds of institutional interplay that shape state policing authority and activity in this context. But beyond this, it is also important to consider the discourses that fuel an insistent ontology of uncertainty in this hybridised context, and how these elements come together to legitimate a restrictive policing of conjugal norms because this is understood to be foundational to the achievement of community order, safety and wellbeing.

In this context, the regulatory authority of custom, and Fijian Methodism, has been described as a normative 'mould' shaping the psyche of Fiji's security agencies,[47] which predominantly comprise Fijian personnel and tend, correspondingly, to assess and police threats to order in ways that reflect an indigenous 'ontology of insecurity'. Narrow norms of conjugal order are upheld by agencies of regulatory authority in this context, not simply because this accords with the dictates of custom or faith, but because these norms are viewed as foundational to the achievement of a broader social order that requires vigilant protection. As I will now demonstrate, this scenario has resulted in practical policing which generates restrictive and sometimes highly punitive outcomes for women and men whose behaviour and expressions of sexuality are deemed to disrupt norms of conjugal order. It is my contention that these trends persist regardless of whether the political elite in power in Fiji advocates strongly nationalist or more reformist political sympathies. The gendered brunt of this hybridised exercise of authority has been particularly felt by Fiji's sex-worker population, gay and lesbian communities, and women seeking protection from gendered forms of violence.

Policing conjugal order: Regulating sexuality

Scrutiny of policing in the years following the Fijian military coup of 2006 indicates the consistent ways in which gender is policed within the country's hybridised system of regulatory authority. Despite its commitments to ending the indigenous capture of the state, the military government that assumed power at this time appointed a conservative and deeply religious senior military officer to the position of police commissioner in 2007. Under this command, the Fiji Police Force then

---

47 Teaiwa, 'Articulated Cultures'.

adopted an evangelistic approach to crime prevention known as the Souls to Jesus campaign which required officers to reflect on their duty to 'be God's Ambassadors'[48] and, through their own example, encourage a 'reconfiguring of public morality' as part of their crime-prevention work.[49] Officers on patrol were instructed to carry bibles as part of their kit, desk officers were required to answer the phone saying 'Praise the Lord' and the police band was instructed to play only Christian songs of worship. Police officers' morality enforcement saw them preach messages of restraint to couples embracing on Suva's sea wall, or young people frequenting Suva's busy nightclub strips.[50]

Those whose behaviour posed more serious threats to norms of conjugal propriety were subject to more serious forms of regulation. This was particularly so for sex workers who were subject to increasing forms of police surveillance. A new crimes decree enacted by the military government in 2009 gave police broader authority to round up and detain sex workers. But in Fiji, sex work is also discussed in ways which suggest it is a powerful source of ontological insecurity. Debates on the legalisation of sex work, for example, are commonly resisted in ways which pathologise this activity or which suggest that decriminalisation will invite 'divine retribution' upon the country.[51] Against this backdrop, regulatory interventions legitimised by the 2009 crimes decree saw detained sex workers subjected to brutal and degrading extrajudicial punishments while in police custody. These included detainees being forced to jump from bridges into the dark waters of sea inlets at night, detainees being stripped and having their heads shaved, and some subjected to forced labour inside military and police barracks.[52]

Fiji Police Force officers' treatment of Fiji's gay and lesbian communities was similarly discriminatory and punitive, despite a military decree in 2010 decriminalising homosexuality. Like the issue of sex work, debate on homosexuality and the rights of gay people in Fiji tends to expose how these questions are publicly framed as posing a challenge to the prevailing conjugal order, and, more broadly, fuel ontological insecurity. My previous work on these questions has shown that, despite more moderate religious

---

48   Trnka, 'Remythologizing the State', 81.
49   Ibid., 82.
50   McGeough, 'An Unholy Alliance'.
51   Pratibha, 'Rooting Out Prostitution and Associated Illicit Practices'; Singh, 'Prostitution Law Changes Fiji's Night Life'; Vakaliwaliwa, 'Question of Prostitution'.
52   McMillan and Worth, *Sex Workers and HIV Prevention in Fiji*.

leadership on this issue, many highly vocal church leaders frame tolerance of homosexuality as a 'cancer' that will invade the country or a 'curse' that will 'swamp' Fiji like a 'tsunami'.[53] This helps to explain why, despite legal and constitutional provisions outlawing discrimination on the basis of sexuality, state regulatory authorities have a well-established history of discriminating and harassing Fiji's homosexual community.[54] In 2007, a new case of this sort brought these broader tendencies into stark and disturbing contrast.

This incident involved the conduct of an auxiliary policeman who was found guilty of raping his sister, an act which he allegedly perpetrated to punish her for her involvement in a same-sex relationship and to rid her of her homosexuality. When this case was later brought to court, the presiding judge found the perpetrator guilty but also exonerated his behaviour in a judgement which stated that his normal reason was impaired by drunkenness. The light sentence, suspended for eight years, required the perpetrator to be jailed only at weekends.[55] This caused outcry among gender and human rights activists and was eventually overturned in the High Court after a long five-year interval. Nonetheless, this case conforms to a longstanding pattern of punitive and discriminatory responses displayed by regulatory authorities towards sex workers and homosexual citizens in Fiji.[56] There exists a pattern suggesting that the violence perpetrated against these groups by regulatory authorities is excusable because it is less grave than the embodied threats these citizens are felt to pose, both personally and collectively, to the ordering of a 'safe community'.

Policing conjugal order: Violence against women

In response to the excessive ways in which policing authority was exercised during the Souls to Jesus campaign, the Fiji Police Force later sought to soften its image through the development of a new community, or Duavata policing program, rolled out across a range of jurisdictions in

---

53 Pratibha, 'Rooting Out Prostitution'.
54 FWCC, Misogyny and Homophobia in the Fiji Police Force; George, 'Contending Masculinities and the Limits of Tolerance'; George, 'In Sickness and in Health'.
55 Narayan, 'Sister Rapist Serves Sentence Only on Weekends'.
56 George, 'In Sickness and in Health'.

2010. The term *duavata* is Fijian and expresses the idea of communities coming together. It is used by the police force to encourage the idea that the police and the community are partners in the effort to 'resolve identified problems in order to prevent crime'.[57] Outwardly, this program seemed to traverse Fiji's communal identifications and involved the participation of both Indian and Fijian industry, cultural and sporting groups, in a shift from the earlier Souls to Jesus campaign, which was exclusively Christian and evangelistic. Nonetheless, deeper scrutiny suggests that even within this new program, there is a hybridised aspect of state security agency operations that continues to function in gender-restrictive ways.

A central component of the Duavata policing program has been a zero-tolerance initiative on violence against women that encourages villages to declare themselves 'violence free' and involves community members as both stakeholders and participants in law and order provision. The program is designed to work in collaboration with state policing, but also aims to build community awareness that gender violence is a crime. Hence community leaders are trained to become designated 'gatekeepers' equipped with skills to reconcile conjugal disputes so that violence in the home or family is de-escalated or avoided altogether.[58] Should community interventions fail, the 2009 Domestic Violence Decree authorises a tough law and order response towards the perpetrators of gender violence.

But the Fiji Police Force's hardline authoritarianism, operating in tandem with informal sites of authority, also undermines the success of this policing program. On one hand, local stakeholders have been found to encourage reconciliation between aggrieved family members so that the customary and religious integrity of the marriage and the family remains intact. Accordingly, women are often urged to return to violent conjugal or familial environments and deterred from seeking external forms of protection or justice by making complaints known to police officers. On the other hand, an under-reporting of incidents of gender violence to police authorities is also said to have occurred because villages who declare themselves 'violence free' are eager to maintain their positive profile with potentially punitive state authorities and have become fearful of unwanted police scrutiny.[59]

---

57 FPF, *Fiji Police Duavata Community Policing Model*.
58 ABC Radio Australia, 'Fiji Women's Minister Defends Domestic Violence Decree'.
59 FWCC, *Somebody's Life, Everybody's Business*; Tukuwasa, 'Fiji Should Not Bank on Zero Reporting'.

Government sources have proudly advocated the successes of this program,[60] but women's non-government organisations in Fiji continue to raise concerns about the efficacy of these initiatives.[61] Allegations that state police officers are themselves perpetrators of this form of violence also undermines government advocacy of the policy gains on violence against women.[62] In this context, reforms designed to improve state agencies' responses to cases of violence against women have been undermined because they are layered over a hybridised system of regulatory authority where threats posed to conjugal and familial integrity are treated as a more serious source of ontological uncertainty than the physical insecurity that women might be exposed to within conjugal and familial settings and at the hands of police themselves. The community policing model may be designed to resonate with the 'the grain of local beliefs',[63] but in practice it has not provided any strong guarantee that women who are exposed to violence in the home and within their families can rely on state protection or intervention to uphold their right to safety.

Conclusion

Hybridity as a concept may presently be much in vogue in the fields of policing studies and in studies of statebuilding, and drawn upon to explain the problematic consequences of international interventions that attempt to layer institutions of governance in contexts 'without peace … without reconciliation'.[64] According to Oliver Richmond, these challenges can be reconciled when there is a prior commitment to 'a mutual process … which negotiates with local customary, cultural, political, social, class, economic and often religious dynamics' in combination with the 'thin cosmopolitan ideas upheld by democracy, human rights, welfare [and] rule of law'.[65]

It is perhaps revealing that Richmond's list of local dynamics does not include a mention of gender. This oversight requires more than a passing acknowledgement. There is a need, in my view, for closer and more nuanced thinking about the vernacularised ontologies of uncertainty

---

60   ABC Radio Australia, 'Fiji Women's Minister Defends Domestic Violence Decree'.
61   FWCC, *Somebody's Life, Everybody's Business*.
62   Tahana, 'Fiji PM's Violence Condemnation Rings Hollow for Some'.
63   Dinnen and Peake, 'More than Just Policing', 572.
64   Richmond, 'Between Peacebuilding and Statebuilding', 174.
65   Ibid.

and insecurity that are generated in hybridised environments, and the potential for restrictive disciplinary outcomes to be legitimated as part of the interplay between state and non-state sites of regulatory authority.

As I have shown, this interplay can 'fashion' (to return to the metaphor invoked at the start of this chapter) the regulatory environment in Fiji so that it delivers strongly gendered forms of policing that do little to address the insecurities of those who are locally understood to pose a threat to norms of conjugal order and the integrity of the political community more generally. More systematic enquiry needs to be undertaken into the interplays that occur between formal and informal sites of regulatory authority and how these shape vernacular definitions of order and security and, ultimately, the conduct of state agencies. The examples discussed in this chapter show that hybridised systems of authority can produce a strong, but not always just, correlation of security ambitions. In practice these may also deliver gender-discriminatory, gender-restrictive and, in some cases, gender-violent forms of policing practice.

16

Hybridity in Port Moresby: Gender, Class and a 'Tiny Bit of Feminism' in Postcolonial Papua New Guinea

Ceridwen Spark

Introduction

In 2007, I was staying at the Holiday Inn in Port Moresby, Papua New Guinea (PNG), with my family. During this time my friend Karuka (a pseudonym) came to visit us. Knowing that my children would appreciate company to combat the boredom of being trapped in a Port Moresby hotel, she brought with her three of her younger siblings. On arrival at the front gate, Karuka and her family were forbidden entry by one of the security guards on duty. It was only when I went to the gate and clarified that the group were there to see us that they were allowed in.

Initially this incident appeared to be a case of 'misreading' Karuka on the part of the security guard. As those who spend time in Port Moresby's hotels can attest, the guards are employed to 'keep out' undesirables as much as to ensure the physical safety of the paying guests. In the colonial era, this was simple—only expatriates or (sometimes) Papua New Guineans who entered with expatriates were allowed in to the more salubrious locations that in practice served as unofficial enclaves allowing expatriates to live separately from those around them.[1] Since independence and the gradual emergence of a middle class in PNG, deciding who may or may not enter a place has become more complicated. My perceptions and anecdotal evidence suggest guards make their boundary-keeping decisions on various aspects of a person's appearance, including skin colour, ethnicity and clothing.

Usually, someone like Karuka—overseas educated and well dressed— would drive in to the premises, thus avoiding scrutiny and being allowed to 'pass' by virtue of having arrived in a car. Cars themselves mark 'class' because of their prohibitive cost in PNG. But, in this instance, having walked up to the gate with other locals, Karuka was vulnerable to the guard's subjective interpretation of her 'status' and his assessment of whether she and her family were allowed to enter the space. Unfortunately, the boundary keeping did not end there. Later that day, the same guard asked Karuka and her family to leave the poolside area because it was only for 'paying guests'. Given that middle class Papua New Guinean families who are not staying at the hotel regularly use the pool on weekends, it is perhaps unsurprising to learn that the guard had something of a vendetta against Karuka and her family.

Karuka recognised the guard as being from Hohola, where she grew up and where her family still lives. Like much of urban PNG, Hohola is characterised by mixed housing including squatter settlements, underlying and sometimes violent ethnic tension, and inadequate and unreliable access to utilities. That the guard from Karuka's area used his role as a (literal) gatekeeper to exercise the form of authority to which he had access needs to be understood through reference to Karuka's perceived privilege. Having won scholarships to attend school and then university overseas, Karuka has lived away from home since the age of 16, making occasional visits to see her family. At the time we coincided in Port Moresby, she was in town staying with her family while on holiday. Karuka said that the guard knew who she and her siblings were and speculated that he refused them entry in an attempt to reassert power over her because he viewed her as a *bikhet meri* ('show-off woman'). As I have noted elsewhere, in urban PNG men have little to gain from supporting greater equality between men and women, at least in the short term.[2] But they can defend their own interests and negate the potential power

---

1   Alpers, 'Medical Research in the Highlands'; Gammage, 'Moresby 1966'.
2   See Spark, 'Gender Trouble in Town'.

of educated and employed women by appealing to idealised versions of gender roles which locate women's 'proper place' as being in the home. As an extension of this they can also refuse women entry to the places that are associated with the benefits of modernity. In my view, this was the dynamic evident between the guard and Karuka.

In their seminal work, *Emerging Class in Papua New Guinea*, anthropologists Gewertz and Errington discuss what they call the 'hidden injuries of class' as these play out between 'grass roots' and middle class Papua New Guineans living in Wewak.[3] Writing in the late 1990s, they note an increasing tendency among middle class Papua New Guineans to construct people from the 'grass roots' as the 'blameworthy poor'.[4] Demonstrating 'what happens to the poor when class has become a *fait accompli*', they construe middle class Papua New Guineans as detaching from less-affluent kin and acquaintances in order to protect their resources.[5] But as Karuka's experience with the guard indicates, people on both sides of the class border harbour stereotypes and prejudices against one another. Importantly, these interactions involve gender, not in an additive sense but at their core. While Karuka may have 'made it out' of the Moresby settlement by virtue of her education, on returning to visit her family in Port Moresby she temporarily inhabits the same world as the security guard, and in this world she is still regarded as a daughter and sister of people known in a particular locality. And here, as in most places now construed as postcolonial, encounters between 'others' reveal a complex interplay between ethnicity, gender and class that inform and underpin ideas about who is entitled to go where. Karuka's difficulty entering and spending time in the spaces of the hotel demonstrates that in contemporary Port Moresby inclusion and exclusion, while class based, also reflect and affect the ways in which gender and ethnicity are constructed and understood.

Such encounters are common in PNG, and other middle-class and tertiary-educated women have told me about similar experiences. In these scenarios, male security guards, who typically have received only primary education, are endowed with a dubious power and responsibility.[6] Policing the boundaries of the city's locations on the basis of their subjective

---

3   Gewertz and Errington, *Emerging Class in Papua New Guinea*.
4   Ibid., 84.
5   Ibid., 84.
6   See Lusby, 'Preventing Violence at Home'; Sharp et al., 'The Formal, the Informal and the Precarious'. See also Lusby, 'Securitisation, Development and the Invisibility of Gender'.

assessment of the class credentials of those seeking to enter, they are well positioned to turn these moments into opportunities to reassert what they perceive to be their 'rightful' place in the gender hierarchy, embarrassing middle class women in the process. As Sharp et al. note, 'employment as a security guard presents one of few options for men with little or no formal education, but wages are barely enough to sustain their families'.[7] The point here is not to 'blame the guards' but rather to note that the rank and file guards who occupy the lowest rungs of PNG's lucrative security industry both reflect and are expected to enact 'a hierarchy of social class and economic privilege in PNG'.[8] As everyday instances of boundary making, such interactions and the hybridity they embody can be analysed to ground discussions of the power dynamics of 'race, gender and class as these are enacted at both the local and global levels'.[9] Below, I describe my approach to reading hybridity in Port Moresby, an approach which is descriptive rather than prescriptive and in which Karuka remains a central character.

There are many ways to explore hybridity in Port Moresby, not least because it is a rapidly expanding city, both in terms of its physical infrastructure, but also with regard to the population, now estimated to be as high as three quarters of a million.[10] But following Laura McLeod's injunction to notice the 'diversity of the personal' and to 'pay deeper attention to the diverse ways in which the personal is political for both international and local actors',[11] I have chosen to consider hybridity as it is represented in the personal views that two 'international' women have about one of the city's new locations, namely Cafe Duffy located in the suburb Gordons.

As one of the new places that is part of the 'dynamic, exciting, dangerous, bewildering, hybrid environment that is Moresby', it would be easy to argue that Duffy merely represents the global spread of cosmopolitan consumerism.[12] But closer inspection reveals the cafe to be a hybrid site. As I argue here, Duffy is characterised by a blending of cultures which underpins and enables the development of perhaps more subversive modes of being than would usually be associated with places made for

---

7   Sharp et al., 'The Formal, the Informal and the Precarious', 3.
8   Ibid.
9   Darling-Wolf, 'Disturbingly Hybrid or Distressingly Patriarchal?', 70.
10   Jones and Kep, 'Understanding Urbanisation in the PNG Context'.
11   McLeod, 'A Feminist Approach to Hybridity', 52.
12   Goddard, 'Introduction: About Moresby', 18; see also Foster, *Materializing the Nation*; Foster, *Coca-Globalization*.

consumption. My analysis of Duffy demonstrates that the site plays a role in the production of new sociospatial practices and identities—with the potential to challenge the dominant constructions of class and gender in Port Moresby.

To make my argument, I draw on a range of sources, including photos and commentary that Karuka shared with me after her November 2015 visit to Port Moresby; my interviews with young middle class women who live in Moresby, including an interview I conducted with Duffy's French owner and manager, Olga Girault; and a postcard that Girault designed to advertise Duffy. Typically, even within conceptualisations of hybridity, the 'international' is represented as being 'a structure or organisation' with the local construed as 'personal'. I challenge this construction, demonstrating that the 'international' can also be 'personal' and deeply imbricated with the 'local'.[13] Invoking the term hybridity in a manner consistent with discussions that occur in postcolonial explorations of identity, place and culture,[14] and which reflect a process in which hybridity has the potential to 'dislocate the process of colonization',[15] I argue that the emergence in Port Moresby of places such as Duffy indicates something other than the 'failures of postcolonial development'[16] or the dominance of consumption-based place making. Allowing young Papua New Guinean women an appealing palette of experience that is otherwise difficult to access in PNG, Duffy enables women to construct themselves as friends and customers—rather than daughters, wives or sisters—and in doing so provides momentary liberation from the ordinary constraints of life in Port Moresby.

Cafe Duffy: Karuka's perspective

Karuka grew up in Hohola, a suburb of Port Moresby then considered a dangerous place.[17] The first of three daughters in a family left by their father she had a profound sense as a child that she and her family were 'at the bottom of the pile', saying 'we were almost like subordinates' and

---

13   McLeod, 'A Feminist Approach to Hybridity'.
14   See Bhabha, 'Questions of Cultural Identity'; Cuninghame, 'Hybridity, Transnationalism, and Identity'; Darling-Wolf, 'Disturbingly Hybrid or Distressingly Patriarchal?'; Jacobs, *Edge of Empire*.
15   Cuninghame, 'Hybridity, Transnationalism, and Identity', 21.
16   Connell, 'Regulation of Space in the Contemporary Postcolonial Pacific City', 245.
17   See Spark, 'Gender Trouble in Town'; Spark, 'An Oceanic Revolution?' and Spark, '"We Only Get the Daylight Hours"' for other discussions of Karuka's background and experience.

that, even at a young age, there was 'already the sense that we were lower'. Perceiving overseas education as something that only the wealthy could afford, she thought 'that happens to those wealthy people, but not to us'. Indeed, Karuka says it was only when she gained a scholarship and left PNG that she came to think that class need not determine opportunity in every case. Though currently completing postgraduate study in New Zealand, Karuka's background and experience growing up in Moresby continue to shape her analysis of class interactions in the city.

Aged 33, Karuka had not been back to Moresby for three years when she went in late 2015. Interested in her impressions of the rapidly changing city, I asked her to send me photos and thoughts about the places she visited. She did this using WhatsApp and later produced a PowerPoint presentation, with accompanying commentary. I have extracted from this in the following discussion. One place Karuka took photos was Cafe Duffy where she went with two friends.

Duffy was established in 2012 by 22-year-old Olga Girault and her partner, local businessman Travers Chue, whose PNG-Chinese father owns Pacific Industries, a company that produces a range of drinks and foodstuffs sold across PNG. In contrast to the 'new Chinese investors in Papua New Guinea' who, as Graeme Smith notes, 'fit Erving Goffman's definition of a group that is "disqualified from full social acceptance" ' on the basis that they tend to be perceived as mercenary and racist,[18] Pacific Industries has existed in PNG for 60 years and both the company and Duffy have an image of having successfully 'localised'.[19] Part of the group of what Smith calls 'old Chinese', they tend to be seen and to see themselves as 'more benevolent' and 'less aggressive' than the 'new Chinese' operating in PNG since 2007.

On one hand, the cafe represents a positive image of national and urban development of the kind dear to 'elites and governments'.[20] Indeed, Duffy has had such a positive reception that PNG's National Airport Corporation invited Girault to establish a second cafe at the international airport when the airport was renovated for the 2015 Pacific Games. In 2016, Girault and Chue opened a third cafe at Harbour City located in Port Moresby's banking and financial hub and, because of gated security,

18   Smith, 'Beijing's Orphans?', 327.
19   Ibid.
20   Connell, 'Regulation of Space', 248.

an area difficult to enter without a car. But despite the cafe's obvious association with the city's professional elites, it would be erroneous to see Duffy merely as an embodiment of wealth, privilege and consumerism in the midst of a 'planet of slums'.[21] As feminist geographer Gillian Rose points out, spaces are 'extraordinarily complicated', allowing for a range of interpretations and meanings.[22] While recognising Harvey's insight that the contemporary urban experience gives (only) those with money 'the aura of freedom of choice',[23] I intend to explore the prospect that Duffy affords a greater range of rights and freedoms than might initially be thought.

Having become interested in Duffy as a site that reflects aspects of the 'new Port Moresby', I interviewed Girault in August 2015. She said the cafe's clientele are 'now around 50/50' in terms of ethnicity (that is, half expatriate and half Papua New Guinean). On the three occasions I have visited (the original) Duffy, the clientele has included professional Papua New Guineans as well as expatriates. But Girault said she noticed that some Papua New Guineans 'will only purchase take away', perhaps suggesting they are not entirely comfortable to spend time in the space of the cafe. Cindy, a 33-year-old Papua New Guinean friend of Karuka's said that when she and her boyfriend went for brunch they were the only Papua New Guineans there 'apart from the ladies behind the counter'. Consequently he was uncomfortable and wanted to 'sit in the corner'. Though Cindy explicitly constructs her boyfriend's discomfort in terms of ethnicity, it is also possible that Papua New Guinean men see Duffy as a feminine space, and that this rather than racism underpins their discomfort.

Duffy sells coffee, pastries, smoothies, juices and fresh bread, alongside a range of lunch items. With the exception of the fresh fruit and vegetables, most of which are locally sourced, the produce comes from Australia and New Zealand.

Along with the range, the quality of the food and beverages is rare in PNG, offering, as Girault says 'the best we can' and 'the best coffee in town'. The commentary accompanying Karuka's photos testifies to this:

---

21   Harvey, 'The Right to the City', 37.
22   Rose, *Feminism and Geography*, 155.
23   Harvey, 'The Right to the City', 31.

Duffy's cafe—[at] 5 mile, had ace food—chocolate croissant —amazeballs. Location is ok as well, although it's in the Gordons industrial area so I had initially been a little hesitant to go. But security was awesome. Duffy however can only be accessed by well to do people. Eg. My sisters mentioned 'only money people go there' and that they hadn't been.

In addition to reporting that her sisters saw Duffy as a place for 'money people', Karuka also told me (in person) that she would not take them there because it would be like 'opening a world to them that they could never have again', once she was not in the country to pay for the experience. Representing a more optimistic perspective, Girault told me 'this coffee shop is open to everyone … and everyone is welcome to come here'. Realistically, however, the cost of the produce (a sandwich and drink costs around 40 PNG kina, which is equivalent to approximately AU$20) means that Duffy can only be afforded by a small proportion of Port Moresby's population.

In advanced capitalist societies, where individualism goes hand in hand with modernity, access by virtue of one's capacity to pay is widely accepted as part of life. But in PNG, places such as Duffy give rise to painful tensions for people like Karuka. On one hand, Duffy represents some of the positives of global capitalism and globalisation, including an opportunity for young women to participate in cosmopolitan consumerism, which, in PNG as elsewhere, tends to be associated with forms of (gendered) freedom and autonomy. For Karuka and her friends who can afford to visit Duffy, the site offers a valued opportunity to take part in the global cosmopolitan culture represented by purchasing quality cakes and coffee in their 'home' town. As Maggie Cummings writes, it is helpful to understand the social change associated with globalisation not as 'something that happens to the people whose lives we study, but rather, something that they themselves do, participate in, drive, and shape through their own choices, actions, feelings, and theories'.[24] Viewed through this focus on agency, we can see that when educated and professional women enter the space of Duffy they are participating in the 'better future'[25] that globalisation can and does deliver to Port Moresby inhabitants who do have money.

24 Cummings, 'Imagining Transnational Futures in Vanuatu', 383.
25 Ibid., 381.

On the other hand, Duffy provides a stark reminder that 'quality' can only be afforded by a few, thus representing the problems associated with urbanisation and reliance on a cash economy.[26] Of course affordability also determines access in advanced capitalist societies, but in PNG, 'hybrid' women like Karuka are related to and otherwise intimately connected with the many who feel uncomfortable about or cannot afford to go inside. As Keith Barber notes in his study of urban households, 'it is not as individuals that people survive in PNG'.[27] Having grown up in a context in which reciprocity and resource sharing continue to form the basis of life and survival for many, including in many instances, themselves, Karuka and other overseas-educated women with whom I have spoken maintain a degree of commitment to this mode of life. Almost all the young women I know help to support their family members, including by paying for housing, food or assisting to educate younger siblings, nephews and nieces. At the same time, like other members of PNG's middle class, they also seek to establish a degree of autonomy from family and tend to reject the financial demands made on them by members of their extended families, preferring to limit their sharing to immediate family members.[28]

While the middle class in PNG are maligned for turning their backs on their grass roots counterparts, internationally educated and cosmopolitan women such as Karuka are acutely aware that they are products of a context in which some are afforded more opportunities than others. Moreover, this perspective is shaped in equal measure by local connections (including, for example, Karuka's relationship with her sisters, whom she financially supports) and experiences such as the one Karuka had with the guard in 2007, as by her international education and outlook. Thus, in this interaction between an apparently 'international' person and a 'local' place, Duffy is a paradoxical space in which both people and place are shown to be hybrid.

---

26   Ibid., 383.
27   Barber, 'Urban Households, Means of Livelihood and Village Identity in Moresby', 95.
28   Cox and Macintyre, 'Christian Marriage, Money Scams, and Melanesian Social Imaginaries'; Gewertz and Errington, *Emerging Class in Papua New Guinea*; Macintyre, 'Money Changes Everything'.

Cafe Duffy: Olga's perspective

To add to the complexities of 'reading' Duffy's hybridity within a modern PNG, it is worth delving further into Girault's perspective as Duffy's manager, for while she initially appears to represent the 'consumption economy',[29] she too complicates easy dichotomies. Two things in particular stand out. The first is Girault's approach to her staff, which, being respectful and mutually supportive, seems positively postcolonial in comparison to the more colonial master–servant relationships between employers and guards evident at most salubrious locations in PNG. Indeed, as Lusby notes, employer–guard relationships are characterised by violence, including 'disciplinary beatings for breaches of the rules'.[30] A closer look at Girault's perspective clarifies that she has transformed the role played by security at Duffy, encouraging them to see would-be entrants as customers rather than as constituting a threat.

Like most places in Moresby that expatriates frequent, there are security guards at the gate outside the entrance to Duffy. But these guards look noticeably different from others in PNG (Figure 16.1). Notably, they are not wearing a police or military style uniform or carrying batons as is commonly the case with guards working for private security companies. On arriving at Duffy, one observes that they appear happy and at ease and have warm and welcoming relationships with customers, rather than the typically deferential ones evident in other expensive locations. Wearing cheerful, rather than mirror sunglasses, they look more like they are on holiday than they do intimidating. As Karuka noted above, 'security was awesome' and Grace, a friend of Karuka's, said she noticed the 'very cheerful and enthusiastic attitude' of the guards. These comments appear to reflect the pleasure that the guards' welcoming attitude gives customers, many of whom, like Karuka, have experienced guards intimidating them and policing their appearance and 'right to the city'.

---

29 Clifford, 'On Collecting Art and Culture', 141.
30 Sharp et al., 'The Formal, the Informal and the Precarious', 3.

Figure 16.1: The friendly security team at Duffy
Source: Karuka (pseudonym), published with permission.

Discussing Duffy's security staff, Girault told me the story of their employment, describing how the guards had become part of the 'Duffy family':

> We had a small number of staff and one of our first security [guards] was a guy who was in the streets actually and he was really malnourished, very skinny, had no family, he looked so sad … And now we're his family pretty much. So it's like all the people that are working with us all have a story with us but we are also a family, we call it the Duffy family so we say you have your family in the village but this is your second family, this is your Duffy family. So they're all very loyal, all our security guards, they have been with us since day one.

Incorporating members of PNG's 'underclass' into 'the Duffy family', Girault reverses the usual anthropological pattern in which the visiting international 'other' is fitted in to local kinship systems. This incorporation represents an implicit critique of those in the middle class who attempt to 'detach' from their less-affluent kin, thus challenging the neoliberal view that people are 'poor because they make bad decisions'—a view Karuka also critiques since leaving PNG. Girault's 'everyday political analysis'[31] of the situation in which the once homeless and hungry guards found themselves before being employed at Duffy is indicative of her border-crossing (as opposed to border-reinforcing) hybrid identity and politics.[32] The 'Duffy family' suggests the need to read the new places of Port Moresby as reflecting and allowing a new mixing between cultures and people, which challenges existing borders of the political and ethnic communities in this context.

As noted above, this mixing between people and cultures is evident in the security guards' interactions with customers. Guards display an obvious familiarity with customers, expatriate and otherwise, and there is a warmth and egalitarianism about their interactions at the entrance to the cafe. Girault says that she and Chue actively encouraged this way of relating, providing 'incentives' for the guards to 'remember the customers' names' and greet them warmly.

> Now we don't need to tell them anything. They love it, they love having relationships with customers and get treated so well by customers. Every Christmas, they get so many gifts because customers love them.

---

31 Hudson et al., *Everyday Political Analysis*, 1.
32 Cuninghame, 'Hybridity, Transnationalism, and Identity', 29.

Matthew, one of Duffy's security guards, confirmed the gift-giving relationship with customers, saying:

> We know our regular customers by name and they know us by our names and that makes us feel good. Sometimes when we become familiar, become friends, with a particular customer, and when he or she leaves to go back to where they come from, we [the guards] give them *bilums* and other PNG gifts. In return they give us gifts like clothes and other things.

Indeed, as Girault told me, some guards became so familiar they were kissing customers when they arrived—perhaps an over emulation of the French Girault—and she had to explain that this was going 'too far'. As Iyall Smith notes: 'those who occupy hybrid spaces benefit from having an understanding of both local knowledge and global cosmopolitanism. Those who can easily cross barriers in a world of amorphous borders have an advantage'.[33] The guards' kissing, which perhaps constitutes a moment of 'excessive' border crossing, serves as a reminder that familiarity with the 'global' language of customer service within a 'local' context is a valuable skill in a hybrid environment.

Girault's hybrid perspective is also captured in a postcard she produced to advertise the cafe. Using Roger Violett's famous image of two French women entitled 'Café et cigarette, Paris, 1925', Girault asked her sister to digitally adapt the image by painting the two French women in bilas, traditional PNG decoration usually worn at celebrations and big events. As Girault explained, the image of women enjoying coffee and the reflection of this as *bilas* and painting on their bodies captures her own experience of drinking Papua New Guinean coffee, a moment, she says, that always makes her 'feel a little bit Papua New Guinean'.[34] Demonstrating the ways in which local and global cultures blend to create something new, the altered image of women enjoying leisure and friendship has a political potency in PNG where women continue to be constructed primarily through reference to their domestic and child-bearing responsibilities.

The desire to refigure local versions of femininity was another of Girault's motivations for adapting and utilising this French image to advertise Duffy.

---

33 Iyall Smith, 'Hybrid Identities', 4.
34 See West, *From Modern Production to Imagined Primitive*, for a comprehensive analysis of the social world of coffee in PNG.

> I really like the picture of these two ladies, and … I'm really trying to empower women here. I guess I'm a tiny bit feminist, a little hint that I'm always for the women. I have meetings with the girls where I'm always you have to be proud independent blah blah blah, because especially in this country. Anyway for me it's symbolic to have those two women having a coffee. Women you know.

Noting 'it is socio-spatial practices that define places and these practices result in overlapping and intersecting places with multiple and changing boundaries',[35] feminist geographer Linda McDowell reminds us that *what women do where* changes the 'nature' of a place. While to a large extent normalised among women in the middle classes of advanced capitalist societies, meeting friends for coffee is still not the norm for most women in PNG. Consequently, when Papua New Guinean women come together in a place like Duffy to do just that, they are perhaps embodying a 'tiny bit of feminism' while simultaneously changing the local place in which they are engaged in this spatial practice. Playfully capturing a more optimistic perspective on the global flows that characterise transnationalism, the revamped postcard encapsulates a different perspective on young women's leisure and consumption practices, demonstrating that while Parisian women can become 'a little bit' Papua New Guinean, so too can Papua New Guinean women become 'a little bit' French.[36]

Conclusion

Taking a descriptive over a prescriptive approach and rather than trying to 'create or administer hybridity',[37] I have sought to demonstrate the value of hybridity for understanding the rapidly developing city of Port Moresby. I have observed how Karuka's and Olga's 'international' perspectives on Duffy, a particular place in their 'home town', enable us to consider hybridity in relation to the power dynamics of race, gender and class in contemporary Port Moresby. As this detailed analysis of their perspectives makes clear, 'exposure to global communication and culture plant the seeds for the formation of a hybrid culture'.[38] Discussing moments and places where this hybridity is embodied, I have shown it is

---

35   McDowell, *Gender, Identity and Place*, 4.
36   Compare with West, *From Modern Production to Imagined Primitive*.
37   Miller, 'Disaggregating Hybridity', 3.
38   Iyall Smith, 'Hybrid Identities', 5.

insufficient to argue that class operates in PNG to produce boundaries on which the 'oppressed' and the 'empowered' exist on opposite sides.[39] Rather, it is useful to take a perspective on everyday boundary making which elucidates 'the mixed and melded cultural forms that [are] ever more common in a globalized world'.[40] The analysis also reveals that 'hybrid' women such as those discussed in this chapter may be best placed to challenge the suspicions and 'othering' narratives that people on both sides of borders 'tend to harbour against each other'[41] and which were manifest in Karuka and the guard's interactions at the Holiday Inn in 2007. Demonstrating that gender intersects with class and ethnicity to produce new versions of people and place that defy neat categorisation, I have shown that Port Moresby both is, and continues to become, a more interesting, complex and hybrid place than it is usually represented to be.

---

39   For a discussion of boundary making, see Kyed, 'Introduction to the Special Issue: Legal Pluralism'.
40   Miller, 'Disaggregating Hybridity', 3.
41   See Cuninghame, 'Hybridity, Transnationalism, and Identity'.

Contributors

Peter Albrecht is a senior researcher at the Danish Institute for International Studies, Copenhagen. He is the co-author of several books on security in Sierra Leone, including *Reconstructing Security after Conflict: Security Sector Reform in Sierra Leone* (Palgrave Macmillan, 2011) and *Securing Sierra Leone, 1997–2013: Defence, Diplomacy and Development in Action* (Taylor and Francis/RUSI, 2014), and co-editor of *Policing and the Politics of Order-Making* (Routledge, 2015). His work is published in several journals, including *Journal of Modern African Studies*, *African Studies Review* and *Ethnos*.

Matthew Allen works at the interstices of geography, political science and anthropology. The unifying theme for his scholarly and policy work in the western Pacific over the past 20 years has been the relationships between social, political and environmental change. Matthew's research interests include extractive resource industries and violence, agrarian change and rural development, and state–society relations. He has published extensively and is author of *Greed and Grievance: Ex-militants' Perspectives on the Conflict in Solomon Islands, 1998–2003* (University of Hawai'i Press, 2013).

Volker Boege is a peace researcher and historian, honorary research fellow at the School of Political Science and International Studies at the University of Queensland, and co-director of Peace and Conflict Studies Institute Australia. His main fields of work are postconflict peacebuilding and state formation, environmental degradation and conflict. From the 1980s through to the early 2000s, Volker worked with a number of peace research institutions in Germany and Switzerland. His most recent research project is titled 'Disentangling international and local understandings in peacebuilding: Insights from the "laboratory" of Bougainville'. Volker has published numerous articles, papers and books in peace research and contemporary history.

Dr Srinjoy Bose is European Union COFUND (Marie Sklowodska-Curie Action) Fellow at the School of Government & International Affairs, Durham University. He is co-editor of *Afghanistan-Challenges and Prospects* (Routledge, 2017) and co–guest editor of the journal special issue *Elections and the State: Critical Perspectives on Democracy Promotion in Afghanistan* (*Conflict, Security and Development*, 2016).

M. Anne Brown is a teacher and researcher at the Centre for Global Research, RMIT University, Melbourne. Anne's research and practice interests focus on political community across division, peacebuilding and state formation in heterogeneous states, social dialogue processes, social resilience and the interface of practice and theory. She worked with the Malvatumauri Council of Chiefs on the Vanuatu Kastom Governance Partnership (2005–2012) and is a director of PaCSIA, a non-government organisation working on dialogue processes. She is author of *Human Rights and the Borders of Suffering: The Promotion of Human Rights in International Politics* (Manchester University Press, 2002), articles and chapters, and an editor of collections.

Imelda Deinla is a fellow in the School of Regulation and Global Governance and director of the Philippines Project at The Australian National University. Her research interests are on legal hybridity; women and peacebuilding in Mindanao, Philippines; rule of law; and ASEAN trade and governance networks. She recently published *The Development of the Rule of Law in ASEAN: The State and Regional Integration* (Cambridge University Press, 2017).

Sinclair Dinnen is a senior fellow with the Department of Pacific Affairs at The Australian National University. With a background in socio-legal studies and criminology, his research examines issues of legal pluralism, policing, security governance, politics and state formation in the south-west Pacific. He is co-editor (with Matthew Allen) of *State-building and State Formation in the Western Pacific—Solomon Islands in Transition?* (Routledge, 2016).

Miranda Forsyth is an associate professor in the School of Regulation and Global Governance, The Australian National University. She formerly lectured in criminal law at the University of the South Pacific, Vanuatu. Miranda's research focuses on the possibilities and challenges of the inter-operation of state and non-state justice and regulatory systems. Her present focus is on examining these issues in the context of the regulation of sorcery- and witchcraft-related violence in Melanesia. Miranda is the author of *A Bird that Flies with Two Wings: Kastom and State Justice Systems in Vanuatu* (ANU E Press, 2009) and co-author with Sue Farran of *Weaving Intellectual Property Policy in Small Island Developing States* (Intersentia, 2015).

Nicole George is a senior lecturer in peace and conflict studies at the University of Queensland. Her research focuses on gender, violence, peacebuilding, conflict transition and security and has been undertaken in Fiji, New Caledonia and Bougainville. She is the author of *Situating Women: Gender Politics and Circumstance in Fiji* (ANU E Press, 2012) and has articles appearing in *International Feminist Journal of Politics, Policing and Society, International Political Science Review, Peacebuilding, Australian Journal of International Affairs, The Contemporary Pacific* and *The Australian Feminist Law Journal.*

Damian Grenfell is a lecturer in undergraduate and postgraduate courses in global studies at RMIT University, Melbourne. He was director of the Centre for Global Research from 2012 to 2017. His research focuses on social conflict and change in postcolonial states, particularly Timor-Leste, with an emphasis on gender, security, justice and reconciliation in the context of nation formation.

Shahar Hameiri is associate professor of international politics and associate director of the Graduate Centre in Governance and International Affairs, School of Political Science and International Studies, University of Queensland. His most recent books are *International Intervention and Local Politics* (Cambridge University Press, 2017), co-authored with Caroline Hughes and Fabio Scarpello, and *Governing Borderless Threats* (Cambridge University Press, 2015), co-authored with Lee Jones. His sole or jointly authored articles have appeared in leading journals, including *International Studies Quarterly, European Journal of International Relations, Review of International Studies* and *Development and Change.* He tweets @ShaharHameiri.

Charles T. Hunt is vice-chancellor's senior research/ARC DECRA fellow at the Centre for Global Research in the School of Global, Urban and Social Studies at RMIT University, Melbourne. He previously lectured in international security in the School of Political Science and International Studies at the University of Queensland. Charles's research focuses on peace and conflict with an emphasis on security and justice system reform in Africa. He is author of *UN Peace Operations and International Policing: Negotiating Complexity, Assessing Impact and Learning to Learn* (Routledge, 2015) and co-author of *Forging New Conventional Wisdom Beyond International Policing* (Brill, 2013).

Victor Igreja teaches international studies, anthropology and peace and conflict studies at the University of Southern Queensland. Recent publications appeared in *Current Anthropology*, *Comparative Studies in Society and History*, *Anthropological Quarterly*, *International Journal of Transitional Justice*, *International Encyclopedia of Anthropology* and *Encyclopedia of Transitional Justice*. He serves on the editorial advisory boards of *Journal of Religion in Africa* and *Revista Estudos Políticos*.

Paul Jackson is professor of African politics at the University of Birmingham. He was formerly the head of the university's School of Government and Society, and director of both the International Development Department (University of Birmingham) and the Global Facilitation Network for Security Sector Reform (Institute of Development Studies). Paul has worked in the fields of politics and security for several governments, the United Nations, the European Union and the World Bank. He is a current member of the Folke Bernadotte Institute working group on security-sector reform. He has published extensively on security and development issues.

Lee Jones is a reader in international politics in the School of Politics and International Relations, Queen Mary University of London. His most recent books are *Societies under Siege* (Oxford University Press, 2015), and *Governing Borderless Threats* (Cambridge University Press, 2015), co-authored with Shahar Hameiri. His sole or jointly authored articles have appeared in leading journals, including *International Studies Quarterly*, *European Journal of International Relations*, *Review of International Studies* and *Development and Change*. He tweets @drleejones.

Lia Kent is a fellow in the School of Regulation and Global Governance, The Australian National University. Since 2000, she has conducted research in and on Timor-Leste. She is currently working on a project titled 'After conflict: Memory frictions in Timor-Leste and Aceh', funded by an ARC Discovery Early Career Researcher Award. Lia is the author of *The Dynamics of Transitional Justice: International Models and Local Realities in East Timor* (Routledge, 2012) and numerous journal articles and book chapters on themes related to transitional justice, peacebuilding, memory politics and gender in Timor-Leste.

Gavin Mount is a lecturer at UNSW Canberra. His primary research is on the global politics of ethnic conflict. He also teaches in the fields of global security, great power politics and conflict transformation and was awarded a Rector's Commendation for Excellence in Classroom Teaching in 2010. His current research explores patterns of postconflict scholarship and the security linkages between non-state actors and non-military issues.

Oliver Richmond is a research professor in International Relations, Peace and Conflict Studies in the Humanitarian Conflict Response Institute at the University of Manchester, United Kingdom. He is also international professor, College of International Studies, Kyung Hee University, Korea and a visiting professor at the University of Tromso, Norway. His publications include *Peace Formation and Political Order in Conflict Affected Societies* (Oxford University Press, 2016), *Failed Statebuilding: Intervention and the Dynamics of Peace Formation* (Yale University Press, 2014), *Peace: A Very Short Introduction* (Oxford University Press, 2014), *A Post-liberal Peace* (Routledge, 2011), *Liberal Peace Transitions: Between Statebuilding and Peacebuilding* (with Jason Franks, Edinburgh University Press, 2009), *Peace in International Relations* (Routledge, 2008) and *The Transformation of Peace* (Palgrave Macmillan, 2005). He is editor of the Palgrave Macmillan book series Rethinking Peace and Conflict Studies and co-editor (with Roger Mac Ginty) of the journal *Peacebuilding*.

James Scambary is a research fellow at the Department of Political and Social Change, The Australian National University. He has worked in the fields of communal conflict, peacebuilding, corruption and governance in East Timor for over a decade, conducting research for a range of agencies including the New York Social Science Research Council, the World Bank and, most recently, the Asia Foundation. He is currently working on a research project on the role of patronage in East Timor's electoral politics.

Ceridwen Spark is a vice-chancellor's senior research fellow in Global, Urban and Social Studies at RMIT University, Melbourne. She conducts research on gender and social change in the Pacific and is widely published in anthropology, feminist and politics journals. Ceridwen has worked collaboratively in Papua New Guinea for over a decade, including most recently with International Women's Development Agency in Bougainville and Equal Playing Field in Port Moresby.

Joanne Wallis is a senior lecturer in the Strategic and Defence Studies Centre, College of Asia & the Pacific at The Australian National University. She completed her PhD at the University of Cambridge and masters degrees in arts (political science) and law at the University of Melbourne. Her research focuses on peacebuilding and security in the Pacific islands, with a special focus on Timor-Leste and Bougainville, Papua New Guinea. Joanne is the author of *Constitution Making during State Building* (Cambridge University Press, 2014) and *Pacific Power? Australia's Strategy in the Pacific Islands* (Melbourne University Publishing, 2017).

Todd Wassel is an international development professional who has worked in more than 15 countries managing complex programs in difficult and politically challenging environments. He is currently the Asia Foundation's country representative in Timor-Leste. Todd has helped develop participatory tenure mapping in Kosovo; managed programs on land disputes, return and restitution for internally displaced persons, gender-based titling and inheritance reform in Sri Lanka; and worked with the police and communities on hybrid justice systems in Timor-Leste. Todd holds a master's degree in international development and conflict resolution from the Fletcher School of Law and Diplomacy, Tufts University, United States.

References

ABC Radio Australia. 'Fiji Women's Minister Defends Domestic Violence Decree'. ABC Radio Australia, 6 December 2012. banabanvoice.ning.com/profiles/blogs/fiji-women-s-minister-defends-domestic-violence-decree

Abinales, Patricio N. *Making Mindanao: Cotabato and Davao in the Formation of the Philippine Nation-State*. Quezon City: Ateneo de Manila University Press, 2000.

Abrahamsen, Rita and Michael C. Williams. *Security beyond the State: Private Security in International Politics*. Cambridge: Cambridge University Press, 2011. doi.org/10.1017/CBO9780511974441

Adam, Jeroen, Boris Verbrugge and Dorien vanden Boer. 'Hybrid Systems of Conflict Management and Community-Level Efforts to Improve Local Security in Mindanao'. *Justice and Security Research Programme Paper* 13. London School of Economics and Political Science, 2014.

Adams, Rebecca (ed.). *Peace on Bougainville—Truce Monitoring Group. Gudpela Nius Bilong Peace*. Wellington, NZ: Victoria University Press, 2001.

Agnew, John A. *Globalization and Sovereignty*. Lanham, MD: Rowman & Littlefield, 2009.

Akin, David W. *Colonialism, Maasina Rule, and the Origins of Malaitan Kastom*. Honolulu: University of Hawai'i Press, 2013. doi.org/10.21313/hawaii/9780824838140.001.0001

Albrecht, Peter. 'The Chiefs of Community Policing in Rural Sierra Leone'. *The Journal of Modern African Studies*, 53(4):611–635, 2015. doi.org/10.1017/S0022278X15000774

Albrecht, Peter. 'Hybridisation in a Case of Diamond Theft in Rural Sierra Leone'. *Ethnos*, online 30 November 2016. doi.org/10.1080/00 141844.2016.1263229

Albrecht, Peter. 'Secrets, Strangers and Order-Making in Rural Sierra Leone'. *Journal of Contemporary African Studies*, 34(4):519–537, 2016. doi.org/10.1080/02589001.2016.1252097

Albrecht, Peter. 'The Hybrid Authority of Sierra Leone's Chiefs'. *African Studies Review*, online 22 August 2017. doi.org/10.1017/asr.2017.87

Albrecht, Peter and Lars Buur. 'An Uneasy Marriage: Non-state Actors and Police Reform'. *Policing and Society*, 19(4):390–405, 2009. doi.org/10.1080/10439460903375182

Albrecht, Peter and Helene Maria Kyed. 'Justice and Security: When the State Isn't the Main Provider'. *DIIS Policy Brief*. Copenhagen: Danish Institute for International Studies, 2010.

Albrecht, Peter and Helene Maria Kyed. 'Introduction: Non-state and Customary Actors in Development Programs'. In P. Albrecht, H.M. Kyed, D. Isser and E. Harper (eds), *Perspectives on Involving Non-state and Customary Actors in Justice and Security Reform* (pp. 3–22). Rome: International Development Law Organization and Danish Institute for International Studies, 2011.

Albrecht, Peter and Helene Maria Kyed (eds). *Policing and the Politics of Order-Making*. Abingdon: Routledge, 2015.

Albrecht, Peter, Helene Maria Kyed, Deborah Isser and Erica Harper (eds). *Perspectives on Involving Non-state and Customary Actors in Justice and Security Reform*. Rome: International Development Law Organization and Danish Institute for International Studies, 2011.

Albrecht, Peter and Louise Wiuff Moe. 'The Simultaneity of Authority in Hybrid Orders'. *Peacebuilding*, 3(1):1–16, 2015. doi.org/10.1080/ 21647259.2014.928551

Alcala, Pilar Riaño and Erin Baines. 'Editorial Note'. *The International Journal of Transitional Justice*, 6(3):385–393, 2012. doi.org/10.1093/ ijtj/ijs027

Alfred, Taiaiake. 'What Is Radical Imagination? Indigenous Struggles in Canada'. *Affinities: A Journal of Radical Theory, Culture, and Action*, 4(2):5–8, 2010.

Alipala, Julie S. 'Abducted Teacher Rescued by Soldiers in Sulu'. Inquirer.net, 11 July 2016. newsinfo.inquirer.net/795387/abducted-teacher-rescued-by-soldiers

Allen, Matthew G. 'Melanesia's Violent Environments: Towards a Political Ecology of Conflict in the Western Pacific'. *Geoforum*, 44(1):152–161, 2013. doi.org/10.1016/j.geoforum.2012.09.015

Allen, Matthew G. and Sinclair Dinnen. 'Solomon Islands in Transition?' *Journal of Pacific History*, 50(4):381–397, 2015. doi.org/10.1080/002 23344.2015.1101194

Allen, Matthew G., Sinclair Dinnen, Daniel Evans and Rebecca Monson. *Justice Delivered Locally: Systems, Challenges, and Innovations in Solomon Islands*. Justice for the Poor Research Report. Washington, DC: World Bank, 2013.

Alpers, Michael P. 'Medical Research in the Highlands: Being Part of the Community Does Make a Difference'. In C. Spark, S. Spark and C. Twomey (eds), *Australians in Papua New Guinea: 1960–1975* (pp. 11–30). St Lucia: University of Queensland Press, 2014.

Andrews, Matt. *The Limits of Institutional Reform in Development: Changing Rules for Realistic Solutions*. New York: Cambridge University Press, 2013. doi.org/10.1017/CBO9781139060974

Aning, Kwesi and Festus Kofi Aubyn. 'Challenging Conventional Understandings of Statehood Based on West African Realities'. In K. Aning, M.A. Brown, V. Boege and C.T. Hunt (eds), *Exploring Peace Formation: Security and Justice in Post-Conflict States*. Abingdon: Routledge, forthcoming.

Appiah, Kwame Anthony. *In My Father's House: Africa in the Philosophy of Culture*. Oxford: Oxford University Press, 1992.

Argenti-Pillen, Alex. *Masking Terror: How Women Contain Violence in Southern Sri Lanka*. Philadelphia, PA: University of Pennsylvania Press, 2003. doi.org/10.9783/9780812201154

Ashcroft, Bill, Gareth Griffiths and Helen Tiffin. *The Empire Writes Back: Theory and Practice in Post-colonial Literatures*. 2nd ed. London: Routledge, 2002.

Ashcroft, Bill, Gareth Griffiths and Helen Tiffin. *Post-colonial Studies: The Key Concepts*. London: Routledge, 2007.

Asia Foundation. *Timor Lorosa'e National Survey of Citizen Knowledge*. Dili: The Asia Foundation, 2002.

Asia Foundation. *Timor-Leste Law & Justice Survey 2013*. Dili: The Asia Foundation, 2013.

Asia Foundation. *Reflections on Law No. 3/2009: Community Leadership and Their Election (II)*. Dili: The Asia Foundation, 2014.

Asia Foundation. *The Proliferation of Security Providers and Assisters in the Context of Community Policing in East Timor*. Dili: The Asia Foundation, 2015.

Asia Foundation. *Understanding Violence against Women and Children in Timor-Leste: Findings from the* Nabilan *Baseline Study – Main Report*. Dili: The Asia Foundation, 2016.

Asian Development Bank. *Indigenous and Ethnic Minorities and Poverty Reduction: Philippines*. Asian Development Bank, 2002.

Augustine (Bishop of Hippo), Saint. *De Civitate Dei Contra Paganos (City of God against the Pagans)* [C. 413–426]. London: Oxford University Press, 1963.

Australian Civil-Military Centre. *Partnering for Peace: Australia's Peacekeeping and Peacebuilding Experiences in the Autonomous Region of Bougainville in Papua New Guinea, and in Solomon Islands and Timor-Leste*. Canberra: Australian Civil-Military Centre, 2012.

Autesserre, Séverine. *The Trouble with the Congo: Local Violence and the Failure of International Peacekeeping*. Cambridge: Cambridge University Press, 2010. doi.org/10.1017/CBO9780511761034

Bain, William (ed.). *The Empire of Security and the Safety of the People*. London: Routledge, 2006.

Baines, Erin. 'Spirits and Social Reconstruction after Mass Violence: Rethinking Transitional Justice'. *African Affairs*, 109(436):409–430, 2010. doi.org/10.1093/afraf/adq023

Baines, Graham. 'Beneath the State: Chiefs of Santa Isabel, Solomon Islands, Coping and Adapting'. *State, Society and Governance in Melanesia Working Paper* 2014/2. Canberra: The Australian National University, 2014. bellschool.anu.edu.au/sites/default/files/publications/attachments/2015-12/WP_2014_2_Baines_0.pdf

Baker, Bruce. 'Beyond the Tarmac Road: Local Forms of Policing in Sierra Leone & Rwanda'. *Review of African Political Economy*, 35(118):555–570, 2008. doi.org/10.1080/03056240802569235

Baker, Bruce. *Security in Post-conflict Africa: The Role of Nonstate Policing*. Boca Raton, FL: CRC Press, 2009. doi.org/10.1201/9781420091946

Baker, Bruce. 'Linking State and Non-state Security and Justice'. *Development Policy Review*, 28(5):597–616, 2010. doi.org/10.1111/j.1467-7679.2010.00500.x

Baker, Bruce. 'Justice and Security Architecture in Africa: The Plans, the Bricks, the Purse and the Builder'. *The Journal of Legal Pluralism and Unofficial Law*, 43(63):25–47, 2011. doi.org/10.1080/07329113.2011.10756656

Baker, Bruce and Eric Scheye. 'Multi-layered Justice and Security Delivery in Post-conflict and Fragile States'. *Conflict, Security and Development*, 7(4):503–528, 2007. doi.org/10.1080/14678800701692944

Balthasar, Domonik. 'From Hybridity to Standardization: Rethinking State-Making in Contexts of Fragility'. *Journal of Intervention and Statebuilding*, 9(1):26–47, 2015. doi.org/10.1080/17502977.2015.993502

Barber, Keith. 'Urban Households, Means of Livelihood and Village Identity in Moresby'. In M. Goddard (ed.), *Villagers and the City: Melanesian Experiences of Port Moresby, Papua New Guinea* (pp. 93–109). Wantage, United Kingdom: Sean Kingston Publishing, 2010.

Barkawi, Tarak and Shane Brighton. 'Conclusion: Absent War Studies? War, Knowledge, and Critique'. In H. Strachan and S. Scheipers (eds), *The Changing Character of War* (pp. 524–541). Oxford: Oxford University Press, 2011. doi.org/10.1093/acprof:osobl/9780199596737.003.0029

Barry, Peter. *Beginning Theory: An Introduction to Literary and Cultural Theory*. Manchester: Manchester University Press, 1995.

Bassetti, Piero. 'Hybridity' (Introduction). *Glocalism: Journal of Culture, Politics and Innovation*. 1, 2013. www.glocalismjournal.net/Issues/HYBRIDITY/Hybridity.kl

Bayart, Jean-François, Stephen Ellis and Beatrice Hibou. *The Criminalization of the State in Africa*. Oxford: James Currey, 1999.

Bell, Duncan. 'What Is Liberalism?' *Political Theory*, 42(6):682–715, 2014. doi.org/10.1177/0090591714535103

Belloni, Roberto. 'Hybrid Peace Governance: Its Emergence and Significance'. *Global Governance: A Review of Multilateralism and International Organizations*, 18(1):21–38, 2012.

Belo, Nélson and Gobie Rajalingam. *Local Leadership of Community Policing Practices in Timor-Leste*. Dili: The Asia Foundation, 2014.

Belo, Nélson, De Sousa C. and Mark R. Koenig. *Institutionalizing Community Policing in Timor-Leste: Exploring the Politics of Police Reform*. Dili: The Asia Foundation, 2011.

Belun and The Asia Foundation. *Tara Bandu: Its Role and Use in Community Conflict Prevention in East Timor*. Dili: Belun and The Asia Foundation, 2013. asiafoundation.org/resources/pdfs/Tara BanduPolicyBriefENG.pdf

Bennett, Judith A. *Pacific Forest: A History of Resource Control and Contest in Solomon Islands, c. 1800–1997*. Cambridge and Leiden: White Horse Press and Brill Academic Publishers, 2000.

Berman, Paul Schiff. 'Jurisgenerative Constitutionalism: Procedural Principles for Managing Global Legal Pluralism'. *Indiana Journal of Global Legal Studies*, 20(2):665–695, 2013. doi.org/10.2979/indjglolegstu.20.2.665

Bertrand, Jacques. 'Peace and Conflict in the Southern Philippines: Why the 1996 Peace Agreement Is Fragile'. *Pacific Affairs*, 73(1):37–54, 2000. doi.org/10.2307/2672283

Bhabha, Homi K. 'Signs Taken for Wonders: Questions of Ambivalence and Authority under a Tree Outside Delhi, May 1817'. *Critical Inquiry*, 12(1):144–165, 1985. doi.org/10.1086/448325

Bhabha, Homi K. *The Location of Culture*. Abingdon: Routledge, 1994.

Bhabha, Homi K. 'Questions of Cultural Identity'. In S. Hall and P. Du Gay (eds), *Cultures in Between*. London: Sage Publications, 1996.

Bierschenck, Thomas and Jean-Pierre Olivier de Sardan. 'Studying the Dynamics of African Bureaucracies: An Introduction to States at Work'. In T. Bierschenck and J-P. Olivier de Sardan (eds), *States at Work: Dynamics of African Bureaucracies* (pp. 1–33). Leiden and Boston: Brill, 2014. doi.org/10.1163/9789004264960_002

Bissell, William Cunningham. 'Engaging Colonial Nostalgia'. *Cultural Anthropology*, 20(2):215–248, 2005. doi.org/10.1525/can.2005.20.2.215

Björkdahl, Annika. 'A Gender-Just Peace? Exploring the Post-Dayton Peace Process in Bosnia'. *Peace and Change*, 37(2):286–317, 2012. doi.org/10.1111/j.1468-0130.2011.00746.x

Björkdahl, Annika and Kristine Höglund. 'Precarious Peacebuilding: Friction in Global–Local Encounters'. *Peacebuilding*, 1(3):289–299, 2013. doi.org/10.1080/21647259.2013.813170

Björkdahl, Annika and Johanna Selimovic. 'Gendering Agency in Transitional Justice'. *Security Dialogue*, 46(2):165–182, 2015. doi.org/10.1177/0967010614552547

Black, Julia. 'Critical Reflections on Regulation'. *Australian Journal of Legal Philosophy*, 27:1–35, 2002.

Bleiker, Roland. 'Conclusion—Everyday Struggles for a Hybrid Peace'. In O.P. Richmond and A. Mitchell (eds), *Hybrid Forms of Peace: From Everyday Agency to Post-liberalism* (pp. 293–309). Basingstoke: Palgrave Macmillan, 2012. doi.org/10.1057/9780230354234_16

Bliesemann de Guevara, Berit. 'Introduction: The Limits of Statebuilding and the Analysis of State-Formation'. *Journal of Intervention and Statebuilding*, 4(2):111–128, 2010. doi.org/10.1080/17502970903 533652

Boddy, Janice. *Wombs and Alien Spirits: Women, Men, and the Zār Cult in Northern Sudan*. Madison, WI: University of Wisconsin Press, 1989.

Boege, Volker. 'Bougainville and the Discovery of Slowness: An Unhurried Approach to State-building in the Pacific'. *Occasional Papers Series 3*. Brisbane: Australian Centre for Peace and Conflict Studies, 2006.

Boege, Volker. 'Legitimacy in Hybrid Political Orders: An Underestimated Dimension of Peacebuilding and State Formation'. Paper presented at European Consortium of Political Research Conference. Potsdam, 10–12 September 2009.

Boege, Volker. 'Potential and Limits of Traditional Approaches in Peacebuilding'. In B. Austin, M. Fischer and H.J. Giessmann (eds), *Advancing Conflict Transformation: The Berghof Handbook II*. Opladen/ Framington Hills: Barbara Budrich Publishers, 2011. www.berghof-handbook.net/documents/publications/boege_handbookII.pdf

Boege, Volker. 'Vying for Legitimacy in Post-conflict Situations: The Bougainville Case'. *Peacebuilding*, 2(3):237–252, 2014. doi.org/ 10.1080/21647259.2014.887616

Boege, Volker, M. Anne Brown and Kevin P. Clements. 'Hybrid Political Orders, Not Fragile States'. *Peace Review: A Journal of Social Justice*, 21(1):13–21, 2009. doi.org/10.1080/10402650802689997

Boege, Volker, M. Anne Brown, Kevin P. Clements, Wendy Foley and Anna Nolan. 'State Building Reconsidered: The Role of Hybridity in the Formation of Political Order'. *Political Science*, 59(1):45–56, 2007.

Boege, Volker, M. Anne Brown, Kevin P. Clements and Anna Nolan. *On Hybrid Political Orders and Emerging States: State Formation in the Context of 'Fragility'*. Berlin: Berghof Research Center for Constructive Conflict Management, 2008.

Boege, Volker, M. Anne Brown, Kevin P. Clements and Anna Nolan. 'States Emerging from Hybrid Political Orders: Pacific Experiences'. *Occasional Papers Series* 11. Brisbane: Australian Centre for Peace and Conflict Studies, 2008. espace.library.uq.edu.au/view/UQ:164904/ Occasional_Paper_No_11__Online_final.pdf

Boege, Volker, M. Anne Brown, Kevin P. Clements and Anna Nolan. 'Building Peace and Political Community in Hybrid Political Orders'. *International Peacekeeping*, 16(5):599–615, 2009. doi.org/ 10.1080/13533310903303248

Boege, Volker, Anne Brown and Louise Wiuff Moe. *Addressing Legitimacy Issues in Fragile Post-conflict Situations to Advance Conflict Transformation and Peacebuilding*. Final Report. Brisbane: University of Queensland, 2012.

Braithwaite, Edward Kamau. *The Development of Creole Society in Jamaica, 1770–1820*. Oxford: Clarendon Press, 1971.

Braithwaite, John. *Restorative Justice and Responsive Regulation*. Oxford: Oxford University Press, 2002.

Braithwaite, John. 'Responsive Regulation and Developing Economies'. *World Development*, 34(5):884–898, 2006. doi.org/10.1016/j.world dev.2005.04.021

Braithwaite, John. 'Partial Truth and Reconciliation in the *Longue Durée*'. *Contemporary Social Science*, 6(1):129–146, 2011. doi.org/10. 1080/17450144.2010.534498

Braithwaite, John. 'Evaluating the Timor-Leste Peace Operation'. *Journal of International Peacekeeping*, 16:282–305, 2012. doi.org/10.1163/ 18754112-1604005

Braithwaite, John, Hilary Charlesworth, Peter Reddy and Leah Dunn. *Reconciliation and Architectures of Commitment: Sequencing Peace in Bougainville*. Canberra: ANU E Press, 2010. press.anu.edu. au/publications/series/peacebuilding-compared/reconciliation-and-architectures-commitment

Braithwaite, John, Hilary Charlesworth and Adérito Soares. *Networked Governance of Freedom and Tyranny: Peace in Timor-Leste*. Canberra: ANU E Press, 2012. doi.org/10.26530/OAPEN_459392

Braithwaite, John, Hilary Charlesworth and Adérito Soares. 'Transitional Justice and Reconciliation'. In J. Braithwaite, H. Charlesworth and A. Soares, *Networked Governance of Freedom and Tyranny: Peace in Timor-Leste* (pp. 175–234). Canberra: ANU E Press, 2012. press. anu.edu.au/publications/series/peacebuilding-compared/networked-governance-freedom-and-tyranny

Braithwaite, John and Philip Pettit. *Not Just Deserts: A Republican Theory of Criminal Justice*. Oxford: Oxford University Press, 1990.

Breen, Bob. 'Coordinating Monitoring and Defence Support'. In M. Wehner and D. Denoon (eds), *Without a Gun: Australians' Experiences Monitoring Peace in Bougainville, 1997–2001* (pp. 43–49). Canberra: Pandanus Books, 2001.

Breen, Bob. *The Good Neighbour: Australian Peace Support Operations in the Pacific Islands, 1980–2006*. Cambridge: Cambridge University Press, 2016.

Brenner, Neil. 'The Limits to Scale? Methodological Reflections on Scalar Structuration'. *Progress in Human Geography*, 25(4):591–614, 2001. doi.org/10.1191/030913201682688959

Brigg, Morgan. 'Relational Peacebuilding: Promise beyond Crisis'. In T. Debiel, T. Held and U. Schneckener (eds), *Peacebuilding in Crisis: Rethinking Paradigms and Practices of Transnational Cooperation* (pp. 56–69). Abingdon: Routledge, 2016.

Brown, M. Anne. 'Security and Development: Conflict and Resilience in the Pacific Islands Region'. In M.A. Brown (ed.), *Security and Development in the Pacific Islands: Social Resilience in Emerging States*. Boulder, CO: Lynne Rienner, 2007.

Brown, M. Anne. *Human Rights and the Borders of Suffering: The Promotion of Human Rights in International Politics*. Manchester: Manchester University Press, 2009.

Brown, M. Anne. 'Security, Development and the Nation-building Agenda: East Timor'. *Conflict, Security and Development*, 9(2):141–164, 2009. doi.org/10.1080/14678800902924971

Brown, M. Anne, Volker Boege, Kevin P. Clements and Anna Nolan. 'Challenging Statebuilding as Peacebuilding—Working with Hybrid Political Orders to Build Peace'. In O.P. Richmond (ed.), *Palgrave Advances in Peacebuilding: Critical Developments and Approaches* (pp. 99–115). Basingstoke: Palgrave MacMillan, 2010. doi.org/10.1057/9780230282681_6

Brown, M. Anne and Alex Freitas Gusmao. 'Peacebuilding and Political Hybridity in East Timor'. *Peace Review: A Journal of Social Justice*, 21(1):61–69, 2009. doi.org/10.1080/10402650802690086

Brown, Michael, Jacqueline Vavra, Jay Singh, Gene Ward and Sidonio Freitas. *Conflict Assessment: East Timor*. Dili: USAID/East Timor and USAID Office of Conflict Management and Mitigation, 2004.

Bubandt, Nils. 'Vernacular Security: The Politics of Feeling Safe in Global, National and Local Worlds'. *Security Dialogue*, 36(3):275–296, 2005. doi.org/10.1177/0967010605057015

Butler, Judith. *Precarious Life: The Powers of Mourning and Violence*. London: Verso, 2005.

Butterworth, David and Pamela Dale. *Local Governance and Community Development Initiatives: Contributions for Community Development Programs in Timor-Leste*. Dili: World Bank, 2011. doi.org/10.1596/27255

Caballero-Anthony, Melly. 'The Philippines in Southeast Asia: An Overview'. In R.C. Severino and L.C. Salazar (eds), *Whither the Philippines in the 21st Century?* (pp. 1–17). Singapore: Institute of Southeast Asian Studies, 2007.

Carroll-Bell, Sam. 'Development Alternatives in Timor-Leste: Recasting Modes of Local Engagement'. *Bijdragen tot de Taal-, Land- en Volkenkunde*, 171(2–3):312–345, 2015. doi.org/10.1163/22134379-17102006

Carvalho, Manuel. *A Guerra que Portugal Quis Esquecer*. Porto: Porto Editora, 2015.

Cassani, Andrea. 'Hybrid What? Partial Consensus and Persistent Divergences in the Analysis of Hybrid Regimes'. *International Political Science Review*, 35(5):542–558, 2014. doi.org/10.1177 /0192512113495756

Castell, Janet. 'Opening Doors'. In R. Adams (ed.), *Peace on Bougainville— Truce Monitoring Group. Gudpela Nius Bilong Peace* (pp. 120–124). Wellington, NZ: Victoria University Press, 2001.

Catholic Relief Services. '*Laletek* Program Final Evaluation'. Dili: Catholic Relief Services East Timor, 2011. (Author's collection.)

CAVR (Commission for Reception, Truth and Reconciliation in East Timor). *Chega! Final Report of the Commission for Reception, Truth and Reconciliation in East Timor*. Dili: CAVR, 2005.

Chabal, Patrick and Jean-Pascal Daloz. *Africa Works: Disorder as Political Instrument*. Oxford: James Currey, 1999.

Chandler, David. 'The Uncritical Critique of "Liberal Peace"', *Review of International Studies*, 36(S1):137–155, 2010. doi.org/10.1017/ S0260210510000823

Chandler, David. 'Peacebuilding and the Politics of Non-linearity: Rethinking "Hidden" Agency and "Resistance"'. *Peacebuilding*, 1(1):17–32, 2013. doi.org/10.1080/21647259.2013.756256

Chandler, David. 'Resilience and the "Everyday": Beyond the Paradox of "Liberal Peace"'. *Review of International Studies*, 41(1):27–48, 2015. doi.org/10.1017/S0260210513000533

Charbonneau, Bruno and Jonathan M. Sears. 'Fighting for Liberal Peace in Mali? The Limits of International Military Intervention'. *Journal of Intervention and Statebuilding*, 8(2–3):192–213, 2014. doi.org/ 10.1080/17502977.2014.930221

Chesterman, Simon. 'Ownership in Theory and in Practice: Transfer of Authority in UN Statebuilding Operations'. *Journal of Intervention and Statebuilding*, 1(1):3–26, 2007. doi.org/10.1080/ 17502970601075873

Choldin, Harvey M. 'Kinship Networks in the Migration Process'. *International Migration Review*, 7(2):163–175, 1973. doi.org/10.2307/ 3002426

Chopra, Jarat and Tanja Hohe. 'Participatory Intervention'. *Global Governance*, 10(3):289–305, 2004.

CIGI (Center for International Governance Innovation). *Security Sector Reform Monitor: Timor-Leste*. Waterloo: CIGI, 2011.

Clausewitz, Carl von. *On War* (ed. and trans. M. Howard and P. Paret). Princeton, NJ: Princeton University Press, 1989 [1873].

Clements, Kevin P., Volker Boege, M. Anne Brown, Wendy Foley and Anna Nolan. 'State Building Reconsidered: The Role of Hybridity in the Formation of Political Order'. *Political Science*, 59(1):45–56, 2007. doi.org/10.1177/003231870705900106

Clifford, James. 'On Collecting Art and Culture'. In R. Ferguson, M. Gever, T.T. Minh-ha and C. West (eds), *Out There: Marginalization and Contemporary Cultures* (pp. 141–169). New York: New Museum of Contemporary Art and MIT Press, 1990.

Cohen, Jean L. and Andrew Arato. *Civil Society and Political Theory*. Cambridge, MA: MIT Press, 1994.

Cohn, Carol and Ruth Jacobson. 'Women and Political Activism in the Face of War and Militarization'. In C. Cohn (ed.), *Women and Wars* (pp. 102–123). Cambridge: Polity Press, 2013.

Connell, John. 'Regulation of Space in the Contemporary Postcolonial Pacific City: Port Moresby and Suva'. *Asia Pacific Viewpoint*, 44(3):243–257, 2003. doi.org/10.1111/j.1467-8373.2003.00213.x

Cox, John and Martha Macintyre. 'Christian Marriage, Money Scams, and Melanesian Social Imaginaries'. *Oceania*, 84(2):138–157, 2014. doi.org/10.1002/ocea.5048

Cox, John and Joanne Morrison. 'Solomon Islands Provincial Governance Information Paper'. Unpublished report prepared for AusAID, 2004.

Craig, David and Doug Porter. 'Political Settlement in Solomon Islands: A Political Economic Basis for Stability after RAMSI?' *State, Society and Governance in Melanesia Working Paper* 2013/1. Canberra: The Australian National University, 2013. ssgm.bellschool.anu.edu.au/sites/default/files/publications/attachments/2015-12/WP_2013_1_Craig_Porter_0.pdf

Crook, Richard C., Kojo Asante and Victor Brobbey. 'Popular Concepts of Justice and Fairness in Ghana: Testing the Legitimacy of New or Hybrid Forms of State Justice'. *African Power and Politics Programme Working Paper* 14. London: Overseas Development Institute, 2010.

Cummings, Maggie. 'Imagining Transnational Futures in Vanuatu'. In A. Quayson and G. Daswani (eds), *A Companion to Diaspora and Transnationalism* (pp. 381–396). Oxford: Wiley Blackwell, 2013. doi.org/10.1002/9781118320792.ch22

Cummins, Deborah. 'The Problem of Gender Quotas: Women's Representatives on Timor-Leste's *Suku* Councils'. *Development in Practice*, 21(1):85–95, 2011. doi.org/10.1080/09614524.2011.530246

Cummins, Deborah. *Local Governance in Timor-Leste: Lessons in Postcolonial State-building*. Abingdon: Routledge, 2015.

Cummins, Deborah and Vicente Maia. *Community Experiences of Decentralised Development in Timor-Leste*. Dili: The Asia Foundation, 2012.

Cuninghame, Patrick Gun. 'Hybridity, Transnationalism, and Identity in the US-Mexican Borderlands'. In K.E. Iyall Smith and P. Leavy (eds), *Hybrid Identities: Theoretical and Empirical Examinations* (pp. 13–40). Leiden: Brill, 2008. doi.org/10.1163/ej.9789004170391.i-411.14

Damaledo, A. 'From Refugee to Citizen: An Examination of the Identity of the Ex–East Timorese Refugees in Indonesia'. Unpublished masters thesis. Brisbane: University of Queensland, 2009.

Darling-Wolf, Fabienne. 'Disturbingly Hybrid or Distressingly Patriarchal? Gender Hybridity in a Global Environment'. In K.E. Iyall Smith and P. Leavy (eds), *Hybrid Identities: Theoretical and Empirical Examinations* (pp. 63–80). Leiden: Brill, 2008. doi.org/10.1163/ej.9789004170391.i-411.28

Das, Veena. *Life and Words: Violence and the Descent into the Ordinary*. Berkeley: University of California Press, 2007.

Das, Veena. 'What Does Ordinary Ethics Look Like?' In M. Lambek, V. Das, D. Fassin and W. Keane, *Four Lectures on Ethics: Anthropological Perspectives* (Chapter 2). Chicago: HAU Books, 2015.

Daurewa, A. 'The Power of Fiji's Women'. *Fiji Times*, 1 May 2009.

Dauvergne, Peter. 'Corporate Power in the Forests of the Solomon Islands'. *Pacific Affairs*, 71(4):524–546, 1998/1999. doi.org/10.2307/2761083

Davenport, William and Gülbün Çoker. 'The Moro Movement of Guadalcanal, British Solomon Islands Protectorate'. *The Journal of the Polynesian Society*, 76(2):123–175, 1967.

de Alwis, Malathi, Julie Mertus and Tazreena Sajjad. 'Women and Peace Processes'. In C. Cohn (ed.), *Women and Wars* (pp. 169–193). Cambridge: Polity Press, 2013.

de Certeau, Michel. *The Practice of Everyday Life*. Berkeley, CA: University of California Press, 2006.

de Coning, Cedric. 'Understanding Peacebuilding as Essentially Local'. *Stability: International Journal of Security & Development*, 2(1):6, 2013. doi.org/10.5334/sta.as

de Guevara, Berit Bliesemann. 'Introduction: The Limits of Statebuilding and the Analysis of State-Formation'. *Journal of Intervention and Statebuilding*, 4(2):111–128, 2010. doi.org/10.1080/1750297090 3533652

Debiel, Tobias and Patricia Rinck. 'Rethinking the Local in Peacebuilding: Moving Away from the Liberal/Post-liberal Divide'. In T. Debiel, T. Held and U. Schneckener (eds), *Peacebuilding in Crisis: Rethinking Paradigms and Practices of Transnational Cooperation*. Abingdon: Routledge, 2016.

Deinla, Imelda and Veronica Taylor. 'Towards Peace: Rethinking Justice and Legal Pluralism in the Bangsamoro'. *RegNet Working Paper* 63. Canberra: Regulatory Institutions Network, The Australian National University, 2015.

Derrida, Jacques. *Writing and Difference* (trans. Alan Bass). Chicago: Chicago University Press, 1978.

DFID (Department for International Development). *Policy Approach to Rule of Law*. London: DFID, 2013.

Dinnen, Sinclair. 'The Solomon Islands Intervention and the Instabilities of the Postcolonial State'. *Global Change, Peace & Security*, 20(3):339–355, 2008.

Dinnen, Sinclair and Matthew G. Allen. 'Paradoxes of Postcolonial Police-Building: Solomon Islands'. *Policing and Society*, 23(2):222–242, 2013. doi.org/10.1080/10439463.2012.696643

Dinnen, Sinclair and Matthew G. Allen. 'State Absence and State Formation in Solomon Islands: Reflections on Agency, Scale and Hybridity'. *Development and Change*, 47(1):76–97, 2016. doi.org/10.1111/dech.12212

Dinnen, Sinclair and Nicole Haley. *Evaluation of the Community Officer Project in Solomon Islands*. Justice for the Poor Research Report. Washington, DC: World Bank, 2012. doi.org/10.1596/26718

Dinnen, Sinclair and Lia Kent. 'Hybridity in Peacebuilding and Development: A Critical Interrogation'. *SSGM In Brief* 2015/50. Canberra: The Australian National University, 2015. ssgm.bellschool. anu.edu.au/sites/default/files/publications/attachments/2016-07/ ib2015.50_dinnen_and_kent.pdf

Dinnen, Sinclair and Gordon Peake. 'More than Just Policing: Police Reform in Post-conflict Bougainville'. *International Peacekeeping*, 20(5):570–584, 2013. doi.org/10.1080/13533312.2013.853961

Dirlik, Arif. 'Bringing History Back In: Of Diasporas, Hybridities, Places, and Histories'. In E. Mudimbe-Boyi (ed.), *Beyond Dichotomies: Histories, Identities, Cultures, and the Challenge of Globalization* (pp. 93–128). Albany, NY: State University of New York Press, 2002.

Dodson, Michael. 'The Human Rights Situation of Indigenous Peoples of Australia'. *Indigenous Affairs*, 1:32–45, 1999.

Donais, Timothy. *Peacebuilding and Local Ownership: Post-conflict Consensus-Building*. London: Routledge, 2012.

Douglas, Bronwen. 'Christian Citizens: Women and Negotiations of Modernity in Vanuatu'. *The Contemporary Pacific*, 14(1):1–38, 2002. doi.org/10.1353/cp.2002.0007

Doyle, Michael W. 'Three Pillars of the Liberal Peace'. *American Political Science Review*, 99(3):463–466, 2005. doi.org/10.1017/S000 3055405051798

Drahos, Peter. 'Intellectual Property and Pharmaceutical Markets: A Nodal Governance Approach'. *Temple Law Review*, 77(2):401–424, 2004.

Drexler, Elizabeth F. 'Fatal Knowledges: The Social and Political Legacies of Collaboration and Betrayal in Timor-Leste'. *The International Journal of Transitional Justice*, 7(1):74–94, 2013. doi.org/10.1093/ijtj/ijs037

Duffield, Mark. *Development, Security and Unending War: Governing the World of Peoples*. Cambridge: Polity Press, 2007.

Dunn, James. *Timor: A People Betrayed*. Milton, Qld: Jacaranda Press, 1983.

Durante, Ofelia L., Norma T. Gomex, Ester O. Sevilla and Howard J. Mañego. 'Management of Clan Conflict and Rido among the Tausug, Magindanao, Maranao, Sama, and Yakan Tribes'. In W.M. Torres III (ed.), *Rido: Clan Feuding and Conflict Management in Mindanao* (pp. 97–126). Makati City: The Asia Foundation, 2007.

Eastmond, Marita. 'Introduction: Reconciliation, Reconstruction and Everyday Life in War-Torn Societies'. *Focaal: Journal of Global and Historical Anthropology*, 57:3–16, 2010. doi.org/10.3167/fcl.2010.570101

Ellis, Stephen. *The Mask of Anarchy: The Destruction of Liberia and the Religious Dimension of an African Civil War*. 2nd ed. London: Hurst, 2007.

Ellis, Stephen and Gerrie ter Haar. *Worlds of Power: Religious Thought and Political Practice in Africa*. New York: Oxford University Press, 2004.

Enloe, Cynthia. *Bananas, Beaches and Bases: Making Feminist Sense of International Politics*. Berkeley, CA: University of California Press, 1990.

Enloe, Cynthia. *The Curious Feminist: Searching for Women in a New Age of Empire*. Berkeley, CA: University of California Press, 2004.

Eriksen, Stein Sundstøl. 'State Effects and the Effects of State Building: Institution Building and the Formation of State-Centred Societies'. *Third World Quarterly*, 38(4):771–786, 2017.

Escobar, Arturo. *Encountering Development: The Making and Unmaking of the Third World.* Princeton, NJ: Princeton University Press, 1995.

Escobar, Arturo. *Territories of Difference: Place, Movements, Life, Redes.* Durham and London: Duke University Press, 2008.

Evans, Daniel, Michael Goddard and Don Paterson. 'The Hybrid Courts of Melanesia: A Comparative Analysis of Village Courts of Papua New Guinea, Island Courts of Vanuatu and Local Courts of Solomon Islands'. *Justice and Development Working Paper Series* 13/2011. Washington, DC: World Bank, 2011. siteresources.worldbank.org/INTJUSFORPOOR/Resources/HybridCourts.pdf

Everett, Silas. *Law and Justice in Timor-Leste: A Survey of Citizen Awareness and Attitudes Regarding Law and Justice.* Dili: The Asia Foundation, 2008.

Everett, Silas and Butch Ragragio. *Decentralisation in Timor-Leste: What's at Stake?* Dili: The Asia Foundation, 2009.

Fawole, W. Alade and Charles Ukeje (eds). *The Crisis of the State and Regionalism in West Africa: Identity, Citizenship and Conflict.* Dakar: Council for the Development of Social Science Research in Africa, 2005.

Feltham, Oliver. *Anatomy of Failure: Philosophy and Political Action.* London: Bloomsbury Publishing, 2013.

Ferguson, James. 'Declarations of Dependence: Labour, Personhood, and Welfare in Southern Africa'. *Journal of the Royal Anthropological Institute*, 19(2):223–242, 2013. doi.org/10.1111/1467-9655.12023

Ferguson, James and Akhil Gupta. 'Spatializing States: Toward an Ethnography of Neoliberal Governmentality'. *American Ethnologist*, 29(4):981–1002, 2002.

Fernandez, Edwin O. '2 Teachers Killed, 2 Hurt in Cotabato City'. Inquirer.net, 13/7/2016. newsinfo.inquirer.net/795706/2-teachers-killed-2-hurt-in-cotabato-city

Fields, Karen E. *Revival and Rebellion in Colonial Central Africa.* Princeton, NJ: Princeton University Press, 1985.

Filer, Colin. 'Compensation, Rent and Power in Papua New Guinea'. In S. Toft (ed.), *Compensation for Resource Development in Papua New Guinea* (pp. 156–189). Canberra: The Australian National University, 1997.

Firth, Stewart. 'Colonial Administration and the Invention of the Native'. In D. Denoon (ed.), *The Cambridge History of the Pacific Islanders* (pp. 253–288). Cambridge: Cambridge University Press, 1997.

Fitzpatrick, Daniel, Andrew McWilliam and Susana Barnes. *Property and Social Resilience in Times of Conflict: Land, Custom and Law in East Timor*. London: Ashgate Publishing, 2012.

Flomoku, Pewee and Lemuel Reeves. 'Formal and Informal Justice in Liberia'. *ACCORD*, 23:44–47, 2012.

Forsyth, Miranda. *A Bird That Flies with Two Wings:* Kastom *and State Justice Systems in Vanuatu*. Canberra: ANU E Press, 2009. press.anu.edu.au/publications/bird-flies-two-wings

Forsyth, Miranda. 'Spinning a Conflict Management Web in Vanuatu: Creating and Strengthening Links between State and Non-state Legal Institutions'. *The Journal of Legal Pluralism and Unofficial Law*, 43(63):179–205, 2011. doi.org/10.1080/07329113.2011.10756661

Forsyth, Miranda and Sue Farran. *Weaving Intellectual Property Policy in Small Island Developing States*. Cambridge: Intersentia, 2015.

Forsyth, Miranda and Blayne Haggart. 'The False Friends Problem for Foreign Norm Transplantation in Developing Countries'. *Hague Journal on the Rule of Law*, 6(2):202–229, 2014. doi.org/10.1017/S1876404514001092

Foster, Robert J. *Materializing the Nation: Commodities, Consumption, and Media in Papua New Guinea*. Bloomington, IN: Indiana University Press, 2002.

Foster, Robert J. *Coca-Globalization: Following Soft Drinks from New York to New Guinea*. New York: Palgrave Macmillan, 2008. doi.org/10.1057/9780230610170

Foucault, Michel. *The Archaeology of Knowledge and the Discourse on Language* (trans. Alan Sheridan). London: Tavistock, 1972.

FPF (Fiji Police Force). *Fiji Police Duavata Community Policing Model.* Suva, 2013.

François, Monika and Inder Sud. 'Promoting Stability and Development in Fragile and Failed States'. *Development Policy Review,* 24(2):141–160, 2006. doi.org/10.1111/j.1467-7679.2006.00319.x

Fritz, V. and A. Rocha Menocal. '(Re)building Developmental States: From Theory to Practice'. *Working Paper* 274. London: Overseas Development Institute, 2006.

Frödin, Olle Jonas. 'Dissecting the State: Towards a Relational Conceptualization of States and State Failure'. *Journal of International Development,* 24(3):271–286, 2012. doi.org/10.1002/jid.1743

Fry, Greg and Tarcisius Tara Kabutaulaka. 'Political Legitimacy and State-building Intervention in the Pacific'. In G. Fry and T.T. Kabutaulaka (eds), *Intervention and State-building in the Pacific* (pp. 1–36). Manchester: Manchester University Press, 2008.

FWCC (Fiji Women's Crisis Centre). *Somebody's Life, Everybody's Business: National Research on Women's Health and Life Experiences in Fiji (2010/2011): A Survey Exploring the Prevalence, Incidence and Attitudes to Intimate Partner Violence in Fiji.* Suva: FWCC, 2013.

FWCC (Fiji Women's Crisis Centre). 'Misogyny and Homophobia in the Fiji Police Force'. Press release, 28 July 2014. www.facebook.com/Drodrolagi.Movement/photos/a.116234978442527.14368.1060 35439462481/710674078998611/

Gadinger, Frank, Wren Chadwick and Tobias Debiel (eds). *Relational Sensibility and the 'Turn to the Local': Prospects for the Future of Peacebuilding.* Global Dialogues 2. Duisburg: Käte Hamburger Kolleg/Centre for Global Cooperation Research, 2013.

Galtung, Johan. 'An Editorial'. *Journal of Peace Research,* 1(1):1–4, 1964. doi.org/10.1177/002234336400100101

Galtung, Johan. *Theories of Peace: A Synthetic Approach to Peace Thinking.* Oslo: International Peace Research Institute, 1967.

Gammage, Bill. 'Moresby 1966'. In C. Spark, S. Spark and C. Twomey (eds), *Australians in Papua New Guinea: 1960–1975* (pp. 235–247). St Lucia: University of Queensland Press, 2014.

Ganson, Brian and Achim Wennmann. 'Operationalising Conflict Prevention as Strong, Resilient Systems: Approaches, Evidence, Action Points'. *Platform Paper* 3. Geneva Peacebuilding Platform, 2012.

Garnsey, Elizabeth and James McGlade (eds). *Complexity and Co-evolution: Continuity and Change in Socio-economic Systems*. Cheltenham: Edward Elgar, 2006. doi.org/10.4337/9781847202925

Gates, Scott, Håvard Mokleiv Nygård and Esther Trappeniers. 'Conflict Recurrence'. *Conflict Trends* 02. Oslo: PRIO, 2016.

George, Nicole. 'Contending Masculinities and the Limits of Tolerance: Sexual Minorities in Fiji'. *The Contemporary Pacific*, 20(1):163–189, 2008. doi.org/10.1353/cp.2008.0012

George, Nicole. '"Just Like Your Mother?" The Politics of Feminism and Maternity in the Pacific Islands'. *The Australian Feminist Law Journal*, 32(1):77–96, 2010. doi.org/10.1080/13200968.2010.10854438

George, Nicole. *Situating Women: Gender Politics and Circumstance in Fiji*. Canberra: ANU E Press, 2012. press.anu.edu.au/publications/situating-women

George, Nicole. 'In Sickness and in Health: Evolving Trends in Gay Rights Advocacy in Fiji'. In N. Besnier and K. Alexeyeff (eds), *Gender on the Edge: Transgender, Gay, and Other Pacific Islanders* (pp. 293–322). Honolulu: University of Hawai'i Press, 2014. doi.org/10.21313/hawaii/9780824838829.003.0013

George, Nicole. '"Starting with a Prayer": Women, Faith, and Security in Fiji'. *Oceania*, 85(1):119–131, 2015. doi.org/10.1002/ocea.5078

Gewertz, Deborah B. and Frederick K. Errington. *Emerging Class in Papua New Guinea: The Telling of Difference*. New York: Cambridge University Press, 1999. doi.org/10.1017/CBO9780511606120

Ghani, Ashraf, Clare Lockhart and Michael Carnahan. 'An Agenda for State-Building in the Twenty-First Century'. *The Fletcher Forum of World Affairs*, 30(1):101–123, 2006.

Goddard, Michael. 'Introduction: About Moresby'. In M. Goddard (ed.), *Villagers and the City: Melanesian Experiences of Port Moresby, Papua New Guinea* (pp. 1–18). Wantage, United Kingdom: Sean Kingston Publishing, 2010.

Goodfellow, Tom and Stefan Lindemann. 'The Clash of Institutions: Traditional Authority, Conflict and the Failure of "Hybridity" in Buganda'. *Commonwealth & Comparative Politics*, 51(1):3–26, 2013. doi.org/10.1080/14662043.2013.752175

Goodhand, Jonathan and David Mansfield. 'Drugs and (Dis)Order: A Study of the Opium Trade, Political Settlements and State-Making in Afghanistan'. *Crisis States Research Centre Working Paper* 83. London School of Economics and Political Science, 2010.

Gow, James. *Legitimacy and the Military: The Yugoslav Crisis*. London: Pinter, 1992.

Gowing, Peter G. *Muslim Filipinos: Heritage and Horizon*. Quezon City: New Day, 1979.

Gready, Paul. *The Era of Transitional Justice: The Aftermath of the Truth and Reconciliation Commission in South Africa and Beyond*. Abingdon: Routledge, 2010.

Grenfell, Damian. 'Governance, Violence and Crises in Timor-Leste: Estadu Seidauk Mai'. In D.J. Mearns (ed.), *Democratic Governance in Timor-Leste: Reconciling the Local and the National* (pp. 85–97). Darwin: Charles Darwin University Press, 2008.

Grenfell, Damian. 'Remembering the Dead from the Customary to the Modern in Timor-Leste'. *Local Global: Identity, Security, Community*, 11:86–109, 2012.

Grenfell, Damian, Meabh Cryan, Kathryn Robertson and Alex McClean. *Beyond Fragility and Inequity: Women's Experiences of the Economic Dimensions of Domestic Violence in Timor-Leste*. Dili: The Asia Foundation, 2015.

Grenfell, Damian, Mayra Walsh, Anna Trembath, Carmenesa Moniz Noronha and Kym Holthouse. *Understanding Community: Security and Sustainability in Four Aldeia in Timor-Leste*. Melbourne: Globalism Research Centre, 2009.

Grenfell, Laura. 'Legal Pluralism and the Rule of Law in Timor Leste'. *Leiden Journal of International Law*, 19(2):305–337, 2006. doi.org/10.1017/S0922156506003323

Grenfell, Laura. 'Promoting the Rule of Law in Timor-Leste'. *Conflict, Security & Development*, 9(2):213–238, 2009. doi.org/10.1080/14678800902925143

Grunebaum, Heidi. *Memorializing the Past: Everyday Life in South Africa after the Truth and Reconciliation Commission*. New Brunswick, NJ: Transaction Publishers, 2011.

Gunningham, Neil. 'Confronting the Challenge of Energy Governance'. *Transnational Environmental Law*, 1(1):119–135, 2012. doi.org/10.1017/S2047102511000124

Gupta, Akhil and James Ferguson (eds). *Culture, Power, Place: Explorations in Critical Anthropology*. Durham and London: Duke University Press, 1997. doi.org/10.1215/9780822382089

Habermas, Jurgen. *Theory of Communicative Action* (trans. Thomas McCarthy). Boston: Beacon Press, 1984.

Hagmann, Tobias, and Didier Péclard. 'Negotiating Statehood: Dynamics of Power and Domination in Africa'. *Development and Change*, 41(4):539–562, 2010. doi.org/10.1111/j.1467-7660.2010.01656.x

Halapua, Winston. *Tradition, Lotu and Militarism in Fiji*. Suva: Fiji Institute of Applied Studies, 2003.

Halliday, Terence and Gregory Shaffer (eds). *Transnational Legal Orders*. Cambridge: Cambridge University Press, 2016.

Hameiri, Shahar. 'State Building or Crisis Management? A Critical Analysis of the Social and Political Implications of the Regional Assistance Mission to Solomon Islands'. *Third World Quarterly* 30(1):35–52, 2009. doi.org/10.1080/01436590802622276

Hameiri, Shahar. *Regulating Statehood: State Building and the Transformation of the Global Order*. Basingstoke: Palgrave Macmillan, 2010. doi.org/10.1057/9780230282001

Hameiri, Shahar. 'The Crisis of Liberal Peacebuilding and the Future of Statebuilding'. *International Politics*, 51(3):316–333, 2014. doi.org/10.1057/ip.2014.15

Hameiri, Shahar. 'Public Administration Reform and the Politics of Scale: The Case of Solomon Islands'. Paper presented at International Studies Global South Caucus Conference, Singapore Management University, 8–10 January 2015. web.isanet.org/Web/Conferences/GSCIS%20Singapore%202015/Archive/e39279f3-9f3f-4fde-a4b3-7653f6153d08.pdf

Hameiri, Shahar and Lee Jones. 'Beyond Hybridity to the Politics of Scale: International Intervention and "Local" Politics'. *Development and Change*, 48(1):54–77, 2017. doi.org/10.1111/dech.12287

Harvey, David. 'The Right to the City'. *New Left Review*, 53:23–40, 2008.

Hayner, Priscilla. *Unspeakable Truths*. New York: Routledge, 2001.

Heathershaw, John. 'Conclusions: Neither Built Nor Formed— The Transformation of Post-conflict States under International Intervention'. In B.B. de Guevara (ed.), *Statebuilding and State-Formation: The Political Sociology of Intervention* (pp. 246–259). Abingdon: Routledge, 2012.

Heathershaw, John. 'Towards Better Theories of Peacebuilding: Beyond the Liberal Peace Debate'. *Peacebuilding*, 1(2):275–282, 2013. doi.org/10.1080/21647259.2013.783260

Henrizi, Annika. 'Building Peace in Hybrid Spaces: Women's Agency in Iraqi NGOs'. *Peacebuilding*, 3(1):75–89, 2015. doi.org/10.1080/21647259.2014.969510

Hensell, Stephan and Felix Gerdes. 'Elites and International Actors in Post-war Societies: The Limits of Intervention'. *International Peacekeeping*, 19(2):154–169, 2012. doi.org/10.1080/13533312.2012.665683

Herlihy, Joan M. 'Always We Are Last: A Study of Planning, Development and Disadvantage in Melanesia'. Unpublished doctoral thesis. Canberra: The Australian National University, 1981.

Herman, Johanna and Olga Martin-Ortega. 2011. 'Narrowing Gaps in Justice: Rule of Law Programming in Liberia'. In C.L. Sriram, O. Martin-Ortega and J. Herman (eds), *Peacebuilding and Rule of Law in Africa: Just Peace?* (pp. 142–160). Abingdon: Routledge, 2011.

Hesselbein, Gabi, Frederick Golooba-Mutebi and James Putzel. 'Economic and Political Foundations of State Making in Africa: Understanding State Reconstruction'. *Crisis States Research Centre Working Paper* 3. London School of Economics and Political Science, 2006.

Hewitt, J. Joseph. 'Trends in Global Conflict, 1946–2009'. In J. Joseph Hewitt, J. Wilkenfeld and T.R. Gurr (eds), *Peace and Conflict 2012.* Abingdon: Routledge, 2012.

Heylighen, Francis. *The Science of Self-Organization and Adaptivity.* Brussels: Center Leo Apostel, Free University of Brussels, 2001.

Hicks, David. *Tetum Ghosts and Kin: Fertility and Gender in East Timor.* 2nd ed. Long Grove, IL: Waveland Press, 2004.

Hicks, David. '*Adat* and the Nation-State: Opposition and Synthesis in Two Political Cultures'. In M. Leach and D. Kingsbury (eds), *The Politics of Timor-Leste: Democratic Consolidation after Intervention.* Ithaca: Cornell University Press, 2013.

Hirblinger, Andreas T. and Claudia Simons. 'The Good, the Bad, and the Powerful: Representations of the Local in Peacebuilding'. *Security Dialogue*,46(5):422–439,2015.doi.org/10.1177/0967010615580055

Hobbes, Thomas. *De Cive (The Citizen): Philosophical Rudiments Concerning Government and Society.* 1998 [1651]. www.constitution.org/th/decive.htm

Hobbes, Thomas. *Leviathan or the Matter, Forme, and Power of a Common-Wealth Ecclesiasticall and Civill.* 2009 [1651]. gutenberg.org

Höglund, Kristine and Camilla Orjuela, 'Hybrid Peace Governance and Illiberal Peacebuilding in Sri Lanka'. *Global Governance: A Review of Multilateralism and International Organizations*, 18(1):89–104, 2012.

Hohe, Tanja. 'The Clash of Paradigms: International Administration and Local Political Legitimacy in East Timor'. *Contemporary Southeast Asia*, 24(3):569–589, 2002. doi.org/10.1355/CS24-3G

Hohe,Tanja. 'Local Governance after Conflict: Community Empowerment in East Timor'. *Journal of Peacebuilding and Development*, 1(3):45–56, 2004. doi.org/10.1080/15423166.2004.681592442113

Hohe, Tanja and R. Nixon. *Reconciling Justice: 'Traditional' Law and State Judiciary in East Timor*. Dili: United States Institute of Peace, 2003.

Holbrook, Justin G. 'Legal Hybridity in the Philippines: Lessons in Legal Pluralism from Mindanao and the Sulu Archipelago'. *Tulane Journal of International and Comparative Law*, 18(2):403–450, 2010.

Hooker, M.B. 'Muhammadan Law and Islamic Law'. In M.B. Hooker (ed.), *Islam in South-East Asia* (pp. 160–182). Leiden, Netherlands: E.J. Brill, 1983.

Howard, Michael. 'The Influence of Clausewitz'. In Carl von Clausewitz, *On War* (ed. and trans. M. Howard and P. Paret) (pp. 27–44). Princeton, NJ: Princeton University Press, 1989 [1873].

Hudson David, Heather Marquette and Sam Waldock. *Everyday Political Analysis*. Birmingham: Developmental Leadership Program, 2016.

Hughes, Bryn, Charles T. Hunt and Jodie Curth-Bibb. *Forging New Conventional Wisdom Beyond International Policing: Learning from Complex, Political Realities*. Leiden: Martinus Nijhoff, 2013. doi.org/10.1163/9789004244825

Hughes, Caroline, Joakim Öjendal and Isabell Schierenbeck. 'The Struggle versus the Song—The Local Turn in Peacebuilding: An Introduction'. *Third World Quarterly*, 36(5):817–824, 2015. doi.org/10.1080/01436597.2015.1029907

Hunt, Charles T. 'Beyond the binaries: towards a relational approach to peacebuilding'. *Global Change, Peace & Security*, 29(3):209–227, 2017. doi.org/10.1080/14781158.2017.1360855

Hunt, Charles T. 'Relational Perspectives on Peace Formation: Symbiosis and the Provision of Security and Justice'. In K. Aning, A. Brown, V. Boege and C.T. Hunt (eds), *Exploring Peace Formation: Security and Justice in Post-colonial States*. Oxford: Routledge, forthcoming.

Hviding, Edvard. 'Re-placing the State in the Western Solomon Islands: The Political Rise of the Christian Fellowship Church'. In E. Hviding and K.M. Rio (eds), *Made in Oceania: Social Movements, Cultural Heritage and the State in the Pacific* (pp. 51–89). Wantage, UK: Sean Kingston, 2011.

Igreja, Victor. "'Why Are There So Many Drums Playing until Dawn?" Exploring the Role of *Gamba* Spirits and Healers in the Post-war Recovery Period in Gorongosa, Central Mozambique'. *Transcultural Psychiatry*, 40(4):460–487, 2003. doi.org/10.1177/1363461503404001

Igreja, Victor. 'Cultural Disruption and the Care of Infants in Post-war Mozambique'. In J. Boyden and J. de Berry (eds), *Children and Youth on the Frontline* (pp. 23–41). Oxford: Berghahn Books, 2005.

Igreja, Victor. 'Memories as Weapons: The Politics of Peace and Silence in Post-civil War Mozambique'. *Journal of Southern African Studies*, 34(3):539–556, 2008. doi.org/10.1080/03057070802259720

Igreja, Victor. 'Justice and Reconciliation in the Aftermath of the Civil War in Gorongosa, Mozambique Central'. In K. Ambos, J. Large and M. Wierda (eds), *Building a Future on Peace and Justice* (pp. 423–437). Berlin: Springer, 2009. doi.org/10.1007/978-3-540-85754-9_16

Igreja, Victor. 'The Politics of Peace, Justice and Healing in Post-war Mozambique'. In C. Sriram and S. Pillay (eds), *Peace versus Justice?* (pp. 277–300). KwaZulu-Natal: University of KwaZulu-Natal Press, 2009.

Igreja, Victor. 'Frelimo's Political Ruling through Violence and Memory in Postcolonial Mozambique'. *Journal of Southern African Studies*, 36(4):781–799, 2010. doi.org/10.1080/03057070.2010.527636

Igreja, Victor. 'Testimonies of Suffering and Recasting the Meanings of Memories of Violence in Post-war Mozambique'. In L. Kapteijns and A. Richters (eds), *Mediations of Violence in Africa* (pp. 141–172). Leiden: Brill, 2010. doi.org/10.1163/ej.9789004185364.i-266.44

Igreja, Victor. 'Traditional Courts and the Struggle against State Impunity for Civil Wartime Offences in Mozambique'. *Journal of African Law*, 54(1):51–73, 2010. doi.org/10.1017/S0021855309990167

Igreja, Victor. 'Negotiating Order in Postwar Mozambique'. In H. Kyed, J. Coelho, A. Souto and S. Araújo (eds), *The Dynamics of Legal Pluralism in Mozambique* (pp. 148–166). Maputo: Centro de Estudos Sociais Aquino de Bragança, 2012.

Igreja, Victor. 'Mozambique'. In L. Stan and N. Nedelsky (eds), *Encyclopedia of Transitional Justice* (pp. 305–311). Vol. II. Cambridge: Cambridge University Press, 2013.

Igreja, Victor. 'Politics of Memory, Decentralisation and Recentralisation in Mozambique'. *Journal of Southern African Studies*, 39(2):313–335, 2013. doi.org/10.1080/03057070.2013.795809

Igreja, Victor. 'Memories of Violence, Cultural Transformations of Cannibals, and Indigenous State-Building in Post-conflict Mozambique'. *Comparative Studies in Society and History*, 56(3):774–802, 2014. doi.org/10.1017/S0010417514000322

Igreja, Victor. 'Amnesty Law, Political Struggles for Legitimacy and Violence in Mozambique'. *International Journal of Transitional Justice*, 9(2):239–258, 2015. doi.org/10.1093/ijtj/ijv004

Igreja, Victor. 'Intersections of Sensorial Perception and Imagination in Divination Practices in Post-war Mozambique'. *Anthropological Quarterly*, 88(3):693–723, 2015. doi.org/10.1353/anq.2015.0042

Igreja, Victor. 'Legacies of War, Healing, Justice and Social Transformation in Mozambique'. In B. Hamber and E. Gallagher (eds), *Psychosocial Perspectives on Peacebuilding* (pp. 223–254). New York: Springer, 2015. doi.org/10.1007/978-3-319-09937-8_7

Igreja, Victor. 'Media and Legacies of War: Responses to Global Film Violence in Conflict Zones'. *Current Anthropology*, 56(5):678–700, 2015. doi.org/10.1086/683107

Igreja, Victor and Béatrice Dias-Lambranca. 'The Thursdays as They Live: Christian Religious Transformation and Gender Relations in Postwar Gorongosa, Central Mozambique'. *Journal of Religion in Africa*, 39(3):262–294, 2009. doi.org/10.1163/157006609X449946

Igreja, Victor, Béatrice Dias-Lambranca and Annemiek Richters. '*Gamba* Spirits, Gender Relations, and Healing in Post–Civil War Gorongosa, Mozambique'. *Journal of the Royal Anthropological Institute*, 14(2):353–371, 2008. doi.org/10.1111/j.1467-9655.2008.00506.x

Igreja, Victor, Wim Kleijn, Béatrice Dias-Lambranca, Douglas A. Hershey, Clara Calero and Annemiek Richters. 'Agricultural Cycle and the Prevalence of Posttraumatic Stress Disorder: A Longitudinal Community Study in Postwar Mozambique'. *Journal of Traumatic Stress*, 22(3):172–179, 2009. doi.org/10.1002/jts.20412

Igreja, Victor and Limore Racin. 'The Politics of Spirits, Justice, and Social Transformation in Mozambique'. In B. Meier and A. Steinforth (eds), *Spirits in Politics* (pp. 181–204). Frankfurt: Campus Verlag, 2013.

Igreja, Victor and Elin Skaar. '"A Conflict Does Not Rot": State and Civil Society Responses to Civil War Offences in Mozambique'. *Nordic Journal of Human Rights*, 31:149–175, 2013.

International Alert. *Rebellion, Political Violence and Shadow Crimes in the Bangsamoro: The Bangsamoro Conflict Monitoring System (BCMS), 2011–2013*. Manila: International Alert, 2014.

International Alert. 'Violence in the Bangsamoro and Southern Mindanao, 2011–2015'. Presentation, 30 March 2017. conflictalert.info/publication/violence-bangsamoro-southern-mindanao-2011-2015/

International Crisis Group. *Timor-Leste: Reconciliation and Return from Indonesia*. Asia Briefing 122. Dili and Brussels: International Crisis Group, 2011.

IPAC (Institute for Policy Analysis of Conflict). *Justice at the Crossroads in Timor-Leste*. Jakarta: IPAC, 2015.

Isser, Deborah H., Stephen C. Lubkemann and Saah N'Tow. *Looking for Justice: Liberian Experiences with and Perceptions of Local Justice Options*. Washington, DC: United States Institute of Peace, 2009.

Iyall Smith and Keri E. 'Hybrid Identities: Theoretical Examinations'. In K.E. Iyall Smith and P. Leavy (eds), *Hybrid Identities: Theoretical and Empirical Examinations* (pp. 3–12). Leiden: Brill, 2008. doi.org/10.1163/ej.9789004170391.i-411.6

Jackson, Paul. 'Chiefs, Money and Politicians: Rebuilding Local Government in Post-war Sierra Leone'. *Public Administration and Development*, 25(1):49–58, 2005. doi.org/10.1002/pad.347

Jackson, Paul. 'Reshuffling an Old Deck of Cards? The Politics of Local Government Reform in Sierra Leone'. *African Affairs*, 106(422):95–111, 2007. doi.org/10.1093/afraf/adl038

Jacobs, Jane M. *Edge of Empire: Postcolonialism and the City*. London and New York: Routledge, 1996. doi.org/10.4324/9780203430903

Jay, Alice and Momoh Taziff Koroma. *From 'Crying' and Clientelism to Rights and Responsibilities*. Study for the Government of Sierra Leone and European Commission on Accountability in Sierra Leone, 2004.

Jayasuriya, Kanishka. 'Institutional Hybrids and the Rule of Law as a Regulatory Project'. In B.Z. Tamanaha, C. Sage and M. Woolcock (eds), *Legal Pluralism and Development: Scholars and Practitioners in Dialogue* (pp. 145–161). New York: Cambridge University Press, 2013.

Jaye, Thomas. 'Understanding and Explaining Hybridity in Liberia'. In K. Aning, A. Brown, V. Boege and C.T. Hunt (eds), *Exploring Peace Formation: Security and Justice in Post-colonial States* (pp. 140–157). Oxford: Routledge, 2018.

Jessop, Bob. *State Power: A Strategic-Relational Approach*. Cambridge: Polity, 2007.

Johnson, Kristin and Marc L. Hutchison. 'Hybridity, Political Order and Legitimacy: Examples from Nigeria'. *Journal of Peacebuilding & Development*, 7(2):37–52, 2012. doi.org/10.1080/15423166.2012.743811

Jolly, Margaret. 'Woman Ikat Raet Long Human Raet o No? Women's Rights, Human Rights and Domestic Violence in Vanuatu'. *Feminist Review*, 52(1):169–190, 1996. doi.org/10.1057/fr.1996.14

Jones, Lee. 'State Theory and Statebuilding: Towards a Gramscian Approach'. In R. Egnell and P. Haldén (eds), *New Agendas in State Building: Hybridity, Contingency and History* (pp. 70–91). London: Routledge, 2013.

Jones, Paul and M. Kep. 'Understanding Urbanisation in the PNG Context'. PNG Symposium 2012: PNG Securing a Prosperous Future. Deakin University, Melbourne, 2012.

Jundam, Mashur Bin-Ghalib. *Tunggal Hulah-Duwa Sarah: Adat and Sharee'ah Laws in the Life of the Tausug*. Quezon City: University of the Philippines, 2006.

Kabutaulaka, Tarcisius Tara. 'Rumble in the Jungle: Land, Culture and (Un)sustainable Logging in Solomon Islands'. In A. Hooper (ed.), *Culture and Sustainable Development in the Pacific*. Canberra: Asia Pacific Press, 2000.

Kaldor, Mary. 'Identity and War'. *Global Policy*, 4(4):336–346, 2013. doi.org/10.1111/1758-5899.12084

Kaldor, Mary and Sabine Selchow (eds). *Subterranean Politics in Europe*. Basingstoke: Palgrave Macmillan, 2015. doi.org/10.1057/9781137441478

Kalyvas, Stathis N. 'The Ontology of "Political Violence": Action and Identity in Civil Wars'. *Perspectives on Politics*, 1(3):475–494, 2003. doi.org/10.1017/S1537592703000355

Kammen, Douglas. 'Subordinating Timor: Central Authority and the Origins of Communal Identities in East Timor'. *Bijdragen tot de Taal-, Land- en Volkenkunde*, 166(2/3):244–269, 2010. doi.org/10.1163/22134379-90003618

Kant, Immanuel. *Perpetual Peace and Other Essays on Politics, History, and Morals* (trans. T. Humphrey). Indianapolis, IN: Hackett Publishing, 1983 [1795].

Kantor, Anna and Mariam Persson. *Understanding Vigilantism: Informal Security Providers and Security Sector Reform in Liberia*. Stockholm: Folke Bernadotte Academy, 2010.

Kapoor, Ilan. 'Acting in a Tight Spot: Homi Bhabha's Postcolonial Politics'. *New Political Science*, 25(4):561–577, 2003. doi.org/10.1080/0739314032000145233

Kelly, John and Martha V. Kaplan. *Represented Communities: Fiji and World Decolonisation*. Chicago: University of Chicago Press, 2001.

Kent, Lia. 'Community Views of Justice and Reconciliation in Timor-Leste'. *Development Bulletin*, 68:62–65, 2005. crawford.anu.edu.au/rmap/devnet/devnet/db-68.pdf

Kent, Lia. 'Narratives of Suffering and Endurance: Coercive Sexual Relationships, Truth Commissions, and Possibilities for Gender Justice in Timor-Leste'. *The International Journal of Transitional Justice*, 8(2):289–313, 2014. doi.org/10.1093/ijtj/iju008

Kent, Lia. 'Remembering the Past, Shaping the Future: Memory Frictions and Nation-Making in Timor-Leste'. *SSGM Discussion Paper* 2015/1. Canberra: The Australian National University, 2015. ssgm.bellschool. anu.edu.au/sites/default/files/publications/attachments/2015-12/ DP_2015_1Kent_Web_0.pdf

Kent, Lia. 'Sounds of Silence: Everyday Strategies of Social Repair in Timor-Leste'. *The Australian Feminist Law Journal*, 42(1):31–50, 2016. doi.org/10.1080/13200968.2016.1175403

Kent, Lia and Naomi Kinsella. '*A Luta Kontinua* (The Struggle Continues): The Marginalization of East Timorese Women within the Veterans' Valorization Scheme'. *International Feminist Journal of Politics*, 17(3):473–494, 2015. doi.org/10.1080/14616742.2014.913383

Kingsbury, Damien. 'East Timor's Political Crisis: Origins and Resolution'. In D.J. Mearns (ed.), *Democratic Governance in East Timor: Reconciling the Local and the National*. Darwin: Charles Darwin University Press, 2008.

Kleinhans, Martha-Marie and Roderick A. MacDonald. 'What Is Critical Legal Pluralism?' *Canadian Journal of Law and Society*, 12(2):25–46, 1997. doi.org/10.1017/S0829320100005342

Kovar, Annika and Andrew Harrington. *Breaking the Cycle of Domestic Violence in Timor-Leste: Access to Justice Options, Barriers, and Decision Making Processes in the Context of Legal Pluralism*. Dili: United Nations Development Programme, 2013.

Kraushaar, Maren and Daniel Lambach. 'Hybrid Political Orders: The Added Value of a New Concept'. *Occasional Papers Series* 14. Brisbane: Australian Centre for Peace and Conflict Studies, 2009.

Kreuzer, Peter. *Political Clans and Violence in the Southern Philippines*. Report No. 71. Frankfurt: Peace Research Institute, 2005.

Kreuzer, Peter. *Philippine Governance: Merging Politics and Crime*. Report No. 93. Frankfurt: Peace Research Institute, 2009.

Kreuzer, Peter. *Violence as a Means of Control and Domination in the Southern Philippines.* Report No. 105. Frankfurt: Peace Research Institute, 2011.

Krogstad, Erlend Grøner. 'Local Ownership as Dependence Management: Inviting the Coloniser Back'. *Journal of Intervention and Statebuilding,* 8(2–3):105–125, 2014. doi.org/10.1080/17502977.2014.901030

Kumar, Chetan and Jos De la Haye. 'Hybrid Peacemaking: Building National "Infrastructures for Peace"'. *Global Governance: A Review of Multilateralism and International Organizations,* 18(1):13–20, 2012.

Kwon, Heonik. *Ghosts of War in Vietnam.* Cambridge: Cambridge University Press, 2008. doi.org/10.1017/CBO9780511807596

Kyed, Helene Maria. 'The Politics of Legal Pluralism: State Policies on Legal Pluralism and Their Local Dynamics in Mozambique'. *The Journal of Legal Pluralism and Unofficial Law,* 41(59):87–120, 2009. doi.org/10.1080/07329113.2009.10756631

Kyed, Helene Maria. 'Introduction to the Special Issue: Legal Pluralism and International Development Interventions'. *The Journal of Legal Pluralism and Unofficial Law,* 43(63):1–23, 2011. doi.org/10.1080/0 7329113.2011.10756655

Laffey, Mark and Suthaharan Nadarajah. 'The Hybridity of Liberal Peace: States, Diasporas and Insecurity'. *Security Dialogue,* 43(5):403–420, 2012. doi.org/10.1177/0967010612457974

Lambek, Michael. *Knowledge and Practice in Mayotte: Local Discourses of Islam, Sorcery, and Spirit Possession.* Toronto: University of Toronto Press, 1993. doi.org/10.3138/9781442676534

Lara, Francisco J., Jr. and Phil Champain. *Inclusive Peace in Muslim Mindanao: Revisiting the Dynamics of Conflict and Exclusion.* London: International Alert, 2009.

Lara, Francisco J., Jr. and Steven Schoofs (eds). *Out of the Shadows: Violent Conflict and the Real Economy of Mindanao.* London: International Alert, 2013.

Larke, Ben. '"… And the Truth Shall Set You Free": Confessional Trade-Offs and Community Reconciliation in East Timor'. *Asian Journal of Social Science,* 37(4):646–676, 2009. doi.org/10.1163/156853109X460237

Larmour, Peter. *Foreign Flowers: Institutional Transfer and Good Governance in the Pacific Islands*. Honolulu: University of Hawai'i Press, 2005.

Larmour, Peter and Ropate Qalo (eds). *Decentralisation in the South Pacific: Local, Provincial and State Government in Twenty Countries*. Suva, Fiji: Institute of Pacific Studies, University of the South Pacific, 1985.

Latour, Bruno. *Reassembling the Social: An Introduction to Actor-Network-Theory*. New York: Oxford University Press, 2005.

Lawler, Peter. 'Peace Research, War, and the Problem of Focus'. *Peace Review: A Journal of Social Justice*, 14(1):7–14, 2002. doi.org/10.1080/10402650220118134

Lears, T.J. Jackson. 'The Concept of Cultural Hegemony: Problems and Possibilities'. *The American Historical Review*, 90(3):567–593, 1985. doi.org/10.2307/1860957

Lederach, John Paul. *The Moral Imagination: The Art and Soul of Building Peace*. Oxford: Oxford University Press, 2005.

Lemay-Hébert, Nicolas. 'The "Empty-Shell" Approach: The Setup Process of International Administrations in Timor-Leste and Kosovo, Its Consequences and Lessons'. *International Studies Perspectives*, 12(2):190–211, 2011. doi.org/10.1111/j.1528-3585.2011.00427.x

Leonardsson, Hanna and Gustav Rudd. 'The "Local Turn" in Peacebuilding: A Literature Review of Effective and Emancipatory Local Peacebuilding'. *Third World Quarterly*, 36(5):825–839, 2015. doi.org/10.1080/01436597.2015.1029905

Levi, Primo. *The Drowned and the Saved*. New York: Simon and Schuster, 1998.

Lubkemann, Stephen. *Culture in Chaos: An Anthropology of the Social Condition of War*. Chicago, IL: University of Chicago Press, 2008.

Lubkemann, Stephen, Deborah Isser and Philip Banks. 'Justice in a Vacuum: The Unintended Consequences of the Constraint of Customary Justice in Post-conflict Liberia'. In D.H. Isser (ed.), *Customary Justice and the Rule of Law in War-Torn Societies* (pp. 193–238). Washington, DC: United States Institute of Peace Press, 2011.

Lubkemann, Stephen, Deborah Isser and Peter Chapman. 'Neither State nor Custom—Just Naked Power: The Consequences of Ideals-Oriented Rule of Law Policy-Making in Liberia'. *The Journal of Legal Pluralism and Unofficial Law*, 43(63):73–109, 2011. doi.org/10.1080 /07329113.2011.10756658

Luckham, Robin and Tom Kirk. 'Security in Hybrid Political Contexts: An End-User Approach'. *The Justice and Security Research Programme Paper* 2. London School of Economics and Political Science, 2012.

Luckman, Robin and Tom Kirk. 'Understanding Security in the Vernacular in Hybrid Political Contexts: A Critical Survey'. *Conflict, Security & Development*, 13(3):339–359, 2013. doi.org/10.1080/146 78802.2013.811053

Luongo, Katherine. *Witchcraft and Colonial Rule in Kenya, 1900–1955*. Cambridge: Cambridge University Press, 2012.

Lusby, Stephanie. 'Preventing Violence at Home, Allowing Violence in the Workplace: A Case Study of Security Guards in Papua New Guinea'. *SSGM In Brief* 2014/49. Canberra: The Australian National University, 2014. ssgm.bellschool.anu.edu.au/sites/default /files/publications/attachments/2015-12/IB-2014-49-Lusby-ONLINE_0.pdf

Lusby, Stephanie. 'Securitisation, Development and the Invisibility of Gender'. In M. Macintyre and C. Spark (eds), *Transformations of Gender in Melanesia* (pp. 23–43). Canberra: ANU Press, 2017. doi.org/10.22459/TGM.02.2017.01

Mac Ginty, Roger. 'Indigenous Peace-Making Versus the Liberal Peace'. *Cooperation and Conflict*, 43(2):139–163, 2008. doi.org/10.1177/ 0010836708089080

Mac Ginty, Roger. 'Gilding the Lily? International Support for Indigenous and Traditional Peacebuilding'. In O.P. Richmond (ed.), *Palgrave Advances in Peacebuilding: Critical Developments and Approaches* (pp. 347–366). Basingstoke: Palgrave Macmillan, 2010. doi.org/10.1057/9780230282681_19

Mac Ginty, Roger. 'Hybrid Peace: The Interaction between Top-Down and Bottom-Up Peace'. *Security Dialogue*, 41(4):391–412, 2010. doi.org/10.1177/0967010610374312

Mac Ginty, Roger. 'Hybrid Peace: How Does Hybrid Peace Come About?' In S. Campbell, D. Chandler and M. Sabaratnam (eds), *A Liberal Peace? The Problems and Practices of Peacebuilding* (pp. 209–225). London: Zed Books, 2011.

Mac Ginty, Roger. *International Peacebuilding and Local Resistance: Hybrid Forms of Peace.* Basingstoke: Palgrave Macmillan, 2011. doi.org/10.1057/9780230307032

Mac Ginty, Roger. 'Everyday Peace: Bottom-Up and Local Agency in Conflict-Affected Societies'. *Security Dialogue*, 45(6):548–564, 2014. doi.org/10.1177/0967010614550899

Mac Ginty, Roger. 'Where Is the Local? Critical Localism and Peacebuilding'. *Third World Quarterly*, 36(5):840–856, 2015. doi.org/10.1080/01436597.2015.1045482

Mac Ginty, Roger and Oliver P. Richmond. 'The Local Turn in Peace Building: A Critical Agenda for Peace'. *Third World Quarterly*, 34(5):763–783, 2013. doi.org/10.1080/01436597.2013.800750

Mac Ginty, Roger and Oliver P. Richmond. 'The Fallacy of Constructing Hybrid Political Orders: A Reappraisal of the Hybrid Turn in Peacebuilding'. *International Peacekeeping*, 23(2):219–239, 2016. doi.org/10.1080/13533312.2015.1099440

Macintyre, Martha. 'Money Changes Everything: Papua New Guinean Women in the Modern Economy'. In M. Patterson and M. Macintyre (eds), *Managing Modernity in the Western Pacific* (pp. 90–120). St Lucia: University of Queensland Press, 2011.

MacKenzie, Megan H. *Female Soldiers in Sierra Leone: Sex, Security, and Post-conflict Development.* New York: New York University Press, 2012. doi.org/10.18574/nyu/9780814761373.001.0001

Madraiwiwi, Joni. 'On Understanding the Fijian People'. In W. Tubman (ed.), *A Personal Perspective: The Speeches of Joni Madraiwiwi* (pp. 19–24). Suva: Institute of Pacific Studies, 2001.

Mallet, Richard. 'Beyond Failed States and Ungoverned Spaces: Hybrid Political Orders in the Post-conflict Landscape'. *eSharp. Uniting Nations: Risks and Opportunities*, 15:65–91, 2010.

Masquelier, Adeline. *Prayer Has Spoiled Everything: Possession, Power, and Identity in an Islamic Town of Niger*. Durham, NC: Duke University Press, 2001. doi.org/10.1215/9780822380559

Massey, Doreen. *For Space*. London: Sage Publications, 2005.

Mastura, Michael O. 'Legal Pluralism in the Philippines'. *Law & Society Review*, 28(3):461–476, 1994. doi.org/10.2307/3054065

McCoy, Alfred W. (ed.). *An Anarchy of Families: State and Family in the Philippines*. Quezon City: Ateneo de Manila University Press, 1994.

McDougall, Debra. 'Sub-national Governance in Post-RAMSI Solomon Islands'. *State, Society and Governance in Melanesia Working Paper* 2014/3. Canberra: The Australian National University, 2014. ssgm. bellschool.anu.edu.au/sites/default/files/publications/attachments/ 2015-12/WP_2014_3_McDougall_0.pdf

McDougall, Debra. 'Customary Authority and State Withdrawal in Solomon Islands: Resilience or Tenacity?' *Journal of Pacific History*, 50(4):450–472, 2015. doi.org/10.1080/00223344.2015.1110102

McDowell, Linda. *Gender, Identity and Place: Understanding Feminist Geographies*. Cambridge: Polity Press, 1999.

McGeough, Paul. 'An Unholy Alliance of Church and State'. *Sydney Morning Herald*, 29 November 2009. www.smh.com.au/world/an-unholy-alliance-of-church-and-state-20091128-jxwu.html

McLeod, Laura. 'A Feminist Approach to Hybridity: Understanding Local and International Interactions in Producing Post-conflict Gender Security'. *Journal of Intervention and Statebuilding*, 9(1):48–69, 2015. doi.org/10.1080/17502977.2014.980112

McMillan, Karen and Heather Worth. *Sex Workers and HIV Prevention in Fiji—After the Fiji Crimes Decree 2009*. Sydney: International HIV Research Group, University of New South Wales, 2011. sphcm. med.unsw.edu.au/sites/default/files/sphcm/Centres_and_Units/Fiji_ Crimes_Decree.pdf

McWilliam, Andrew. 'Houses of Resistance in East Timor: Structuring Sociality in the New Nation'. *Anthropological Forum*, 15(1):27–44, 2005. doi.org/10.1080/0066467042000336698

McWilliam, Andrew. 'Customary Governance in Timor-Leste'. In D.J. Mearns (ed.), *Democratic Governance in Timor-Leste: Reconciling the Local and the National*. Darwin: Charles Darwin University Press, 2008.

McWilliam, Andrew, Lisa Palmer and Christopher Shepherd. '*Lulik* Encounters and Cultural Frictions in East Timor: Past and Present'. *The Australian Journal of Anthropology*, 25(3):304–320, 2014. doi.org/10.1111/taja.12101

Meagher, Kate. 'The Strength of Weak States? Non-state Security Forces and Hybrid Governance in Africa'. *Development and Change*, 43(5):1073–1101, 2012. doi.org/10.1111/j.1467-7660.2012.01794.x

Meagher, Kate, Tom De Herdt and Kristof Titeca. *Unravelling Public Authority: Paths of Hybrid Governance in Africa*. London: London School of Economics, 2014.

Meiksin, Rebecca, Dominique Meekers, Susan Thompson, Amy Hagopian and Mary Anne Mercer. 'Domestic Violence, Marital Control, and Family Planning, Maternal, and Birth Outcomes in Timor-Leste'. *Maternal and Child Health Journal*, 19(6):1338–1347, 2015. doi.org/10.1007/s10995-014-1638-1

Melander, Erik, Therése Pettersson and Lotta Themnér. 'Organized Violence, 1989–2015'. *Journal of Peace Research*, 53(5):727–742, 2016. doi.org/10.1177/0022343316663032

Menkhaus, Ken. 'Traditional Conflict Management in Contemporary Somalia'. In I.W. Zartman (ed.), *Traditional Cures for Modern Conflicts: African Conflict 'Medicine'* (pp. 183–199). Boulder and London: Lynne Rienner, 2000.

Menkhaus, Ken. 'Governance without Government in Somalia: Spoilers, State Building and the Politics of Coping'. *International Security*, 31(3):74–106, 2007. doi.org/10.1162/isec.2007.31.3.74

Merry, Sally Engle. 'Legal Pluralism'. *Law & Society Review*, 22(5):869–896, 1988. doi.org/10.2307/3053638

Mesaki, Simeon. 'Witchcraft and the Law in Tanzania'. *International Journal of Sociology and Anthropology*, 1(8):132–138, 2009.

Metz, Steven and Phillip Cuccia. *Defining War for the 21st Century*. 2010 Strategic Studies Institute Annual Strategy Conference Report, 2011.

Millar, Gearoid. 'Disaggregating Hybridity: Why Hybrid Institutions Do Not Produce Predictable Experiences of Peace'. *Journal of Peace Research*, 51(4):501–514, 2014. doi.org/10.1177/0022343313519465

Millar, Gearoid. *An Ethnographic Approach to Peacebuilding: Understanding Local Experiences in Transitional States*. Abingdon: Routledge, 2014.

Mitchell, Audra. 'Quality/Control: International Peace Interventions and "the Everyday"'. *Review of International Studies*, 37(4):1623–1645, 2011. doi.org/10.1017/S0260210511000180

Mitchell, Melanie. *Complexity: A Guided Tour*. Oxford: Oxford University Press, 2009.

Moore, Sally Falk. 'Law and Social Change: The Semi-Autonomous Social Field as an Appropriate Subject of Study'. *Law & Society Review*, 7(4):719–746, 1973. doi.org/10.2307/3052967

Moreiras, Alberto. 'Hybridity and Double Consciousness'. *Cultural Studies*, 13(3):373–407, 1999. doi.org/10.1080/095023899335149

Mortlock, Roger. 'A Good Thing to Do'. In R. Adams (ed.), *Peace on Bougainville—Truce Monitoring Group. Gudpela Nius Bilong Peace* (pp. 69–82). Wellington, NZ: Victoria University Press, 2001.

Mueggler, Erik. *The Age of Wild Ghosts*. Berkeley, CA: University of California Press, 2001.

Muizarajs, Miks, Prerna Choudhury, Erin Steffen, Amanda Kuppers, Yuhki Tajima and Andrew Beath. *Programa Nasional Dezenvolvimentu Suku Research and Evaluation Program: Omnibus Baseline Survey and Process Monitoring Report*. Dili: World Bank, 2015.

Myat Thu, Pyone. 'Displacement and Informal Repatriation in a Rural Timorese Village'. In S. Ingram, L. Kent and A. McWilliam (eds), *A New Era? Timor-Leste after the UN* (pp. 251–263). Canberra: ANU Press, 2015. doi.org/10.22459/NE.09.2015.17

Nadarajah, Suthaharan and David Rampton. 'The Limits of Hybridity and the Crisis of Liberal Peace'. *Review of International Studies*, 41(1):49–72, 2015. doi.org/10.1017/S0260210514000060

Nandy, Ashis. *The Intimate Enemy: Loss and Recovery of Self under Colonialism*. New Delhi: Oxford University Press, 1983.

Narayan, Vijay. 'Sister Rapist Serves Sentence Only on Weekends'. Fijivillage.com, 15 March 2013. fijivillage.com/news/Sister-rapist-serves-sentence-only-on-weekends-9s25rk/

National Statistics Directorate. *Timor-Leste Demographic and Health Survey 2009–10*. Dili: Ministry of Finance, 2010.

Nbebele, Njabulo S. 'The Rediscovery of the Ordinary: Some New Writings in South Africa'. *Journal of Southern African Studies*, 12(2):143–157, 1986. doi.org/10.1080/03057078608708118

Newland, Lynda. 'New Methodism and Old: Churches, Police and State in Fiji, 2008–09'. *The Round Table: The Commonwealth Journal of International Affairs*, 101(6):537–555, 2012. doi.org/10.1080/003 58533.2012.749094

Newman, Edward. 'A Human Security Peace-building Agenda'. *Third World Quarterly*, 32(10):1737–1756, 2011. doi.org/10.1080/014365 97.2011.610568

Nicole, Robert. *Disturbing History: Resistance in Early Colonial Fiji*. Honolulu: University of Hawai'i Press, 2011.

Niner, Sara. '*Hakat Klot*, Narrow Steps: Negotiating Gender in Post-conflict Timor-Leste'. *International Feminist Journal of Politics*, 13(3):413–435, 2011. doi.org/10.1080/14616742.2011.587371

Nordstrom, Carolyn. *A Different Kind of War Story*. Philadelphia, PA: University of Pennsylvania Press, 1997.

Norval, Aletta J. 'Memory, Identity and the (Im)possibility of Reconciliation: The Work of the Truth and Reconciliation Commission in South Africa'. *Constellations*, 5(2):250–265, 1998. doi.org/10.1111/1467-8675.00091

Nye, Andrea. *Feminism and Modern Philosophy*. New York: Routledge, 2004.

OECD-DAC (Organisation for Economic Co-operation and Development—Development Assistance Committee). *The OECD DAC Handbook on Security System Reform: Supporting Security and Justice.* OECD Publishing, 2008.

OECD-DAC (Organisation for Economic Co-operation and Development—Development Assistance Committee). 'Improving Security and Justice Programming in Fragile Situations: Better Political Engagement, More Change Management'. *OECD Development Policy Papers* 3. OECD Publishing, March 2016.

Ojendal, Joakim, Isabell Schierenbeck and Caroline Hughes (eds). 'The "Local Turn" in Peacebuilding: The Liberal Peace Challenged'. *Third World Quarterly*, Special Issue 36(5), 2015.

Orend, Brian. *War and International Justice: A Kantian Perspective.* Waterloo, Canada: Wilfrid Laurier University Press, 2000.

Orend, Brian. 'Justice after War'. *Ethics & International Affairs*, 16(1):43–56, 2002. doi.org/10.1111/j.1747-7093.2002.tb00374.x

Osborn, Bruce. 'Role of the Military Commander'. In M. Wehner and D. Denoon (eds), *Without a Gun: Australians' Experiences Monitoring Peace in Bougainville, 1997–2001* (pp. 51–58). Canberra: Pandanus Books, 2001.

Ospina, Sofi and Tanja Hohe. 'Traditional Power Structures and the Community Empowerment Project and Local Governance Project: Final Report'. 2001.

Ostergaard, L. *East Timor Youth Social Analysis Mapping and Youth Institutional Assessment.* Dili: World Bank, 2005.

Ostrom, Vincent. 'Polycentricity (Parts 1&2)'. In M.D. McGinnis (ed.), *Polycentricity and Local Public Economies: Readings from the Workshop in Political Theory and Policy Analysis.* Ann Arbor: University of Michigan Press, 1999.

Paffenholz, Thania. 'Unpacking the Local Turn in Peacebuilding: A Critical Assessment towards an Agenda for Future Research'. *Third World Quarterly*, 36(5):857–874, 2015. doi.org/10.1080/01436597.2015.1029908

Pahuka, Sundhya. *Decolonising International Law: Development, Economic Growth and the Politics of Universality.* New York: Cambridge University Press, 2011. doi.org/10.1017/CBO9781139048200

Paris, Roland. *At War's End: Building Peace after Civil Conflict.* Cambridge: Cambridge University Press, 2004. doi.org/10.1017/CBO9780511790836

Paris, Roland. 'Saving Liberal Peacebuilding'. *Review of International Studies,* 36(2):337–365, 2010. doi.org/10.1017/S0260210510000057

Paris, Roland and Thomas Sisk (eds). *The Dilemmas of Statebuilding: Confronting the Contradictions of Postwar Peace Operations.* Abingdon: Routledge, 2009.

Parry, Trina. 'Peace Monitoring in Wakunai, 1998'. In M. Wehner and D. Denoon (eds), *Without a Gun: Australians' Experiences Monitoring Peace in Bougainville, 1997–2001* (pp. 103–107). Canberra: Pandanus Books, 2001.

Pels, Peter. *A Politics of Presence: Contacts between Missionaries and Waluguru in Late Colonial Tanganyika.* Chur, Switzerland: Harwood Academic Publishers, 1999.

Pereira, Martinho and Maria Madalena Lete Koten. 'Dynamics of Democracy at the *Suku* Level'. *Local–Global: Identity, Security, Community,* 11:222–232, 2012.

Peterson, Jenny H. '"Rule of Law" Initiatives and the Liberal Peace: The Impact of Politicized Reform in Post-conflict States'. *Disasters,* 34(1):S15–S39, 2010. doi.org/10.1111/j.1467-7717.2009.01097.x

Peterson, Jenny H. 'A Conceptual Unpacking of Hybridity: Accounting for Notions of Power, Politics and Progress in Analyses of Aid-Driven Interfaces'. *Journal of Peacebuilding & Development,* 7(2):9–22, 2012. doi.org/10.1080/15423166.2012.742802

Pettman, Jan Jindy. 'Boundary Politics: Women, Nationalism and Danger'. In M. Maynard and J. Purvis (eds), *New Frontiers in Women's Studies: Knowledge, Identity and Nationalism* (pp. 187–202). London: Taylor & Francis, 1996.

Pieterse, Jan Nederveen. 'Hybridity, So What? The Anti-hybridity Backlash and the Riddles of Recognition'. *Theory, Culture & Society*, 18(2–3):219–245, 2001. doi.org/10.1177/026327640101800211

Pieterse, Jan Nederveen. *Ethnicities and Global Multiculture: Pants for an Octopus*. Lanham: Rowman & Littlefield, 2007.

Piiparinen, Touko. *The Transformation of UN Conflict Management: Producing Images of Genocide from Rwanda to Darfur and Beyond*. Abingdon: Routledge, 2010.

Piot, Charles. *Remotely Global: Village Modernity in West Africa*. Chicago: University of Chicago Press, 1999.

Porter, Doug. 'Some Implications on the Application of Legal Pluralism to Development Practice'. In B.Z. Tamanaha, C. Sage and M. Woolcock (eds), *Legal Pluralism and Development: Scholars and Practitioners in Dialogue* (pp. 162–174). New York: Cambridge University Press, 2013.

Poulantzas, Nicos. *State, Power, Socialism*. London: New Left Books, 1976.

Pouligny, Béatrice. *Peace Operations Seen from Below: UN Missions and Local People*. Bloomfield, CT: Kumarian Press, 2006.

Pratibha, Jyoti. 'Rooting Out Prostitution and Associated Illicit Practices'. *Fiji Sun* online, 10 March 2015. fijisun.com.fj/2015/03/10/editorial-rooting-out-prostitution-and-associated-illicit-practices/

Prokhovnik, Raia and Gabriella Slomp (eds). *International Political Theory after Hobbes: Analysis, Interpretation and Orientation*. Basingstoke: Palgrave Macmillan, 2011.

Pupavac, Vanessa. 'Therapeutic Governance: Psycho-social Intervention and Trauma Risk Management'. *Disasters*, 25(4):358–372, 2001. doi.org/10.1111/1467-7717.00184

Quijano, Aníbal. 'Coloniality and Modernity/Rationality'. *Cultural Studies*, 21(2–3):168–178, 2007. doi.org/10.1080/09502380601164353

Quimpo, Nathan Gilbert. 'Back to War in Mindanao: The Weaknesses of a Power-Based Approach in Conflict Resolution'. *Philippine Political Science Journal*, 21(44):99–126, 2000. doi.org/10.1080/01154451.2 000.9754216

Quimpo, Nathan Gilbert. 'Mindanao: Nationalism, Jihadism and Frustrated Peace'. *Journal of Asian Security and International Affairs*, 3(1):64–89, 2016. doi.org/10.1177/2347797015626046

Radio New Zealand. 'Decree in Fiji Aimed at Tackling Domestic Violence'. Radio New Zealand, 10 August 2009. www.radionz.co.nz/international/pacific-news/185322/decree-in-fiji-aimed-at-tackling-domestic-violence

Raeymaekers, Timothy, Ken Menkhaus and Koen Vlassenroot. 'State and Non-state Regulation in African Protracted Crises: Governance without Government'. *Afrika Focus*, 21(2):7–21, 2008.

Rajagopal, Balakrishnan. *International Law from Below: Development, Social Movements and Third World Resistance*. Cambridge: Cambridge University Press, 2004.

Ramsbotham, Oliver, Tom Woodhouse and Hugh Miall. *Contemporary Conflict Resolution*. 3rd ed. Cambridge: Polity Press, 2011.

Ranck, Stephen R. 'Recent Rural–Urban Migration to Dili, Portuguese Timor: A Focus on the Use of Households, Kinship and Social Networks by Timorese Migrants'. Unpublished masters thesis. Sydney: Macquarie University, 1977.

Randazzo, Elisa. 'The Paradoxes of the "Everyday": Scrutinising the Local Turn in Peace Building'. *Third World Quarterly*, 37(8):1351–1370, 2016. doi.org/10.1080/01436597.2015.1120154

Ranger, Terence. 'The Local and Global in Southern African Religious History'. In R. Hefner (ed.), *Conversion to Christianity* (pp. 65–98). Berkeley, CA: University of California Press, 1993.

Rawls, John. *A Theory of Justice*. Cambridge: Belknap Press, 1971.

Rawls, John. *The Law of Peoples*. Cambridge, MA: Harvard University Press, 1999.

RDTL (Democratic Republic of East Timor). '*Simu Malu* and *Fila Fali:* Policy Framework for the Return of IDPs in East Timor'. Dili: Ministry of Labour and Community Reinsertion, 2006.

RDTL (Democratic Republic of East Timor). *2010 Population Census.* Dili: Department of Statistics, 2010.

Regan, Anthony J. 'Lessons from a Successful Peace Process in Bougainville, Papua New Guinea, 1997–2005'. Expert Report. Washington, DC: United States Institute of Peace, 2005. www.usip.org/events/lessons-successful-peace-process-bougainville-papua-new-guinea-1997-2005

Regan, Anthony J. 'The Bougainville Intervention: Political Legitimacy and Sustainable Peace-building'. In G. Fry and T.T. Kabutaulaka (eds), *Intervention and State-building in the Pacific: The Legitimacy of 'Cooperative Intervention'* (pp. 184–208). Manchester: Manchester University Press, 2008.

Regan, Anthony J. *Light Intervention: Lessons from Bougainville.* Washington, DC: Unites States Institute of Peace, 2010.

Reid, Elizabeth. 'Re-thinking Human Rights and the HIV Epidemic: A Reflection on Power and Goodness'. In V. Luker and S. Dinnen (eds), *Civic Insecurity: Law, Order and HIV in Papua New Guinea* (pp. 265–274). Canberra: ANU E Press, 2010. press.anu.edu.au/publications/series/state-society-and-governance-melanesia/civic-insecurity

Renders, Marleen and Ulf Terlinden. 'Negotiating Statehood in a Hybrid Political Order: The Case of Somaliland'. *Development and Change*, 41(4):723–746, 2010. doi.org/10.1111/j.1467-7660.2010.01652.x

Richards, Rebecca. 'Bringing the Outside In: Somaliland, Statebuilding and Dual Hybridity'. *Journal of Intervention and Statebuilding*, 9(1):4–25, 2015. doi.org/10.1080/17502977.2014.991074

Richmond, Oliver P. 'Becoming Liberal, Unbecoming Liberalism: Liberal–Local Hybridity via the Everyday as a Response to the Paradoxes of Liberal Peacebuilding'. *Journal of Intervention and Statebuilding*, 3(3):324–344, 2009. doi.org/10.1080/17502970903086719

Richmond, Oliver P. 'A Post-liberal Peace: Eirenism and the Everyday'. *Review of International Studies*, 35(3):557–580, 2009. doi.org/10.1017/S0260210509008651

Richmond, Oliver P. 'The Romanticisation of the Local: Welfare, Culture and Peacebuilding'. *The International Spectator*, 44(1):149–169, 2009. doi.org/10.1080/03932720802693044

Richmond, Oliver P. 'Between Peacebuilding and Statebuilding, between Social Engineering and Post-colonialism'. *Civil Wars*, 12(1–2):167–175, 2010. doi.org/10.1080/13698249.2010.484909

Richmond, Oliver P. 'Post-colonial Hybridity and the Return of Human Security'. In D. Chandler and N. Hynek (eds), *Critical Perspectives on Human Security: Rethinking Emancipation and Power in International Relations* (pp. 43–55). Abingdon: Routledge, 2010.

Richmond, Oliver P. 'Resistance and the Post-liberal Peace'. *Millennium: Journal of International Studies*, 38(3):665–692, 2010.

Richmond, Oliver P. 'De-romanticising the Local, De-mystifying the International: Hybridity in Timor Leste and the Solomon Islands'. *The Pacific Review*, 24(1):115–136, 2011. doi.org/10.1080/0951274 8.2010.546873

Richmond, Oliver P. *A Post-liberal Peace*. Abingdon: Routledge, 2011.

Richmond, Oliver P. 'A Pedagogy of Peacebuilding: Infrapolitics, Resistance, and Liberation'. *International Political Sociology*, 6(2):115–131, 2012. doi.org/10.1111/j.1749-5687.2012.00154.x

Richmond, Oliver P. 'The Dilemmas of a Hybrid Peace: Negative or Positive?' *Cooperation and Conflict*, 50(1):50–68, 2015. doi.org/ 10.1177/0010836714537053

Richmond, Oliver P. 'The Paradox of Peace and Power: Contamination or Enablement?' *International Politics*, 54(5):637–658, 2017. doi.org/ 10.1057/s41311-017-0053-9

Richmond, Oliver P. and Roger Mac Ginty. 'Where Now for the Critique of the Liberal Peace?' *Cooperation and Conflict*, 50(2):171–189, 2014. doi.org/10.1177/0010836714545691

Richmond, Oliver P. and Audra Mitchell (eds). *Hybrid Forms of Peace: From Everyday Agency to Post-liberalism*. Basingstoke: Palgrave Macmillan, 2012. doi.org/10.1057/9780230354234

Richmond, Oliver P. and Audra Mitchell. 'Introduction—Towards a Post-liberal Peace: Exploring Hybridity via Everyday Forms of Resistance, Agency and Autonomy'. In O.P. Richmond and A. Mitchell (eds), *Hybrid Forms of Peace: From Everyday Agency to Post-liberalism* (pp. 1–38). Basingstoke: Palgrave Macmillan, 2012. doi.org/10.1057/9780230354234_1

Richmond, Oliver P. and Audra Mitchell. 'Peacebuilding and Critical Forms of Agency: From Resistance to Subsistence'. *Alternatives: Global, Local, Political*, 36(4):326–344, 2011. doi.org/10.1177/0304375411432099

Ring, Laura A. *Zenana: Everyday Peace in a Karachi Apartment Building*. Bloomington: Indiana University Press, 2006.

Robbins, Joel. 'Recognition, Reciprocity, and Justice: Melanesian Reflections on the Rights of Relationships'. In K.M. Clarke and M. Goodale (eds), *Mirrors of Justice: Law and Power in the Post–Cold War Era* (pp. 171–190). New York: Cambridge University Press, 2010.

Roberts, David. 'Everyday Legitimacy and Postconflict States: Introduction'. *Journal of Intervention and Statebuilding*, 7(1):1–10, 2013. doi.org/10.1080/17502977.2012.655611

Robertson, Robert Thomas and William M. Sutherland. *Government by the Gun: The Unfinished Business of Fiji's 2000 Coup*. Melbourne: Pluto, 2001.

Robinson, Geoffrey. *East Timor 1999: Crimes against Humanity*. Dili: United Nations Office of the High Commissioner for Human Rights, 2003. www.etan.org/etanpdf/2006/CAVR/12-Annexe1-East-Timor-1999-GeoffreyRobinson.pdf

Robinson, Geoffrey. *'If You Leave Us Here We Will Die': How Genocide Was Stopped in East Timor*. Princeton, NJ: Princeton University Press, 2010.

Rodman, William. 'Men of Influence, Men of Rank: Leadership and the Graded Society on Aoba, New Hebrides'. Unpublished doctoral thesis. University of Chicago, 1973.

Rose, Gideon. *How Wars End: Why We Always Fight the Last Battle*. New York: Simon & Schuster, 2010.

Rose, Gillian. *Feminism and Geography: The Limits of Geographical Knowledge*. Cambridge: Polity Press, 1993.

Ross, Fiona C. *Bearing Witness: Women and the Truth and Reconciliation Commission in South Africa*. London: Pluto Press, 2003.

Ross, Fiona C. *Raw Life, New Hope: Decency, Housing and Everyday Life in a Post-apartheid Community*. Claremont, Cape Town: UCT Press, 2010.

Rousseau, Jean-Jacques. *The Social Contract and Other Later Political Writings* (ed. and trans. V. Gourevitch). Cambridge: Cambridge University Press, 1997.

Ruiz-Avila, Katherine. 'Peace Monitoring in Wakunai, 1998'. In M. Wehner and D. Denoon (eds), *Without a Gun: Australians' Experiences Monitoring Peace in Bougainville, 1997–2001* (pp. 97–100). Canberra: Pandanus Books, 2001.

Ryan, Stephen. *The Transformation of Violent Intercommunal Conflict*. Aldershot: Ashgate Publishing, 2007.

Sabaratnam, Meera. 'Avatars of Eurocentrism in the Critique of the Liberal Peace'. *Security Dialogue*, 44(3):259–278, 2013. doi.org/10.1177/0967010613485870

Sahak, Nabi. 'Afghanistan's Enslaved Children'. *Foreign Policy*, 25 September 2015. foreignpolicy.com/2015/09/25/afghanistans-enslaved-children/

Sahin, Selver B. 'Building the State in Timor-Leste'. *Asian Survey*, 47(2):250–267, 2007. doi.org/10.1525/as.2007.47.2.250

Santos, Boaventura de Sousa. 'Law: A Map of Misreading. Toward a Post-modern Conception of Law'. *Journal of Law and Society*, 14(3):279–302, 1987. doi.org/10.2307/1410186

Santos, Boaventura de Sousa. *Towards a New Legal Common Sense*. 2nd ed. Cambridge: Cambridge University Press, 2006.

Santos, Romeo Raymond C. 'Not a Lot to Allot: A Review of Legislative, Executive and Judicial Decisions on Internal Revenue Allotment (IRA)'. *Philippine Law Journal*, 85(4):846–895, 2011.

Sawyer, Amos. 'Social Capital, Survival Strategies, and Their Potential for Post-conflict Governance in Liberia'. *WIDER Research Paper* 2005/15. Helsinki: World Institute for Development Economics Research, 2005.

Scambary, James. 'Anatomy of a Conflict: The 2006–2007 Communal Violence in East Timor'. *Conflict, Security & Development*, 9(2):265–288, 2009. doi.org/10.1080/14678800902925184

Scambary, James. 'Conflict and Resilience in an Urban Squatter Settlement in Dili, East Timor'. *Urban Studies*, 50(10):1935–1950, 2013. doi.org/10.1177/0042098012470396

Schafer, Jessica. *Soldiers at Peace: Veterans and Society after the Civil War in Mozambique*. New York: Palgrave Macmillan, 2007. doi.org/10.1057/9780230605718

Scheper-Hughes, Nancy and Philippe Bourgois. 'Introduction'. In N. Scheper-Hughes and P. Bourgois (eds), *Violence in War and Peace: An Anthology*. Malden, MA: Blackwell Publishing, 2004.

Schiavo-Campo, Salvatore and Mary Judd. 'The Mindanao Conflict in the Philippines: Roots, Costs, and Potential Peace Dividend'. *Social Development Papers: Conflict Prevention and Reconstruction Paper* 24. Washington, DC: World Bank, 2005.

Schlichte, Klaus and Alex Veit. 'Coupled Arenas: Why State-building Is so Difficult'. *Working Papers Micropolitics of Armed Groups* 3/2007. Berlin: Humboldt University, 2007.

Schmidt, Jessica. *Rethinking Democracy Promotion in International Relations: The Rise of the Social*. London: Routledge, 2016.

Schon, Donald Alan. *The Reflective Practitioner: How Professionals Think in Action*. New York: Basic Books, 1983.

Schroeder, Ursula and Fairlie Chappuis. 'New Perspectives on Security Sector Reform: The Role of Local Agency and Domestic Politics'. *International Peacekeeping*, 21(2):133–148, 2014. doi.org/10.1080/13533312.2014.910401

Scott, Colin. 'Analysing Regulatory Space: Fragmented Resources and Institutional Design'. *Public Law*, Summer:329–353, 2001.

Scruton, Roger. 'Immanuel Kant and the Iraq War'. *Open Democracy*, 19 February 2004. www.opendemocracy.net/faith-iraqwar philoshophy/article_1749.jsp

Scruton, Roger. 'Why Iraq Is a Write-Off'. *Forbes / Opinion*, 23 June 2014. www.forbes.com/sites/rogerscruton/2014/06/23/why-iraq-is-a-write-off/

Seigworth, Gregory J. and Michael E. Gardiner. 'Rethinking Everyday Life: And Then Nothing Turns Itself Inside Out'. *Cultural Studies*, 18(2–3):139–159, 2004. doi.org/10.1080/0950238042000201455

Sending, Ole Jacob. 'The Effects of Peacebuilding: Sovereignty, Patronage and Power'. In S. Campbell, D. Chandler and M. Sabaratnam (eds), *A Liberal Peace? The Problems and Practices of Peacebuilding* (pp. 55–68). London: Zed Books, 2011.

Sharp, Tim, John Cox, Ceridwen Spark, Stephanie Lusby and Michelle Rooney. 'The Formal, the Informal and the Precarious: Making a Living in Urban Papua New Guinea'. *SSGM Discussion Paper* 2015/2. Canberra: The Australian National University, 2015. ssgm.bellschool. anu.edu.au/sites/default/files/publications/attachments/2015-12/ DP_2015_2_Sharp_Cox_Spark_Lusby_Rooney_0.pdf

Shearing, Clifford and Jennifer Wood. 'Nodal Governance, Democracy, and the New "Denizens"'. *Journal of Law and Society*, 30(3):400–419, 2003. doi.org/10.1111/1467-6478.00263

Shepley, Susan. 'The Social and Cultural Context of Child Soldiering in Sierra Leone.' Paper presented at PRIO workshop on Techniques of Violence in Civil War, Oslo, 20–21 August 2004. www.academia. edu/334441/The_Social_and_Cultural_Context_of_Child_ Soldiering_In_Sierra_Leone

Shoesmith, Dennis. 'Timor-Leste: Interpreting Violence in a Post-conflict State'. In D. Shoesmith (ed.), *The Crisis in Timor-Leste: Understanding the Past, Imagining the Future*. Darwin: Charles Darwin University Press, 2007.

Silva, Kelly. 'Foho versus Dili: The Political Role of Place in East Timor National Imagination'. *REALIS—Revista de Estudos AntiUtilitaristas e PosColoniais*, 1(2):144–165, 2011.

Singh, Shailendra. 'Prostitution Law Changes Fiji's Night Life'. *Indian Weekender*, 15 April 2010. www.indianweekender.co.nz/Pages/Article Details/14/1008/Fiji/Prostitution-law-changes-Fijis-night-life

Smith, Graeme. 'Beijing's Orphans? New Chinese Investors in Papua New Guinea'. *Pacific Affairs*, 86(2):327–349, 2013. doi.org/10.5509/2013862327

Smith, Linda. *Decolonizing Methodologies: Research and Indigenous People*. New York: Zed Books, 1999.

Smith, Neil. *Uneven Development: Nature, Capital, and the Production of Space*. 2nd ed. Cambridge, MA: Blackwell, 1990.

Smith, Neil. 'Remaking Scale: Competition and Cooperation in Pre-national and Post-national Europe'. In N. Brenner, B. Jessop, M. Jones and G. MacLeod (eds), *State/Space: A Reader* (pp. 227–238). Malden: Blackwell Publishing, 2003. doi.org/10.1002/9780470755686.ch13

Smith, Sarah. 'When "Gender" Started: The United Nations in Post-occupation Timor-Leste'. *Global Change, Peace & Security*, 27(1):55–67, 2015. doi.org/10.1080/14781158.2015.994489

Smits, Rosan and Deborah Wright. *Engagement with Non-state Actors in Fragile States: Narrowing Definitions, Broadening Scope*. The Hague: Conflict Research Unit, Clingendael Institute, 2012.

Snyder, Francis G. 'Colonialism and Legal Form: The Creation of "Customary Law" in Senegal'. *The Journal of Legal Pluralism and Unofficial Law*, 13(19):49–90, 1981. doi.org/10.1080/07329113.1981.10756258

Spark, Ceridwen. 'Gender Trouble in Town: Educated Women Eluding Male Domination, Gender Violence and Marriage in PNG'. *The Asia Pacific Journal of Anthropology*, 12(2):164–180, 2011. doi.org/10.1080/14442213.2010.546425

Spark, Ceridwen. 'An Oceanic Revolution? *Stella* and the Construction of New Femininities in Papua New Guinea and the Pacific'. *The Australian Journal of Anthropology*, 25(1):54–72, 2014. doi.org/10.1111/taja.12066

Spark, Ceridwen. '"We Only Get the Daylight Hours": Gender, Fear and "Freedom" in Urban Papua New Guinea'. *Security Challenges*, 10(2):15–32, 2014.

Spear, Thomas. 'Neo-traditionalism and the Limits of Invention in British Colonial Africa'. *Journal of African History*, 44(1):3–27, 2003. doi.org/10.1017/S0021853702008320

Spivak, Gayatri Chakravorty. 'Can the Subaltern Speak?' In C. Nelson and L. Grossberg (eds), *Marxism and the Interpretation of Culture* (pp. 271–313). Urbana, IL: University of Illinois Press, 1988.

Stacey, Ralph D. *Complexity and Creativity in Organizations*. San Francisco, CA: Berrett-Koehler Publishers, 1996.

Steger, Manfred B. *The Rise of the Global Imaginary: Political Ideologies from the French Revolution to the Global War on Terror*. New York: Oxford University Press, 2009. doi.org/10.1093/acprof:oso/9780199286942.001.0001

Stephens, Matthew. 'Islamic Law in the Philippines: Between Appeasement and Neglect'. *Islam, Syari'ah and Governance Background Paper Series* 9. Melbourne: Centre for Islamic Law and Society, University of Melbourne, 2011.

Stockhammer, Philipp W. 'Questioning Hybridity'. In P.W. Stockhammer (ed.), *Conceptualizing Cultural Hybridization: A Transdisciplinary Approach* (pp. 1–3). Heidelberg: Springer-Verlag, 2012. doi.org/10.1007/978-3-642-21846-0_1

Strachan, Hew and Sibylle Scheipers (eds). *The Changing Character of War*. Oxford: Oxford University Press, 2011. doi.org/10.1093/acprof:osobl/9780199596737.001.0001

Stroeken, Koen. *Moral Power: The Magic of Witchcraft*. New York: Berghahn Books, 2010.

Swaine, Aisling. *Traditional Justice and Gender Based Violence*. Research Report. International Rescue Committee, 2003.

Swyngedouw, Erik. 'Neither Global nor Local: "Glocalization" and the Politics of Scale'. In K.R. Cox (ed.), *Spaces of Globalization: Reasserting the Power of the Local* (pp. 137–166). New York: The Guildford Press, 1997.

Sylvester, Christine. *War as Experience: Contributions from International Relations and Feminist Analysis*. London: Routledge, 2013.

Tahana, Jamie. 'Fiji PM's Violence Condemnation Rings Hollow for Some'. Radio New Zealand, 18 February 2014. www.radionz.co.nz/international/programmes/datelinepacific/audio/2586031/fiji-pm%27s-violence-condemnation-rings-hollow-for-some

Tamanaha, Brian Z. 'Understanding Legal Pluralism: Past to Present, Local to Global'. *Sydney Law Review*, 30(3):375–411, 2008.

Tamanaha, Brian Z., Carolyn Sage and Michael Woolcock (eds). *Legal Pluralism and Development: Scholars and Practitioners in Dialogue*. New York: Cambridge University Press, 2013.

Tan, Samuel K. *Decolonization and Filipino Muslim Identity*. Quezon City: University of the Philippines, 1989.

Tanikella, Leela. 'The Politics of Hybridity: Race, Gender, and Nationalism in Trinidad'. *Cultural Dynamics*, 15(2):153–181, 2003. doi.org/10.1177/0921374003015002002

Tansey, Oisín. *Regime-Building: Democratization and International Administration*. Oxford: Oxford University Press, 2009. doi.org/10.1093/acprof:oso/9780199561032.001.0001

Teaiwa, Teresia K. 'Articulated Cultures: Militarism and Masculinities in Fiji during the Mid 1990s'. *Fijian Studies: A Journal of Contemporary Fiji*, 3(2):201–222, 2005.

Thornton, John K. 'Legitimacy and Political Power: Queen Njinga, 1624–1663'. *Journal of African History*, 32(1):25–40, 1991. doi.org/10.1017/S0021853700025329

Timmer, Jaap. '*Kastom* and Theocracy: A Reflection on Governance from the Uttermost Part of the World'. In S. Dinnen and S. Firth (eds), *Politics and State Building in Solomon Islands* (pp. 194–212). Canberra: ANU E Press and Asia Pacific Press, 2008. press.anu.edu.au/publications/politics-and-state-building-solomon-islands

Tobin, Brendan M. 'Bridging the Nagoya Compliance Gap: The Fundamental Role of Customary Law in Protection of Indigenous Peoples' Resource and Knowledge Rights'. *Law, Environment and Development Journal*, 9(2):142–162, 2013.

Tomlinson, Matthew Akim. *In God's Image: The Metaculture of Fijian Christianity*. Berkley, CA: University of California Press, 2009.

Torres, Wilfred Magno, III (ed.). *Rido: Clan Feuding and Conflict Management in Mindanao*. Makati City: The Asia Foundation, 2007.

Totilo, Matthew Alan. 'Development in the Shadows: How the World Bank and the Frente Clandestina Almost Built a New Government in Timor-Leste'. Unpublished masters thesis. Massachusetts Institute of Technology, 2009. www.cultura.gov.tl/sites/default/files/Totilo_Development_in_the_Shadows_How_the_World_Bank_and_the_Frente_Clandestina_Almost_Built_a_New_Government_in_Timor-Leste.pdf

Traube, Elizabeth G. 2007. 'Unpaid Wages: Local Narratives and the Imagination of the Nation'. *Asia Pacific Journal of Anthropology*, 8(1):9–25, 2007. doi.org/10.1080/14442210601161724

Trnka, Susanna. 'Remythologizing the State: Public Security, the "Jesus Strategy" and the Fiji Police'. *Oceania*, 81(1):72–87, 2011. doi.org/10.1002/j.1834-4461.2011.tb00094.x

True, Jacqui. 'The Political Economy of Violence against Women: A Feminist International Relations Perspective'. *Australian Feminist Law Journal*, 32(1):39–59, 2010. doi.org/10.1080/13200968.2010.10854436

Tsing, Anna Lowenhaupt. *Friction: An Ethnography of Global Connection*. Princeton, NJ: Princeton University Press, 2005.

Tukuwasa, Epeli. 'Fiji Should Not Bank on Zero Reporting: FWCC'. Fiji Broadcasting Corporation, 11 December 2013. www.fbc.com.fj/fiji/16126/fiji-should-not-bank-on-zero-reporting-fwcc

Tully, James. *Strange Multiplicity: Constitutionalism in an Age of Diversity*. Cambridge: Cambridge University Press, 1995.

Turcot DiFruscia, Kim. 'Listening to Voices: An Interview with Veena Das'. *Alterites*, 7(1):136–145, 2010.

UNDP (United Nations Development Programme). 'Human Development Index Highlights Inequality, Slow Pace of Progress'. UNDP, 29/7/2013. www.ph.undp.org/content/philippines/en/home/presscenter/pressreleases/2013/07/29/human-development-index-highlights-inequality-slow-pace-of-progress.html

UNFPA (United Nations Population Fund). *Gender-Based Violence in Timor-Leste: A Case Study*. New York: UNFPA, 2005.

United Nations. *An Agenda for Peace: Preventive Diplomacy, Peacemaking and Peace-keeping* (UN Doc A/47/277-S/24111). 17 June 1992. www.un-documents.net/a47-277.htm

United Nations Secretary General. *The Rule of Law and Transitional Justice in Conflict and Post-conflict Societies* (UN Doc S/2004/616). New York: United Nations Security Council, 2004.

United Nations Secretary General. *The Rule of Law and Transitional Justice in Conflict and Post-Conflict Societies* (UN Doc S/2011/634). New York: United Nations Security Council, 2011.

UNOHCHR and UNMIT (United Nations Office of the High Commissioner for Human Rights and United Nations Integrated Mission in Timor-Leste). *Facing the Future: Periodic Report on Human Rights Developments in Timor-Leste, 1 July 2009 – 30 June 2010*. Dili: UNOHCHR and UNMIT, 2010.

USAID. *Rule of Law in Timor-Leste*. Dili: Freedom House, USAID and the ABA Rule of Law Initiative, 2007.

Vakaliwaliwa, Savenaca. 'Question of Prostitution'. Letters to the Editor, *Fiji Times* online, 4 January 2014. www.fijitimes.com/story.aspx?ref=archive&id=255966

van der Burg, Wibren. *The Dynamics of Law and Morality: A Pluralist Account of Legal Interactionism*. Farnham: Ashgate, 2014.

van Klink, Bart. 'Facts and Norms: The Unfinished Debate between Eugen Ehrlich and Hans Kelsen'. *Tilburg Working Paper Series On Jurisprudence And Legal History* 06-03. Amsterdam, 2006. ssrn.com/abstract=980957

Vilhena, Maria. *Gungunhana*. Lisboa: Edições Colibri, 1999.

Vinthagen, Stellan and Anna Johansson. '"Everyday Resistance": Exploration of a Concept and Its Theories'. *Resistance Studies Magazine*, 1:1–46, 2013.

Visoka, Gëzim. 'Three Levels of Hybridisation Practices in Post-conflict Kosovo'. *Journal of Peacebuilding & Development*, 7(2):23–36, 2012. doi.org/10.1080/15423166.2012.743807

Wainwright, Elsina. *Our Failing Neighbour: Australia and the Future of Solomon Islands*. Canberra: Australian Strategic Policy Institute, 2003.

Waldorf, Lars. 'Mass Justice for Mass Atrocity: Rethinking Local Justice as Transitional Justice'. *Temple Law Review*, 79(1):1–87, 2006.

Waldorf, Lars. 'Local Transitional Justice: Customary Law, Healing Rituals, and Everyday Justice'. In O. Simić (ed.), *An Introduction to Transitional Justice: A Textbook* (pp. 157–176). Abingdon: Routledge, 2017.

Walker, Robert B.J. *Inside/Outside: International Relations as Political Theory*. Cambridge: Cambridge University Press, 1993.

Wallis, Joanne. 'A Liberal–Local Hybrid Peace Project in Action? The Increasing Engagement between the Local and Liberal in Timor-Leste'. *Review of International Studies*, 38(4):735–761, 2012. doi.org/10.1017/S0260210511000787

Wallis, Joanne. *Constitution Making during State Building*. Cambridge: Cambridge University Press, 2014. doi.org/10.1017/CBO9781107587700

Wallis, Joanne, Renee Jeffery and Lia Kent. 'Political Reconciliation in Timor Leste, Solomon Islands and Bougainville: The Dark Side of Hybridity'. *Australian Journal of International Affairs*, 70(2):159–178, 2016. doi.org/10.1080/10357718.2015.1113231

Walzer, Michael. *Arguing about War*. New Haven, CT: Yale University Press, 2006.

Wassel, Todd and Gobie Rajalingam. *A Survey of Community-Police Perceptions in Timor-Leste 2015*. Dili: The Asia Foundation, 2015.

Wehner, Monica and Donald Denoon (eds). *Without a Gun: Australians' Experiences Monitoring Peace in Bougainville, 1997–2001*. Canberra: Pandanus Books, 2001.

Weil, Simone. *The First and Last Notebooks* (trans. Richard Rees). Oxford: Oxford University Press, 1970.

Wellman, Barry. 'Network Analysis: Some Basic Principles'. *Sociological Theory*, 1:155–200, 1983. doi.org/10.2307/202050

West, Harry. *Kupilikula: Governance and the Invisible Realm in Mozambique*. Chicago, IL: University of Chicago Press, 2005.

West, Paige. *From Modern Production to Imagined Primitive: The Social World of Coffee from Papua New Guinea*. Durham, NC: Duke University Press, 2012. doi.org/10.1215/9780822394846

Wiegink, Nikkie. 'Why Did the Soldiers Not Go Home? Demobilized Combatants, Family Life, and Witchcraft in Postwar Mozambique'. *Anthropological Quarterly*, 86(1):107–132, 2013. doi.org/10.1353/anq.2013.0014

Williams, J. Michael. *Chieftaincy, the State, and Democracy: Political Legitimacy in Post-apartheid South Africa*. Bloomington: Indiana University Press, 2009.

Williams, Philippa. 'Reproducing Everyday Peace in North India: Process, Politics, and Power'. *Annals of the Association of American Geographers*, 103(1):230–250, 2013. doi.org/10.1080/00045608.2011.652878

Wiuff Moe, Louise. 'Hybrid and "Everyday" Political Ordering: Constructing and Contesting Legitimacy in Somaliland'. *The Journal of Legal Pluralism and Unofficial Law*, 43(63):143–177, 2011. doi.org/10.1080/07329113.2011.10756660

Wiuff Moe, Louise. 'The "Turn to the Local": Hybridity, Local Ordering and the New Governing Rationalities of Peace and Security Interventions in Somalia'. Unpublished doctoral thesis. Brisbane: The University of Queensland, 2014.

Wiuff Moe, Louise and Peter Albrecht. 'Hybridity and Simultaneity in the Global South'. In P. Jackson (ed.), *Handbook of International Security and Development* (pp. 332–348). Cheltenham: Edward Elgar Publishing, 2015.

World Bank. *Violence in the City: Understanding and Supporting Community Responses to Urban Violence*. Washington, DC: World Bank, 2010.

World Bank. *World Development Report 2011: Conflict, Security, and Development*. Washington, DC: World Bank, 2011.

Young, Iris Marion. 'The Logic of Masculinist Protection: Reflections on the Current Security State'. *Signs: Journal of Women in Culture and Society*, 29(1):1–25, 2003. doi.org/10.1086/375708

Young, Robert J.C. *Colonial Desire: Hybridity in Theory, Culture and Race*. London: Routledge, 1995.

Zack-Williams, A.B. 'Child Soldiers in the Civil War in Sierra Leone'. *Review of African Political Economy*, 28(87):73–82, 2001. doi.org/10.1080/03056240108704504

Zaum, Dominik. 'Beyond the "Liberal Peace"'. *Global Governance: A Review of Multilateralism and International Organizations*, 18(1):121–132, 2012.

Zifcak, Spencer. 'Restorative Justice in Timor-Leste: The Truth and Reconciliation Commission'. *Development Bulletin*, 68:51–55, 2005. crawford.anu.edu.au/rmap/devnet/devnet/db-68.pdf

Zwitter, Andrej and Michael Hoelzl. 'Augustine on War and Peace'. *Peace Review: A Journal of Social Justice*, 26(3):317–324, 2014. doi.org/10.1080/10402659.2014.937987

www.ingramcontent.com/pod-product-compliance
Lightning Source LLC
Chambersburg PA
CBHW040151270326
41926CB00071B/4581